CQ GUIDE TO

CURRENT AMERICAN
GOVERNMENT

CQ GUIDE TO

CURRENT AMERICAN
GOVERNMENT

Spring 2001

CQ PRESS

A Division of Congressional Quarterly Inc.

Washington, D.C.

Congressional Quarterly Inc.

Congressional Quarterly Inc., an editorial research service and publishing company, serves clients in the fields of news, education, business, and government. It combines the specific coverage of Congress, government, and politics contained in the CQ *Weekly* with the more general subject range of an affiliated service, the CQ *Researcher*.

Under the CQ Press imprint, Congressional Quarterly also publishes college political science textbooks and public affairs paperbacks on developing issues and events, information directories, and reference books on the federal government, national elections, and politics. Titles include the *Guide to the Presidency*, the *Guide to Congress*, the *Guide to the U.S. Supreme Court*, the *Guide to U.S. Elections*, and *Politics in America*. CQ's A-Z Collection is a four-volume reference series that provides essential information about American government and the electoral process. The CQ *Almanac*, a compendium of legislation for one session of Congress, is published each year. *Congress and the Nation*, a record of government for a presidential term, is published every four years.

CQ publishes the *Daily Monitor*, a report on the current and future activities of congressional committees. An online information system, CQ.com on Congress, provides immediate access to CQ's databases of legislative action, votes, schedules, profiles, and analyses.

CQ Press
A Division of Congressional Quarterly Inc.
1414 22nd St. N.W.
Washington, DC 20037
(202) 822-1475; (800) 638-1710

www.cqpress.com

Printed in the United States of America
04 03 02 01 00   5 4 3 2 1

♾ The paper used in this publication meets the minimum requirements of the American National Standard for Information Sciences—Permanence of Paper for Printed Library Materials, ANSI Z39.48-1992.

ISSN 0196-612-X
ISBN 1-56802-560-2

Contents

Introduction

Congressional Quarterly's *Guide to Current American Government* reprints articles selected from the *CQ Weekly* and related CQ publications. The editors chose articles that would complement existing texts with up-to-date examinations of current issues and controversies. The *Guide* is divided into four sections—elections 2000, Congress and the nation 2001, politics and public policy, and foundations of American government—that correspond to standard introductory American government courses.

Elections 2000. The articles in this section look at the outcome of the House and Senate races and examine the effects of the new party split in both chambers of Congress. This section concludes with articles on the newly elected governors and the results of ballot initiatives in the states.

Congress and the Nation 2001. In the wake of the November 2000 congressional elections, CQ editors discuss the likely organization and agenda of the 107th Congress, which convenes in January 2001. Unresolved issues, from health care to education, are likely to greet the new Congress.

Politics and Public Policy. This section provides in-depth coverage of major social policy issues, including articles on prescription drug benefits for Medicare recipients, tax cuts, the budget surplus, and violence in entertainment.

Foundations of American Government. Articles in this section examine current issues that have implications for interpretation of the U.S. Constitution or the broad workings of the federal government. The first article provides an overview of the Supreme Court's 1999 term; the remaining articles focus on two recent decisions that demonstrate the Court's insistence on the separation of powers.

By reprinting *CQ Weekly* articles as they originally appeared, the editors provide a handy source of information about contemporary political issues. The original date of publication is noted with each article to give readers a time frame for the events that are described. Although new developments inevitably occur, the editors provide updates only when they are essential to an understanding of the basic operations of American government. Page number references to related articles in the *CQ Weekly* and the *CQ Almanac* facilitate additional research on topical events. Both publications are available in many school and public libraries.

Note: As *Guide to Current American Government* went to press in November 2000, the outcome of a number of elections—including the presidential election—remained uncertain. The winner of the presidential contest depended on recounts and legal actions in Florida. In a few House races, close votes held out the prospect of recounts. In the state of Washington, an extremely close vote for senator left in doubt whether a Democratic challenger would unseat the Republican incumbent; this election had important ramifications for control of the Senate in the 107th Congress.

Readers of articles in this edition of the *Guide* should keep in mind that these unsettled races may significantly affect the politics and policies of the federal government in 2001. They should keep abreast of new information by consulting the *CQ Weekly*, available in many libraries, and through their local news outlets.

Elections 2000

The articles in this section of the *Guide* report on and interpret the results of the congressional races. The 2000 elections kept the Republicans in power in both houses of Congress, but their majority was diminished.

The presidential election ended without a clear winner on election day. Although the Democratic candidate, Vice President Al Gore, led the popular vote with 49 percent of the total, the winner of the crucial electoral vote was undecided as the *Guide* went to press in November. At issue were Florida's 25 electoral votes, which each candidate needed to win the presidency. (A candidate must have at least 270 electoral votes to be declared the president.) At press time, Gore had 255 electoral votes, while Texas governor George W. Bush, the Republican candidate, had 246. Because the vote was so close in Florida, the Gore campaign requested a manual recount in certain counties. If, after the final recount, Bush prevails and wins Florida's electoral votes, he will be the first president since Benjamin Harrison, in 1888, to win the electoral college vote but lose the popular vote.

The Democratic Party picked up five seats in the Senate, leaving the Republicans with a bare majority at best. With results of the Senate race in Washington state between incumbent GOP senator Slade Gorton and former representative Maria Cantwell still undecided in mid-November, the Republicans were faced with a 50–50 split if Cantwell were to win the race, leaving the new vice president to cast the tie-breaking votes.

Although House Democrats picked up some seats, the Republicans maintained their six-year hold on that chamber. With four races still undecided in mid-November, it appeared that the Democrats picked up no more than two seats for a 221–212 party split. Not since the 83rd Congress, in 1953–1955, have the margins in both chambers been this close.

CQ editors also review the fate of the propositions on the state ballots, including a gun control effort to allow background checks at gun shows in Colorado and Oregon and a ban on same-sex unions in Nebraska and Nevada. Unofficial Senate, House, and gubernatorial election results are located on page 106 of the appendix.

A Divided Nation Has Much to Lose In Battle of Ballots

The only clear mandate for the new president and Congress: Work together

In 212 years of presidential and congressional campaigns, there may never have been one that ended with such a collective gasp, the candidates like marathon runners who collapsed in a heap — with no one quite sure who was first across the finish line. There have been close presidential elections, shaky House margins, and paper-thin Senate majorities. In modern times, however, all three have never happened at once.

If Republican Gov. George W. Bush of Texas ultimately wins the 43rd presidency of the United States, as he claims he has, he will have the slimmest possible majorities in both the House and Senate. That would make his power all the more precarious, even as lingering questions about the validity of the Florida results hang over his head.

If Democratic Vice President Al Gore prevails, he will face a GOP Congress weaker than any President Clinton has had to deal with. But the narrowness of his victory could make him more vulnerable than Clinton was, while Gore's protracted challenge to the Florida vote may have poisoned his relationship with Republicans beyond repair.

Days after the vote, the exact party makeup in Congress was still in flux, and the only sure thing was that the Republicans had lost seats. They had been whittled down to, at best, a two-seat margin of control in the Senate — 52-48 — and possibly a 50-50 split if Republican Sen. Slade Gorton loses the Washington Senate race, which remains too close to call. *(Senate, p. 9)*

The House was likely to end up with a 221-212 party split, with several recounts under way. Republicans came away from the election wounded, but the Democrats, who mounted an all-out effort to take the House back, came away with almost nothing to show for it. *(House, p. 17)*

"It is safe to say that never in our history have we ever had a partisan balance across the country as even as this," Norman

Ornstein, a resident scholar at the American Enterprise Institute, said at a Nov. 9 forum.

Not since the 83rd Congress, in 1953-55, have the margins been nearly this close in both chambers. At the time, newly elected President Dwight D. Eisenhower had to deal with narrow congressional majorities from his own party; the Republicans held the Senate with a 48-47 split and the House by only 221-211.

Then again, Eisenhower's own election was a landslide, not a jaw-dropping cliffhanger. If Bush prevails, he will be the first president since Benjamin Harrison in 1888 to win the electoral college vote but lose the popular vote. Harrison, too, worked with a tight Republican margin. Since then, no president who worked with such a narrow majority from his own party ever had to face questions about whether he truly was the people's choice.

Gore, who is leading in the popular vote, would not have that distinction, but would be forever tagged as the man who ran to continue a presidential administration during economic prosperity and almost lost. And there is this warning for Bush and congressional Republicans, should they end up working together: Eisenhower lost his majority in Congress after two years.

Mutual Dependence

The combination means the new president and the 107th Congress will be desperately dependent on each other for political survival. Whether they can actually do what it takes to succeed is another question.

"It is chaos, and the scenarios are endless," said Bruce Buchanan, a government professor at the University of Texas at Austin and an expert on the presidency.

Somehow, the new president will have to unite a country that is ideologically divided. And he must find a way to work with Congress despite the current legal challenges and recounts that have turned the fight for the presidency into a

bitter, vicious battle. The fight could become still more divisive, with an Electoral College challenge no longer out of the question. (*Electoral College, p. 4*)

The electoral picture has been changing with dizzying speed. As of Nov. 10, a vote recount in the make-or-break state of Florida forced Bush's lead over Gore down to 327 votes out of the nearly 6 million cast, according to the Associated Press. Gore led Bush in the popular vote nationwide, 49.2 million to 48.9 million, a number that was still in flux. Florida's 25 Electoral College votes would put either candidate officially over the top; Gore had 255 electoral votes to Bush's 246, both within inches of the 270 needed to win.

The Gore campaign, sensing victory within its grasp, asked for more detailed recounts in four Florida counties and raised the legal possibility of a new election in Palm Beach County. The Bush campaign said the election was over — but considered asking for its own recounts in Iowa and Wisconsin if Gore proceeded with the Florida challenges. The final outcome in Florida, which hangs on the mail-in ballots from state residents living overseas, might not be known until Nov. 17.

In the meantime, the lawyers have been unleashed. Eight lawsuits, one later withdrawn, were filed in Florida to challenge the election results. And the National Association for the Advancement of Colored People, raising the possibility of Voting Rights Act violations in a Florida precinct, asked Attorney General Janet Reno to send in federal marshals to monitor the recount.

In looking for historical parallels, both sides cited 1960, when Richard M. Nixon lost narrowly to John F. Kennedy and allegations of vote fraud in Cook County, Ill., hung in the air. One big difference: Nixon chose not to challenge the results to avoid dividing the country.

The shadow of the virtual electoral tie is sure to hang over a lame-duck session set to start the week of Nov. 13. An election that was supposed to help lawmakers resolve several ideologically polarized disputes, from school construction to immigration policy to worker safety, appears to have instead muddied things further. It is one thing for a lame-duck Congress not to have a mandate on the issues. It is another not even to know who the new president is. (*Lame duck, 2000 CQ Weekly, p. 2639*)

'A Mandate to Be Modest'

The most glaring reality that will confront the new president is the view — voiced by lawmakers from both parties — that in order to operate at all, the White House and the leaders of the 107th Congress will have to find what until now has been an elusive balance between the two parties.

The power of individual lawmakers, whether moderates or simply mavericks, will be stronger than ever. As retiring Sen. Bob Kerrey, D-Neb., put it, "There's potentially 100 kings in the Senate."

"We're going to have a power-sharing situation," said Senate Minority Leader Tom Daschle, D-S.D., who will now have even more leverage in passing or blocking legislation than he has had in the 106th Congress.

"There will be a coalition government," Rep. Mark Foley, R-Fla., a deputy House Republican whip, declared Nov. 8.

What does that mean for Bush or Gore? The conventional wisdom solidified quickly. Controversial issues will become off limits, lawmakers and experts said, and only bite-sized initiatives have a real chance to become law. That would seem to require a delay, or at least a smaller-scale ap-

proach, for some of the ambitious proposals that dominated the presidential race: expanding the federal role in education, overhauling Social Security, adding Medicare prescription drug coverage for senior citizens, and, in Bush's case, providing $1.3 trillion in tax relief over the next 10 years.

"I think the new president has a mandate to be modest," said Stephen Wayne, a professor of government at Georgetown University and an expert on the presidency. "I think you're going to have a government that moves slowly, casually, incrementally."

The makeup of the 107th Congress alone would make the job difficult for any president. For Bush, "if you're going to strike out in any dramatic way, the Democrats can stop you because they hold the filibuster card," said Christopher J. Deering, a congressional expert and professor of political science at The George Washington University in Washington, D.C.

As for Gore, Deering said, "his agenda would be largely dead. I don't think the Republicans have any more incentive to cooperate with a Gore presidency than a Clinton presidency."

Others, however, said the new president could slowly build a base of support, from which he could tackle the large issues later. Sheila Burke, chief of staff to former Senate Majority Leader Bob Dole, R-Kan. (1969-96), suggested a strategy of scoring a few "quick wins" by carefully picking out issues with potential for consensus and working to pass those bills first.

"Pick the two or three issues where you show the willingness to let the Congress win with you," said Burke, now an adjunct lecturer in public policy at the John F. Kennedy School of Government at Harvard University.

Finding those issues, however, can be a problem. At the beginning of the 106th Congress, the Clinton administration thought patients' rights legislation had the potential for a "quick win," since both Democrats and Republicans claimed to want it. In reality, the insurance industry and business groups pushed Republicans in one direction and provider and consumer groups sent Democrats in another, tangling endlessly over the right to sue managed-care plans. The legislation (HR 2990) is stuck in a House-Senate conference committee and appears to be dead for the year.

With some issues, it is easy to see incremental strategies that could move legislation forward. Bush might not be able to move his entire education package through a Congress with a powerful Democratic minority. Democrats, and many Republicans, furiously oppose his proposal to let parents pull their kids out of failing schools and use federal funds to send them to private or religious schools. These opponents, who killed several congressional voucher amendments this session, may have new ammunition now that voucher initiatives failed on Nov. 7 in California and Michigan.

Both parties, however, generally have lined up behind tougher strategies to hold states and schools accountable for what students learn, including more regular testing for students, bonus payments for states that improve their schools and financial penalties for states that do not. Those pieces of either the Bush education plan or the Gore education plan could move through on their own. (*Issues, 2000 CQ Weekly, p. 2669*)

Step by Step

Likewise, Gore's "step by step" plan to expand health coverage for the uninsured is a patchwork of ideas that includes

Capitol Hill: Final Campus For Electoral College?

With the closest presidential election in decades hinging on the outcome in Florida, lawsuits, recounts and absentee ballots could combine to force Congress into an unusual role in determining the winner of the state, and its 25 electoral votes.

A muddle of scenarios being weighed by constitutional scholars include several ways in which Congress could be called upon to resolve disputes that could be pivotal in determining whether GOP Texas Gov. George W. Bush or Democratic Vice President Al Gore becomes the 43rd president.

"We're dealing in uncharted territory," said Rutgers University law professor Frank Askin. "We are really in the midst of a constitutional conundrum."

If the confusion over the presidential race continues in the Sunshine State beyond Dec. 12 — six days before the Electoral College is supposed to meet and cast the votes that formally decide the presidency — it is possible Congress will end up having to rule on the legitimacy of the electors Florida sends. It is possible, according to experts, that Florida could send electors for both Bush and Gore, which then would leave Congress in the position of deciding which to accept.

State Power

Under a federal law passed in the wake of the closest Electoral College presidential election in history — in 1876 — states have the ultimate authority to arbitrate election disputes, unless the issue is not resolved in time for the Electoral College.

At least two law professors with expertise in election law said it is possible the election of a president could be held without including the electoral votes of a state, such as Florida.

Although experts have traditionally held that the election of a president requires an absolute majority of

270 Electoral College votes, the Constitution says a candidate wins with "a majority of the whole numbers of Electors appointed."

Should it miss the deadline, Florida could still attempt to present a slate of electors to Congress after the vote of the Electoral College has passed. Congress meets Jan. 6 to certify that vote. A certified slate of electors would probably be acepted unless both the House and the Senated voted to reject it.

It also is possible for electors to change their votes. Electors are expected — but not constitutionally bound — to cast votes in line with their state's popular vote winner.

The heart of these problems is in the Electoral College, America's hybrid system of choosing presidents that combines popular voting with representative balloting. Although disputes have long existed over the wisdom of having an Electoral College that could award the presidency to a candidate who loses the popular vote, those arguments have, until this year, been largely hypothetical background noise.

"Americans are about to engage in a great civics lesson," said Democratic Sen. Robert G. Torricelli of New Jersey on Nov. 8. "The president of the United States is chosen by the people of the states, not the people of the nation."

Electors to the college, who typically are chosen by their state parties, are scheduled to meet in their state capitals Dec. 18 to cast ballots for president. But if Florida's electoral results remain in dispute six days before, the state's results may not be counted at all, experts said.

That deadline could bring Congress into the dispute.

Gore and Bush are in a bitter fight over Florida's final vote count. Bush won by almost 1,800 votes, but the automatic recount triggered by that slim margin cut the difference to just over 300 out of nearly 6 million votes

cast. Gore's campaign has requested hand counts in four Democratic counties, and absentee ballots from Floridians abroad will be accepted until Nov. 17.

In addition, allegations of voting irregularities in the Democratic stronghold of Palm Beach County have resulted in lawsuits and cries for a new vote. Democrats contend that the county's ballot layout confused voters, leading many Gore supporters to accidentally cast ballots for Reform Party candidate Patrick J. Buchanan.

The arch-conservative Buchanan did garner a striking number of votes in Palm Beach County and said in a television interview the week of Nov. 6 that he suspects he got votes that were intended for Gore.

The same ballot problem is being blamed for the loss of about 19,000 ballots that were thrown out because voters punched them wrong, in some cases voting for two candidates for president.

According to the Associated Press, eight lawsuits have been filed in state and federal courts to challenge the Florida results, including six in Palm Beach County and two in the state capital of Tallahassee. Democratic Party-backed lawsuits won't be filed until next week, party officials said.

And in Palm Beach County a state circuit court judge issued a stay Nov. 9, preventing any certified election results in the county from being sent to the state. Palm Beach will do a hand count of ballots in three precincts over the weekend to determine whether a complete hand recount of the voting is necessary.

All of this could leave Congress to decide during its lame-duck session, which begins the week of Nov. 13, whether to postpone the date for the Electoral College vote. Only Congress can change that date, but no one has yet requested that such action be considered.

provisions Republicans have never liked, such as expanding Medicaid and the State Children's Health Insurance Program to cover low-income parents. Both he and Bush have proposed tax credits to help pay for health insurance, however, and the idea has drawn enough interest from both parties — even though experts have questioned its effectiveness — that it could stand a chance as a stand-alone health care proposal.

As for Bush's tax relief plan, the incremental strategy is simple: scale it back. "We're going to have tax cuts. They may not be as large as [Bush] wants, but there will be tax cuts," Rep. Christopher Shays, R-Conn., said in a Nov. 9 interview.

"The cards are still in the Republicans' hands," Deering said, and Bush would be able to make some headway on such issues as tax cuts, higher defense spending, and perhaps even a narrow campaign finance overhaul. "There's no reason George Bush can't have some modest successes, and probably with an agenda that looks pretty Republican."

It is hard to break down Social Security overhauls or Medicare prescription drug coverage into incremental strategies, however, and not everyone agrees that the new president should avoid them because they are controversial.

"I couldn't disagree more," Kerrey said. "If Bush wins Florida, it's because he campaigned on the partial privatization of Social Security. . . . If he's seen as being gutsy, even if people disagree, they'll respect him."

"We don't want the new president to be timid," said Rep. Benjamin L. Cardin, D-Md. "We want the new president . . . to set out a bold agenda for what he thinks is best for the nation. Then he needs to work with Democrats and Republicans to implement those programs, and he needs to listen."

That is where either Bush or Gore will find that their personalities count every bit as much as their leadership skills.

Calling a Truce

"It just can't happen without bipartisan cooperation," Rep. Michael N. Castle, R-Del., said in a Nov. 8 interview.

"It simply will not occur in any other way," Daschle said at a Nov. 8 press conference. "They don't have the votes, we don't have the votes, and I think that realization could actually change this."

But lawmakers said much the same thing in 1996 and 1998, and the initial bipartisan glow faded quickly. Indeed, the 106th Congress became all about point-scoring, as both parties maneuvered to embarrass each other in a battle for the majority in the 107th Congress — and the Democrats will have a lower hurdle to clear in the next election than they did this time. (*2000 CQ Weekly, p. 2518*)

"The Democrats will be saying, 'There but for the grace of God, one more shot and we've got the Senate,' " said Burke. "All of the incentives will be in the wrong direction, and that's why it's going to be so important for the new president to set the tone and bring everyone together."

Cabinet and staff appointments will be crucial, according to lawmakers and former congressional staffers. The president should surround himself with people "who are known to be consensus builders," Burke said. Cardin said the appointments will be important, but also the pre-inauguration meetings — which should include leaders of both parties — and the tone of the statements the new president makes in the early days.

"It starts with process," Cardin said. "I understand that the Republicans felt excluded from the process when the Democrats were in power. I can tell you the Democrats were excluded from the process when the Republicans [came to]

power. That's got to come to an end, and the new president can help that happen."

Others said the first few months will be important. When Clinton, in the beginning of his new administration, rammed his 1993 budget reconciliation package through Congress (PL 103-66) without a single Republican vote, said Buchanan of the University of Texas, it set a tone that made his later health care overhaul effort "nearly impossible." (*1993 CQ Almanac, p. 107*)

The health care effort itself misfired with Republicans, Burke recalled, when Clinton appointed first lady Hillary Rodham Clinton — now a newly elected senator from New York — to head a task force that drafted the plan in closed-door meetings without inviting any Republican staffers. "That would be high on my list, is not excluding people from the conversations" that craft major legislation, Burke said. (*Senate women, p. 10*)

One step lawmakers and experts are recommending for Bush or Gore, for example, is to appoint Cabinet members from the other party. Clinton did that, but not until the beginning of his second term. He named William Cohen, the former Republican senator from Maine (1979-97), as Defense secretary.

By 1997, Clinton reached out to Republicans to negotiate a balanced-budget package (PL 105-33) that included milder versions of the same things Clinton had criticized in the Republican balanced-budget package of 1995 (HR 2491), such as measures to slow the growth of Medicare spending. (*1997 Almanac, p. 2-3; 1995 Almanac, p. 2-44*)

"He took a lot of criticism, including from me, for triangulating" by working with Republicans on issues such as the budget and the welfare overhaul of 1996, Kerrey said. Still, Clinton's efforts did little to temper a growing animus. By the end of 1998, the president had been impeached by the House. This session, the two sides spent most of the year holding dueling press conferences as Clinton badgered Republicans on hot-button political issues, issued lengthy veto threats, and followed through with generous use of his veto pen.

Baggage

That last chapter of the Clinton legacy could easily rub off on Gore, despite his efforts to campaign as his own man. Should he prevail, Republicans and outside experts say, he will have far less political capital to spend than Bush — partly because Republicans' relations with Clinton were so bad, but partly because Gore adopted much of the same partisan, win-at-any-cost rhetoric during his campaign.

"If Gore is the president and he takes the posture that Clinton has taken, the atmosphere is going to be toxic," said Sen. Robert F. Bennett, R-Utah.

Even if Gore wanted to move into a more conciliatory mode, analysts say, he might not have enough political breathing room to do so. If he wins, "Gore owes his election to the labor unions and African-Americans, and he won't be able to walk out on them," Ronald M. Peters Jr., chairman of the political science department at the University of Oklahoma, said in an interview. The two groups are generally on the left side of the political spectrum.

Bush, on the other hand, is the man who famously promises to be "a uniter, not a divider." He says his experience in Texas has taught him the importance of working with Democrats: Republicans hold the Texas Senate by one seat — 16-15 — while Democrats narrowly control the House, 79-71.

The Presidential Contenders' Key Contacts on the Hill

If Republican Texas Gov. George W. Bush wins the White House, his key GOP contacts on Capitol Hill would include:

- Tennessee Sen. Bill Frist, a cardiac surgeon who was named Senate liaison to the Bush campaign after the death of Georgia Sen. Paul Coverdell.
- Texas Sen. Phil Gramm, a longtime home-state ally of the governor. The fellow Texan is a staunch supporter of tax cuts and would probably be a key ally on this issue.
- Texas Rep. Henry Bonilla, one of a small number of Hispanic Republicans, is a member of the House Appropriations Committee and close to the GOP leadership.
- Missouri Rep. Roy Blunt, a chief deputy whip and fiscal conservative who has tried to work out deals.
- Washington Rep. Jennifer Dunn, a member of the House Ways and Means Committee. She has spearheaded efforts to attract more female voters to the Republican Party.
- Ohio Rep. Rob Portman, who served in Bush's father's White House as associate counsel and legislative affairs director. Portman was at the forefront of efforts to overhaul the IRS. He also is a member of the Ways and Means panel.

Should Vice President Al Gore capture the presidency, his key Democratic contacts on Capitol Hill would include:

- Washington Rep. Norm Dicks, a longtime member of the House Appropriations Committee. Dicks and Gore have been close since they served in the House together and worked jointly on military issues.
- Rep. Bart Gordon. A fellow Tennessean, Gordon is one of the moderate New Democrats who hew to a more conservative line on fiscal issues.
- Senate Minority Leader Tom Daschle of South Dakota. Daschle is certain to have more power in the 107th Congress, now that Democrats have picked up Senate seats. He has closely coordinated legislative strategy with the Clinton administration and the Gore campaign.

That is why congressional Republicans, along with some outside experts, say Bush would start off with more good will than Gore. "George Bush will say to [Democrats], 'If your side is willing to be Americans first and Democrats second, and my side is willing to be Americans first and Republicans second, we can get a lot done,'" Shays said.

Texas Democrats, however, say the image of Bush as a truly bipartisan figure is mostly a facade.

"He reached out to Democrats who . . . are very friendly to Republicans, if you know what I mean," state Sen. Gonzalo Barrientos, chairman of the Texas Senate Democrats, said in a Nov. 8 interview. If congressional Democrats are waiting for a truly bipartisan Bush who would listen to the broad spectrum of views, Barrientos said, "tell them not to hold their breath."

If Eisenhower's experience is any guide, Bush would have no choice but to reach out. In 1953, Eisenhower often had to rely on Democratic support to carry out his programs because he could not count on Republicans to hold together.

The Harrison experience was different. He let congressional Republicans run the true show and, in the words of historian John A. Garraty, "cheerfully submitted to being practically a figurehead."

The 'Personality Issue'

One area where Bush gets better marks than Gore is intangible: good personal skills. It is far from trivial; it can mean the difference when working with key lawmakers who can either help your agenda or block it. If nothing else, it can keep political tensions from boiling over.

A congenial relationship was the reason President Ronald Reagan and former House Speaker Tip O'Neill, for all their deep ideological differences, never lunged for each other's throats. Even Republicans say Clinton was saved by his personality. They say Bush has the same advantage, and therefore will be able to put much of the election's fury behind him.

They do not have the same view of Gore.

"He's very opinionated, he's very partisan, and he's made no attempt to work with anybody," said Foley. With Bush, he said, "I can see relaxing sessions at the White House. I can see members getting together for Super Bowl parties. . . . That's the kind of thing you'd never, ever see under Gore."

Even Kerrey, a fellow Democrat, said Gore has "a personality issue that he's going to have to deal with." But it is easily overcome, he said, when a president starts working with Congress and giving members public credit at press conferences for the legislation they pass. "Once the praise starts flowing their way," he said, "it all changes."

Even the best schmoozing skills are unlikely to save Bush from the inevitable questions about how much authority he has if he does not win a majority of the popular vote. Gore's challenges could undermine the healing public statements made by other Democrats. Sen. Robert G. Torricelli, D-N.J., said Nov. 8 that "if George Bush wins this election in Florida, I will not look back, question his election or his authority, or anything else that he does."

By contesting the Florida vote, Gore may be hurting himself with Republicans he would have to work with later. "The Gore people are playing a dangerous game," said Shays, one of the moderate Republicans whom Gore would have to court.

The one saving grace, according to Bennett, is that a president has time to build public support that he may not have had going in, making the narrow vote totals a distant memory. "John F. Kennedy got fewer votes percentage-wise than either of these guys," Bennett said, "and he captured the imagination of the American people."

Ultimately, Congress will have to be part of the healing process. The model may come from a leading political figure from the Eisenhower era. At an April 17, 1953, speech to the American Society of Newspaper Editors, Rep. Sam Rayburn, a Texas Democrat who would later become Speaker of the House, offered this backhanded but memorable olive branch to Eisenhower: "We are determined that we shall not, and will not, hate the president of the United States."

If the 107th Congress can manage the same feat after the most bitter presidential election in modern times, that could be its first big accomplishment. ◆

Survival of the Surplus

Budget hawks expect the almost even split in Congress to spell failure for new president's most generous proposals on taxes and spending

Defenders of the budget surplus are among the few people these days who are finding a silver lining in the stasis looming over Washington.

They see their cause as benefiting no matter who is eventually inaugurated president and begins to work with a 107th Congress that will be historic for its partisan equilibrium. The outcome, they are confident, is that the most grandiose — and expensive — spending increases and tax reductions proposed by either Al Gore or George W. Bush will be abandoned quickly. And with the campaign platforms consigned to the shelf, the chances will grow that the predictions of swelling surpluses during the next decade will come true.

"Given the nature of Congress and the closeness of the election, whoever wins the presidency, I don't see how they will enact any of the major proposals that they're talking about," John F. Bibby, a professor emeritus at the University of Wisconsin in Milwaukee, said in a Nov. 9 interview.

Bibby, a widely published congressional scholar, said the crucial factor will be how Congress interprets the instructions from the voters on Nov. 7. Twenty years ago, he noted, the House was run by a solid Democratic majority, but President Ronald Reagan was able to win many of their votes anyway for his program of tax cuts and spending reductions, because many Democrats felt compelled to abide by Reagan's solid electoral mandate from the year before. (*1981 CQ Almanac, p. 14*)

Such a scenario is unlikely next year, he said. Regardless of who becomes president, the opposing party in Congress is not likely to feel much obligation to support his agenda, given the astonishingly even split of the electorate. (*Overview, 2000 CQ Weekly p. 2628*)

Until the presidential outcome is final, however, some risk exists for the surplus because the nation's financial markets — a key component in much of the current wave of federal revenue — are not likely to stand idly by for long.

"The markets do not like uncertainty; the uncertainty about the outcome is not a favorable thing, " noted George G. Kaufman, professor of business administration at Loyola University in Chicago. But if the result of the election turns out to be continued gridlock, businesses and the markets could find contentment in the knowledge that no sweeping policy changes are likely for the next few years — and Alan Greenspan remains firmly entrenched as chairman of the Federal Reserve.

The most expensive item proposed during the 2000 campaign was the centerpiece of Bush's agenda. He has called for a $1.3 trillion tax cut over 10 years, including lowering of income tax rates, eliminating the estate tax, doubling the per-child tax credit, reducing the code's "marriage penalty" and giving tax breaks for charitable contributions. But as president he should expect little chance for such an ambitious program, said Robert Bixby, executive director of the Concord Coalition, a watchdog group that advocates federal fiscal prudence. "Gridlock is good for paying down the debt," he said.

Both Plans Based on CBO's Projected Surplus

Both Bush and Gore have unveiled their proposals in the context of the cumulative $4.6 billion unified surplus that the Congressional Budget Office (CBO) projects will accrue by 2010. But $2.4 trillion of the money would come from Social Security revenue considered "off budget," which both candidates have promised to tap only to ensure the solvency of the retirement income system. That leaves a projected $2.2 trillion "on-budget" surplus.

In addition to his tax cut, Bush has proposed $475 billion in spending, mostly on Medicare and other health care programs. He says his agenda would require $313 billion in additional interest payments in the next decade, because not as much money would be available to pay down the federal debt.

Gore has proposed a net $480 billion tax cut, the biggest piece of which would be to enhance retirement savings options, and $1 trillion in spending, like Bush's with Medicare and health care at the center. He says his program would cost $253 billion in extra interest payments.

The CBO assumes that economic growth will average about 2.7 percent annually in the next decade, and that spending will increase by no more than the rate of inflation, which it says will generally be in the 3 percent range. At least initially, the new president will inherit such an economy. (*Chart, p. 8*)

Several nonpartisan number-crunchers have warned that these assumptions nonetheless yield overly optimistic surplus projections — because Congress has been pushing to enact laws that have increased discretionary spending much faster than the rate of inflation since 1998, when the federal government began running surpluses. Although Congress will return the week of Nov. 13 to resume haggling over fiscal 2001 appropriations bills, almost all of the remaining ar-

guments are about policies, not spending levels. The total is expected to be about $637 billion, 8.7 percent more than in fiscal 2000. (*Lame-duck session*, *2000 CQ Weekly, p. 2639*)

The Concord Coalition says continuing this pace of spending increases will yield a cumulative surplus of $712 billion in the next decade — less than one-third what CBO expects. The Brookings Institution, a leading Washington think tank, projects an on-budget surplus of only $352 billion, because it makes several additional assumptions about how Congress will operate — including the assumption that it will continue its practice of renewing tax breaks set to expire. (*Background*, *2000 CQ Weekly, pp. 2319, 2388*)

The American Academy of Actuaries, meanwhile, says the Medicare and Social Security proposals of both Gore and Bush are "potentially misleading" and fiscally unsound. An analysis by the trade association released Oct. 26 said Bush's plan to allow some Social Security savings to be invested in the markets would plunge the budget, including both the on-budget and off-budget accounts, into deficit around 2015, and make it impossible for Bush to pay off the $3.4 trillion publicly held national debt by 2016 as he has promised. Gore's Social Security and Medicare proposals, which place a greater emphasis on debt reduction, stretch the solvency of those programs somewhat but lack any structural reforms that would improve their long-term solvency, the actuaries concluded.

Moderates on the Rise

If Bush is sworn in and reaches out to centrist Democrats in Congress, such as the Blue Dog coalition in the House, he will be able to enact at least a smaller package of targeted tax cuts, Bixby predicted, adding, "I think the public would respond very well to small but noticeable accomplishments."

Robert D. Reischauer, a former head of the Congressional Budget Office, agreed that the Blue Dogs and moderate Democrats in the Senate will ascend in importance in the 107th Congress. "The real question in a Bush administration is whether the White House pressures the congressional leaders to moderate their partisanship and their ideological fervor," he said in a Nov. 9 interview. "This is what has to happen to make a Bush presidency a significant factor in American history." (*New Democrats, p. 12*)

It could be politically difficult, however, for Bush to build bridges with moderate Democrats without alienating the GOP. This is particularly true in the House, where the Blue Dogs have repeatedly hammered Republican leaders for rebuffing their offers of compromise.

Reischauer still gives Bush's tax plan a good chance. With President Clinton, he said, Democrats have felt they had an effective and articulate leader, and the result was a relatively high degree of party unity in big-picture fights. With a Republican administration, congressional Democrats would be more likely to splinter, giving Bush the crossover votes he will need to enact his agenda, Reischauer said. "Democrats will speak with many voices, and their voices won't be loud," he said.

A key factor in whether large tax cuts can be enacted will be the new surplus estimates from OMB and CBO due in January. If the surplus forecast gets better, as it has with each new revision in the past few years, opposition to a Bush-sized tax cut would erode substantially, Reischauer said.

Reliance on a rosier CBO forecast — it now pegs the 10-year surplus at $4.6 trillion — seems safe. Agency officials held their semiannual meeting Nov. 8 with a group of professional economists whose advice is factored in to CBO pro-

jections. CBO officials made comments at that session suggesting they will make a "significant adjustment" upward of their surplus estimates, according to a high-ranking Republican congressional staff aide who attended. Although CBO officials mentioned no specific new numbers, "they expect that the surpluses will continue to increase," the aide said.

Critics say CBO's projections are insufficiently optimistic about the productive capacity of the U.S. economy. But not everyone agrees that the economic future is bright. The American Enterprise Institute for Public Policy Research, a business-oriented Washington think tank, predicted this month that a "sharp" domestic and possibly global recession is likely in 2001. CBO projects that the gross domestic product will grow 3.1 percent next year. ◆

Inherited Economies

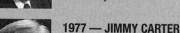

1969 — RICHARD M. NIXON

■ Gross domestic product:	$949.4 billion
■ Annual economic growth:	3 percent
■ Federal balance, FY '69:	$3.2 billion surplus
■ Publicly held debt:	$278.1 billion

1977 — JIMMY CARTER

■ Gross domestic product:	$1,974.6 billion
■ Annual economic growth:	4.6 percent
■ Federal balance, FY '77:	$53.7 billion deficit
■ Publicly held debt:	$549.1 billion

1981 — RONALD REAGAN

■ Gross domestic product:	$3,060.3 billion
■ Annual economic growth:	2.5 percent
■ Federal balance, FY '81:	$79 billion deficit
■ Publicly held debt:	$789.4 billion

1989 — GEORGE BUSH

■ Gross domestic product:	$5,406.6 billion
■ Annual economic growth:	3.5 percent
■ Federal balance, FY '89:	$152.5 billion deficit
■ Publicly held debt:	$2,191 billion

1993 — BILL CLINTON

■ Gross domestic product:	$6,560.9 billion
■ Annual economic growth :	2.7 percent
■ Federal balance, FY '93:	$255.1 billion deficit
■ Publicly held debt:	$3,248.8 billion

2001 — PROJECTIONS FOR A NEW PRESIDENT

■ Gross domestic product:	$10,041.3 billion
■ Annual economic growth:	3.2 percent
■ Federal balance, FY '01:	$239 billion surplus
■ Publicly held debt:	$3,224 billion

SOURCES: Office of Management and Budget, Department of Commerce

Searching for the Vital Center

Republicans' ability to run the traditionally freewheeling institution may depend on a handful of moderates

The extent to which the next president is able to advance his agenda will depend a lot on whether the U.S. Senate can change its ways.

The Senate is a difficult institution to run on a good day with a healthy majority. Years of Clinton-era partisanship and gridlock have strained relations between Republican and Democratic leaders. Efforts at coalition-building by moderates mostly have been shoved aside. Partisans on both sides already are looking ahead to midterm elections in 2002 that could well tip the Senate to the Democrats.

Now, protracted bitterness over a contested presidential election that remains undecided a week after the polls closed could conspire with an excruciatingly narrow margin of control to make running the Senate all but impossible.

"I call it gridlock plus — a president with no mandate and no honeymoon and an evenly divided Congress that couldn't run itself when it had a wider majority," Larry J. Sabato, political science professor at the University of Virginia told Reuters. "It puts the next president in a terrible position."

The Nov. 7 election produced not only a late, poll-defying surge for Vice President Al Gore, but major gains for Democrats that bring the Senate near the tipping point. Beyond the obvious threat of Democratic filibusters, the prospects for operational control are in peril, with a handful of Republican moderates poised to play a pivotal role in determining whether GOP leaders can avoid day-to-day chaos.

Republicans lost a net of at least three seats and very possibly a fourth, leaving their margin of control so close, at 51-49 or 50-50, that bipartisanship will be a necessity instead of a talking point. The still uncertain presidential election and an unresolved Senate race in Washington leave the exact numbers unclear. GOP control could be as close as 50-50 under a Bush presidency, which would then require Vice President Dick Cheney to break ties. If Gore wins and Republicans win in Washington, a resignation by Sen. Joseph I. Lieberman, Gore's vice presidential running mate, would produce a 52-48 margin.

In any case, the margin of control will be the narrowest since 1953, when, after the death of Majority Leader Robert Taft, R-Ohio (1939-53), President Dwight D. Eisenhower faced a Senate with 47 Republicans and 48 Democrats that remained under GOP control only because Independent Wayne Morse of Oregon (1945-69) voted with Republicans.

If Gore or Texas Gov. George W. Bush is going to successfully advance his agenda, he will have to forge centrist coalitions in a body where the model of late has been partisanship over coalition-building.

For Majority Leader Trent Lott, R-Miss., the challenge is enormous. His predecessors, such as Democrat George J. Mitchell of Maine (1980-1995), who led the Senate from 1989 through 1994, typically had the luxury of larger margins and a pool of people in the other party with whom they could work. But Lott is unpopular among Democrats and figures to be constantly refereeing intraparty squabbles.

"For all those who claim to be interested in bipartisanship, the next two years will be the ultimate test in the United States Senate," said Sen. Robert G. Torricelli, D-N.J.

The poisonous atmosphere in the Senate in recent years stemmed not just from Clinton's impeachment trial, but also from the way Lott has run the traditionally difficult-to-control body. He has sought rigid control in a chamber where the rules favor freewheeling debate and maximize the opportunity for the minority party to win consideration of its agenda. One of Lott's goals over the past two years was to protect vulnerable Republicans from having to cast politically challenging votes, a luxury he will not have if he wants to move the agenda of a Republican president.

Minority Leader Tom Daschle, D-S.D., has responded with delaying tactics and repeated attempts to force votes on Democrats' issues.

Making the Senate Work

Once the presidential election is decided, the big question is whether Lott and Daschle can get the Senate to function. The majority will have to share power, and the minority will have to resist the impulse to pepper the majority with difficult votes designed to create political advantage. The news media was replete the week of Nov. 6 with predictions of gridlock, but others held out hope.

"If Bush is the president and he says, 'Okay, let's tackle the big problems in as bipartisan a way as we possibly can,' and the Democrats decide it's to their advantage to get along with him, then we're going to be in much better shape," said Sen. Robert F. Bennett, R-Utah. "Whether the Senate will repair itself, I don't know. I think that's a question, quite frankly, you ask Tom Daschle."

"It might create the opportunity for the center to be recreated in the United States Senate. You're not going to be able to accomplish anything with strict party line votes,"

Clinton the Most Visible in New Wave Of New Women in Congress

One out of eight members of the 107th Congress will be a woman, but only Hillary Rodham Clinton will arrive at the Capitol in January as an international celebrity.

Along with Edward M. Kennedy, D-Mass., Strom Thurmond, R-S.C., and a handful of others in the Senate, the presence of New York's new junior Democratic senator on the floor will be met with pointed fingers, knowing gazes and whispered asides in the spectators' galleries above. (*Security,* 2000 CQ *Weekly,* p. 2625)

The unprecedented election of a first lady to public office has overshadowed the stronger-than-ever showing of women candidates for federal office. Eighteen Republican women and 41 Democratic women were elected to the House, 13.6 percent of the membership. For the first time, women will hold a similar share of the Senate seats, as well.

There will be at least a dozen female senators at the start of the 107th Congress — there were just two a decade ago — and 13 if the Washington state seat goes to Democrat Maria Cantwell, an Internet executive and former House member (1993-95). The outcome of that race may not be final for two weeks. But if Cantwell were to defeat GOP incumbent Slade Gorton, all six female nominees will have prevailed. That would be a better outcome than in 1992, touted as the "Year of the Woman," when 11 were nominated but only five were elected. (All were re-elected in 1998 except Carol Moseley-Braun, D-Ill.)

Three women were re-elected overwhelmingly on Nov. 7: Dianne Feinstein, D-Calif.; Kay Bailey Hutchison, R-Texas; and Olympia J. Snowe, R-Maine. Besides Clinton, the women who have won certain membership in the Class of 2000 are fellow Democrats who are taking vastly different paths to the Senate. Rep. Debbie Stabenow of Michigan, who has represented the 8th District in the House since 1997, campaigned for more than a year to oust GOP incumbent Spencer Abraham. Jean Carnahan of Missouri is the latest in a long line of widows to fill their husbands' shoes. She will be named to fill the first two years of the term to which her husband, Gov. Mel Carnahan, was elected even though he died in an airplane crash Oct. 16.

The arrival of another female senator is possible early next year. If Sen. Joseph I. Lieberman, D-Conn., emerges as the vice president-elect, Republican Gov. John G. Rowland would appoint a replacement to serve until the 2002 election. The leading prospect is Rep. Nancy L. Johnson, the second most senior House Republican woman, just elected to a 10th term.

Positioning to Run for President

The growing caucus of women in Congress is heartening to many of those already there. "That's going to be a pretty impressive visual: 13 women, all in different color suits, different styles, different sizes, different accents, dif-

said J. Keith Kennedy, a former longtime Senate GOP aide, now a lobbyist. "The only way anything happens is if you get a bipartisan vote. And once people get used to it, that that's the way you make it happen, who knows, it may catch on."

Still, the Democratic minority has the potential to wrest working control of the Senate floor from Republicans on a host of issues, should they force votes on the agenda they took to the voters: a "patient's bill of rights" for those whose health care is covered by health maintenance organizations, raising the minimum wage, and trying again to overhaul campaign finance laws. The prospect of Republicans having to mount filibusters to stop those popular issues is a potential public relations disaster. Even more damaging might be for a Republican president to veto bills sent to him by a GOP-controlled Congress.

And thin control maximizes freelancing opportunities for

rogue senators such as Arizona Republican John McCain, who vows to revisit campaign finance early next year.

On the other hand, if everyone is serious about bipartisanship and centrist coalition-building, the bodies are there.

"This is a situation that is made for mainstream coalition-building. . . . The Republicans will have no choice," said John B. Breaux, a moderate Democrat from Louisiana. "What [Bush's] mandate will be if he is elected is to build a bipartisan coalition to govern from the center."

And it was not lost on Republicans that every GOP incumbent who was defeated — Rod Grams of Minnesota, John Ashcroft of Missouri, Spencer Abraham of Michigan, William V. Roth Jr., of Delaware, and perhaps Slade Gorton of Washington — was a conservative. Three New England GOP moderates: Lincoln Chafee of Rhode Island, James M. Jeffords of Vermont and Olympia J. Snowe of Maine, sailed

ferent parties," said Mary L. Landrieu, a Louisiana Democrat elected to the Senate in 1996.

Three of the five female gubernatorial candidates were elected. Such statewide victories — which generally require greater name recognition and political sophistication than winning a seat in the House of Representatives — are a boon for those who aspire to someday elect a woman to the nation's highest office. (*Governors*, 2000 *CQ Weekly*, p. 2668)

"The increased number of women in the Senate and governors' mansions will bear fruit in years to come by expanding the pool of women who are poised to seek the presidency," said Roselyn O'Connell, president of the National Women's Political Caucus, an organization that identifies, recruits, trains and supports women seeking public office.

That, of course, is what many of Clinton's opponents fear. At a news conference the morning after the election, she was asked if she would seek to return to the White House in four years — as president. "No, I'm going to serve my six years as the junior senator from New York," she replied, and she promised that her first bill would be to enhance upstate New York's economy.

Some Senate Republicans were already openly skeptical. "I have a hard time seeing her as Senator Pothole," Robert F. Bennett of Utah said in a Nov. 9 interview. "I think she's going to be out on the fundraising trail. I think she's going to give speeches. I think she's going to have high public visibility, but I don't think she's going to be involved in the day-to-day work of the Senate."

Majority Leader Trent Lott, R-Miss., urged Clinton to refute that prediction. "She'll be one of 100 co-equals; she'll have to get used to that," he said on election night. "Getting a lot of attention and getting something done in the Senate don't always go hand in hand. If she's smart, she'll keep a pretty low profile for a while."

The Women's Vote

Most of the women who won seats in the Senate have other women to thank.

In New York, for instance, exit polls showed women preferred Clinton to Republican Rick A. Lazio, 60 percent to 39 percent, in a race she won with 55 percent. At her news conference, she said female voters "played a decisive

role. . . . It was a very powerful statement about what women voters care about, which is what I care about."

Similar gender gaps were evident in Stabenow's and Cantwell's races. Exit polls showed Stabenow won 54 percent of the female vote, and Abraham won 54 percent of the male vote, in an election she won by a percentage point. Preliminary returns showed precisely the same split in the Washington state race.

This is not altogether surprising. In this presidential election and in 1996, the gender gap was at least 10 percent, up from 4 percent in 1992, according to the Center for American Women and Politics at Rutgers University.

Preliminary numbers from the Voter News Service show that Democratic Vice President Al Gore won the votes of 54 percent of women and 42 percent of men, while 43 percent of women and 53 percent of men voted for Republican Texas Gov. George W. Bush. With 58 percent, Gore won his strongest support from working women.

Experts at Rutgers say such gaps generally are based on party, not gender. For example, Hutchison won re-election in Texas with 65 percent overall, but with 68 percent of the male vote and 63 percent of the female vote.

Party-based gender gaps in voting may exist because female voters tend to be more concerned about education, care for the elderly and several other issues that generally play to Democrats' strengths. In addition, female candidates often are seen as more credible than their male opponents on such issues, Landrieu said.

Gender gaps also existed in House races, but women candidates were unable to leverage them as often as their Senate counterparts. Of the 122 women who were nominated, only 59 (48 percent) have been declared the winners; three others are in extremely close races are awaiting recounts or the counting of absentee ballots. House newcomers include Republicans Jo Ann Davis of Virginia, Melissa Hart of Pennsylvania and Shelley Moore Capito of West Virginia and Democrats Susan Davis and Hilda Solis of California and Betty McCollum of Minnesota.

Many of those who lost were nominated to run against entrenched and well-financed incumbents. Once elected, however, the power of incumbency appears gender-neutral. All 52 congresswomen who sought re-election won it.

to easy victories. (*Story*, p. 14)

Meanwhile, an influx of moderate Democrats such as Thomas R. Carper of Delaware, Ben Nelson of Nebraska and Bill Nelson of Florida will come to Washington to replenish the thinned roster of centrist Democrats.

"You have some pretty conservative guys taking a dive and being replaced by moderate Democrats," said Robert D. Reischauer, president of the Urban Institute, a Washington think tank. "I think the Republicans are going to be more pragmatic."

Furthermore, if one examines the roster of senators up for reelection in 2002, there are a host of moderate Democrats such as Mary L. Landrieu of Louisiana, Max Cleland of Georgia, Max Baucus of Montana and Torricelli. "Some of the Democratic moderates are up, too, and they may be less willing to simply follow their leadership and may be actually

willing to work with Republicans," said a senior Senate GOP aide. "The dynamic is unclear at this point. You can't really predict it. You can only opine about it."

"If it's Bush, he's got to come in with the style and attitude that he at least projected during the campaign, of working across the aisle," said Charles O. Jones, professor emeritus of political science at the University of Wisconsin-Madison. "Congress is no Texas state legislature, and Tom Daschle and [House Minority Leader Richard A.] Gephardt [D-Mo.] are sure as hell not Texas Democrats. So it's going to take tremendous resourcefulness on his part."

Added Jones: "It's very important to set the tone very early, so that the media don't begin to set the theme of potential conflict."

But even in the event there is the will on both sides to work together, there are fewer in the Senate with the gravi-

New Democrats Looking For Larger Role in 107th Congress

The New Democrats are hoping that the 107th Congress will give them new clout.

Whether Republican Texas Gov. George W. Bush or Democratic Vice President Al Gore ultimately becomes president, the New Democratic coalition believes the Nov. 7 election was a validation of its middle-of-the road platform of targeted tax cuts, entitlement overhaul and efforts to improve education.

Electoral victories by the self-described moderates helped the Democrats increase their Senate membership to at least 49, and possibly 50, and aided the House Democrats' likely pickup of two seats. The narrower GOP margin of control should give the group more clout.

"You cannot lead this Congress in a liberal direction and pass anything," said Rep. Charles W. Stenholm, D-Texas. He belongs to a group of about 30 fiscally conservative Democrats, known as the Blue Dogs, some of whom are also New Democrats.

Simon Rosenberg, president of the New Democrat Network, a political fundraising affiliate of the coalition, said the group's Senate membership will increase from 16 to at least 17. One Senate race, between Slade Gorton, R-Wash., and another New Democrat, former Rep. Maria Cantwell (1993-95), is still undecided. Rosenberg estimated that the number of House New Democrats could increase from 64 to more than 70, depending on how many incoming members formally join the coalition. (*2000 CQ Weekly, p. 1985*)

He said that it was unclear whether some newly elected lawmakers, including Sen.-elect Hillary Rodham Clinton, D-N.Y., would join.

In the case of a Gore presidency, New Democrats and moderate Republicans could be allies in an effort to move one of his top priorities: legislation similar to a campaign finance overhaul bill (S 1593) sponsored by Sens. John McCain, R-Ariz., and Russell D. Feingold, D-Wis. It would ban "soft money," or unrestricted donations to political parties.

Rep. Amo Houghton, R-N.Y., said several New Democrats met in October with some members of his own group of 55 GOP moderates, known as the Main Street Partnership, and discussed joining forces to promote the

Evan Bayh, left, with Sen. Arlen Specter, R-Pa., is a moderate "New Democrat."

McCain-Feingold bill. "We may work together," he said.

Joseph I. Lieberman, D-Conn., Gore's running mate, founded the Senate New Democrat coalition this year. Gore himself was a member of the Democratic Leadership Council, founded to move the party toward the center.

During the campaign, however, some of the moderates distanced themselves from Gore's attacks on oil and pharmaceutical firms and his criticism of tax breaks for the wealthy.

In the case of a Bush presidency, New Democrats probably would be vital to efforts to promote tax cuts, changes in the Social Security system and a proposal to give the president expedited authority to work out trade deals. Bush has proposed the creation of private investment accounts under Social Security, a proposal many of the Democrats support.

"The president, whoever he is, will have to look to moderate centrists to get his agenda passed," said Sen. John B. Breaux, D-La.

With Bush as president, Charles Bullock, a professor at the University of Georgia, said New Democrats could play a role similar to the "Boll Weevils," conservative Southern Democrats who helped President Ronald Reagan win passage of tax and spending cuts in 1981. (*1981 Almanac, p. 245*)

Bullock added that it could be harder to cut deals in 2001 than in 1981. "Reagan had a mandate. There is no sense of that this time," Bullock said.

Republican moderates such as Michigan Rep. Fred Upton agree that New Democrats could be allies of the GOP. "The margins in both chambers will be narrow. New Democrats may play an important role," he said.

In the 107th Congress, one of the prominent new leaders of the New Democrats will likely be Sen. Evan Bayh of Indiana. Even if he does not become vice president, Lieberman is expected to step down from his post as chairman of the DLC, which represents a national network of elected officials and community leaders.

Breaux said Lieberman's likely successor would be Bayh. "Joe has been there a long time. He's ready to pass the baton," he said.

tas to make it happen. A generation of senators cut their teeth in the unrelentingly partisan Clinton era.

"When Reagan was elected president, he had Howard Baker [R-Tenn., 1967-85], Bob Dole [R-Kan., 1969-96], Paul Laxalt [R-Nev., 1974-87], Bob Packwood [R-Ore., 1969-95] — all these guys were actually grownups and knew how to pass legislation, and had been legislating for years and years and years," said the chief of staff to a senior Senate Democrat. "What Bush has is Trent Lott, Don Nickles [R-Okla.], Rick Santorum [R-Pa.] — nobody who's ever passed anything. So it's going to be hard."

Factor in an election that produced no mandate for the next president, one whose very legitimacy is being questioned, and it is clear either Bush or Gore faces an uphill climb.

"If Bush has . . . a Reaganesque ability to market ideas, he can govern," said a senior Senate GOP aide. "If he proves inept at building these coalitions, or if the Democrats decide they have no interest in allowing him to govern successfully, we have utter and absolute gridlock."

The Agenda

The early agenda of Congress in general and the Senate in particular depends, naturally, on who is in the White House. But for the Senate, where it effectively requires 60 votes to pass bills without letting them bog down in endless debate, the early weeks and months of the session will prove a time of testing. There probably will be pressure to act quickly on the fiscal 2002 budget resolution, which then would permit action on a budget reconciliation bill or bills. Such bills, which are available exclusively for tax and spending issues, are the only filibuster-proof vehicles in the Senate.

"They have a huge impediment in the Senate," a top Democratic aide said of a Republican government led by Bush. "They could maybe get through a couple of . . . things, but I think at some point it bogs down."

The chaotic presidential race was mirrored by a delay in knowing the precise party ratio in the Senate. Republicans will continue to control the chamber, but the exact makeup of the Senate depends on the outcome of both the presidential race and the results of a nail-biter in Washington, where a huge tally of absentee ballots means Republican Slade Gorton will not know until the week of Nov. 13, at the earliest, whether he will keep his seat. If Gorton hangs on and if Bush wins the White House, Republicans would control the Senate 51-49. That number would rise to 52-48 if Gore wins and Connecticut Democrat Lieberman becomes vice president because Connecticut GOP Gov. John G. Rowland would almost certainly appoint a Republican to replace Lieberman.

If Democrat Maria Cantwell defeats Gorton, the Senate would be evenly divided for the first time since 1881. Democrats predicted a big absentee vote from Democratic-tilting Seattle would give Cantwell the seat. But Cheney, as president of the Senate, would be the decisive vote. Again, however, a Gore victory in that scenario would shift the balance fully to Republicans.

The dizzying array of possibilities cast uncertainty over how the Senate will organize when it convenes Jan. 3. The first battle may be over committee ratios.

"We're at 50-50 in the Senate. It would seem to me we ought to be 50-50 in committees," Daschle said Nov. 8. "I don't see why that should be any different."

Republicans' aides said there is no way committees would be evenly divided in the event the Senate is. But already narrow ratios on powerful panels such as Finance and Appropriations are likely to close. Finance's present 11-9 split, for example, would shift to 10-9 or 11-10.

"All of that will be negotiated," said Sen. Mitch McConnell, R-Ky.

It is possible that a couple of committees that typically work on a bipartisan basis, such as Armed Services, could be evenly split. Until the Gorton race is sorted out, any such talk would be premature. But the prospect of a battle over how to organize a 50-50 Senate would bode ill for a body eager to display a bipartisan desire to work together.

Challenge Unlikely

Despite the disappointing election results for Senate Republicans, there appeared to be little serious talk of a potential challenge to Lott as majority leader. It was the second consecutive election cycle that went poorly for Republicans who did not make any net gains in 1998, despite hopes for a filibuster-proof 60-vote majority. But unlike the 1998 disappointment, which some Republicans partially attributed to a massive "omnibus" spending bill that conceded much to Clinton, the new Senate results did not spawn anger at Lott.

"I would be very surprised if Lott were challenged by anybody," said a senior GOP aide.

Said another GOP insider: "Somebody asked me if I thought there would be a challenge to Lott. Who would want to be leader with a 50, 51 vote majority?"

Adding yet another wrinkle is the possibility of someone giving up a seat for health-related reasons. The death of Paul Coverdell, R-Ga. (1993-2000), earlier this year delivered his GOP seat to the Democrats. Republican Strom Thurmond of South Carolina, 97, has been hospitalized several times this year, and 79-year-old Jesse Helms, R-N.C., also has had recent health problems. Both come from states with Democratic governors. Of the nine senators over the age of 70, seven represent states that have, or will have, Democratic governors.

If this came to pass and shifted the majority to the Democrats, the Senate presumably would reorganize in midstream. But nobody knows precisely how that might work; it has never happened.

In addition, the narrow margin in the Senate very well may have erased the chances of any Senator serving in the Cabinet of either Bush or Gore.

More than one Senate race made history. Hillary Rodham Clinton, who was the only first lady to run for public office, won a New York Senate seat. Clinton is a polarizing figure, and many Republicans are skeptical that she will fit in in the Senate. (Story, p. 2642)

Democrat Mel Carnahan beat incumbent John Ashcroft, R-Mo., even though Carnahan had died in a plane crash Oct. 16. It was the first time someone has been elected posthumously to the Senate — it has happened three times in House elections. Carnahan's widow, Jean, is expected to be named to the seat. The strange circumstances had some Republicans threatening to challenge the election, but Ashcroft, in a graceful and heartfelt concession speech Nov. 8, said he would not support such an effort. "I hope that the outcome of this election is a matter of comfort to Mrs. Carnahan," he said. "I believe the will of the people has been voiced with compassion, and I believe the will of the people should be respected and heard." ◆

Momentum Swing

Voters' ongoing purge of Class of '94 combines with untimely deaths to leave Senate GOP with a bare majority at best

Six years ago, a "revolution" swept Republicans to power in the House and Senate. But it took only two years for the pendulum to start swinging back in the House, as 12 of the 73 Republican freshmen elected in 1994 were swiftly booted out by voters in 1996.

That "purging" process may be the only way to explain the unexpected fate of Senate Republicans on Nov. 7. Having started the year with a 55-45 seat majority, they now face the prospect of holding — at best — a one-seat, 51-49 margin going into the 107th Congress.

Of the four GOP incumbents who were defeated on Nov. 7, three of them — Spencer Abraham of Michigan, John Ashcroft of Missouri and Rod Grams of Minnesota — were facing re-election for the first time since entering the Senate in that halcyon GOP year of 1994. The fourth, William V. Roth Jr. of Delaware, began his tenure in 1971.

A fifth GOP senator, Slade Gorton of Washington, remains virtually deadlocked with former Rep. Maria Cantwell (1993-95) as state election officials count absentee ballots. Gorton was elected to a third term in the Senate in 1994, but his checkered electoral history includes a defeat in 1986, resulting in a two-year hiatus from the chamber. (*Cantwell profile, 2000 CQ Weekly, p. 2678*)

Democrats, meanwhile, lost only one incumbent — Charles S. Robb of Virginia. In fact, they were defending only 15 seats, compared with 19 held by Republicans, and their only freshman was Zell Miller of Georgia, who was appointed to his seat July 24 to fill the vacancy caused by the death of Republican Sen. Paul Coverdell (1993-2000).

Democrats also lost the open seat of retiring Democrat Richard H. Bryan in Nevada to former GOP Rep. John Ensign (1995-99).

While Democrats made remarkable gains in the Senate on Tuesday, it was not enough to give them majority control. They will reach a 50-50 tie only if Cantwell wins in Washington. But because Sen. Joseph I. Lieberman of Connecticut would have to resign if Vice President Al Gore prevails in the presidential contest, there is no scenario that could give Democrats full control of the Senate. (*Story, p. 9*)

Republicans clearly were dismayed at the unexpected loss of power in the Senate. Mitch McConnell, R-Ky., chairman of the National Republican Senatorial Committee, tried to put the best face on the outcome by noting that "our goal for this cycle was to maintain our majority in the Senate for four [election] cycles," which had not happened since the election of 1930.

McConnell blamed the setbacks on the deaths of Coverdell and, ironically, of Democratic Missouri Gov. Mel

Carnahan three weeks ago. "These intervening events altered the landscape and made it tough for us to be in the majority," McConnell said.

The shocking death of Carnahan in an Oct. 16 plane crash produced an outpouring of support and sympathy that led to a stunning victory for the late governor over the embattled Ashcroft. The state's interim Democratic governor, Roger Wilson, has promised to appoint Carnahan's widow, Jean, to the seat.

Democrats, on the other hand, were ebullient, with Democratic Senatorial Campaign Committee Chairman Robert G. Torricelli, N.J., calling the election "an enormous, even historic victory."

Democratic Pickups

Missouri: The most dramatic and surprising Democratic victory came in Missouri, where Carnahan's death put Ashcroft in the awkward position of running against a dead man and his widow. In unofficial returns, Carnahan outpolled Ashcroft 50 percent to 48 percent. (*Results, p. 108*)

Missouri Republicans had grumbled before Tuesday that they might challenge a Carnahan victory on the basis that, according to the Constitution, only an "inhabitant" of the state could win election. Ashcroft, however, said Nov. 8 that he would neither contest the election nor support others who did. McConnell subsequently said the party would honor that concession.

Still, the state's senior senator, Republican Christopher S. Bond, asked the U.S. Attorney's office to look into possible election fraud in St. Louis County, whose voters contributed heavily to Carnahan's winning margin.

Before Carnahan's death, his "battle of the titans" contest with Ashcroft was vigorous and, at times, heated. But after Oct. 16, Ashcroft had no opponent to juxtapose himself against. He tried to focus on his experience as a senator, governor (1985-93) and state attorney general (1976-85), but also blamed his faltering campaign on his decision to suspend activities for eight days after Carnahan's death.

Jean Carnahan stayed out of the public eye, for the most part, after giving a news conference Oct. 30 indicating she would accept an appointment to the Senate should her husband receive more votes than Ashcroft. She did appear in a late TV ad asking Missourians to vote for her late husband. (*New member profile, 2000 CQ Weekly, p. 2675*)

Michigan: Democratic Rep. Debbie Stabenow appeared to eke out a 49 percent to 48 percent victory over Abraham, with 3 percent going to third-party candidates, according to unofficial returns.

Abraham's superior fundraising and qualified support for prescription drug benefits gave him a perceived edge

through much of the fall campaign. But Stabenow, who has represented Michigan's 8th District for two terms, got a desperately needed helping hand from organized labor, whose cash contributions and get-out-the-vote campaign worked to put her over the top. (*New member profile, 2000 CQ Weekly, p. 2674*)

Minnesota: GOP one-termer Grams never seemed to gain traction in his re-election bid. Former state auditor and department store heir Mark Dayton scored a relatively comfortable 49 percent to 43 percent victory. Independence Party candidate James Gibson garnered 6 percent.

Grams' campaign was dogged from the beginning by his surprisingly low name recognition, the result of a quiet and unassuming tenure in the Senate.

Dayton, on the other hand, pumped nearly $10 million of his own money into the race and focused his message on tried and true Democratic issues such as health care and education. His victory revived what had been a flagging political career: He nearly upset Republican Sen. Dave Durenberger in 1982, but finished fourth in the 1998 Democratic primary for governor. (*New member profile, 2000 CQ Weekly, p. 2674*)

Delaware: In the close but largely congenial Delaware Senate race, five-term GOP Sen. Roth lost his seat to popular two-term Democratic Gov. Thomas R. Carper, 56 percent to 44 percent, in unofficial returns.

Roth — the 79-year-old chairman of the Senate Finance Committee who is best-known for authoring legislation creating the "Roth IRA" retirement accounts — fainted twice during the campaign. This made his age a more overt issue than Carper had been employing under his low-key but unmistakably worded slogan, "A Senator for Our Future."

Carper served 10 years in the House before winning the gubernatorial race in 1992. (*New member profile, 2000 CQ Weekly, p. 2673*)

Florida: Democrats also netted the sole open GOP-held seat. Democratic state Insurance Commissioner Bill Nelson beat Republican Rep. Bill McCollum, 52 percent to 47 percent, to succeed retiring Sen. Connie Mack.

McCollum, an Orlando-area congressman first elected to the House in 1980, was best known as a House manager during the impeachment trial of President Clinton.

Nelson, a centrist who served in the House in 1979-91, established himself as a Democrat in the mold of Sen. Bob Graham, the state's popular senior senator. (*New member profile, 2000 CQ Weekly, p. 2673*)

Republican Pickups

Virginia: In a conservative-leaning state where Republican voting became more habitual in the 1990s, former GOP Gov. George F. Allen was able to oust Robb 52 percent to 48 percent, in unofficial returns.

Allen represented Virginia's version of the dream Republican candidate: conservative enough to appeal to the state's ample religious conservative constituency, but not so much as to make it easy for Democrats to portray him as an extremist. (*New member profile, 2000 CQ Weekly, p. 2677*)

Nevada: When Democratic incumbent Bryan decided to retire last year, Republicans saw a golden opportunity for Ensign to wrench the seat from Democratic control.

Ensign had lost a 1998 Senate bid against Democratic Sen. Harry Reid by just 428 votes. This time, he outpolled Democratic Las Vegas lawyer Ed Bernstein by 55 percent to 40 percent in unofficial returns. (*New member profile, 2000 CQ Weekly, p. 2676*)

Other Close Races

Three Democratic open seat contests also were close, but in the end the status quo prevailed.

New York: The Empire State's historic election between Democratic first lady Hillary Rodham Clinton and Republican Rep. Rick A. Lazio was the biggest political story through much of the election year. It was eventually overtaken by Missouri's bizarre race and the closeness of the presidential race.

Nonetheless, Clinton becomes the first sitting presidential spouse ever elected to office, and she was able to do it in impressive style, prevailing over Long Island congressman Lazio by 55 percent to 43 percent to take the seat left open by retiring Democratic Sen. Daniel Patrick Moynihan.

Clinton's victory can, in part, be attributed to her better than expected support from upstate New Yorkers, who traditionally vote Republican. She promised to make the flagging upstate economy one of her top priorities. (*New member profile, 2000 CQ Weekly, p. 2677*)

New Jersey: For the seat of retiring Democratic Sen. Frank R. Lautenberg, former Wall Street CEO Jon Corzine, also a Democrat, spent more than $50 million of his own money to put himself narrowly over the top of Republican Rep. Bob Franks, 50 percent to 47 percent, in unofficial returns.

Franks criticized Corzine — the former head of the Wall Street brokerage firm of Goldman Sachs — for trying to buy the election and saw the Democrat's once wide lead shrink. But with only about $5 million to spend, Franks could not compete over the airwaves with Corzine.

Although his background is in business and finance, Corzine ran on a liberal agenda that included calls for universal health care coverage. (*New member profile, 2000 CQ Weekly, p. 2676*)

Nebraska: In his second try for the Senate, former Democratic Gov. Ben Nelson triumphed over Republican state Attorney General Don Stenberg for the seat of retiring Democrat Bob Kerrey. In unofficial returns, Nelson led Stenberg 51 percent to 49 percent. (*New member profile, 2000 CQ Weekly, p. 2675*)

Georgia: While former Republican Sen. Mack Mattingly (1981-87) tried mightily to keep Miller below 50 percent of the vote to force a runoff, his efforts were thwarted in the special Senate election to fill the remaining four years of Coverdell's term. The enormously popular Miller beat Mattingly 57 percent to 39 percent.

Three Republican incumbents also narrowly weathered tough challenges.

In Montana, two-term Sen. Conrad Burns scored a 51-47 percent victory over farmer/rancher Brian Schweitzer. In Rhode Island, Lincoln Chafee made short work of Democratic Rep. Bob Weygand with 57 percent of the vote, retaining the seat he was appointed to after his father, GOP Sen. John H. Chafee, died in October 1999.

In Pennsylvania, Rick Santorum, once considered the most vulnerable member of the GOP Class of 1994, easily bested Pittsburgh-area Democratic Rep. Ron Klink, 52 percent to 45 percent. Santorum set out a couple of years ago to moderate his strongly conservative image, and Klink suffered from lagging fundraising. ◆

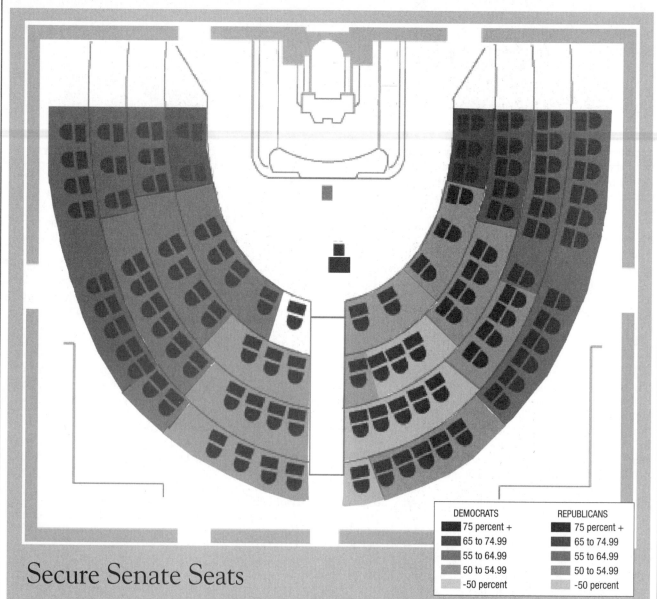

	DEMOCRATS	
	75 percent +	
	65 to 74.99	
	55 to 64.99	
	50 to 54.99	
	-50 percent	

	REPUBLICANS	
	75 percent +	
	65 to 74.99	
	55 to 64.99	
	50 to 54.99	
	-50 percent	

Secure Senate Seats

Of the 32 senators elected this year — one race remained in doubt — two-thirds won with at least 55 percent of the vote and one-third won with 65 percent or more, a group generally secure from challenge and with little reason to compromise. The trend has largely held through the last three Senate election cycles: 60 percent of all senators have won their offices with more than 55 percent of the vote; 25 percent have won with more than 65 percent of the vote. The most competitive races were in 1996. Of the 33 senators elected that year, 14 won with 50 to 55 percent of the vote, and five squeaked through with less than 50 percent.

	DEMOCRATS	REPUBLICANS
Senators unopposed:	0	0
Elected with 75 percent or more:	3	2
65-75 percent:	5	15
55-65 percent:	19	16
50-55 percent:	16	14
less than 50 percent:	5	4

The Limits of Outreach

Hastert and Gephardt talk hopefully of better cooperation, but partisan positions are already beginning to harden

The Nov. 7 elections loosened but did not break the Republican Party's six-year hold on the House majority. It did, however, break the long and bitter silence between the Republican and Democratic leaders in that chamber.

Hours after the election results showed that Democrats picked up some but not all of the seven seats needed to retake the majority, Minority Leader Richard A. Gephardt, D-Mo., called Speaker J. Dennis Hastert, R-Ill., to congratulate him.

It was the first time the two had formally spoken in months.

Harsh partisanship has permeated Congress this session, as both parties sought over the last two years to position themselves for an election that each hoped would vault them into solid control. Instead, the Republicans' slim majority got slightly smaller, and the Democrats' expected return to power fell short.

Hastert and Gephardt promised in their phone call to try working more closely in the future. "They both agreed that things need to improve and they said they should get together soon to talk about things," said a Gephardt aide.

But mixed into the conciliatory talk from both sides could be heard hints of the same hard-nosed positioning that led to so much partisan paralysis in the past. In addition, the lingering recount of the paper-thin presidential race in Florida set some members at loggerheads by the end of election week, and Democrats and Republicans still are disputing the results of half a dozen House races. More recounts are expected in several districts across the country.

It is far from certain whether relations between the two parties will improve next year. And most Congress watchers agree that the narrow House margin makes prospects for enacting broad legislation extremely dim.

"It is unlikely they will pass any dramatic reform," said Ronald M. Peters Jr., chairman of political science at the University of Oklahoma. "That would really split the parties."

While party leaders may instinctively say they want to work across party lines to pass "common sense" legislation, they were quick to point fingers and lay blame at each other's feet in the days following the election.

"We want to work with Democrats who want to get things done. Democrats seeking political advantage make that very hard," said John Feehery, press secretary for Hastert. "Our biggest obstacle has been the Democratic leader. Instead of running for Speaker for the first three months of the session like he did last year, we hope we'll see a more constructive effort."

Gephardt sent a similarly conflicting message the day after the elections.

"Democrats are determined to work with Republicans on a bipartisan agenda," Gephardt said in a written statement Nov. 8.

But the statement immediately went on to list as priorities for the new Congress the same controversial and partisan issues that choked the current Congress. Gephart's list included a patients' bill of rights, an increase in the minimum wage, campaign finance restructuring and expansion of hate crimes legislation.

Neither party has yet offered any concrete proposals on reaching a middle ground.

Democrats contend there are several visible ways Republicans could take the first step. For instance, they want the GOP to recalculate party ratios on committees and give them more seats to reflect the new, narrower majority. Democrats made a similar request in 1998 after picking up five seats, but were rejected.

Democrats say they also want more office space in the Capitol to hold party meetings. They say it would be a small but symbolic move on behalf of the Republicans.

Hastert's office said no decisions have yet been made on either request.

Democrats say there is little they can do to reach out a friendly hand to their Republican counterparts.

"They have all the control," said one Democratic leadership aide. "We don't have anything to give them."

Leadership Challenges?

A day after the elections, House Republicans crowed at their historic victory, the first time the party has won a fourth term in the majority since 1924. But it also is the third straight election since winning control in 1994 that they have lost seats.

Former Speaker Newt Gingrich was ousted following the party's poor election day showing in 1998, and while Republicans said Hastert doesn't face the same threat, that may not be true for Majority Leader Dick Armey of Texas.

One day after the elections, moderate Republicans held a conference call to discuss a feeling that they had been ignored by party leaders. During the call, members discussed the possibility of leadership challenges — especially to Armey.

"I think Denny Hastert is held in tremendous esteem by the members," said moderate GOP Rep. Michael N. Castle of

Delaware. "I suppose Dick Armey is OK, although I'm not as sure about him."

During the call, Castle said, the moderates agreed they should not pledge their support to any leaders until they know who may be running for the top posts.

"We're urging everyone to keep their powder dry," he said. "I don't think most people are inclined to be very committal at this stage."

However, Rep. Thomas M. Davis III, R-Va., chairman of the National Republican Congressional Committee, was pleased with results and said Democrats had lost a "once in a generation" opportunity to reclaim the House.

Before Election Day, even Democrats acknowledged that failing to retake the House this year could trigger a slew of retirements over the next two years. At the same time, the upcoming redistricting process following the 2000 census is expected to make it even more difficult for Democrats to win enough seats to take the majority in 2002, because Republicans control many of the state capitals where redistricting will be decided. (*2000 CQ Weekly, p. 2578*)

Republicans also are courting a number of conservative House Democrats to switch parties, hoping to shore up a more solid GOP majority.

"We'll probably get three or five members who will switch parties as a result of our retaining the majority," said GOP deputy whip Rep. Mark Foley of Florida. "Under the best circumstances, they did not prevail. I think they'll recognize that this is the time to switch. The times aren't going to get any better than this."

Among the possible party switchers Foley named were Rep. James A. Traficant Jr. of Ohio, who already has said he will support Hastert for Speaker, and Rep. Virgil H. Goode of Virginia, who earlier this year left the Democratic party to become an Independent, and has since met with the Republican Party conference.

But Rep. Charles W. Stenholm of Texas, a co-chair of the moderate Democratic Blue Dog caucus, said he did not expect any of his caucus colleagues to jump ship.

"There's no reason to believe any one is seriously making that decision," Stenholm said. "We have not had any serious communications about switchers."

Slim Majority

The final makeup of the House in the 107th Congress may not be determined for a week or more, but it appears that Democrats will pick up no more than two seats for a 221-212 party split, with two independents.

The last time there was such a close party ratio in the House was during the 83rd Congress from 1953-55, when the GOP held the majority. Republican President Dwight D. Eisenhower sent 44 legislative proposals to Congress during the first session, and won action on 32. (*CQ 1953 Almanac, p. 87*)

Political observers say such legislative success would be unlikely during the narrowly divided 107th Congress.

"I'm sure they will be well intentioned, but I'm sure political pressures will work against bipartisanship," said John J. Pitney, associate professor of

government at Claremont McKenna College in California.

Pitney said Eisenhower had a cordial personal relationship with Democratic congressional leaders and was able to work in a bipartisan way to enact legislation. Such a friendly relationship is unlikely next year should Texas Gov. George W. Bush, who remains ahead of Vice President Al Gore in the disputed Florida recount, win the White House.

Republicans would then control the House, Senate and the White House. Pitney said Democrats would quickly turn into partisan warriors.

"They are now in the same position as the Republicans were in 1993 and 1994," he said. "With no institutional responsibility, they are liberated to throw as many bombs as they like."

This year's race for congressional control came down to just a few dozen seats on both sides of the aisle; the result of each party being firmly entrenched in most of their districts. Very few swing seats still exist that can be captured by the opposing party, meaning there is little political reason for most lawmakers to move to the ideological center and abandon their base constituencies.

"It is more problematic now than in the 1950s. You had less-partisan parties then," said Barbara Sinclair, professor of political science at University of California-Los Angeles. "I don't expect a period of sweetness and light next year."

With no clear mandate from the voters — whose party splitting largely sanctioned the status quo — neither party is likely to budge from their ideological stands.

The election of the president, likely to come down to a few hundred votes, will not give the ultimate winner strong political authority to push his party's priorities. If Bush wins the White House with only the Electoral College votes, as appears possible, Democrats will be in a position to continually remind Republicans that he lost the popular vote.

And the narrow House split, coupled with a surprisingly close Senate margin, will give each party more reason to score political points in preparation for the 2002 elections.

"It will be hard for Republicans not to take advantage of the fact that they have all three branches of government," Sinclair said. "There will be a push by conservatives to get through things that have been stymied."

Moderate members of both parties, however, say they will keep a close eye on their leaders and make sure there is greater bipartisanship next year.

"We have to change the way we're doing business around here," said Stenholm. "This confrontational business was a leadership call on both sides."

Republicans said the rank and file may have to forge the bipartisan path on their own, dragging their leaders behind them.

"It may well be that members will have to send word to their leadership that we need to find issues where we can work in a bipartisan way," another moderate member said.

Stenholm said his leaders will have no choice but to incorporate Blue Dog proposals into the Democratic agenda. He said his moderate Democratic colleagues also have begun to reach out across the aisle.

Elected with less than 50 percent			
Betty McCollum	D	MN	48.04%
Bill Luther	D	MN	49.56
Heather A. Wilson	R	NM	46.96
James A. Traficant Jr.	D	OH	49.95
Jane Harman	D	CA	48.38
Mark Kennedy	R	MN	48.17
Mike Ferguson	R	NJ	49.49
Mike Rogers	R	MI	48.85
Shelley Moore Capito	R	WV	47.55
Steve Horn	R	CA	48.44
Steven Israel	D	NY	47.68
Susan A. Davis	D	CA	49.79

"There's no other path to pursue," Stenholm said.

Five new Blue Dogs were elected to the House on Nov. 7. After factoring in several retirements and one likely defeat — Blue Dog Rep. David Minge, D-Minn., has filed for a recount on his race in which he is currently trailing — the group's ranks are expected to grow by two.

"I really expect things will be a little different next year. I think the other side will reach out to us a little more than in the past," Stenholm said. "I would anticipate the White House would be reaching out to the other side of the aisle."

Even conservative Republicans said they believe the two parties will have to find common ground if any legislation is to pass next session.

"If we don't, nothing will get done next year," said Rep. John Shadegg, R-Ariz., chair of the GOP Conservative Action Team. "I do believe it's important for Republicans to work with Democrats."

However, Sinclair at the University of California said Republicans will have to be careful if they simply work with moderate Blue Dogs and ignore the Democratic leadership.

"If Republicans are not willing to deal with the Democratic leadership and just try to peal off votes from the middle, they will win a few issues," she said, "but it will poison the well even further."

Women in Leadership

On the Democratic side, it appears possible a woman could launch a challenge for at least one top position. Currently, no women are in the top elected Democratic leadership.

"I think we have to reinforce once again it's the women who are the backbone of this party, the ones who we can count on to support the party," said Rep. Louise M. Slaughter, D-N.Y.

Slaughter declined to say if there would in fact be an outright challenge to any leaders. But she said female Democratic members will meet early next week to discuss their plans.

"We'll do some plotting," she said.

Rep. Nancy Pelosi, D-Calif., had been running for what would have been the majority whip's position had the Democrats won control of the House. That position, however, evaporated with the GOP victories.

Pelosi said she does not plan to challenge any of the current leadership, but will keep a close eye on any openings. "I won't be challenging Gephardt or [Democratic Whip David] Bonior," Pelosi said. "I will continue to seek a position in the top leadership when there is an opportunity to run."

Pelosi said she would not be interested in any newly created leadership positions aimed at expanding female representation among the top ranks. In 1998, after women failed to win any leadership positions in the party, Gephardt created a new post to which he appointed Rep. Rosa DeLauro, D-Conn. She was confirmed in a vote by the caucus.

Rep. Steny H. Hoyer, D-Md., who with Pelosi had been vying for the majority whip position, said he is not actively seeking any new leadership positions either.

He, however, said it is "impossible to really talk intelligently about what we do now until we know the outcome of the presidential election."

Democratic sources said a change in the party hierarchy is unlikely unless the party rank and file pressure Gephardt or Bonior, D-Mich., to step down before the Democrats officially organize themselves. Gephardt and Bonior say they intend to run for re-election to their posts, but several Democrats suggested the two might consider stepping down because they failed to bring the party into the majority.

Both parties are scheduled to elect their leaders the week of Nov. 13. Republicans are slated to meet Nov. 14-15. Democrats will gather Nov. 15-16.

Currently, the only contested leadership race in either party is for the open seat of Republican Conference Secretary. Three women are expected to run for the post, which is being vacated by Rep. Deborah Pryce, R-Ohio, who is running unopposed for the vice chairmanship position.

Those running for secretary are Reps. Anne M. Northup of Kentucky, Kay Granger of Texas, and Barbara Cubin of Wyoming. Rep. Judy Biggert, R-Ill., also is mentioned as a possible contender.

Neither party is expected to begin selecting their committee memberships until late December and early January.

Outstanding Races

At press time, Democrats and Republicans were still disputing the results of at least six races.

The most hotly contested race was between New Jersey Democratic Rep. Rush D. Holt and former Rep. Dick Zimmer. By the end of election week, New Jersey's Department of Elections reported Zimmer leading Holt by 371 votes. Democrats, however, say Holt is leading by a few dozen votes. Both campaigns said it may be a week before the ongoing review of the results is completed. Zimmer represented the district from 1991-97, leaving the House for an unsuccessful 1996 Senate bid.

Officials are checking absentee ballots, the accuracy of vote totals at each precinct and "provisional" ballots cast by people who said they were registered but whose names were not found on voter rolls. Both sides say it is still too early to ask for an official recount.

A recount, however, has been requested in the district of Democrat Minge in his loss to Republican Mark Kennedy in Minnesota's 2nd District.

As of Nov. 10, the Minnesota secretary of state gave Kennedy, a businessman and first-time candidate, a 150-vote lead over Minge.

The count will not be certified until Nov. 21, however, and a recount could not be done until then. Minge contends that mangled ballots, software problems and the tightness of the race warrant the action. Kennedy, meanwhile, has claimed victory.

Another recount has been called in Michigan's 8th District race between Democratic state Sen. Dianne Byrum and Republican state Sen. Mike Rogers.

According to unofficial results posted by the Michigan secretary of state, Rogers led Byrum by 152 votes out of 297,510 cast in a race that included four third-party candidates.

In Florida, a recount confirmed GOP Rep. E. Clay Shaw Jr.'s victory over Democratic State Rep. Elaine Bloom. The final tally showed Shaw with a 586-vote edge. But Bloom's campaign urged patience.

"It's premature for anyone to rush to judgment," said Bloom spokesman Jeff Garcia, who said Bloom would take the next seven days to confirm the outcome of the race.

Both parties say they are also awaiting the count of absentee ballots in the California races of GOP Reps. Steve Horn and Steven T. Kuykendall. ◆

GOP Maintains Thin Edge

Despite a reversal of party control in several hotly contested races, Republicans manage to retain a hold on the House

Republicans withstood an aggressive Democratic attempt to win control of the U.S. House of Representatives. With a handful of races still undecided and subject to recounts, Republicans' seven-seat majority was only slightly eroded, with the most likely outcome a one- or two-seat Democratic gain.

That virtual electoral stalemate guarantees that the 107th Congress again will be sharply divided and that the 2002 elections, to be held under redrawn House districts, will be just as hard-fought as the Nov. 7 slugfest.

Next January, it appears that Republicans will hold a majority of 221-212, with two independents. That would be the smallest House majority since the 1952 elections produced a House of 221 Republicans, 213 Democrats and one independent. That was also the last year Republicans won control of the presidency, House and Senate, a trifecta scenario that will occur again if George W. Bush wins the presidency.

Ebullient Republicans noted that this year's elections marked the first time in 70 years that Republicans won a majority of U.S. House seats for the fourth consecutive election. "Without a doubt, House Republicans last night made history," said National Republican Congressional Committee (NRCC) Chairman Thomas M. Davis III of Virginia.

Republicans turned in an impressive performance in open-seat races, which were presumed to be the party's Achilles heel.

Of the 35 seats left open by incumbents who retired, sought other office or were defeated in primary elections, Republicans had to defend 26, while Democrats were defending nine. But Republicans held on to most of their vulnerable open seats, picked off a few Democratic open seats and minimized their incumbents' losses. *(New member profiles, 2000 CQ Weekly, pp. 2680-2693)*

Davis said that Republican candidates ran highly localized campaigns tailored to each district's demographics and political predilections.

Democratic officials, while falling short of their goal of winning the House majority, noted that Democrats scored a net gain in House seats for the third consecutive election. After losing a net of 52 seats and control of the House in 1994, Democrats gained nine seats in 1996 and five seats in 1998.

"We lost a lot of very close races," said David Plouffe, executive director of the Democratic Congressional Campaign Committee, in his interpretation of why the party failed to get over the top.

In fact, several House races were decided by the slimmest of margins. In at least five races, the winner's margin was fewer than 2,000 votes; in 1998, just one race was decided by fewer than 2,000 votes. At least three of those five Republicans appear to have won races by fewer than 600 votes.

Davis said Nov. 8 that the GOP expects to augment its House majority through Democratic defections, though he declined to identify any of "several" Democrats he said could switch parties. And he also expects to gain in 2002 through the states' post-census redistricting process, which Republicans will be in a far better position to control than a decade ago. Nearly all of the 435 House districts will be redrawn in time for the 2002 elections.

"I think what you're going to see is, in the coming months, Democrats will face a steep electoral challenge in redistricting and a wave of potential retirements in their ranks," Davis said.

Democrats dismiss GOP talk of Democratic party switches as wishful thinking. Erik Smith, communications director for the Democratic Congressional Campaign Committee, said Nov. 8 that any House Democrats who have harbored thoughts of switching parties already would have done so, because Republicans have "already offered these guys everything under the sun," including plum committee assignments.

The elections, as usual, were friendly to incumbents. Of the 403 House members who sought re-election, three lost in the primaries and six lost in the general election, an incumbent retention rate of 97.8 percent. That total does not include Democratic Rep. Rush D. Holt, who may lose his seat to Republican former Rep. Dick Zimmer (1991-97) in New Jersey's 12th District.

That incumbent retention percentage is only slightly lower than the 98 incumbent retention rate in the 1998 elections.

Flip-Flopping Districts

Republicans held the House majority in part by successfully defending 20 of their 26 open seats. And they severely wounded Democrats by capturing six of their nine open seats.

One clear Republican victory in an open Democratic district came in New York's 1st, where Republican fireworks executive Felix J. Grucci Jr. beat Democrat Regina Seltzer

by 56 percent to 40 percent. Grucci was aided by Seltzer's primary victory in September over incumbent Democratic Rep. Michael P. Forbes, who had been elected under the GOP banner in 1998 before switching parties in 1999.

In Pennsylvania's 4th District, Republican state Sen. Melissa Hart trounced Democratic state Rep. Terry Van Horne by 18 percentage points to win the seat left open by four-term Democratic Rep. Ron Klink, who ran unsuccessfully for the Senate. Hart raised twice as much money as Van Horne, who failed to capitalize on the district's Democratic lean.

In West Virginia's 2nd District, Republican state Rep. Shelley Moore Capito overcame the heavy spending of Democratic former state Sen. Jim Humphreys to win the seat of Democratic Rep. Bob Wise, who ran successfully for governor. Humphreys, a wealthy trial lawyer, lent his campaign more than $6.1 million. But the NRCC came to Capito's aid, including airing a television advertisement for her in the Washington, D.C., market during ABC's "Monday Night Football." The Washington media market reaches a few counties in the 2nd, which includes West Virginia's Eastern panhandle and is the least Democratic-leaning district in the state.

In Virginia's 2nd District, Republican state Sen. Edward L. Schrock overcame a spirited challenge by Democratic lawyer Jody Wagner to capture the seat of retiring Democratic Rep. Owen B. Pickett. If Schrock's margin of 4 percentage points was uncomfortably and uncharacteristically close, his victory was long assumed by Republicans and political analysts. The 2nd District, which includes all of Virginia Beach and some of Norfolk, has a Republican lean and a strong military presence.

The race in Missouri's 6th District was indicative of Democrats' poor performance in rural areas. Retiring Democratic Rep. Pat Danner easily held the conservative-leaning northwestern district for four terms, winning in 1998 with 71 percent of the vote. But that popularity did not transfer to her son Steve, the Democratic nominee and a former state senator. Republican state Sen. Sam Graves beat Steve Danner by 51 percent to 47 percent.

In Michigan's 8th District, Republican state Sen. Mike Rogers apparently scored a narrow victory over Democratic state Sen. Dianne Byrum. Rogers, the majority floor leader in the Michigan Senate, led Byrum by 524 votes out of 294,845 cast in a race that included four third-party candidates.

But Byrum is likely to seek a recount after the state board of elections certifies the results on or before Nov. 27. A recheck of results in Democratic-leaning Ingham County netted Byrum 371 votes, reducing Rogers' margin to 152 out of more than 290,000 cast.

If Rogers' lead holds, as GOP officials expect, he will succeed Democratic Rep. Debbie Stabenow, who narrowly defeated Republican incumbent Spencer Abraham in the Senate contest.

Defending the Veterans

For the third consecutive election, Democrats did a good job defending their incumbents. Other than Holt's race in New Jersey, which is yet to be decided, just two House Democrats were defeated for re-election Nov. 7.

In Connecticut's 2nd District, Republican state Rep. Rob Simmons unseated Democratic Rep. Sam Gejdenson, who was seeking an 11th term. Simmons surmounted Democratic strength at the top of a Connecticut ballot that included Sen. Joseph I. Lieberman, the Democratic vice-presidential nominee. Simmons outpolled Republican presidential nominee George W. Bush in the district by more than 20,000 votes. Though his district has a Democratic lean, Gejdenson's left-of-center voting record made him vulnerable to charges that he is too liberal for the district.

In Minnesota's 2nd District, voters appear to have elected Republican businessman Mark Kennedy over four-term Democratic Rep. David Minge. As of Nov. 10, Kennedy led Minge by 150 votes out of more than 288,000 votes cast in a race that included three minor candidates. Minge will file a lawsuit requesting a recount.

Kennedy, most recently the chief financial officer for the giftware company Department 56, ran a meticulous 18-month campaign and capitalized on the district's conservative underpinnings. Both Bush and defeated Republican Sen. Rod Grams comfortably carried the 2nd District in their races.

For Minge, the result was eerily similar to the cliffhanger 1992 election that brought him into office. That year, Minge defeated Republican Cal R. Ludeman by 569 votes.

For most of the campaign season, Gejdenson and Minge were not considered particularly vulnerable. Several Democratic incumbents whom Republicans aggressively targeted wound up winning: Dennis Moore of Kansas beat Republican state Rep. Phill Kline by 50 percent to 47 percent in a GOP-leaning district in suburban Kansas City; and Joseph M. Hoeffel of Pennsylvania beat Republican state Sen. Stewart Greenleaf by 53 percent to 46 percent in a GOP-leaning district in suburban Philadelphia.

Two Republicans who sought rematches against vulnerable Democrats fell well short of victory.

In Connecticut's 5th District, two-term Rep. Jim Maloney beat Republican former state Sen. Mark Nielsen by 54 percent to 44 percent in a rematch of a 1998 race Maloney won by just 2,300 votes. In Illinois' 17th District, nine-term Democrat Lane Evans beat Republican Mark Baker for the third consecutive time. Evans won by 55 percent to 45 percent after winning just 52 percent of the vote in 1996 and 1998.

In Minnesota's 6th District, Republican John Kline narrowly lost to Democratic Rep. Bill Luther in a rematch attempt. The 50-48 percent margin was slightly closer than in their 1998 race, which Luther won by 4 percentage points.

GOP Loses a Handful of Open Seats

Democrats captured just six Republican open seats, well short of what they expected and needed to win.

Democrats won one Republican open seat almost automatically, capturing California's 31st District seat after incumbent Matthew G. Martinez was defeated in the Democratic primary by state Sen. Hilda Solis. Martinez subsequently switched parties but was not on the ballot.

In California's 15th District, Democratic state Rep. Mike Honda comfortably defeated Republican state Rep. Jim Cunneen in a Silicon Valley-based area that Republican Rep. Tom Campbell gave up for an unsuccessful Senate bid. Honda, personally recruited to run by President Clinton, won by 55 percent to 42 percent in a district with a sizable Democratic registration advantage.

A Republican would have had a rough time in any case,

but Cunneen's campaign was hurt in late October by an NRCC mail piece that placed Honda's head over a jail cell to illustrate what Republicans argued was Honda's weak record on combating crime. Democrats and newspaper editorials blasted the attack as insensitive, noting that Honda and his family spent time in an internment camp during World War II.

Perhaps the poorest showing by Republicans in an open-seat race was in New York's 2nd District, which four-term Republican Rep. Rick A. Lazio left open in an unsuccessful run for the Senate. Democrat Steve Israel, the majority leader of the Huntington town board, beat Republican Joan Johnson, the Islip city clerk, by 48 percent to 34 percent.

Johnson, a moderate who was bidding to become the first black Republican woman to be elected to Congress, was hurt by the presence of conservative candidates on the Conservative and Right-to-Life ballot lines who took a combined 12 percent of the vote.

David Bishop, whom Israel defeated in the Democratic primary but whose name remained on three general election ballot lines, took 6 percent.

In Utah's 2nd District, Democratic energy consultant Jim Matheson beat Republican Internet entrepreneur Derek Smith with 56 percent of the vote to succeed Rep. Merrill Cook, whom Smith defeated in the primary.

In Oklahoma's 2nd District, Democratic lawyer Brad Carson easily beat Republican car dealer Andy Ewing for the seat of three-term Republican Rep. Tom Coburn, who retired to honor a term-limits pledge. Carson, who at 33 will be one of the youngest House freshmen, had 55 percent of the vote in a northeast Oklahoma district that has a conservative lean but a wide Democratic registration advantage.

A term-limits pledge also worked to the Democrats' advantage in Washington's 2nd District, where Democratic county councilman Rick Larsen defeated Republican state Rep. John Koster to succeed three-term Republican Rep. Jack Metcalf. Tens of thousands of absentee ballots are being counted, but Larsen held a 10,000 vote lead as of Nov. 10.

In several other critical Republican-held open districts, Democratic candidates fell just short.

In Illinois' 10th District, Republican lawyer Mark Steven Kirk beat Democratic state Rep. Lauren Beth Gash by 51 percent to 49 percent to succeed retiring Republican Rep. John Edward Porter. Kirk, who most recently served as counsel to the House International Relations Committee, emphasized his support of abortion rights, gun control and environmental protections, and brandished an impressive resume that included service in the Naval Reserves, World Bank and State Department. Kirk also benefited from his association with the popular Porter; Kirk once served as Porter's chief of staff.

In New Jersey's 7th District, which was left open by Republican Rep. Bob Franks' unsuccessful Senate bid, Republican educator Michael Ferguson beat Democratic former Fanwood Mayor Maryanne Connelly by 50 percent to 48 percent.

In Florida's 8th District, conservative lawyer Ric Keller narrowly outpolled Democratic former county chairwoman Linda Chapin to succeed Republican Bill McCollum, who ran unsuccessfully for the Senate. Keller overcame an aggressive primary campaign — one that concluded with an Oct. 5 runoff — and impressions that the moderate Chapin

was a better political match for the district. But Keller drew strength from the Orlando-area's strong Republican base.

In Montana, Republican former Lt. Gov. Dennis Rehberg beat Democrat Nancy Keenan, the state superintendent of public instruction, with 52 percent of the vote. Keenan was highly touted by national Democratic officials, but her liberalism on social issues did not sit well with conservative-leaning Montanans. Rehberg, who nearly beat Democratic Sen. Max Baucus in 1996, succeeds retiring two-term Republican Rick Hill.

Golden State Warriors

Democrats claimed that numerous Republican incumbents were vulnerable, but they knocked off only four of them Nov. 7. Excepting the GOP banner year of 1994, it was the best year for GOP incumbents since 1988, when four Republicans were defeated. Democrats defeated 18 Republican incumbents in 1996 and five in 1998.

Three of the four Republican losses came in California, where the GOP has performed terribly in the last three elections.

Topping the list was two-term Rep. James E. Rogan, who lost by 8 percentage points to Democratic state Sen. Adam Schiff in California's 27th District. Rogan and Schiff were on pace to spend more than $10 million combined, and the parties and outside groups chipped in more.

Republicans said Rogan's defeat was attributable to the district's Democratic trend and not to his role as a House manager in the politically unpopular impeachment trial of Clinton in early 1999. Davis said the 27th District, which includes the cities of Burbank and Pasadena, has a 7-point Democratic registration advantage just one decade after having had a 7-point Republican registration advantage.

In California's 36th District, also located in Los Angeles County, Democrat Jane Harman narrowly defeated freshman Republican Rep. Steven T. Kuykendall to claim the seat she held for three terms (1993-99) before pursuing a gubernatorial bid in 1998 that proved unsuccessful.

Farther south in the 49th District, three-term Republican Rep. Brian P. Bilbray was felled by Democratic state Rep. Susan Davis, who was well-funded.

Outside of the Golden State, the only Republican incumbent who lost was Jay Dickey of Arkansas, who was beaten by Democratic state Sen. Mike Ross. President Clinton, who was born and raised in the 4th District, campaigned for Ross, who won 51 percent of the vote.

Several Republican incumbents appeared to hold on to their seats by wafer-thin margins. In Florida's 22nd District, Rep. E. Clay Shaw Jr. apparently won an 11th term by defeating Democratic state Rep. Elaine Bloom by 586 votes after a recount.

In California's 38th District, Republican Rep. Steve Horn, who regularly underperforms at the polls, beat Democrat Gerrie Schipske by just 1,600 votes, but with thousands of absentee ballots still to be counted. Neither Bloom or Schipske has conceded.

In New Mexico's 1st District, Rep. Heather A. Wilson won re-election by about 2,200 votes over Democrat John Kelly, a former U.S. attorney.

For the third consecutive election, Wilson won with just a plurality of votes; the Green Party candidate received more votes than the difference between Wilson and the Democratic candidate. ◆

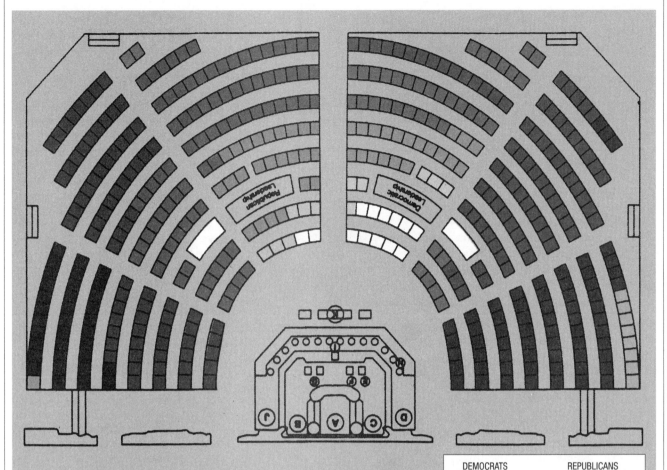

Small Room for Compromise

Not only does the next president face a narrowly divided House of Representatives, most lawmakers will have little incentive to strike bargains with the opposing party. Fully 87 percent of Republicans and Democrats were elected with more than 55 percent of the vote. Half of the Republicans and 63 percent of Democrats received more than 65 percent of the vote, leaving them virtually impregnable.

DEMOCRATS		REPUBLICANS	
■ 75 percent +		■ 75 percent +	
■ 65 to 74.99		■ 65 to 74.99	
■ 55 to 64.99		■ 55 to 64.99	
■ 50 to 54.99		■ 50 to 54.99	
□ -50 percent		□ -50 percent	
■ Unopposed		■ Independent	

	DEMOCRATS	REPUBLICANS	INDEPENDENTS
House members unopposed:	8	1	
Elected with 75 percent or more:	63	34	
65-75 percent:	64	75	2
55-65 percent:	52	80	
50-55 percent:	20	24	
less than 50 percent:	6	6	
Total:	**213**	**220**	**2**

States With the Most Secure House Delegations
(Average winning vote percentages)

Alabama	80%
Tennessee	78%
Florida	77%
West Virginia	76%
Virginia	74%
Louisiana	74%
Massachusetts	73%
Texas	72%
Nebraska	71%
Pennsylvania	71%

GOP Primed for Redistricting

Republican governors will play a key role in 29 states as congressional maps are redrawn in accordance with new census information

State elections have left Republicans well-positioned to try to increase their scant House majority in 2002 after congressional maps are redrawn with the latest Census data.

After the Nov. 7 elections, the GOP is set to hold 29 governorships while Democrats hold 19, with independents in Maine and Minnesota. Legislative dominance is even, with Democrats and Republicans each tentatively controlling 17 states. In 15 states, control is divided. Nebraska's unicameral legislature is nonpartisan.

Democrats say gains in Colorado, where they took control of the Senate, and Texas, where they maintained their control of the House, will help them during redistricting.

"We are as well-positioned as we could be," said Kevin Mack, executive director of the Democratic Legislative Campaign Committee, in a Nov. 9 interview. "We have fought back" since 1994, when Republicans held a majority of seats and chambers on the state level, "and protected those chambers in 2000."

For their part, Republicans point to Pennsylvania, where they gained control of the House, kept control of the Senate and hold the governorship, effectively giving them control of the redistricting process. That could help the GOP add seats even though the state's House delegation could shrink by two spots in 2002.

In increasingly populous Florida — which is likely to add a seat when districts are redrawn — Republicans maintained control of state government, holding off Democrats' efforts to retake the Senate. The GOP also gained in South Carolina and Missouri, with the senates going from Democratic control to ties.

The bottom line is that nine Democratic governors will lead Democrat-controlled legislatures, and 13 Republicans will govern GOP-controlled states. In most instances, if a party controls both the legislature and governorship, it can dictate the redistricting process.

"The story was how successfully the two parties did in terms of protecting their majority in states they already held," said Tim Storey, a redistricting analyst for the National Conference of State Legislatures, in a Nov. 9 interview.

Female Governors

In 2001, for the first time, five women will be serving as state governors.

GOVERNOR	STATE
Jane Dee Hull (R)	Arizona
Judy Martz (R)*	Montana
Ruth Ann Minner (D)*	Delaware
Jeanne Shaheen (D)**	New Hampshire
Christine Todd Whitman (R)	New Jersey

*Elected Nov. 7.
**Re-elected Nov. 7.

Storey also noted that the courts will have a say in the redistricting process, pointing out that they have not been shy in recent years about throwing out maps that are blatantly partisan.

"There are so many wild cards in the deck, and one is the role of the courts. Tuesday's election was just the first step in the journey," Storey said.

Gubernatorial Races

In the 11 states with gubernatorial races this year, issues such as education and welfare reform figured prominently, with many of the winners campaigning on a moderate agenda against opponents they were able to cast as too driven by ideology.

The elections also will usher in a record number of female governors: Five women will be the chief executives of their states, and Sila Calderon will govern Puerto Rico.

The only Democratic gain — and the only seat where party control changed — came in West Virginia, where Democratic Rep. Bob Wise defeated Republican Gov. Cecil H. Underwood.

In other gubernatorial races:
- North Carolina Attorney General Mike Easley defeated Republican Richard Vinroot, a former mayor of Charlotte.
- Missouri Treasurer Bob Holden beat four-term Republican Rep. James M. Talent.
- Montana Lt. Gov. Judy Martz topped Democratic state Auditor Mark O'Keefe.
- North Dakota banker John Hoevena, a Republican, defeated Democratic state Attorney General Heidi Heitkamp.
- Vermont Democrat Howard Dean was re-elected, defeating Republican Ruth Dwyer.
- New Hampshire Democratic Gov. Jeanne Shaheen narrowly defeated former Republican Sen. Gordon Humphrey (1979-91).
- Delaware Lt. Gov. Ruth Ann Minner, a Democrat, defeated Republican John Burris.
- Indiana Democratic Gov. Frank L. O'Bannon prevailed over Republican Rep. David M. McIntosh.
- Washington Democratic Gov. Gary Locke defeated radio talk show host John Carlson, a Republican.
- Utah Gov. Michael O. Leavitt, a Republican, beat former Democratic Rep. Bill Orton (1991-97). ◆

Voters Tackle Issues Cautiously

Far-reaching measures including assisted suicide and same-sex marriage are defeated, while gun control effort passes

Voters around the country tackled some of the contentious issues Congress has been avoiding when they considered ballot initiatives on Nov. 7, approving measures such as gun control while rejecting others, including assisted suicide.

Although victories were won for both conservative and liberal causes, experts said there was a discernible trend: "The overriding theme of this election when discussing ballot measures is that the voters were cautious," said M. Dane Waters of the Washington-based Initiative & Referendum Institute. "Almost every measure that could be labeled 'far-reaching' was voted down."

Still, 48 percent of the 71 state initiatives on ballots around the country were approved, up from the 100-year average of 41 percent. Some key results from the Nov. 7 election:

Taxes

Though tax cuts failed on the congressional agenda and were overshadowed in the presidential campaign, fiscal conservatives did see some victories through the initiative process. The most high-profile of these was in Massachusetts, where Republican Gov. Paul Cellucci's effort to lower the state income tax was supported by state voters, despite a Boston Globe editorial that said the measure would benefit only "the richest taxpayers." Other victories were in South Dakota, where citizens voted to abolish the state inheritance tax, and possibly Washington state, where voters appeared to have passed a measure that would abolish some tax or fee increases that were adopted without voter approval. An initiative that would reduce property taxes for seniors passed in Colorado. At the same time, several tax decreases were defeated: a property tax cut in Alaska, a measure in Oregon that would have made federal income taxes deductible from state income taxes, and a Colorado initiative that would have reduced utility, vehicle, income and property taxes.

Guns

Gun control advocates scored two major victories this election, as voters in Colorado and Oregon approved background checks at gun shows. Parents of victims of the Columbine High School shootings in Littleton, Colo., campaigned heavily for their state's gun measure, and Republican Gov. Bill Owens and Republican Rep. Tom Tancredo of Littleton — who survived a tough re-election contest — signed the petition to get the initiative on the ballot. It

passed with 70 percent of the vote.

The two decisions were a blow to the National Rifle Association, which scaled back its efforts in Colorado in the face of overwhelming emotional support for the measure. Gun control advocates hope to parlay their victories into momentum in Congress, but opponents say the victories carry less weight because they occurred in less populous states.

Education

Although more than $35 million was raised in support of two school voucher measures on the ballot, both were defeated decisively. The initiatives — Proposition 38 in California and Proposal 1 in Michigan — each took only about 30 percent of the vote. A charter schools initiative in Washington backed by Microsoft co-founder Paul Allen seemed to be headed for a narrow defeat, although mail-in ballots still are being counted. In the past decade, 10 voucher proposals have been put to voters across the country and each has been defeated.

Social Issues

Social conservatives scored on the issue of same-sex marriage, winning overwhelming victories in Nebraska and Nevada when 70 percent of voters in each state supported bans on same-sex unions. A Maine initiative to ban discrimination based on sexual orientation failed, 51 percent to 49 percent. Gay rights leaders say they may try to have the bans overturned in court. Previously, voters passed similar prohibitions in California, Hawaii and Alaska. Waters said restricting same-sex marriage is "the new trend to watch at the ballot box." Gay rights supporters won, though, on a measure in Oregon that would have prohibited "public school instruction encouraging, promoting or sanctioning homosexual or bisexual behaviors." It failed 51 percent to 49 percent. Opponents of abortion rights lost in Colorado, where a mandatory 24-hour waiting period for abortion won 40 percent of the vote.

Euthanasia

After a big defeat in Michigan in 1998, physician-assisted suicide suffered another loss the week of Nov. 6, when Maine's "death with dignity" initiative narrowly failed, 48 percent to 52 percent. Supporters of the measure were looking for a more moderate approach — the initiative would have allowed a mentally competent adult to "request and obtain medication from a physician to end that patient's own life in a humane and dignified manner, with safeguards to ensure that the patient's request is voluntary and based on an informed decision." ◆

Senate Membership in 107th Congress

ALABAMA
Richard C. Shelby, R
Jeff Sessions, R

ALASKA
Ted Stevens, R
Frank H. Murkowski, R

ARIZONA
John McCain, R
Jon Kyl, R

ARKANSAS
Tim Hutchinson, R
Blanche Lincoln, D

CALIFORNIA
Dianne Feinstein, D
Barbara Boxer, D

COLORADO
Ben Nighthorse Campbell, R
Wayne Allard, R

CONNECTICUT
Christopher J. Dodd, D
Joseph I. Lieberman, D

DELAWARE
Joseph R. Biden Jr., D
Thomas R. Carper, D *

FLORIDA
Bob Graham, D
Bill Nelson, D *

GEORGIA
Max Cleland, D
Zell Miller, D

HAWAII
Daniel K. Inouye, D
Daniel K. Akaka, D

IDAHO
Larry E. Craig, R
Michael D. Crapo, R

ILLINOIS
Richard J. Durbin, D
Peter G. Fitzgerald, R

INDIANA
Richard G. Lugar, R
Evan Bayh, D

IOWA
Charles E. Grassley, R
Tom Harkin, D

KANSAS
Sam Brownback, R
Pat Roberts, R

KENTUCKY
Mitch McConnell, R
Jim Bunning, R

Lineup

Republicans: 50 or 51
Democrats: 49 or 50

* Denotes new members

LOUISIANA
John B. Breaux, D
Mary L. Landrieu, D

MAINE
Olympia J. Snowe, R
Susan Collins, R

MARYLAND
Paul S. Sarbanes, D
Barbara A. Mikulski, D

MASSACHUSETTS
Edward M. Kennedy, D
John Kerry, D

MICHIGAN
Carl Levin, D
Debbie Stabenow, D *

MINNESOTA
Paul Wellstone, D
Mark Dayton, D *

MISSISSIPPI
Thad Cochran, R
Trent Lott, R

MISSOURI
Christopher S. Bond, R
Jean Carnahan, D *

MONTANA
Max Baucus, D
Conrad Burns, R

NEBRASKA
Chuck Hagel, R
Ben Nelson, D *

NEVADA
Harry Reid, D
John Ensign, R *

NEW HAMPSHIRE
Robert C. Smith, R
Judd Gregg, R

NEW JERSEY
Robert G. Torricelli, D
Jon Corzine, D *

NEW MEXICO
Pete V. Domenici, R
Jeff Bingaman, D

NEW YORK
Charles E. Schumer, D
Hillary Rodham Clinton, D *

NORTH CAROLINA
Jesse Helms, R
John Edwards, D

NORTH DAKOTA
Kent Conrad, D
Byron L. Dorgan, D

OHIO
Mike DeWine, R
George V. Voinovich, R

OKLAHOMA
Don Nickles, R
James M. Inhofe, R

OREGON
Ron Wyden, D
Gordon H. Smith, R

PENNSYLVANIA
Arlen Specter, R
Rick Santorum, R

RHODE ISLAND
Jack Reed, D
Lincoln Chafee, R

SOUTH CAROLINA
Strom Thurmond, R
Ernest F. Hollings, D

SOUTH DAKOTA
Tom Daschle, D
Tim Johnson, D

TENNESSEE
Fred Thompson, R
Bill Frist, R

TEXAS
Phil Gramm, R
Kay Bailey Hutchison, R

UTAH
Orrin G. Hatch, R
Robert F. Bennett, R

VERMONT
Patrick J. Leahy, D
James M. Jeffords, R

VIRGINIA
John W. Warner, R
George F. Allen, R

WASHINGTON
Patty Murray, D
— †

WEST VIRGINIA
Robert C. Byrd, D
John D. Rockefeller IV, D

WISCONSIN
Herb Kohl, D
Russell D. Feingold, D

WYOMING
Craig Thomas, R
Michael B. Enzi, R

† Maria Cantwell, D, or Slade Gorton, R, depending on final results

House Membership in 107th Congress

ALABAMA
1	Sonny Callahan, R
2	Terry Everett, R
3	Bob Riley, R
4	Robert B. Aderholt, R
5	Robert E. "Bud" Cramer, D
6	Spencer Bachus, R
7	Earl F. Hilliard, D

ALASKA
AL	Don Young, R

ARIZONA
1	Jeff Flake, R *
2	Ed Pastor, D
3	Bob Stump, R
4	John Shadegg, R
5	Jim Kolbe, R
6	J.D. Hayworth, R

ARKANSAS
1	Marion Berry, D
2	Vic Snyder, D
3	Asa Hutchinson, R
4	Mike Ross, D *

CALIFORNIA
1	Mike Thompson, D
2	Wally Herger, R
3	Doug Ose, R
4	John T. Doolittle, R
5	Robert T. Matsui, D
6	Lynn Woolsey, D
7	George Miller, D
8	Nancy Pelosi, D
9	Barbara Lee, D
10	Ellen O. Tauscher, D
11	Richard W. Pombo, R
12	Tom Lantos, D
13	Pete Stark, D
14	Anna G. Eshoo, D
15	Mike Honda, D *
16	Zoe Lofgren, D
17	Sam Farr, D
18	Gary A. Condit, D
19	George P. Radanovich, R
20	Cal Dooley, D
21	Bill Thomas, R
22	Lois Capps, D
23	Elton Gallegly, R
24	Brad Sherman, D
25	Howard P. "Buck" McKeon, R
26	Howard L. Berman, D
27	Adam Schiff, D *
28	David Dreier, R
29	Henry A. Waxman, D
30	Xavier Becerra, D
31	Hilda Solis, D *
32	Julian C. Dixon, D
33	Lucille Roybal-Allard, D
34	Grace F. Napolitano, D
35	Maxine Waters, D
36	Jane Harman, D *
37	Juanita Millender-McDonald, D
38	Steve Horn, R[1]
39	Ed Royce, R
40	Jerry Lewis, R
41	Gary G. Miller, R
42	Joe Baca, D
43	Ken Calvert, R
44	Mary Bono, R
45	Dana Rohrabacher, R
46	Loretta Sanchez, D
47	Christopher Cox, R
48	Darrell Issa, R *
49	Susan A. Davis, D *
50	Bob Filner, D
51	Randy "Duke" Cunningham, R
52	Duncan Hunter, R

COLORADO
1	Diana DeGette, D
2	Mark Udall, D
3	Scott McInnis, R
4	Bob Schaffer, R
5	Joel Hefley, R
6	Tom Tancredo, R

CONNECTICUT
1	John B. Larson, D
2	Rob Simmons, R *
3	Rosa DeLauro, D
4	Christopher Shays, R
5	Jim Maloney, D
6	Nancy L. Johnson, R

DELAWARE
AL	Michael N. Castle, R

FLORIDA
1	Joe Scarborough, R
2	Allen Boyd, D
3	Corrine Brown, D
4	Ander Crenshaw, R *
5	Karen L. Thurman, D
6	Cliff Stearns, R
7	John L. Mica, R
8	Richard "Ric" Keller, R *
9	Michael Bilirakis, R
10	C.W. Bill Young, R
11	Jim Davis, D
12	Adam Putnam, R *
13	Dan Miller, R
14	Porter J. Goss, R
15	Dave Weldon, R
16	Mark Foley, R
17	Carrie P. Meek, D
18	Ileana Ros-Lehtinen, R
19	Robert Wexler, D
20	Peter Deutsch, D
21	Lincoln Diaz-Balart, R
22	E. Clay Shaw Jr., R
23	Alcee L. Hastings, D

Lineup

Republicans: 221 or 222
Democrats: 211 or 212

* Denotes new members

GEORGIA
1	Jack Kingston, R
2	Sanford D. Bishop Jr., D
3	Mac Collins, R
4	Cynthia A. McKinney, D
5	John Lewis, D
6	Johnny Isakson, R
7	Bob Barr, R
8	Saxby Chambliss, R
9	Nathan Deal, R
10	Charlie Norwood, R
11	John Linder, R

HAWAII
1	Neil Abercrombie, D
2	Patsy T. Mink, D

IDAHO
1	C. L. "Butch" Otter, R *
2	Mike Simpson, R

ILLINOIS
1	Bobby L. Rush, D
2	Jesse L. Jackson Jr., D
3	William O. Lipinski, D
4	Luis V. Gutierrez, D
5	Rod R. Blagojevich, D
6	Henry J. Hyde, R
7	Danny K. Davis, D
8	Philip M. Crane, R
9	Jan Schakowsky, D
10	Mark Steven Kirk, R *
11	Jerry Weller, R
12	Jerry F. Costello, D
13	Judy Biggert, R
14	J. Dennis Hastert, R
15	Timothy V. Johnson, R *
16	Donald Manzullo, R
17	Lane Evans, D
18	Ray LaHood, R
19	David D. Phelps, D
20	John Shimkus, R

INDIANA
1	Peter J. Visclosky, D
2	Mike Pence, R *
3	Tim Roemer, D
4	Mark Souder, R
5	Steve Buyer, R
6	Dan Burton, R
7	Brian D. Kerns, R *
8	John Hostettler, R
9	Baron P. Hill, D
10	Julia Carson, D

IOWA
1	Jim Leach, R
2	Jim Nussle, R
3	Leonard L. Boswell, D
4	Greg Ganske, R
5	Tom Latham, R

KANSAS
1	Jerry Moran, R
2	Jim Ryun, R
3	Dennis Moore, D
4	Todd Tiahrt, R

KENTUCKY
1	Edward Whitfield, R
2	Ron Lewis, R
3	Anne M. Northup, R
4	Ken Lucas, D
5	Harold Rogers, R
6	Ernie Fletcher, R

LOUISIANA
1	David Vitter, R
2	William J. Jefferson, D
3	W.J. "Billy" Tauzin, R
4	Jim McCrery, R
5	John Cooksey, R
6	Richard H. Baker, R
7	Chris John, D

MAINE
1	Tom Allen, D
2	John Baldacci, D

MARYLAND
1	Wayne T. Gilchrest, R
2	Robert L. Ehrlich Jr., R
3	Benjamin L. Cardin, D
4	Albert R. Wynn, D
5	Steny H. Hoyer, D
6	Roscoe G. Bartlett, R
7	Elijah E. Cummings, D
8	Constance A. Morella, R

MASSACHUSETTS
1	John W. Olver, D
2	Richard E. Neal, D
3	Jim McGovern, D
4	Barney Frank, D
5	Martin T. Meehan, D
6	John F. Tierney, D
7	Edward J. Markey, D
8	Michael E. Capuano, D
9	Joe Moakley, D
10	Bill Delahunt, D

MICHIGAN
1	Bart Stupak, D
2	Peter Hoekstra, R
3	Vernon J. Ehlers, R
4	Dave Camp, R
5	James A. Barcia, D
6	Fred Upton, R
7	Nick Smith, R
8	Mike Rogers, R * [1]
9	Dale E. Kildee, D
10	David E. Bonior, D
11	Joe Knollenberg, R
12	Sander M. Levin, D
13	Lynn Rivers, D
14	John Conyers Jr., D
15	Carolyn Cheeks Kilpatrick, D

[1] Recount expected

16 John D. Dingell, D

MINNESOTA
1 Gil Gutknecht, R
2 Mark Kennedy, R * [1]
3 Jim Ramstad, R
4 Betty McCollum, D *
5 Martin Olav Sabo, D
6 Bill Luther, D
7 Collin C. Peterson, D
8 James L. Oberstar, D

MISSISSIPPI
1 Roger Wicker, R
2 Bennie Thompson, D
3 Charles W. "Chip" Pickering Jr., R
4 Ronnie Shows, D
5 Gene Taylor, D

MISSOURI
1 William Lacy Clay Jr., D *
2 Todd Akin, R *
3 Richard A. Gephardt, D
4 Ike Skelton, D
5 Karen McCarthy, D
6 Sam Graves, R *
7 Roy Blunt, R
8 Jo Ann Emerson, R
9 Kenny Hulshof, R

MONTANA
AL Denny Rehberg, R *

NEBRASKA
1 Doug Bereuter, R
2 Lee Terry, R
3 Tom Osborne, R *

NEVADA
1 Shelley Berkley, D
2 Jim Gibbons, R

NEW HAMPSHIRE
1 John E. Sununu, R
2 Charles Bass, R

NEW JERSEY
1 Robert E. Andrews, D
2 Frank A. LoBiondo, R
3 H. James Saxton, R
4 Christopher H. Smith, R
5 Marge Roukema, R
6 Frank Pallone Jr., D
7 Mike Ferguson, R *
8 Bill Pascrell Jr., D
9 Steven R. Rothman, D
10 Donald M. Payne, D
11 Rodney Frelinghuysen, R
12 — [2]
13 Robert Menendez, D

NEW MEXICO
1 Heather A. Wilson, R
2 Joe Skeen, R
3 Tom Udall, D

NEW YORK
1 Felix J. Grucci Jr., R *
2 Steven Israel, D *
3 Peter T. King, R
4 Carolyn McCarthy, D
5 Gary L. Ackerman, D
6 Gregory W. Meeks, D
7 Joseph Crowley, D
8 Jerrold Nadler, D
9 Anthony Weiner, D
10 Edolphus Towns, D
11 Major R. Owens, D
12 Nydia M. Velazquez, D
13 Vito J. Fossella, R
14 Carolyn B. Maloney, D
15 Charles B. Rangel, D
16 Jose E. Serrano, D
17 Eliot L. Engel, D
18 Nita M. Lowey, D
19 Sue W. Kelly, R
20 Benjamin A. Gilman, R
21 Michael R. McNulty, D
22 John E. Sweeney, R
23 Sherwood Boehlert, R
24 John M. McHugh, R
25 James T. Walsh, R
26 Maurice D. Hinchey, D
27 Thomas M. Reynolds, R
28 Louise M. Slaughter, D
29 John J. LaFalce, D
30 Jack Quinn, R
31 Amo Houghton, R

NORTH CAROLINA
1 Eva Clayton, D
2 Bob Etheridge, D
3 Walter B. Jones Jr., R
4 David E. Price, D
5 Richard M. Burr, R
6 Howard Coble, R
7 Mike McIntyre, D
8 Robin Hayes, R
9 Sue Myrick, R
10 Cass Ballenger, R
11 Charles H. Taylor, R
12 Melvin Watt, D

NORTH DAKOTA
AL Earl Pomeroy, D

OHIO
1 Steve Chabot, R
2 Rob Portman, R
3 Tony P. Hall, D
4 Michael G. Oxley, R
5 Paul E. Gillmor, R
6 Ted Strickland, D
7 David L. Hobson, R
8 John A. Boehner, R
9 Marcy Kaptur, D
10 Dennis J. Kucinich, D
11 Stephanie Tubbs Jones, D
12 Pat Tiberi, R *
13 Sherrod Brown, D
14 Tom Sawyer, D
15 Deborah Pryce, R
16 Ralph Regula, R
17 James A. Traficant Jr., D
18 Bob Ney, R
19 Steven C. LaTourette, R

OKLAHOMA
1 Steve Largent, R
2 Brad Carson, D *
3 Wes Watkins, R
4 J.C. Watts Jr. (R)
5 Ernest Istook, R
6 Frank D. Lucas, R

OREGON
1 David Wu, D
2 Greg Walden, R
3 Earl Blumenauer, D
4 Peter A. DeFazio, D
5 Darlene Hooley, D

PENNSYLVANIA
1 Robert A. Brady, D
2 Chaka Fattah, D
3 Robert A. Borski, D
4 Melissa Hart, R *
5 John E. Peterson, R
6 Tim Holden, D
7 Curt Weldon, R
8 James C. Greenwood, R
9 Bud Shuster, R
10 Donald L. Sherwood, R
11 Paul E. Kanjorski, D
12 John P. Murtha, D
13 Joseph M. Hoeffel, D
14 William J. Coyne, D
15 Patrick J. Toomey, R
16 Joseph R. Pitts, R
17 George W. Gekas, R
18 Mike Doyle, D
19 Todd Platts, R *
20 Frank R. Mascara, D
21 Phil English, R

RHODE ISLAND
1 Patrick J. Kennedy, D
2 Jim Langevin, D *

SOUTH CAROLINA
1 Henry Brown, R *
2 Floyd D. Spence, R
3 Lindsey Graham, R
4 Jim DeMint, R
5 John M. Spratt Jr., D
6 James E. Clyburn, D

SOUTH DAKOTA
AL John Thune, R

TENNESSEE
1 Bill Jenkins, R
2 John J. "Jimmy" Duncan Jr., R
3 Zach Wamp, R
4 Van Hilleary, R
5 Bob Clement, D
6 Bart Gordon, D
7 Ed Bryant, R
8 John Tanner, D
9 Harold E. Ford Jr., D

TEXAS
1 Max Sandlin, D
2 Jim Turner, D
3 Sam Johnson, R
4 Ralph M. Hall, D
5 Pete Sessions, R
6 Joe L. Barton, R
7 John Culberson, R *
8 Kevin Brady, R
9 Nick Lampson, D
10 Lloyd Doggett, D
11 Chet Edwards, D
12 Kay Granger, R
13 William M. "Mac" Thornberry, R
14 Ron Paul, R
15 Ruben Hinojosa, D
16 Silvestre Reyes, D
17 Charles W. Stenholm, D
18 Sheila Jackson-Lee, D
19 Larry Combest, R
20 Charlie Gonzalez, D
21 Lamar Smith, R
22 Tom DeLay, R
23 Henry Bonilla, R
24 Martin Frost, D
25 Ken Bentsen, D
26 Dick Armey, R
27 Solomon P. Ortiz, D
28 Ciro D. Rodriguez, D
29 Gene Green, D
30 Eddie Bernice Johnson, D

UTAH
1 James V. Hansen, R
2 Jim Matheson, D *
3 Christopher B. Cannon, R

VERMONT
AL Bernard Sanders (I)

VIRGINIA
1 Jo Ann Davis, R *
2 Edward L. Schrock, R *
3 Robert C. Scott, D
4 Norman Sisisky, D
5 Virgil H. Goode Jr., I
6 Robert W. Goodlatte, R
7 Eric I. Cantor, R *
8 James P. Moran, D
9 Rick Boucher, D
10 Frank R. Wolf, R
11 Thomas M. Davis III, R

WASHINGTON
1 Jay Inslee, D
2 Rick Larsen, D *
3 Brian Baird, D
4 Richard "Doc" Hastings, R
5 George Nethercutt, R
6 Norm Dicks, D
7 Jim McDermott, D
8 Jennifer Dunn, R
9 Adam Smith, D

WEST VIRGINIA
1 Alan B. Mollohan, D
2 Shelley Moore Capito, R *
3 Nick J. Rahall II, D

WISCONSIN
1 Paul D. Ryan, R
2 Tammy Baldwin, D
3 Ron Kind, D
4 Gerald D. Kleczka, D
5 Thomas M. Barrett, D
6 Tom Petri, R
7 David R. Obey, D
8 Mark Green, R
9 F. James Sensenbrenner Jr., R

WYOMING
AL Barbara Cubin, R

[1] Recount expected; [2] Dick Zimmer, R, or Rush D. Holt, D, depending on final results

Congress and the Nation 2001

This section of the *Guide* examines how the outcome of the 2000 elections will affect the organization and agenda of the 107th Congress. The section begins with an article on the unresolved issues from 2000 that were likely to make up the agenda of the 107th Congress. Concerns such as tax relief, education reform, missile defense, and health care were waiting to confront the new Congress when it convened in January 2001.

Also included are articles on expected changes in committee membership and leadership. With an almost even split between the two parties, the Senate prepared for changes in its committee ratios. In the House, as a result of the six-year term limit on committee chairs imposed in 1995 as part of the Republican's "Contract with America," leadership changes were expected on almost every panel.

This section closes with "Decision Time," written by CQ staff a month before the November elections. These articles look at six key policy areas that are likely to present the new president with the toughest dilemmas as he begins his first term and Congress as it starts its 107th session.

Fast Start on a Familiar Agenda

'Honeymoon' may be brief as Congress confronts a host of leftover issues; GOP leaders predict progress, but cooperation with Democrats will be key

The legislative menu for the 107th Congress will feature a heaping serving of leftovers. Lawmakers could discover, though, that they go down easier the second time around.

Unresolved issues from this year, ranging from health care to storage for high-level nuclear waste, will confront Congress when it convenes in January to begin working with a new administration. At the same time, lawmakers are expected to revisit other topics from the not-too-distant past, including welfare, agriculture and fast-track negotiating authority for the president to pursue trade agreements.

The bitterness of the elections and the shrinking Republican majorities in both chambers likely will mean that the "honeymoon" period, when Congress grants a new president considerable legislative leeway, may be a thing of the past.

"The honeymoon this time is a one-night stand," quipped veteran Washington lobbyist Tom Korologos of Timmons & Co.

Despite the narrow voting margins in the House and Senate, Republican leaders predict they should be able to get more done without President Clinton to confound or co-opt their plans.

"I think the issues of tax relief, tax reform, balancing the budget, paying down the debt, education reform, health care reform are some things that we can do, and we want to be working on that right away to get it done," House Speaker J. Dennis Hastert, R-Ill., told CBS News on Nov. 8, the day after the election.

More so than before, however, it will take close cooperation between Democrats and Republicans to get legislation passed.

Attention-Getters

Though neither party has unveiled a formal legislative wish list, here are some of the areas that are widely regarded as most likely to occupy Congress' attention in 2001:

• **Taxes.** Despite a narrower Republican majority in the House and a possible 50-50 deadlock in the Senate, renewed calls for tax relief are a certainty, especially if Texas Gov. George W. Bush is declared the winner over Vice President Al Gore.

"Bush has a much broader-based appeal to tax relief than Gore has," said Dorothy Coleman, vice president for tax policy at the National Association of Manufacturers.

Bush made across-the-board personal income tax cuts a centerpiece of his campaign, although he is expected to have difficulty finding the support for a sizable reduction.

According to Coleman, while Bush did not devote as much public attention to addressing tax cuts for businesses, he has supported cuts for business partnerships and some corporations.

A business proposal that Coleman would expect to see in the 107th Congress, no matter who wins, is a permanent tax credit for businesses that conduct research and development. Another proposal Bush supports is repealing the estate tax, a top priority for small companies.

Coleman said additional tax relief, such as changes in alternative minimum taxes and a major overhaul of the tax code like that in 1986 (PL 99-514), are possible in a Bush administration. (*1986 CQ Almanac, p. 491*)

• **Trade.** Renewal of fast-track authority is expected to surface early, especially in a Bush administration. It would allow the president to submit trade agreements to Congress for up-or-down votes with no amendments. Supporters say it is needed to ensure competitiveness with countries whose leaders have similar powers. Critics fear it would mute Congress' role and put American workers and companies in jeopardy.

American presidents had this authority from 1974 to 1994. Clinton and Republican leaders led efforts to renew it in 1997, but failed when a bloc of House Democrats and Republicans refused to give their support. A second attempt a year later also failed. (*1997 Almanac, p. 2-85; 1998 Almanac, p. 23-3*)

Some observers believe that a Bush administration would have to devote considerable attention to forging a new consensus among business groups that support fast-track authority and the labor and environmental groups that oppose it.

"A lot of work is going to have to be done to stimulate dialogue among those groups," said Sherman Katz, an international trade specialist at the Center for Strategic and International Studies (CSIS), a Washington think tank.

Christopher Sands, another CSIS scholar, said the narrow Republican majority means that additional provisions may need to be added to trade packages to make them more palatable — something he said angers other nations.

"The horse-trading in a close Congress to move legislation often sideswipes foreign interests," Sands said.

• **Health care.** Legislation that would give the federal government more oversight of private health insurance plans is sure to resurface, especially since Democrats, who prefer a broader federal role, will have at least 49 Senate seats.

In the House, such legislation likely will retain the broad bipartisan support it received in October 1999, when 68 Republicans voted with Democrats to pass a bill (HR 2990) sponsored by Reps. Charlie Norwood, R-Ga., and John D. Dingell, D-Mich., that would give consumers expanded rights in the private health insurance system. (*1999 CQ Almanac, p.16-3*)

Lawmakers of both parties in both chambers also are expected to focus on the issue of prescription drugs for seniors, but likely will do so in the context of a broader Medicare overhaul. House Republicans passed a prescription drug bill (HR 4680) in June, but Senate Republican leaders have been unwilling to move on the issue, saying that new benefits should not be added to Medicare — especially a costly prescription drug benefit — until the entire program is overhauled. Millions of Baby Boomers are expected to begin flooding Medicare in 2010, placing additional strain on the federal health insurance program that provides medical care to nearly 40 million elderly and disabled Americans. (*2000 CQ Weekly, p. 1584*)

• **Welfare.** Congress must decide by the end of 2002 whether to continue the structure of block grants to states established in the 1996 law (PL 104-193) that swept away six decades of federal welfare policy. It was the first time the federal government had transformed a major federal entitlement program into a block grant to the states. (*1996 Almanac, p. 6-3*)

Many observers assume that Congress will continue the block grant structure, but considerable debate is expected about whether a stronger federal role is needed. Some lawmakers are likely to argue that, with declines in caseloads since 1996, federal funding is too high.

• **Education.** With better schools and improved test scores at the top of voters' priority lists, Congress is expected to continue work on reauthorization of the Elementary and Secondary Education Act (ESEA). Lawmakers have learned, though, that public support for a broad overhaul of education does not translate into being able to surmount the partisan maneuvering on Capitol Hill and among interest groups.

Bush already has raised eyebrows by suggesting during an Oct. 3 presidential debate that the federal government should require annual testing of teachers, something that even many House Republicans are likely to resist. (*2000 CQ Weekly, p. 2394*)

• **Missile Defense.** Of all the defense and foreign policy issues awaiting the next administration, few are as potentially difficult as to how to blend weaponry and diplomacy to protect the country from long-range ballistic missiles.

The new president will unveil a formula for balancing two goals: blunting the threat posed by hostile nations that might have a handful of ballistic missiles, while not alienating Russia, which has thousands of missiles and remains committed to the 1972 Anti-Ballistic Missile (ABM) Treaty prohibiting anti-missile defenses.

Bush has made it clear that if the Russians did not budge, he would abrogate the treaty. However, to fund whatever system he wants to deploy, he would need the support of as many as 10 Democrats to get the 60 votes needed to break a filibuster. (*2000 CQ Weekly, p. 2398*)

• **Electricity deregulation.** Another issue likely to resurface in the 107th Congress is the restructuring of the national $217 billion electricity market, long a goal of industry and other heavy users of electric power.

Legislation that would allow competition has not gone anywhere in each of the previous two Congresses, but the legislation could proceed next year, thanks to the retirement of Thomas J. Bliley Jr., R-Va., chairman of the House Commerce Committee.

Bliley's departure would remove a significant roadblock that held up a restructuring bill (HR 2944) for more than a year. Republicans are eager to place much of the power to restructure electricity markets in the hands of individual states, a position Bliley opposed.

The legislation still would face an uncertain fate in the Senate, where members of the Energy and Natural Resources Committee must agree to the amount of oversight the Federal Energy Regulatory Commission should exercise in a restructured market.

• **Nuclear waste.** Republicans believe that a Bush election could end the impasse over where and how to store high-level spent fuel from commercial nuclear reactors in 34 states, an impasse that has persisted since the GOP took control of Congress in 1994. The Energy Department is studying Nevada's Yucca Mountain, 100 miles northwest of Las Vegas, as the potential permanent storage site.

Under Yucca Mountain's current schedule, the secretary of Energy is expected to decide next year whether to recommend the site to the president. The president, in turn, is to decide whether to submit the recommendation to Congress. If Congress agrees and the site is designated, the Energy Department would ask the Nuclear Regulatory Commission for a license to operate it. The site could begin receiving waste from power plants across the country in 2010 if everything goes according to plan. There is no guarantee that will happen, given the unyielding opposition of Nevada lawmakers and environmentalists.

• **Minimum wage.** If efforts fall short in the lame-duck session to pass a wide-ranging tax bill (HR 2614) that would include a $1 increase in the minimum wage over two years to $6.15 an hour, Congress can be expected to take up the issue next year. Despite misgivings by Republican leaders, a minimum wage increase is widely supported by labor groups and has broad bipartisan support.

In addition, both parties support targeted tax breaks that would offset higher costs generated by the wage increase, though they would have to negotiate the size of the tax package for businesses.

• **Agriculture.** A new farm bill will be at the top of the agenda of both the House and Senate Agriculture committees. Although the 1996 farm law (PL 104-127) does not expire until the end of 2002, critics of the measure have called for early action on a comprehensive overhaul. They say the so-called Freedom to Farm law does not provide an adequate safety net and has required Congress to pass emergency aid packages for farmers.

• **Campaign finance.** Supporters of overhauling campaign finance laws, led by Sens. John McCain, R-Ariz., and Russell D. Feingold, D-Wis., are likely to point to the election results as proof that another crack at the issue is warranted.

According to the Center for Responsive Politics, the average winning House campaign cost $636,000 through Oct. 18, or $4.90 per vote. Winning Senate campaigns averaged $5.6 million or $6.07 per vote, although that figure was skewed by the free-spending race of New Jersey Democrat Jon Corzine. ◆

Power Plays and Term Limits

Seniority doesn't rule as GOP leaders orchestrate a bruising game of musical chairs to fill committee positions

Major changes are in store for committees in the 107th Congress, as House Republican leaders sort out a tangle of competing interests and egos among lawmakers jockeying for chairmanships, and as the Senate changes its committee ratios to reflect an almost even split between the parties.

In the House, a six-year term limit for committee chairmen imposed in 1995 as part of the Republican "Contract With America" will force a change in leadership on virtually every panel, sparking several intense races for powerful committees including Commerce, Ways and Means, and Banking. *(2000 CQ Weekly, p. 628; 1995 CQ Almanac, p. 1-12)*

The contests have created an intricate web of power plays, seniority questions and jurisdictional issues that House Republican leaders will have to resolve in the months leading up to their votes on chairmanships — scheduled for Jan. 4 — without further fracturing their fragile majority.

While Republicans will retain control of the committees in the Senate, they will do so by a razor-thin margin, since Senate panels usually reflect the percentage of seats held by each party. Retirements and defeats also will prompt changes in Senate committee rosters, most notably the Senate Finance Committee.

The Ripple Effect

The race to replace retiring House Commerce Committee Chairman Thomas J. Bliley Jr., R-Va., is one of the most heated, and an example of the difficult task GOP leaders face. Second-ranking Republican W. J. "Billy" Tauzin of Louisiana is vying with third-ranking Michael G. Oxley of Ohio to head the panel. Choosing Tauzin, who was allowed to retain his seniority when he switched to the Republican party in 1995, would signal a willingness on the part of GOP leaders to accommodate party-switchers and perhaps entice other desertions that would improve the GOP's narrow margin.

"This would be a terribly, terribly important signal" to potential Democratic party-switchers, said Kenneth A. Guenther, executive vice president of the Independent Community Bankers of America, who closely follows financial issues on Capitol Hill. "I think Republicans will continue to make a major effort to have people switch."

Some conservative Republicans are pushing a scenario in which financial securities, Oxley's area of expertise, would be pulled out of the Commerce Committee's jurisdiction and handed over to the Banking and Financial Services Committee with Oxley as chairman. That could alienate Marge Roukema of New Jersey — the most senior Banking Committee Republican after Chairman Jim Leach of Iowa, who must step aside because of the term limit, and Bill McCollum of Florida, who just lost a bid for the Senate. Roukema could be the GOP's only female chairman and a key moderate voice.

"As the herding of cats goes forward," said one financial services lobbyist, "there is a consideration of the fact that the person who has seniority on the Banking Committee is, one, a woman, and, two, a moderate. This is not something they can necessarily afford to ignore."

One plan being discussed would be to transfer housing from the Commerce Committee to Small Business and offer that to Roukema. Small Business Chairman James M. Talent, R-Mo., ran for governor and lost, and the next ranking Republican, Larry Combest of Texas, is expected to remain as chairman of the Agriculture Committee.

House Handicapping

Maneuvering will be most aggressive in the House, where Speaker J. Dennis Hastert, R-Ill., signaled in an Oct. 29 letter to Republicans that he will consider more than just seniority in choosing committee chairmen. The GOP Conference will meet the week of Nov. 13 to select a Steering Committee, which will convene in December "to interview those members seeking a chairmanship," Hastert's letter said.

"Communication is an important component in chairmanships, and the ability to communicate your committee's agenda to the American people is going to be important," one Republican leadership aide said. "This is going to be a natural selection process."

Others argue that there is nothing natural about the interview process — which one GOP aide compared to fraternity rush — or the six-year limits that have made it necessary.

"It certainly creates the possibility for mischief," said David C. King, associate professor of public policy at Harvard University's John F. Kennedy School of Government, and the author of "Turf Wars: How Congressional Committees Claim Jurisdiction."

"If it's a political process, then it undermines the committee system in a deplorable way," King said.

Five senior Republicans whose terms as committee chairmen were running out chose to retire: Ways and Means Com-

mittee Bill Archer of Texas; Commerce Committee Chairman Bliley; Education and the Workforce Committee Chairman Bill Goodling of Pennsylvania; Budget Committee Chairman John R. Kasich of Ohio; and John Edward Porter of Illinois, chairman of the Appropriations Subcommittee on Labor, Health and Human Services and Education.

"House Republicans, by holding to these term limits for committee chairs, undermine the expertise of their own committees," King said. "These are the little legislatures . . . they're where expertise is brought to bear on policy issues."

Still, some lawmakers say Republican leaders have made up in energy and enthusiasm what they will have lost in experience.

"There is a great loss there on the one hand, but on the other hand there are gains," said Ken Johnson, Tauzin's spokesman. "It has energized things. You bring in new people with new blood and new ideas . . . It keeps hope alive that you don't have to make Washington a career in order to get ahead in the conference."

Not all House chairmen face term limits this year, of course. Combest took over the Agriculture Committee in 1999, so he has four more years, as does Rules Committee Chairman David Dreier, R-Calif., who replaced former Chairman Gerald B.H. Solomon, R-N.Y. (1979-99) when he retired.

C.W. Bill Young, R-Fla., also potentially has another four years as chairman of the House Appropriations Committee. He was picked to replace Chairman Robert L. Livingston, R-La., late in 1998 when Livingston ran for Speaker. Livingston (1977-99) quit the race and Congress after admitting to an extramarital affair. (*1998 Almanac, p. 7-7*)

Consensus in the Senate

The unexpectedly tight margins in the Senate pose new challenges for Majority Leader Trent Lott, R-Miss., and Minority Leader Tom Daschle, D-S.D., who will have to strike a compromise on allocating committee seats in order to ensure that any work gets done during the next session.

The exact margin of GOP control in the Senate is still uncertain, but it has become clear that Republicans will not have an edge of more than a few seats.

If the margin is 50-50, Senate leaders will have to bargain to determine which committees will retain a larger GOP advantage.

"I would doubt that any committees will be even, but I think you'll have one committee that [has a two-vote margin] and the rest of them not," said a top Lott aide. If the margin is 51-49 in favor of Republicans, the aide added, "one committee may have a two-seat margin and the rest of them one-seat majorities."

Senate Republicans and Democrats are expected to organize during the first week of December. While there likely will be maneuvering for seats on key panels such as Appropriations, Finance and Banking, chairmen and ranking members are almost always selected according to seniority.

Charles E. Grassley, R-Iowa, who is in line to be the next chairman of the Senate Finance Committee, has had his differences with Lott and Banking Committee Chairman Phil Gramm, R-Texas, but he is not expected to face a challenge.

"Senate committee procedures are far more collegial," said King of the Kennedy School. "I don't think that things will change there very much at all."

SENATE

★Agriculture

Legislation dealing with trade barriers and agriculture industry concentration will be at the top of the agenda for Chairman Richard G. Lugar, R-Ind., in the 107th. The lead architect of the 1996 farm policy overhaul (PL 104-127), Lugar — who long had resisted efforts to re-open the law — is expected to begin work on a replacement measure that would take effect when the so-called Freedom to Farm bill expires in 2002.

Lugar also expects the panel to take up legislation he has long championed that would promote the use of agricultural products to produce energy. Other issues likely to come up include food safety and genetically engineered crops.

It is unclear who will chair the Marketing, Inspection and Product Promotion Subcommittee. No replacement was named for Paul Coverdell, R-Ga. (1993-2000), after his death.

Tim Johnson of South Dakota is likely to become ranking Democrat on the Production and Price Competitiveness Subcommittee, replacing Bob Kerrey, D-Neb., who is retiring.

★Appropriations

A nail-biting finish to the Washington state Senate race leaves one of the panel's 13 prestigious subcommittee chairmanships hanging in the balance, with Slade Gorton, R-Wash., chairman of the Interior Subcommittee, locked in a very tight contest with former Democratic Rep. Maria Cantwell (1993-95).

The only other wild card among the "cardinals," as subcommittee chairmen are known, is Arlen Specter, R-Pa., who chairs the Labor, Health and Human Services and Education Subcommittee. Frustrated with the gridlock surrounding that panel's bill this year, Specter has said on more than one occasion he would like to swap chairs with another cardinal.

It is not clear whether Specter actually will surrender the high-profile post, however. His bill is the biggest domestic discretionary measure of the 13 annual appropriations measures and a sure attention-grabber.

A pair of veteran senators will continue to lead the committee. Ted Stevens, a 76-year-old Alaska Republican, will remain chairman and West Virginia's Robert C. Byrd, 82, will continue as the ranking Democrat.

On the Democratic side, Frank R. Lautenberg of New Jersey is retiring, leaving open the party's top slot on the Transportation Subcommittee. The next Democrat in line on that subcommittee is Byrd, who has not decided whether to give up his ranking slot on the Interior subcommittee for the Transportation seat.

A move by Byrd could set in motion a number of other subcommittee changes. If Byrd passes on Transportation, Barbara A. Mikulski, D-Md., would be next in line. But aides said Mikulski was not likely to give up her position as ranking Democrat on the VA-HUD Subcommittee.

That means Harry Reid of Nevada could take the slot if he were willing to step down as the top Democrat on the Energy and Water Development Subcommittee. He has not decided whether to make the move, his spokesman said.

★ Armed Services

No changes are likely in the leadership of the Senate Armed Services Committee, which is expected to continue its focus on improving the military's readiness for combat and modernizing its aging weapons.

John W. Warner, R-Va., will remain chairman, a position he has held since 1998; Carl Levin of Michigan is expected to continue as ranking Democrat. The two men generally have worked smoothly together.

Although Warner said he was pleased with the defense authorization bill for fiscal 2001 (PL 106-398) produced by his committee, he also has said more effort is needed to retain troops and modernize the military. Committee members will work from the Quadrennial Defense Review, the Pentagon-produced blueprint of its needs and priorities that is updated every four years.

"Our military forces are presently involved in overseas deployments at an unprecedented rate," Warner said. "More and more, we are being forced to confront the problems that result from trying to do too much with too little."

The committee also is expected to continue looking at a proposed national missile defense, likely to be a leading priority in a George W. Bush administration.

At the same time, Warner has promised to put closing military bases near the top of the committee's agenda next year. The Defense Department has sought congressional approval to conduct additional rounds of base closures to save money. In 1996, Republicans accused President Clinton of politicizing the process in order to win votes in California and Texas. (*1996 CQ Almanac, p. 9-19*)

The only certain membership change will come on the Democratic side, where Charles S. Robb of Virginia was defeated. Vice President Al Gore's running mate, Joseph I. Lieberman, D-Conn., is awaiting the final outcome of the presidential election.

★ Banking, Housing and Urban Affairs

A priority for Chairman Phil Gramm, R-Texas, will be to monitor implementation of the landmark financial services overhaul that carries his name: the Gramm-Leach-Bliley Act of 1999 (PL 106-102).

Gramm is watching the incoming administration's implementation of the law, which aims to enhance competition in the financial services industry by reducing barriers among the banking, insurance and securities industries. He also is expected to review enforcement of the 1997 Community Reinvestment Act (PL 95-128), which requires banks to document efforts to invest in all segments of the communities they serve.

Another item expected to return to the committee's agenda is stalled legislation (S 1712) to create an export review process for so-called dual-use items, which have both military and commercial applications. The measure, which was supported by the high-tech industry, is designed to streamline the process for approving the export of computers and software similar to products that are widely available overseas.

The panel likely will play a key role in the debate of privacy protection for personal financial information. Gramm also is expected to revive a bill (S 2107) that would limit fees the Securities and Exchange Commission (SEC) may collect on stock trades.

The committee also plans to review an SEC proposal to prohibit accounting firms from offering both auditing and consulting services to corporate clients. The agency has encouraged the firms to divide auditing and consulting services into separate units.

Two committee members are retiring: Richard H. Bryan, D-Nev., ranking member of the Financial Institutions Subcommittee, and Connie Mack, R-Fla., chairman of the Economic Policy Subcommittee. Rod Grams, R-Minn., chairman of the Securities Subcommittee, was defeated.

★ Budget

Chairman Pete V. Domenici, R-N.M., is likely to find himself on familiar ground if George W. Bush prevails in the presidential election. Domenici became Budget Committee chairman when President Ronald Reagan took office in 1981, and found himself supporting Reagan's call for spending cuts while resisting his tax-cut proposals.

Domenici faces a difficult task in the 107th Congress. With an extremely slim margin of control, Republicans most likely will need to forge a centrist governing coalition with moderate Democrats. Domenici, a fiscal moderate, has faced opposition in the past from conservatives on the committee led by Phil Gramm, R-Texas, who pushed for spending limits that Domenici considered unrealistically low.

Domenici must find common ground with House Republicans as well, who also have wanted tight-fisted spending levels that Domenici considered unrealistic.

Prairie populist Kent Conrad of North Dakota will be the Budget panel's new ranking Democrat, replacing Frank R. Lautenberg of New Jersey, who is retiring.

Panel Republicans Spencer Abraham of Michigan and Rod Grams of Minnesota were defeated, and Slade Gorton, R-Wash., is locked in a race too tight to call.

★ Commerce, Science and Transportation

No longer distracted by his 2000 presidential campaign, Chairman John McCain, R-Ariz., is expected to lead the committee through an activist agenda.

Ernest F. Hollings of South Carolina remains the ranking Democrat, but the panel's GOP ranks will change significantly following the defeat of John Ashcroft of Missouri, chairman of the Consumer Affairs, Foreign Commerce and Tourism Subcommittee; and Spencer Abraham of Michigan, chairman of the Manufacturing and Competitiveness Subcommittee. Sam Brownback, R-Kan., likely will have his choice of which panel to head.

If Slade Gorton, R-Wash., loses a tight race to former Rep. Maria Cantwell, D-Wash. (1993-95), the Aviation Subcommittee chairmanship would also be open. Democrats, meanwhile, must seek a replacement for Richard H. Bryan of Nevada, ranking Democrat on the Consumer Affairs subcommittee, who retired.

The full panel's jurisdiction is wide-ranging: aviation, consumer issues, sports, the Internet, space, trade and surface transportation.

The committee could be ground zero for the privacy de-

bate in the next Congress, as McCain has shown a desire to move legislation covering online privacy standards. In the 106th Congress, McCain introduced legislation (S 2928) with John Kerry, D-Mass., that would require online businesses to let consumers decide whether to share personal information with third parties. The measure also would require commercial Internet sites to post privacy policies.

One issue sure to crop up is the moratorium on Internet-specific taxes (PL 105-277), which expires in October 2001. McCain backs a five-year extension of the moratorium, but the issue is tied to a wider dispute over efforts by states to collect sales taxes on online purchases.

States and a bipartisan group of senators, including Byron L. Dorgan, D-N.D., want to tie the moratorium extension to an agreement on language that would give states authority to develop a system for collecting sales taxes from out-of-state vendors.

At the urging of Communications Subcommittee Chairman Conrad Burns, R-Mont., the committee also is expected to examine ways to extend high-speed Internet access to rural areas.

In the non-technology arena, McCain has shown a keen interest in curbing the tobacco industry's influence on children, and he is monitoring the way states are using their tobacco settlement money. The panel also is expected to review voluntary efforts by movie studios and video game makers to scale back the marketing of graphic violent films and software to children.

★Energy and Natural Resources

Frank H. Murkowski, R-Alaska, is returning for another stint as chairman and again will push comprehensive deregulation of the electric power industry.

Murkowski also wants to work on legislation that would reduce the United States' dependence on foreign oil. He has pushed for increased drilling in his home state, particularly in the Arctic National Wildlife Refuge, a move Democrats vehemently oppose.

The committee again will try to come up with a solution to storing nuclear waste in the wake of President Clinton's veto of a measure (S 1287) that would have set a schedule for the development of a permanent waste repository at Nevada's Yucca Mountain.

Jeff Bingaman of New Mexico will remain the committee's top-ranking Democrat. The subcommittee chairmen and ranking members who served during the 106th Congress are expected to remain the same in the 107th Congress.

The only potential membership change is on the Republican side, where Slade Gorton of Washington is locked in a race too close to call.

★Environment and Public Works

Chairman Robert C. Smith, R-N.H., who took the committee's helm after John H. Chafee, R-R.I., died Oct. 24, 1999, is expected to focus his agenda in the 107th Congress on an overhaul of the Clean Air Act and some unfinished business from his first term.

Smith is likely to take up legislation — bogged down during the 106th by disputes between the agriculture and oil in-

dustries — that would ban the clean-burning fuel additive methyl tertiary butyl ether (MTBE), a possible carcinogen that has seeped into many states' water supplies. Farm states are seeking greater use of ethanol, a clean-burning additive made from corn.

Also left undone in the 106th were efforts to clean up polluted and abandoned industrial sites known as brownfields.

The panel's Republican lineup should not change, but Democrats will be shuffling some top slots and welcoming some new faces.

Minority Whip Harry Reid, D-Nev., is expected to move into the ranking slot on the committee, replacing Max Baucus, D-Mont., who will assume that post on the Senate Finance Committee while remaining a member of the Environment panel. Reid wants to retain his leadership post as well and will lobby to hold both jobs.

After Baucus, the next two senior Democrats on the panel are retiring: Daniel Patrick Moynihan of New York and Frank R. Lautenberg of New Jersey.

Reid, who was the ranking Democrat on the Fisheries, Wildlife and Water Subcommittee, may turn those reins over to Barbara Boxer of California, who had been acting as ranking Democrat while Reid handled whip duties. Boxer is also in line to become the most senior Democrat on the Superfund, Waste Control and Risk Assessment Subcommittee.

★Finance

The committee, which will have jurisdiction over some of the biggest issues before the 107th Congress, is facing more upheaval than any other standing Senate panel.

Not only will it have a new chairman and ranking Democrat, it also will see at least six, and perhaps seven, new members.

The new chairman will be Charles E. Grassley, R-Iowa, who cultivates an understated and straight-talking image and often describes himself as "just a farmer from Butler County." As such, he has been an unwavering advocate for his state's agricultural interests, most recently by urging trade expansion. In a statement Nov. 8, he said his priorities as chairman would be updating Medicare, cutting taxes for families and married couples and crafting "an aggressive trade agenda to open up new markets."

Grassley will succeed William V. Roth Jr., R-Del., who was defeated in his bid for a sixth term. As chairman since late 1995, Roth concentrated much of his efforts on expanding tax incentives for retirement savings.

The new ranking Democrat, Max Baucus of Montana, will take over from Daniel Patrick Moynihan of New York, who retired. Baucus may bring a sharper partisan edge to the table than Moynihan, who worked closely and amiably with Roth. But he shares Grassley's concern for rural areas, which could make them allies on many issues.

Baucus is expected to push for more open debate and decision-making on tax and trade bills instead of backroom deals designed to ensure speedy approval.

The committee writes tax, trade, health care, welfare and Social Security legislation. In the next Congress it will be called on to reauthorize the law (PL 105-193) that overhauled the welfare system in 1996; to consider reviving fast-

track trade powers for the president; to consider proposals to shore up the solvency of Social Security and Medicare — and, of course, to alter the tax code.

One other committee member, Charles S. Robb, D-Va., was defeated for re-election. In addition to Moynihan, three other panel members are retiring: Democrats Richard H. Bryan of Nevada and Bob Kerrey of Nebraska and Republican Connie Mack of Florida.

Another vacancy on the committee could be created by Larry E. Craig, R-Idaho, who was assigned to Finance temporarily this year to fill the seat opened by the death of Paul Coverdell, R-Ga. (1993-2000). Craig is also on the Appropriations Committee, where he is in line for a subcommittee chairmanship. He cannot serve on both Finance and Appropriations and will have to choose which seat to relinquish. A spokesman said he has not yet made a decision.

★Foreign Relations

Chairman Jesse Helms, R-N.C, will continue to lead the panel. Ranking Democrat Joseph R. Biden Jr., of Delaware, and former chairman Richard G. Lugar, R-Ind., also will stay.

The remaining Republicans, however, have less tenure on the committee and may seek to shift to more popular committees. Republicans also will have to find a new chairman for the International Operations Subcommittee with the defeat of Rod Grams, R-Minn. Little movement is expected on the Democratic side.

Next year is likely to see the panel tackling several nuclear weapons issues as well as helping to build the GOP case for an expanded U.S. national missile defense, an issue that has met with strong resistance from Russia and some European nations.

The committee also will work on a foreign aid authorization bill that likely would include additional assistance to Serbia and other parts of the Balkan region to complement existing initiatives.

The committee also may hold preparatory hearings leading toward NATO's expected expansion, as well as hearings on Colombia, North Korea, China's relationship with Taiwan and nuclear proliferation in India and Pakistan. Export promotion could become another priority, and lawmakers may spend more time on child immunization programs and on overseas efforts to fight diseases such as AIDS, malaria and tuberculosis.

★Governmental Affairs

The Governmental Affairs Committee probably will see little change in membership from the 106th Congress. The only election casualty was William V. Roth Jr., R-Del.

Fred Thompson, R-Tenn., will retain the chairmanship he has held since 1997. Vice-presidential nominee Joseph I. Lieberman of Connecticut, ranking Democrat since 1999, is awaiting the outcome of the presidential election.

Thompson plans to address what the committee has identified as management problems in the executive branch. He also said he would continue working to stem the proliferation of weapons of mass destruction.

The Permanent Subcommittee on Investigations, chaired

by Susan Collins, R-Maine, is likely to continue using the panel's broad investigative jurisdiction to focus on money-laundering schemes.

★Health, Education, Labor and Pensions

Not a single panel member retired or lost a re-election bid, so no changes in leadership or focus are expected for the 107th Congress.

James M. Jeffords, R-Vt., returns as chairman for a third consecutive Congress, and Edward M. Kennedy of Massachusetts will remain the ranking Democrat. No subcommittee chairmanships are likely to shift.

The committee's first priority is reauthorization of the 1965 Elementary and Secondary Education Act (ESEA). Although the panel approved a rewrite (S 2) last March, the package fell victim to partisan deadlock on the floor.

The ESEA is the primary blueprint for federal support of public education, sending billions of dollars to states and local school districts each year.

Senators of both parties also plan to continue to work on health issues, which could include a possible revival of stalled legislation to give the federal government more regulatory power over managed-care plans.

★Indian Affairs

Committee Chairman Ben Nighthorse Campbell, R-Colo., and ranking Democrat Daniel K. Inouye of Hawaii will be returning to lead the panel.

The only uncertainty on the panel is the fate of Slade Gorton, R-Wash., who was locked in a tight re-election contest. Indian groups poured time and money into the effort by former Democratic Rep. Maria Cantwell (1993-95) to defeat Gorton, the fourth-ranking Republican on the committee, whom they view as opposing their efforts to gain more self-determination.

★Judiciary

On the GOP side, the defeat of two subcommittee chairmen — Spencer Abraham of Michigan and John Ashcroft of Missouri — guarantees some changes, although Chairman Orrin G. Hatch, R-Utah, and the panel's top Democrat, Patrick J. Leahy of Vermont, will return.

Jeff Sessions, R-Ala., currently chairman of the Youth Violence Subcommittee, could claim the more influential Immigration Subcommittee. Or Robert C. Smith, R-N.H., could take that gavel. Smith does not currently head a subcommittee on Judiciary, nor does Arlen Specter, R-Pa. Both have high-profile chairmanships elsewhere.

Two newly elected senators — George F. Allen, R-Va., and Hillary Rodham Clinton, D-N.Y. — would like to join Judiciary, while Charles E. Schumer, D-N.Y., may leave the panel if he wins a seat on the Finance Committee.

Republicans' razor-thin majority will make it even more difficult than usual for the committee — which tends to deal with such controversial issues as the criminal justice system — to get time on the floor for its agenda. It could also make confirmation of judges, especially Supreme Court justices,

very difficult.

Hatch intends to continue his effort to write rules for Internet security and privacy issues in the 107th Congress. He also will try again to move legislation that would increase penalties for violent teen criminals and provide state grants for crime prevention. In the 106th, the House and Senate passed juvenile crime bills (S 254, HR 1501) but the measures died in conference because of a dispute over gun control provisions.

The panel may try to revive legislation to overhaul the bankruptcy process, and Hatch may also explore legislation that would permit post-conviction DNA testing and facilitate the exchange of DNA information among law enforcement agencies.

★Rules and Administration

After gaining new leaders at the start of the 106th Congress, the committee will have few changes in the 107th. Mitch McConnell, R-Ky., will remain as chairman and only one member is leaving — retiring Daniel Patrick Moynihan, D-N.Y.

While the panel's housekeeping activities rarely draw much attention, it will have a busy January because it will be in charge of arrangements for the presidential inauguration. The panel also decides the budgets of Senate committees and has jurisdiction over federal elections challenges.

The panel is likely to continue its perpetual hearings on campaign finance issues. John McCain, R-Ariz., is already vowing to force a floor fight on that topic in February, ensuring that the Rules Committee will have to address it.

The committee, which has little other legislative jurisdiction, will focus some of its oversight on the Office of the Architect of the Capitol. That office is handling a major new construction project — the planned Capitol visitors center.

★Select Ethics

Appointments to this evenly divided, six-member committee are made by the majority and minority leaders, who can appoint new members at any time.

While Pat Roberts, R-Kan., is expected to remain chairman, the vice chairman, Harry Reid, D-Nev., may give up his slot because of his post as minority whip and his plan to take the ranking member slot on the Environment and Public Works Committee.

There are no cases currently before the committee, which conducts its business behind closed doors. The panel plans to post a new version of the Senate Code of Official Conduct on its website in December.

★Select Intelligence

Turnover is taking a toll on the 15-member Select Intelligence Committee.

Richard C. Shelby, R-Ala., will continue as chairman, but ranking Democrat Richard H. Bryan of Nevada is retiring. So are Connie Mack, R-Fla., and Frank R. Lautenberg, D-N.J. Charles S. Robb, D-Va., lost his bid for re-election.

Four other members are scheduled to step down due to the eight-year term limits for committee members: Republican Richard G. Lugar of Indiana and Democrats Bob Graham of Florida, John Kerry of Massachusetts and Max Baucus of Montana. That leaves only one returning Democrat — Carl Levin of Michigan. However, Levin is expected to keep his ranking spot on the Armed Services Committee, leaving a newcomer to become the ranking Democrat on the Intelligence Committee.

Several Democrats, including Graham, have said they would like to see the eight-year term limit waived to bring stability and experience to the committee. Shelby and other Republicans have promised to consider the idea, but they have noted that the panel remains a popular assignment for many senators and that ending term limits would deny them a chance to serve.

Shelby plans to continue his emphasis on restructuring the National Security Agency, the super-secret eavesdropping arm of the intelligence community. The panel also will focus on counter-terrorism and ensuring that the CIA and other agencies are prepared to properly collect, analyze and disseminate information about threats — an issue that intensified after the Oct. 12 attack on the USS Cole in Yemen.

★Small Business

With no leadership changes expected, the committee is likely to pick up pretty much where it left off once the 107th Congress gets under way.

Returning Chairman Christopher S. Bond, R-Mo., plans to continue scrutinizing the "bundling" by federal agencies of contracts for different services into a single contract. The practice is intended to save administrative expenses, but critics say it makes the contracts too big for smaller businesses to make competitive bids.

Bond wants agencies to divide service contracts into smaller pieces, giving small businesses a better chance to win them. The committee also is expected to review the controversial practice known as "slotting," in which retailers force product suppliers to pay fees to have their items prominently displayed. The practice affects businesses ranging from computer companies to food producers, according to committee staff.

The panel also is expected to continue promoting efforts by federal agencies to simplify government red tape and paperwork to help small businesses save time and money.

Committee member Spencer Abraham, R-Mich., was defeated for re-election, while Joseph I. Lieberman of Connecticut, the Democratic vice-presidential nominee, is awaiting the outcome of the presidential election. The ranking Democrat, John Kerry of Massachusetts, is retiring.

★Special Aging

The leadership of the committee is in question because Chairman Charles E. Grassley, R-Iowa, is expected to relinquish the gavel to head the Finance Committee following the defeat of William V. Roth Jr., R-Del..

James M. Jeffords, R-Vt., is next on the GOP seniority list, but he already chairs the Health, Education, Labor and Pensions Committee. Larry E. Craig, R-Idaho, is third in se-

niority, followed by Conrad Burns, R-Mont.

According to Republican aides, no decisions have yet been made about who will chair the committee. The panel has no authority to report legislation, but it can hold hearings and conduct investigations to spotlight issues affecting the elderly.

John B. Breaux of Louisiana, who will remain the panel's ranking Democrat, hopes to focus on such areas as assisted-living services for seniors, preventing abuse of the elderly, consumer fraud and new technologies that can help seniors.

★ Veterans' Affairs

If the 106th Congress is any indication, the pace of this committee will be slow and steady in the 107th Congress.

Arlen Specter, R-Pa., is likely to build on his four years as chairman. Veterans' groups have praised Specter for being evenhanded, though some also have criticized him for what they saw as the panel's slow pace. The committee held only two markups during the 106th Congress, approving omnibus bills at each that covered a broad range of matters. The committee also held far fewer hearings than its House counterpart, prompting complaints from veterans' groups that some issues did not receive a public airing.

Of special interest to Specter is Gulf War syndrome. He would make it easier for Persian Gulf War veterans to receive compensation for the illness.

John D. Rockefeller IV of West Virginia returns as ranking Democrat. The rest of the panel's makeup is likely to be unchanged.

HOUSE

★ Agriculture

With the farm economy in the doldrums and Congress recovering from several years of costly agriculture bailouts, the committee will focus much of its agenda on overhauling the 1996 Freedom to Farm law (PL 104-127), which expires in 2002. Returning GOP Chairman Larry Combest of Texas believes the measure, which sought gradually to wean farmers from federal agriculture subsidies, left them without a safety net and needs a "permanent fix."

The panel's ranking Democrat, Charles W. Stenholm of Texas, is expected to work closely with Combest, as he did during the 106th Congress.

The committee also is expected to monitor new Environmental Protection Agency water quality rules — slated to take effect in October 2001 — that target agricultural runoff from farms, ranches and timber operations.

Livestock and Horticulture Subcommittee Chairman Richard W. Pombo, R-Calif., is likely to continue his crusade to revise the 1996 Food Quality Protection Act (PL 104-70), which eliminated a law barring traces of any cancer-causing substances — including pesticides used on crops — in processed foods. Pombo says the EPA, which is required by the law to use a standard of "reasonable certainty of no harm" for processed foods, is not implementing the statute.

Two new subcommittee chairmen will be named as a result of retirements.

John A. Boehner, R-Ohio, is in line to succeed Bill Barrett, R-Neb., as chairman of the General Farm Commodities, Resource Conservation and Credit Subcommittee, but he may have chairmanship options on other committees. Nick Smith, R-Mich., is the likely replacement for Thomas W. Ewing, R-Ill., at the helm of the Risk Management, Research and Specialty Crops Subcommittee.

★ Appropriations

The most dramatic shakeup in six years is in store, with prized subcommittee chairmanships up for grabs.

Chairman C.W. Bill Young, R-Fla., will be back, along with ranking Democrat David R. Obey of Wisconsin. Two of the 13 subcommittee chairmen are retiring, however, and term limits will force five others to switch panels.

In theory, the picking of subcommittee chairmen rests with Young, but the GOP leadership is certain to be involved when such plum assignments are at stake. The choices generally go by seniority on the full committee.

The most important opening is at the Labor, Health and Human Services and Education Subcommittee, where John Edward Porter, R-Ill., is retiring. That panel writes the largest and frequently the most contentious of the 13 annual spending bills. House leaders will be cautious in choosing a successor to Porter, a moderate who was popular even as Democrats and Republicans fought over priorities.

Also retiring is Ron Packard, R-Calif., who heads the Energy and Water Development Subcommittee.

Ralph Regula, R-Ohio, now at the helm of the Interior Subcommittee, may hold the key to the musical chairs game. He is second in seniority on the full committee, and GOP leaders may press him to take the Labor-HHS panel.

Some appropriators are openly angling for specific chairs. For example, Ernest Istook, R-Okla., current District of Columbia Subcommittee chairman, is trying to position himself for the Labor-HHS-Education gavel. These chairmanships are also in play:

• Transportation Subcommittee Chairman Frank R. Wolf, R-Va., has made clear he would like to head the Foreign Operations Subcommittee.

• Agriculture Subcommittee Chairman Joe Skeen, R-N.M., would like to replace Regula at Interior.

• VA, HUD and Independent Agencies Subcommittee Chairman James T. Walsh, R-N.Y., is eyeing the Agriculture panel.

• Sonny Callahan, R-Ala., now Foreign Operations chairman, is looking at Energy and Water Development or Transportation.

Other appropriators may be satisfied to stay put. Defense Subcommittee Chairman Jerry Lewis, R-Calif., and Military Construction Subcommittee Chairman David L. Hobson, R-Ohio, appear satisfied with their current assignments.

Some subcommittee chairmen are not looking forward to the changes. "It's a terrible waste of expertise and knowledge to disqualify chairmen just because they have been serving" for six years, said Harold Rogers, R-Ky., chairman of the Commerce-Justice-State panel. "The six-year rule is idiocy." Rogers refused to say what new assignment he would like.

Few if any changes are expected among the subcommittees' ranking Democrats.

★Armed Services

The House Armed Services Committee could be the setting for a rough-and-tumble fight for the chairman's gavel.

Chairman Floyd D. Spence, R-S.C., must step aside because of term limits. Although Bob Stump, R-Ariz., is in line to head the panel, Curt Weldon, R-Pa., currently chairman of the Military Research and Development Subcommittee, said he hopes to leapfrog Stump and two other members to become chairman.

A spokesman for Duncan Hunter, R-Calif., chairman of the Military Procurement Subcommittee and second in seniority to Stump, said Hunter does not plan to challenge Stump. James V. Hansen, R-Utah, also outranks Weldon, but is likely to become Resources Committee chairman.

Weldon, an outspoken conservative and one of Congress' leading advocates of a national missile defense, informed party leaders in the spring that he was going to seek the chairmanship. Since then, he has thrown himself into party-building activities. "I want to present a new idea for how the Armed Services Committee should operate," he said. He wants the committee to work more closely with its Senate counterpart and with appropriators.

Spence is eyeing the Military Procurement Subcommittee, headed by Hunter, who must give up his position because of term limits. Saxby Chambliss, R-Ga., is in line to take over the Military Readiness Subcommittee. He would replace the late Herbert H. Bateman, R-Va. (1982-2000).

The ranking Democrat, Ike Skelton of Missouri, has been on the committee for two decades and is an advocate of greater defense spending, especially pay increases to improve personnel retention.

In addition to the annual defense authorization bill and missile defense-related issues, the committee is likely to look at improving the readiness of U.S. troops, a subject of heavy debate in the presidential campaign.

★Banking and Financial Services

Marge Roukema, R-N.J., and Richard H. Baker, R-La., are vying to succeed term-limited Chairman Jim Leach, R-Iowa. Both now head subcommittees but are term-limited and must change their panel assignments.

If Roukema, serving her 11th term and the more senior of the two, succeeds, she will be the only female chairman of a major committee in the 107th Congress. She insists she has the full support and confidence of Republican leaders, including Speaker J. Dennis Hastert of Illinois, who campaigned for her this fall. But many conservatives distrust Roukema and some actively campaigned against her.

Baker, just elected to an eighth term, has positioned himself well through his fundraising for other Republicans. His conservatism also puts him more in line with GOP leaders.

John J. LaFalce of New York will return for a second term as the committee's ranking Democrat.

The panel will have a full agenda in the 107th Congress. Republicans plan close oversight of implementation of the 1999 financial services overhaul (PL 106-102). It also will continue to grapple with financial privacy issues.

Roukema, broadening her focus from the Financial Institutions and Consumer Credit Subcommittee she has headed for six years, said she would lead a study of the lending practices of Freddie Mac and Fannie Mae, which finance a large percentage of the nation's home mortgages. Baker has given sharp scrutiny to the politically powerful institutions as chairman of the Subcommittee on Capital Markets, Securities and Government-Sponsored Enterprises.

With the terms of Roukema and Baker as subcommittee chairmen limited, and Rick A. Lazio, R-N.Y., the Housing and Community Opportunity Subcommittee chairman, leaving the House after an unsuccessful Senate race, there will be at least three new subcommittee chairmen.

★Budget

Retiring Chairman John R. Kasich, R-Ohio, will give way probably to either Jim Nussle, R-Iowa, or Saxby Chambliss, R-Ga. Nussle, a leading proponent of two-year budget cycles, is favored to win the job. Chambliss, who was named to the Budget Committee at the beginning of the 106th Congress by Speaker-designate Robert L. Livingston, R-La. (1977-99), is a contender for the chairmanship because, as a Speaker's appointee, he is the vice chairman.

Since 1995, the annual budget resolutions produced by the GOP-controlled committee have set the stage for appropriations battles with President Clinton.

If Republican nominee George W. Bush becomes president, the Budget Committee is likely to endorse his budget recommendations. House Republicans, after seeing their tax agenda scuttled for years, probably will make room in budget resolutions for sizable tax cuts to move as part of budget reconciliation measures.

There will be a vacancy on the GOP side of the committee as a result of Bob Franks' unsuccessful bid for a New Jersey Senate seat. The Democrats also will see turnover, with the departure of Bob Weygand of Rhode Island and possibly David Minge of Minnesota, whose election results remain unsettled. Another Democratic vacancy would be created if Rush D. Holt, of New Jersey, loses his re-election campaign against Republican Dick Zimmer.

Nussle headed a bipartisan task force during the 106th Congress that recommended procedural changes that would have given the Budget Committee more power. The annual budget resolution would be given the force of law, continuing resolutions would be triggered automatically, and new rules would make it easier to enact tax cuts.

The measure (HR 853) was blocked by House GOP leaders and appropriators, but Nussle can be expected to try to carve out a more prominent role for the committee.

The panel's top Democrat will remain John M. Spratt Jr., an amiable South Carolinian with ties to both House Minority Leader Richard A. Gephardt, D-Mo., and the more conservative "Blue Dog" Democrats.

★Commerce

With Chairman Thomas J. Bliley Jr., R-Va., retiring, W.J. "Billy" Tauzin, R-La., and Michael G. Oxley, R-Ohio — who have waged a bitter fight to succeed him — could both end up winning.

One scenario being floated has GOP leaders splitting the Commerce panel. Oxley would chair a new financial services committee, while Tauzin would lead a Commerce pan-

el that concentrated on telecom and energy issues.

The two men have been rivals on the committee since Tauzin switched parties in 1995. In a compromise in the 104th Congress, GOP leaders divided a subcommittee into two parts, making Tauzin chairman of a new Telecommunications, Trade and Consumer Protection Subcommittee, and giving Oxley control of a Hazardous Materials panel.

John D. Dingell of Michigan will remain the full committee's ranking Democrat, and Bart Stupak of Michigan is in line to replace Ron Klink of Pennsylvania as the top Democrat on the Oversight and Investigations Subcommittee. Klink gave up his House seat for an unsuccessful Senate bid.

A wild card on the Democratic side is Edward J. Markey of Massachusetts, who could become ranking Democrat on the Resources Committee. If Markey takes that job, Rick Boucher of Virginia is in line to replace him as the Telecommunications subcommittee's ranking member.

Electric utility deregulation and privacy protection are expected to be on the committee's agenda next year. The panel is also expected to review the telecommunications overhaul of 1996 (PL 104-104) and to consider a proposal to let the Baby Bells transmit high-speed data over long-distance telephone lines.

Members are also likely to deal with a managed-care overhaul proposal similar to a bill (HR 2990) sponsored by Charlie Norwood, R-Ga., and Dingell. The measure stalled in the 106th Congress.

In addition, the panel is expected to consider a proposal to reduce stock transaction fees collected by the Securities and Exchange Commission and to review implementation of a new law (PL 106-414) requiring the automobile industry to share with the government a broad range of information on possible product defects.

★ Education and the Workforce

Tom Petri, R-Wis., is in line to succeed retiring Chairman Bill Goodling, R-Pa., but he may be challenged by Marge Roukema, R-N.J., second in seniority on the panel, if she loses her bid to become chairman of the Banking Committee. Other lawmakers could also vie for the top spot.

Peter Hoekstra, R-Mich., who must leave his post as chairman of the Oversight and Investigations Subcommittee because of term limits, has indicated he would like to lead the committee. Hoekstra has made his mark on the education debate mainly by exposing cases of fraud and bad bookkeeping in the Department of Education.

John A. Boehner, R-Ohio, chairman of the Employer-Employee Relations Subcommittee, is another possibility if he decides to ask the leadership for a chairmanship.

Howard P. "Buck" McKeon, R-Calif., chairman of the Postsecondary Education, Training and Life-Long Learning Subcommittee, faces a term limit, as does Cass Ballenger, R-N.C., chairman of the Workforce Protections Subcommittee. Michael N. Castle, R-Del., chairman of the Early Childhood, Youth and Families Subcommittee, is expected to keep the job.

With ranking Democrat William L. Clay of Missouri retiring, George Miller of California is expected to move into that spot.

One of the committee's most pressing tasks will be reauthorization of the 1965 Elementary and Secondary Education Act, the primary blueprint for federal support of public education. Petri, if he takes the chair, is also interested in legislation that would help low-skilled working parents retain government benefits when they leave the welfare rolls.

★ Government Reform

The partisan battles that have consumed the committee since the 105th Congress are likely to continue.

Coming back for another stint as chairman is Dan Burton, R-Ind., who since 1997 has used the position to launch a series of probes into the Clinton administration. Henry A. Waxman of California returns as the most senior Democrat.

Aides said the committee will continue its investigations of anthrax vaccine, alternative cancer treatments and how children develop autism. The committee also may continue its investigation into campaign finance practices.

Committee term limits will result in several new faces on subcommittees. Thomas M. Davis III, R-Va., who was given the gavel of the District of Columbia Subcommittee when he came to the House in 1995, must relinquish the chairmanship. Also term-limited are Steve Horn, R-Calif., who now heads the Government Management, Information and Technology Subcommittee; and John McHugh, R-N.Y., currently chairman of the Postal Service Subcommittee.

The departure of unsuccessful gubernatorial candidate David M. McIntosh, R-Ind., leaves open the chairmanship of the National Economic Growth, Natural Resources and Regulatory Affairs Subcommittee.

Subcommittee chairmanships are generally determined by seniority on the full committee, not subcommittee, and it is unclear which members will move into vacant spots.

★ House Administration

The leadership of the committee that handles the House's internal affairs is up in the air. Bill Thomas, R-Calif., has served as chairman for the past six years while also serving as the Ways and Means Health Subcommittee chairman. Under GOP term limits, he must relinquish both gavels.

Republican rules prohibit members from chairing more than one committee or subcommittee at a time, but Thomas received a waiver to head both panels.

He is expected to campaign to be Ways and Means chairman, and he might seek permission to stay on at the top of House Administration if he loses that contest.

If he steps down as Administration chairman, John A. Boehner, R-Ohio, is next in line. Boehner now serves as chairman of the Education and the Workforce Subcommittee on Employer-Employee Relations, but his aides say he would give up that position to lead House Administration.

Boehner is also interested in chairing the full Education Committee. If he takes that panel, next in line for the Administration chairmanship is Vernon J. Ehlers, R-Mich.

If Democrat Steny H. Hoyer of Maryland declines the ranking member slot in favor a party leadership position or post on another committee, Chaka Fattah, D-Pa., is next in line.

The committee handles housekeeping tasks, which range from investigating contested elections to revising campaign finance rules. The committee also will have an oversight role in the construction of the $265 million Capitol visitors' center, which is scheduled to open in 2005.

★ International Relations

The House International Relations Committee could see major changes in the 107th Congress: The chairman's gavel is up for grabs, and the collegiality that the panel has enjoyed in recent years may be endangered.

Chairman Benjamin A. Gilman, R-N.Y., and ranking Democrat Sam Gejdenson of Connecticut have not always agreed on policy but usually have worked together to ensure that the committee operates smoothly.

Now Gilman has to step down because of term limits, and Gejdenson lost his bid for re-election. The ranking Democrat is expected to be Tom Lantos of California, who has brought an assertive and sometimes confrontational approach to his role on the committee's Asia and the Pacific Subcommittee.

Gilman has requested a waiver to allow him to remain chairman. If he is turned down, he may become chairman of a newly created Europe and Middle East Subcommittee.

A long line of Republicans may attempt to replace Gilman. The committee's second-ranking Republican, Bill Goodling of Pennsylvania, is retiring and Jim Leach, R-Iowa, might eye the position, since term limits will force him to give up his Banking and Financial Services Committee chairmanship.

Leach likely will be challenged by Asia and the Pacific Subcommittee Chairman Doug Bereuter, R-Neb., who is two rungs down the seniority ladder and passed up a Senate bid in hopes of landing the chairmanship.

Christopher H. Smith, R-N.J., also may be interested, since his term is up as chairman of the International Operations and Human Rights Subcommittee. Smith also is in line to succeed Bob Stump, R-Ariz., as chairman of the Veterans Affairs Committee.

Right behind Leach in seniority is Judiciary Chairman Henry J. Hyde, R- Ill., who may be in the market for a new post because of term limits.

No matter who is at the helm, the committee will seek to reassert its authority as the authorizing committee for foreign affairs agencies. For more than a decade, at least one-third of the agencies' funding has been authorized through the Appropriations Committee rather than coming through Interior Relations first. The committee is also certain to focus next year on the Middle East.

★ Judiciary

The committee will see major leadership changes in the 107th Congress, including a new chairman. Henry J. Hyde, R-Ill., has hit the three-term limit, and his place will probably be taken by F. James Sensenbrenner Jr., R-Wis. There was talk of granting Hyde an exemption from the term-limits rule, but that would require action from the GOP leadership and could open the door for other chairmen who want to retain their panels, so it seems unlikely.

In addition to the full committee chairmanship, four of the five subcommittees will see new leaders. Hyde is not likely to take a subcommittee chairmanship.

Constitution Subcommittee Chairman Charles T. Canady, R-Fla., is retiring, and the Crime Subcommittee's Bill McCollum, R-Fla., left the House for a Senate bid that failed.

Howard Coble, R-N.C., plans to keep his post as chairman of the Courts and Intellectual Property Subcommittee. George W. Gekas, R-Pa., could take over the Crime Subcommittee.

Lamar Smith, R-Texas, has completed his term as Immigration and Claims Subcommittee chairman and may take over the Constitution Subcommittee. Elton Gallegly, R-Calif., could head either the Immigration panel or the Commercial and Administrative Law Subcommittee.

The Judiciary panel's agenda is likely to feature familiar issues — bankruptcy overhaul, Internet security and privacy, and legislation to ban Internet gambling.

The committee also may revisit juvenile crime legislation (S 254, HR 1501) that stalled in conference over gun control provisions. In addition, the panel may consider legislation that would expand the use of DNA testing in criminal cases by giving offenders access to such analysis if it was unavailable at the time of their convictions.

John Conyers Jr. of Michigan will remain the committee's top-ranking Democrat, and the subcommittee ranking posts also are unlikely to change. Gun control, broadening the definition of hate crimes and granting amnesty to some illegal immigrants are key issues for the minority.

★ Resources

James V. Hansen, R-Utah, will take the helm of the full committee after heading the National Parks and Public Lands Subcommittee for the past six years. Don Young of Alaska, one of several term-limited GOP chairmen, will make a lateral move to assume the chairmanship of the House Transportation and Infrastructure Committee.

Hansen, who wants to rename the Parks and Public Lands Subcommittee as the Parks and Recreation Subcommittee, shares with his predecessor a passion for protecting access to public lands. Energized in 1996 by President Clinton's designation of 1.7 million acres in his home state as the Grand Staircase-Escalante National Monument over the objections of local officials, Hansen has steadfastly represented the viewpoint of many Westerners, who want the federal government to leave land management to property owners and state officials.

A review and overhaul of the 1964 Wilderness Act (PL 88-577) and the Endangered Species Act of 1973 (PL 93-205) are high on Hansen's agenda.

With Hansen's promotion and the retirement of Forests and Forest Health Subcommittee Chairwoman Helen Chenoweth-Hage, R-Idaho, two subcommittee chairmanships will be open. Elton Gallegly, R-Calif., is in line for the Parks panel unless he opts for the Judiciary Subcommittee on Immigration. John J. "Jimmy" Duncan Jr., R-Tenn., is in line for the Forests subcommittee.

George Miller of California will step down as the committee's top Democrat to become ranking member of the Education and the Workforce Committee. Either Edward J. Markey of Massachusetts or Nick J. Rahall II of West Virginia is expected to take over as ranking Democrat.

Markey has been on a leave of absence from Resources so he could serve on the Budget Committee, but retains his seniority. If Markey becomes ranking member, he would have to surrender his ranking position on the Commerce Committee's Telecommunications, Trade and Consumer Protection Subcommittee.

★Rules

David Dreier, R-Calif., returns for a second term as chairman of the Rules Committee, which sets procedures for legislative action on the House floor.

Republicans are appointed by the Speaker and are party loyalists. "The Rules Committee is the Speaker's committee," Dreier said. "My goal is to make sure we help to implement the plan that he has."

Because Republicans will hold such a narrow majority, the leadership will again have to craft rules that can command the support of all Republicans. Defections by either moderates or conservatives could doom any rule on the floor.

Joe Moakley of Massachusetts, who was ousted as Rules chairman in the Republican takeover of Congress after the 1994 elections, is expected to remain the panel's ranking Democrat and a persistent critic of the majority.

★Select Intelligence

The Intelligence Committee is losing several key members, but not its chairman — at least, not yet.

Former CIA agent Porter J. Goss, R-Fla., will head the panel for a final two years — unless he is tapped to be director of Central Intelligence in a Republican administration. Goss, who will not seek re-election in 2002, said recently he would be interested in the administration job but is not actively seeking it.

The second-ranking Republican, Jerry Lewis of California, is at the end of his term on the panel and Bill McCollum, R-Fla., is leaving the House after an unsuccessful Senate bid. House rules do not permit lawmakers to serve on the committee longer than eight years.

McCollum's departure probably will mean that Charles Bass, R-N.H., will take over the Human Intelligence, Analysis and Counterintelligence Subcommittee. Michael N. Castle of Delaware will be the panel's second-ranking Republican and will return as chairman of the Technical and Tactical Intelligence Subcommittee.

Julian C. Dixon of California returns as the ranking Democrat. Second-ranking Nancy Pelosi of California is at the end of her eight-year term.

The committee will focus on upgrading technology at the National Security Agency and continue to monitor efforts to correct security lapses. It may follow up on the investigation of former CIA Director John M. Deutch, who was reprimanded for storing classified information on a personal computer. Members will also work on initiatives to improve counterintelligence and counterterrorism programs, especially in light of the Oct. 12 bombing attack on the USS *Cole* in the Mideast.

★Science

A leadership change is coming, as term-limited Science Chairman F. James Sensenbrenner Jr., R-Wis., prepares to replace Henry J. Hyde, R-Ill., as chairman of the Judiciary Committee.

Sensenbrenner's most likely successor is Sherwood Boehlert of New York, the Science panel's second-ranking

Republican. However, it is unclear whether conservatives in the House leadership may be tempted to pass over the moderate from central New York, who tends to vote with Democrats on environmental issues.

Technology Subcommittee Chairwoman Constance A. Morella, R-Md., will have to relinquish that post because of term limits imposed by House rules. The other three subcommittee chairmen — Nick Smith, R-Mich., Basic Research; Dana Rohrabacher, R-Calif., Space and Aeronautics; and Ken Calvert, R-Calif., Energy and Environment — are expected to remain.

Ralph M. Hall, D-Texas, will remain the committee's ranking minority member and push an agenda that favors more basic science research.

★Small Business

With the departure of Chairman James M. Talent, R-Mo., the leadership of the committee will change. Talent narrowly lost a race for governor of Missouri on Nov. 7.

Next in seniority is Larry Combest, R-Texas, but he plans to continue as chairman of the Agriculture Committee. Joel Hefley, R-Colo., would be a logical candidate, but he is eyeing a Resources subcommittee chairmanship.

Donald Manzullo, R-Ill., is next in line, and is now chairman of the Tax, Finance and Exports Subcommittee. Sue W. Kelly, R-N.Y., the chairwoman of the Regulatory Reform and Paperwork Reduction Subcommittee, is also interested.

Nydia M. Velazquez of New York is likely to remain the ranking Democrat on the committee.

Republican members are expected to pursue tax relief for small businesses, including repeal of the estate tax. The panel also is expected to consider monitoring the federal practice of "bundling" smaller service contracts into a single, large contract. The bigger contracts are designed to cut administrative costs, but opponents argue that bundling favors large companies in the bidding process at the expense of smaller competitors.

Additionally, the panel is expected to continue its scrutiny of the Small Business Administration's lending programs and to encourage government agencies to reduce paperwork requirements for small businesses.

★Standards of Official Conduct (Ethics)

The 10-member panel, known informally as the House ethics committee, divides its seats evenly between the parties. The Speaker and minority leader appoint members, and the assignments are not coveted.

Chairman Lamar Smith, R-Texas, has not reached his term limit, but will ask the GOP leadership to step down next year. His request is expected to be granted.

Next in line is Joel Hefley, R-Colo. Howard L. Berman of California is expected to return as ranking Democrat.

Although the panel conducts business in private, it is known that at least one probe will carry over from the 106th Congress — the investigation into the alleged misuse of campaign funds by Earl F. Hilliard, D-Ala. The committee is also continuing work on a comprehensive ethics manual.

★Transportation and Infrastructure

Observers will need a scorecard to keep track of the changes on Transportation and Infrastructure, the largest panel in Congress. Each of the six subcommittees, as well as the full committee, is likely to have a new chairman.

Don Young, R-Alaska, is expected to take over as chairman, replacing Bud Shuster, R-Pa. Young will relinquish the gavel he has held for six years at the Resources Committee. Shuster is expected to replace Tom Petri, R-Wis., as chairman of the Ground Transportation Subcommittee, which writes the highway and mass transit authorization bill.

Petri is expected to seek the chairmanship of the Education and the Workforce Committee.

John J. "Jimmy" Duncan Jr., R-Tenn., the Aviation Subcommittee chairman, and Sherwood Boehlert, R-N.Y., the Water Resources and Environment Subcommittee chairman, face term limits.

Wayne T. Gilchrest, R-Md., who served as the chairman of the Coast Guard and Maritime Transportation Subcommittee, may take Boehlert's place on the Water Resources subcommittee; Boehlert is expected to become Science Committee chairman.

Two other subcommittee chairmen are leaving the House. Bob Franks, R-N.J., the Economic Development, Public Buildings, Hazardous Materials and Pipeline Transportation Subcommittee chairman, lost a Senate bid. And Tillie Fowler, R-Fla., Oversight, Investigations and Emergency Management Subcommittee chairman, is keeping her pledge to leave Congress after four terms.

The committee is expected to tackle unfinished business from the 106th Congress, including an overhaul of pipeline safety laws and changes to the federal railroad retirement system. The House passed a bill on the railroad retirement issue (HR 4844), but it ran into problems in the Senate. Similarly, a Senate-passed pipeline safety bill (S 2438) ran into problems in the House.

James L. Oberstar, D-Minn., will remain as ranking member of the full committee.

★Veterans Affairs

Term limits will end the tenure of Chairman Bob Stump, R-Ariz., and his replacement will be selected with less than military precision.

If things proceeded in an orderly fashion, Christopher H. Smith, R-N.J., would become chairman. Smith, who has served on the committee since he was first elected in 1980, is from a district with a large number of veterans.

However, Smith — a proponent of human rights and opponent of international abortion funding — also is within striking distance of the chairmanship of the International Relations Committee and is undecided about whether to pursue the post. While he is first in line for the Veterans Affairs chairmanship, he would have to tussle with three or four other Republicans to gain the leadership of International Relations.

Next in line after Smith for the Veterans committee helm is Michael Bilirakis, R-Fla., who has said he will not compete against Smith but would be interested in the job if it were uncontested. No changes are expected in the chairmanships of the Veterans' Affairs subcommittees.

Democrat Lane Evans of Illinois, who has served on the panel since 1982, is expected to remain as ranking member, his third term in that post.

★Ways and Means

The battle to succeed Ways and Means Chairman Bill Archer, R-Texas, who is retiring, is shaping up as one of the House's hottest chairmanship contests.

Philip M. Crane, R-Ill., and Bill Thomas, R-Calif., are seeking to take over from Archer, who served six tumultuous years that saw the passage of major trade legislation and an IRS overhaul but did not deliver on GOP promises to slash taxes.

Crane, left, and Thomas

Crane, who has more seniority than Thomas, is counting on his decision to seek treatment for alcoholism earlier this year to persuade colleagues that he has earned the chairmanship. He has been chairman of the Trade Subcommittee since the GOP took control of the House in 1995, working for liberalized trade rules with members on both sides of the aisle.

Thomas, whose relations with fellow lawmakers are often contentious, has made his mark as chairman of the Health Subcommittee, leading the GOP effort to overhaul Medicare by increasing the role of managed-care plans and adding a voluntary prescription drug plan through the private sector.

House Republican leaders have not publicly endorsed either candidate. A key factor in the race will be the preference of Speaker J. Dennis Hastert, whose Illinois district borders Crane's district in suburban Chicago.

Thomas and Crane have aggressively sought support and both have been generous with campaign funds. Thomas has not officially declared his intention to seek the chairmanship, however. If he does, that could open a pandora's box in which other members would also challenge for the chairmanship.

Third in line on the committee is E. Clay Shaw Jr., R-Fla. He might put his hat in the ring if Thomas does not acquiesce to Crane's seniority. Some lobbyists and staff say Jim McCrery, R-La., a quiet but knowledgeable member further down the committee roster, might also be a candidate if the race becomes a free-for-all.

Term limits will force the selection of new chairmen for both Crane's Trade Subcommittee and Thomas' Health Subcommittee. The loser in the chairmanship race could possibly take the other's subcommittee gavel.

If Shaw moves, that would open up the chairmanship of the Social Security Subcommittee. The new chairman would have a prominent place in the debate on the future of the retirement program expected in the 107th Congress.

Few changes will be seen on the other side of the ornate Ways and Means hearing room. With 30 years in Congress under his belt, Charles B. Rangel, D-N.Y., will return as ranking member. The top-ranking Democrat on the key Health Subcommittee will again be Pete Stark of California. ◆

Decision Time

Some of the biggest problems and opportunities that await the new chief executive have received comparatively little attention on the campaign trail

KEY ISSUES, AS SELECTED BY CQ'S EDITORS:

■ Surplus Politics 45	■ Education 51
■ Technology 47	■ Health Care 53
■ Trade, Globalization 49	■ Foreign Affairs 55

When Bill Clinton won re-election in 1996, the federal government was mired in deficits, and experts were warning that the nascent economic recovery would be impossible to sustain throughout his second four-year term.

They were wrong.

Whoever wins the White House in November will inherit an economy in its ninth year of expansion and a budget surplus that, at least on paper, gives the chief executive enough cash to offer generous tax cuts or new spending. The financial boom, by generating more revenue for Social Security and Medicare, has led to rosier projections about the near-term financial health of those programs, quieting calls for dramatic overhauls.

If there is a downside to these good times, it is that they may breed complacency among the public, which could see little compelling reason to vote come Election Day, and the candidates, who have narrowed their focus to a relatively small band of poll-tested, middle-class, domestic issues.

Democratic Vice President Al Gore and Republican Texas Gov. George W. Bush have run targeted campaigns keyed on education, a Medicare prescription drug benefit, tax reduction and Social Security. Until the latest outbreak of violence in the Middle East, the two largely shied away from foreign affairs or an in-depth discussion of national defense.

History is rife, however, with the lesson that political campaigns often bear little relation to presidential achievements or defeats. Lyndon B. Johnson ran on economic and civil rights in 1964, only to be undone by Vietnam. Clinton sailed into a second term by focusing on the economy — and was sullied by a sex scandal that led to impeachment by the House.

As Congressional Quarterly's editors looked at the key issues likely to confront the next president, a paradox became clear: Many of the problems (or opportunities) that could require immediate attention from the new chief executive have received scant attention in the campaign — and therefore little effort to develop public consensus.

One of the first big decisions the new president will face after taking office in January is whether the United States should deploy an anti-missile defense system that critics warn could violate the 1972 Anti-Ballistic Missile (ABM) Treaty and strain relations with Russia. Foreign affairs could come to the top of the agenda, with recent events in Israel and Lebanon showing that the Middle East peace process, a focus of the Clinton administration, is much more fragile than many had hoped.

Congress' decision this year to grant China permanent normal trade status ended a long debate about U.S. policy toward that nation, but did little to resolve an increasingly bitter argument about the role that labor and environmental standards should play in future trade deals. Several trade agreements are ready for submission to Congress, but have been held back until after the election to avoid controversy.

Even on domestic issues that have been the foundation of the campaign, change could be difficult. The direction of policy depends not just on who wins the presidency, but whether Republicans retain control of the House and Senate. Whatever the outcome of the congressional races, the next president is almost certain to be working with a Congress ruled by a slim majority and possibly unwilling to take bold steps.

Nearly 43 million Americans do not have health insurance, but the political fallout from Clinton's failed 1993 plan for universal coverage has made politicians skittish about endorsing sweeping government changes.

Washington's clunky bureaucracy has not kept pace with the real-time Internet, partly because lawmakers and the White House have not wanted it to. Concerns about privacy, access and taxation may force politicians to act rather than react on technology issues in the next four years. Likewise, the next president faces safety, ethical and scientific questions about genetically modified foods and organisms.

D-day, or deficit day, for Social Security and other entitlements has been delayed slightly, thanks to the economy, but the huge programs still face enormous financing issues over the next several decades as the Baby Boom generation retires, life expectancy increases, and there are fewer workers to cover promised benefits. Should the forecast surplus shrink, so will the options for fixing the programs, and the chances for new tax cuts and government aid to the poor and elderly.

Ironically, the one issue that has dominated the campaign — education — may be the area where the president is least able to effect broad change. Washington provides less than a dime of every public education dollar. While Democrats are more willing than the GOP to expand the federal role, neither party is pushing for changes to usurp local control, such as a national curriculum or standards.

The Surplus And the Baby Boomers

Managing the current prosperity to deal with a looming fiscal burden

The day of reckoning for the next president will not come solely in four years, when he may stand for re-election; history may impose a more enduring verdict in four decades, when a demographic time bomb explodes.

He will be the first president elected in a period of multi-year budget surpluses since Dwight D. Eisenhower won his second term in 1956. This will give him an extraordinary perch from which to direct the nation's fiscal policy — on a spending spree, a tax-cutting spree or a more circumspect middle course.

A presidential focus on budgetary discipline could put Washington on a firmer financial footing to deal with the retirement of the Baby Boomers, the youngest of whom will turn 40 during the next administration. Such an attitude from the Oval Office also might set the tone for subsequent administrations that will have to remain vigilant, even under the best economic circumstances, if the long-term solvency of the nation's growing smorgasbord of entitlement benefits is to be ensured.

If the next president sends Washington in a different direction, the nation will reel under the weight of the crushing demand of supporting the Baby Boomers in their retirement. The warning signs are obvious and ominous:

• The surplus now accumulating in the Social Security trust funds will disappear in about 15 years, the program's administrators warn. The "on-budget" surpluses generated primarily by unspent income tax receipts could be used to help finance the income program for the elderly for only about another decade.

• Even if the national debt is paid in the next 10 years, the federal budget will be back in the red before 2030, and debt will begin accumulating again. This could be delayed only if, once the debt is retired, a substantial share of the surplus is used to buy stocks or other assets — a highly unlikely scenario.

• Unless entitlement costs are trimmed, the fiscal dam will burst somewhere around 2040, when demographic pressures overwhelm the government's ability to meet its obligations.

According to Congressional Budget Office (CBO) calculations made public Oct. 6, there will be only about two workers for each elderly person receiving Social Security benefits. The national debt will have begun doubling every few years — to roughly twice the size of the gross domestic product by 2040. (In the mid-1990s, as the years of deepest deficits began to recede, the debt was two-thirds the size of the economy.) All discretionary programs, for defense and all domestic endeavors, would be competing for a small fraction of the

budget. Entitlement spending — mostly on senior citizens — and interest on the ballooning debt would consume the rest.

It would be a blueprint for generational warfare.

And perhaps the most frightening part of this forecast: CBO assumes there will be no changes in government policy and that discretionary spending will grow at the rate of inflation — a dubious assumption based on the trend set in the past few years. Any new spending programs, tax cuts or entitlements could result in a substantially more bleak fiscal picture.

Short-Term Surplus Overstated

Looking only at the coming decade, the fiscal picture at first glance seems bright. The CBO projects that surpluses totaling about $4.6 trillion will accumulate — although more than half would be Social Security revenues that both presidential nominees have vowed not to touch. That leaves an on-budget surplus of $2.2 trillion over the next 10 years. Although they differ on their priorities, Republican George W. Bush, now the governor of Texas, and Democrat Al Gore, now the vice president, have proposed tax cuts and new programs that would consume most of that on-budget surplus.

However, nonpartisan budget watchdog groups say the two are proposing to spend money that does not exist, because the CBO forecast is based on faulty assumptions — in particular, the premise that Washington's spending appetite is no more ravenous than inflation. The Concord Coalition, a non-partisan group that advocates fiscal conservatism, calculates that discretionary outlays have grown at an average rate of 5.5 percent annually since fiscal 1998, when the federal government ran its first surplus in three decades. If that rate of increase continues, all but $712 billion of the CBO's projected on-budget surplus will have evaporated in fiscal 2010. The Brookings Institution paints an even starker picture. Using a more complex analysis of likely tax and spending patterns during the next 10 years, the institution expects a 10-year surplus of only $352 billion.

Both of these projections do not account for any of the new proposals of Gore and Bush. If the programs of either were fully implemented, the national books would be back in the red before the end of the decade.

The impact of the surplus on politics and policy is that candidates no longer feel obligated to explain the means of paying for their promises, said David C. Colander, a historian of economic thought at Middlebury College. "It has changed the whole nature of the discussion," he said. "Both sides are trying to give people more."

Solutions Elusive

There is no firm agreement among economists on how best to leverage today's prosperity to cope with the looming fiscal burden. Some economists maintain that tax cuts designed to spur additional economic expansion would be worthwhile immediately — even if they delay paying down the debt — because tax receipts would actually grow if the economy grows more. And some liberal think tanks maintain that some of the surplus should be invested in social programs, such as education, that would make the work force more productive.

There is near universal accord among budget watchdogs, however, that eliminating or at least reducing the debt should be the top priority, because funds that otherwise would be used for interest payments could instead be spent on entitlements. These are programs whose eligibility requirements are in law, so anyone who meets the specified criteria is entitled to pay-

ment. Social Security, Medicare, Medicaid, unemployment benefits, food stamps and federal pensions are examples.

There is widespread agreement, as well, that there should be no big expansions of entitlements unless they are accompanied by proposals to ensure their long-term solvency. The promises from the campaign trail this fall do not fill that bill. Gore and Bush both would expand Medicare, the medical insurance for the elderly and disabled, by adding a prescription drug benefit. Although they disagree on the details, both would dramatically increase the government's commitment to its graying population. But there has been no substantial discussion about cost-saving changes to entitlements.

"You should not be pushing major tax cuts or major entitlement increases until you have dealt with the long-term problem," said James Horney, a former top CBO analyst who is now a senior fellow at the liberal-leaning Center on Budget and Policy Priorities. "This is a crucial time in the sense that we're getting closer to the beginning of the demographic problem."

Even AARP — the leading lobby for the elderly, and long viewed as a major obstacle to reining in entitlement spending — agrees that changes need to be made. Its public policy director, John Rother, cited the increase in the Social Security retirement age to 67 from 65, which was enacted in 1983 but is only beginning to be phased in, as an example of how entitlement changes should take effect over time and with enough advance notice for beneficiaries to plan. "Our position on Social Security is that we need to enact fairly modest adjustments now in order to assure younger people that the system will be there and adequately funded for them," Rother said.

The next president has an opportunity to leverage the surplus to extend the solvency of entitlement programs even if no changes in their rules are enacted. Promptly paying off the $3.1 trillion in debt held by the public would delay the onset of deficits for perhaps a decade. If the government paid off its debt and then invested additional surpluses in securities, the nation's books would stay in the black until about 2050, according to the CBO.

But with both parties busily chipping away at the surplus that might be dedicated to debt service, the likelihood that Washington could both clear its debts and squirrel away funds for a rainy day seems remote at best.

Lessons From the Past

Just a decade ago, deficit spending seemed intractable, the possibility of paying off most of the debt almost unthinkable. The demands placed on the federal government were too great, and the political obstacles to cutting funding for any established programs were insurmountable, as the Republicans learned when they took control of Congress in 1995. Even Ronald Reagan, whom conservatives still revere as the modern messiah of smaller government, was unable to make any substantial dent in domestic spending and was forced to press his agenda of tax cuts and increased defense spending without offsetting spending reductions. The result were deficits that pushed past $100 billion in fiscal 1982 and did not come back below that mark for 15 years.

What few expected was technological change so radical that it would force revisions in basic economic models. In the later 1990s, job growth and wages climbed rapidly. Enhanced by increased worker productivity, inflation and interest rates stayed relatively low, allowing the economic boom — which continues today — to be longer and stronger than economists previously thought possible.

The failure of past fiscal projections may comfort those who want to ignore the dire warnings of budget watchdogs. There are two risks in taking a Pollyanna approach. First, projections that are far off could be much worse than expected, instead of much better. Second, the possible range of economic variations in long term budget projections, while significant, are relatively small compared to the massive demographic shifts that are at the root of the nation's long-term budgetary challenges.

In history, economic matters have ranked second only to war in defining presidencies. With no protracted conflict since Vietnam, the role of the president as economic steward has taken center stage. Reagan's fiscal legacy remains the most hotly debated facet of his presidency: The GOP credits his tax cuts with laying the groundwork for long-term prosperity, while Democrats say those tax cuts combined with his military buildup caused the depths of the current debt.

The Persian Gulf War, the most lopsided military victory in U.S. history, propelled George Bush to unparalleled popularity. Yet he was defeated the following year, largely because he was perceived as not aggressive enough in combatting a recession that turned out to be mild and brief.

Bill Clinton walked a path just slightly left of center; he pushed a tax increase in the name of deficit reduction early on and has advanced relatively modest expansions in domestic spending. He unsuccessfully promoted two big expansions to entitlements: universal health care at the start of his presidency, and Medicare prescription drug coverage at the end. But in between, he signed one of the biggest entitlement reductions ever, ending 61 years of federally guaranteed cash welfare to poor mothers and their children. (That 1996 law will be up for renewal on the next president's watch.)

Clinton also was president at a benchmark in American budget history, when the deficit era ended and surpluses began. How much credit historians will give him for this turnaround remains to be seen.

For the 43rd president, properly managing the surplus will neither be any easier, nor less important, than his predecessors' task of shrinking the deficit. History may expect even more from a leader fortunate enough to inherit a windfall that could be a down payment on the nation's long-term obligations.

THE NARROWING RATIOS

■ In 1960, 5.1 workers backed each Social Security beneficiary. The ratio now is 3.4 to 1. In 2040, it will be 2.1 to 1.

■ Spending on Social Security, Medicare and Medicaid now totals about 7.5 percent of the nation's gross domestic product. By 2040, the figure will be 16.7 percent.

■ Interest payments on the $3.1 trillion in publicly held federal debt will consume about 11 percent of the $1.8 trillion that the federal government will spend on all programs in fiscal 2001.

Information Technology's Anxious Side

Economic engine of 1990s, e-commerce will draw increasing regulatory scrutiny

Being the engine of economic growth has its advantages. As the information technology sector kept good times rolling by creating most of the new high-paying jobs in the 1990s, it acquired virtual immunity from federal regulation. With a few exceptions, most notably the antitrust case against Microsoft Corp., Washington policymakers fairly shuddered at the prospect of drawing up ground rules for the digital economy and its myriad Internet companies, fearing they would stifle innovation and scare away new investment.

That may be about to change. The next president will have to confront growing anxiety about electronic privacy and information security, as well as an intensifying high-stakes battle over the proposed taxation of electronic commerce. He also will likely be thrust into thorny debates over intellectual property on the Internet, high-tech mega-mergers, the "digital divide" and biotechnology.

Navigating all of those issues will be challenging. The new president will have to balance the needs of the high-tech industry and its cadre of powerful campaign donors with those of consumers and local governments. He must do so knowing that Washington's cumbersome bureaucracy cannot possibly keep up with rapid developments in the marketplace and that many key decisions may wind up being made by the courts. Many in the industry hope that the next president, through agencies such as the Federal Communications Commission (FCC), the Department of Justice and the Federal Trade Commission (FTC), may try to establish rules for fair play and propose suitable remedies for wrongdoing.

The president's possible role as digital referee may bring about a significant shift in Washington's political thinking. Unlike education or health care, digital economy issues tend to be diffuse and do not fall along the political fault lines established by long-running debates over Great Society programs such as Medicare and Head Start. Conservatives suspicious of government surveillance on the Internet already have found themselves allied with civil libertarians and liberals on some privacy issues. And politicians from both major parties are learning that even short-term legislative fixes based on established laws and regulations can be elusive in a world where innovations blending entertainment, computers and telecommunications crop up almost daily.

"There still is the sense that government should somehow dictate to private industry what is good, but it can provide a real powerful lesson in humility," said William E. Lee, professor of telecommunications at the University of Geor-

gia. "Many politicians don't yet understand the changes in communications patterns. That makes it difficult to cling to old ways of looking at the world on a subject like copyright issues every time some kid invents another Napster," the controversial music file-swapping software.

Another new economy issue that will force policymakers to change their world view is biotechnology. While genetic engineering of foods has the potential to boost yields and feed starving millions around the world, critics say there is a need for better labeling and testing. Concerns over food safety that already have swept Europe could prompt the next president to work with Congress to set new standards.

The Privacy Debate

Experts believe electronic privacy will likely be the preeminent digital economy issue to confront the next administration. Public concern over market researcher DoubleClick Inc.'s in-depth tracking of consumers' online habits last year, and the more recent controversy swirling around Carnivore, the FBI's e-mail "wiretap" system, prompted a flurry of hearings and privacy legislation in Congress and a package of electronic surveillance and cybercrime proposals from the Clinton administration. While no sweeping legislation was enacted, the bills offered represent a broader move to control what Internet companies can do with personal information.

"Technology is challenging individuals' ability to seek out information and engage in activities without being monitored and identified," Jerry Berman, executive director of the Center for Democracy and Technology, a Washington-based Internet civil liberties group, recently told a Senate Commerce Committee hearing on Internet privacy.

Two areas of concern that are certain to be addressed are medical and financial information. The profusion of medical websites and online pharmacies that collect personal information has raised questions about who has access to individuals' medical histories and whether that information could be used to deny employment or health insurance. The issue has become even more complicated in light of the recent decoding of the complete human genome. This could lead to the storage of individuals' DNA sequences in cyberspace, where access to their genetic profile could yield information about any medical conditions and reveal whether they or their children are predisposed to specific gene-based diseases.

In the area of finance, last year's overhaul of financial services laws (PL 106-102) placed new restrictions on the ability of banks, brokerages and insurers to transfer customer data to third parties. However, recent cases of identity theft and hacker attacks on commercial websites have reinforced the perception that personal information is not secure — and that security measures vary so much among online sites that a comprehensive solution may be elusive. An increased focus on privacy issues would mean a more prominent role for the FTC, which oversees most conduct and business practices on the Internet. Such an expansion of authority would cause heartburn for high-tech executives, who worry that federal privacy mandates will make them more liable for enforcement actions over alleged deceptive acts. Crafting a uniform set of standards and enforcing them could also prove difficult for federal authorities, who might have to scrutinize millions of websites. (*1999 CQ Almanac, p. 5-3*).

The Taxation Dilemma

While the privacy issue is fraught with technical chal-

lenges, the debate over taxing e-commerce centers more around legal and political considerations. The expiration next October of a three-year congressional moratorium (PL 105-277) on Internet-specific taxes will renew calls from state and local governments for a nationwide system to more easily collect them for online purchases. Groups such as the National Governors' Association have argued there should be parity between the digital world — which essentially operates as a tax-free zone — and Main Street businesses, which account for a sizable share of local tax bases and are already losing customers to cyberspace. (*1998 Almanac, p. 21-19*)

The issue has forced Washington policymakers to balance the preservation of state and local governments' taxing authority with the need to keep interstate e-commerce free of potentially burdensome new taxes. Few politicians, including the two major presidential candidates, have taken a position. The notable exception is former candidate Sen. John McCain, R-Ariz., who opposes new taxes in cyberspace.

With consumer spending on the Internet expected to exceed $20 billion this year by some estimates, action is likely. One possible approach would be to allow local taxes to be levied only on companies with a "substantial physical presence" in the taxing jurisdiction. For that to happen, the next president would have to work with Congress to clarify what type of e-businesses are subject to taxation at what point in the borderless realm of the World Wide Web.

"The solution is to let mayors and governors impose taxes on those Internet companies located within their jurisdictions," said Adam D. Thierer, economic policy fellow at the Heritage Foundation, a conservative Washington think tank. "Companies could shop around for more hospitable tax locales if their current jurisdictions become overzealous."

Thierer questions, however, whether a state should be able to tax an Internet service provider or a Web-hosting service that accepts and processes orders for a Web site in another state. He and other experts believe the issue's legal complexity may lead policymakers to defer to the courts to avoid alienating localities and the high-tech industry.

Copyrights and Wrongs

Another difficult legal issue is how to apply existing copyright and intellectual property laws to the digital world. A court ruling against the digital music site MP3.com and a pending case against Napster have focused attention on whether the Web services violated record labels' copyrights by providing downloadable music files. Proponents say the services allow people to use new technologies to share music and movies and thus expand the audience for such fare. The entertainment industry says the services are using the Internet to commit outright piracy and wants stronger copyright protection. The next administration may have to take sides and consider a rewrite of existing laws.

Similarly, the new president likely will have to consider whether telecommunications laws need to be updated in order to expand and enhance Internet service. Many policymakers have proposed giving regulatory relief to local phone companies so they can use their fiber optic lines to deliver the Internet over long distances at speeds many times faster than what is currently available on ordinary copper cable. The 1996 telecommunications law (PL 104-104) requires the FCC first to certify that the companies have opened up their local franchises to competition by allowing new vendors to hook up to their central switches. This "broadband"

debate is an important component of larger discussions over the digital divide and how to bring high-speed Internet to outlying and underserved areas. (*1996 Almanac, p. 3-43*)

The next president could choose to streamline the FCC approval process or take other steps to "build out" the Internet backbone. However, many observers say the regional Bells and other vendors should not get access to the lucrative, long-distance data transmission market until they can prove they have opened their local markets to rivals. An alternative would be to offer telecommunications vendors tax credits to build fiber optic systems in more remote areas.

The posture the next administration adopts toward big telecommunications companies also will be reflected in actions by its Justice Department, which became a powerful check on the high-tech market during the Clinton administration through its antitrust division.

Mergers such as the proposed AOL-Time Warner Inc. deal have raised questions about whether consolidation will limit consumer choice in areas such as selecting an Internet service provider. AOL-Time Warner, for example, would own significant stakes in entertainment and news content, operate cable television systems and phone networks capable of carrying Internet traffic and control the nation's most popular Internet portal. Such a market giant could easily bundle services and offer price discounts to steer consumers to its products even while offering rivals "open access" to their Internet lines.

Analysts believe antitrust could offer a big digital economy distinction between Bush and Gore administrations. They believe Gore would be less sympathetic to takeovers and combinations involving broadcasters and telecommunications companies, while Bush would be expected to take more of a laissez-faire approach.

"It is unlikely that Bush would have brought a case against [computer chip maker] Intel Corp. for refusing to share technology or pursue the antitrust case against Microsoft Corp.," said Sherman E. Katz of the Center for Strategic and International Studies, a Washington think tank. "It boils down to whether you believe competition is better than regulation."

TECHNOLOGY'S GROWING ROLE

■ 85 million Internet users are expected to purchase goods online annually by the end of 2003, compared with 28.8 million in 1999.

■ The computer industry has contributed $22 million to federal candidates in the current election cycle, compared with $1.26 million a decade ago. According to the Center for Responsive Politics, 54 percent of the money has gone to Democrats and 45 percent to Republicans.

■ At least 14 major Internet privacy bills have been introduced in the 106th Congress, most dealing with consumer protection or enhanced law enforcement.

The Many Shades of Trade Policy

U.S. dependence on global commerce intersects with calls for economic justice

When George Bush assumed the presidency in 1989, he had a luxury of sorts: He could view much of the globe in black and white. Most nations either were in the camp of the "bad guys," led by the communist Soviet Union, or the "good guys," led by the capitalist United States. The threat of an apocalyptic nuclear conflict between the two sides shaded all foreign policy.

Just a year after Bush took office, the picture began to change. The Soviet bloc started dissolving, as Poland and Hungary broke away. Other nations followed suit, and then the Soviet Union itself fell apart at the end of 1991. U.S. foreign policy began to pay more attention to the trade alliances of the world, and less on military pacts.

As a result, the president who takes office in 2001 will see the world in a startling array of colors.

Imagine the map that George W. Bush or Al Gore will inherit. Across the Atlantic, there is a 15-nation bloc of blue known as the European Union. Another six countries — picture them in yellow — have banded together to the south to form Latin American trade ties. And across the Pacific, in shades of red, are 10 Asian nations increasingly affiliated in trade and economic matters. A spattering of aquamarine, fuchsia, burnt sienna are scattered throughout, representing lesser alliances.

A mapmaker with a sense of humor — and an awareness of current geopolitics — might be tempted to cover the entire thing with a layer of vellum. It would be green, like the dollar.

In a world in which capitalism is the only strong soldier left standing, it is the U.S. greenback that drives relations between the world's only superpower and all the other countries. More trading opportunities are the result, but the landscape is far less certain than during the polarizing days of the free market versus state control.

Europeans — viewed primarily as our most loyal military allies for the last half century — are now often our testiest economic competitors. Battles over shelf space for U.S. products in European supermarkets and the trade fairness of the U.S. tax code have strained relations. And many nations termed "Third World" when the elder Bush was president, India and Brazil among them, are emerging economic forces. China's membership in the World Trade Organization (WTO), which could come before the inauguration, will lend further strength to the causes of the so-called "lesser developed countries."

Those are not the next president's only challenges in managing the U.S. relationship with the new world order. The most complicating factor is on our shores.

Opponents of a globalized economy — who lament its homogenizing and sometimes exploitative side effects — are beginning to make headway with the leaders of some institutions, such as the World Bank, who now acknowledge that the status quo may not be lifting all boats. The new president will be pressed to juggle two forceful groups: social activists, who want trade policy to focus on more than financial reward, and business leaders, for whom reduction in trade barriers may be critical for continued profitability.

The stakes for balancing the two and piecing together a renewed force for trade expansion are at the heart of the next president's top priority: sustaining the record economic expansion of the past eight years.

American wealth is increasingly linked to trade. The nation's appetite for consumer products could not be met without cheap imports; its output of top-of-the-line goods and services could not be sustained without plenty of overseas markets; its standard of living, highlighted by the strong dollar, could not stand without record foreign investment in both U.S. companies and U.S. government securities.

Still, the mix has resulted in a record gap between the value of goods and investments coming into the United States and the value being exported. (The trade deficit through June was on pace to be $354 billion for this year; that would be $89 billion, or 34 percent, higher than in 1999.) The next president may need to address this trade deficit with the same urgency that compelled his predecessors to tackle the budget deficit.

Catherine L. Mann, in her 1999 book "Is the U.S. Trade Deficit Sustainable?," says the imbalance could continue for "two or three more years" unless U.S. leaders substantially win access to more foreign markets for services, a sector in which the United States has a significant advantage, or spur the national savings rate, now at a negative 0.4 percent, a record low. Both actions would lower the trade deficit.

If neither happens, the United States could become a less attractive investment for foreigners and the value of the dollar — now high compared to other currencies — could fall, as it did from 1985 to 1987. That would raise the prices Americans pay for imports and increase the costs of doing business for their employers. It could also depress the stock market.

Challenge No. 1: Finding a Way in the New World

The next president's efforts to make a big splash on the international scene would be helped immeasurably by fast-track trading authority, a procedure that allows the administration to negotiate trade pacts without fear that they will be rewritten at the Capitol. Instead, Congress must endorse or reject the deal within 90 days of being formally informed of it. That procedure expired in 1994, and President Clinton was unable to win it back. (*1998 Almanac, p. 23-3*)

His failure was due in part to a surge of protectionism after enactment of the 1993 law (PL 103-182) that implemented the North American Free Trade Agreement between Mexico, Canada and the United States. (*1993 Almanac, p. 171*)

For lawmakers and their constituents in Southern states such as Florida and Rust Belt states such as Ohio, NAFTA was associated with the flight to Mexico of old-time industries and a subsequent loss of jobs, many of them unionized positions that paid well and afforded good benefits. Defeating fast-track, which would have made more such trade agree-

ments possible, became the Holy Grail for organized labor and others who sided with unions.

The new president could feel the full brunt of that force against an effort to revive fast-track authority, unless he found a way to appease groups whose issues are not now considered central to trade strategy. Any concessions to them would likely subject either Bush or Gore to business group criticism.

Some members of Congress, and the leaders of the World Bank and International Monetary Fund (IMF), believe it is possible to find some middle ground on international economic issues, however.

This acknowledgement that the current system may need tweaking comes as a victory for the forces against globalization. They have taken their protests against worldwide corporate interests from Seattle to Washington to Prague in the last year. Their cause has won headlines, but it is not clear whether the nerves they have touched — among world leaders and the public — will change the course of U.S. trade policy or simply increase the polarization of the haves and have-nots.

Neither the Texas governor nor the vice president has talked about trade much in his campaign. Each would likely approach the issue quite differently if elected.

Gore has promised that trade agreements he would sign would address labor and environmental standards. It is unclear how strong his language might be, although U.S. Trade Representative Charlene Barshefsky is attempting to set a precedent by negotiating rules on treatment of workers in Jordan as part of an agreement with that Middle Eastern nation.

Bush is more likely to embrace the status quo, and will probably succeed if Congress stays Republican. But trade has not historically been a party-line issue, and a Bush effort to continue business as usual could alienate most Democrats. Even pro-trade Democrats such as Rep. Robert T. Matsui of California insist a new consensus will be necessary to win fast track.

In addition to prodding Congress to revive fast track and approve trade pacts with Jordan and Vietnam, the 43rd president will be pushed by the business community — farmers in particular — to limit congressional efforts to punish enemies with economic sanctions. They will advocate more open relations with Cuba, the lone communist nation in the Western Hemisphere, and may attempt to weaken sanctions on Iran and Libya when a law (PL 104-172) restricting trade with those nations lapses next year. Some business leaders are also pushing lawmakers to rethink sanctions on India, imposed because of its nuclear weapons program.

Europe and Beyond

With the European Union and the United States increasingly playing rough under the world's trade rules, Bush or Gore will play a role in determining how to bridge the differences. The current disputes being adjudicated by the WTO involve Europe's barriers to Central American bananas sold by U.S. companies, hormone-treated beef sold by U.S. ranchers, and income tax breaks the United States gives its exporters.

If the differences remain and cross-Atlantic sniping continues or escalates, many on both continents say the world trading system is jeopardized. It is questionable whether the WTO, created in 1994 as the successor to the weaker adjudication system of the General Agreement on Tariffs and Trade, could withstand barrages from its two main benefactors. Other disagreements, including one over Europe's ban on equipment — known as "hush kits" — to soften the sound of aircraft, are simmering.

Thus far, the system appears to be working. The United States has won the right to retaliate against Europe for a failure to abide by WTO rulings on bananas and beef, and Congress is pushing to pass a bill (HR 4986) to alter its taxation of income earned abroad in order to avoid punitive tariffs the WTO would otherwise authorize. (*2000 CQ Weekly*, p. 2264)

The next president's handling of globalization issues will only be made more complicated by the emergence of more voices on the world's economic stage.

The WTO will face one of its biggest challenges when China joins its ranks. The world's most populous nation is slowly emerging from its state-run economy, and its progress in meeting the high standards set by the WTO will likely occur in fits and starts. The United States put its imprimatur on China's WTO membership Oct. 10, when Clinton signed a bill (HR 4444 — PL 106-286) granting the country, upon its accession to the WTO, the same permanent normal tariff rate as all but a handful of nations. (*2000 CQ Weekly*, p. 2223)

Toward the end of his term the new president will likely feel increasing pressure to help Russia join the rest of the world's largest nations in the WTO. That still appears several years off, although Barshefsky says that leaders are trying to speed negotiations.

Before that emerges as a major issue, the United States and the other major industrial nations will face more immediate challenges, namely how to jump-start global negotiations on reducing trade barriers. Led by China, India and Brazil, emerging nations will pose significant challenges there, especially if leaders attempt to address the cry from the Western left for international environmental and labor standards. Less-developed countries fear that such rules will disadvantage them in world competition.

If the United States and Europe are unable to agree on a course for trade liberalization, the emerging voices will have an opening to exploit the gap. Their desire for a greater say in world matters, and their anger at Clinton's suggestion of sanctions against labor-exploiting countries, led in part to the failure of the WTO to launch a comprehensive round of trade negotiations at a Seattle meeting last year.

FRIENDS AND WHAT WE OWE

■ About 30 percent of the real Gross Domestic Product of the United States is directly affected by trade.

■ Friends are hard to discern from trade balances. In July, the top surpluses were with the Netherlands, Australia and Belgium. Top deficits were with China, Japan and Canada.

■ The trade deficit would be larger if exports of services were not growing. In July, $65 billion in goods were exported, down $1.5 billion from June. Service exports stood at $24.7 billion, up $200 million.

Education: High Expectations, Limited Means

Leveraging the limited federal investment to fulfill promises of 'accountability'

The next president could easily conclude that he had a green light from the public to propose the biggest changes in years to the nation's school system.

With a strong economy and no wars to dominate the country's attention, education leapt to the top of voters' priority lists in the mid-1990's and has stayed there ever since. The nation has gone through spasms of public concern about education before: Dwight Eisenhower focused the country's attention on math and science education after the Soviet Union launched Sputnik in 1957, Lyndon B. Johnson won billions of dollars for disadvantaged students with the Elementary and Secondary Education Act (ESEA) in 1965, and George Bush hammered out a set of education goals with the nation's governors in 1989.

This time around, the buzzword is accountability.

Both major presidential candidates are promising dramatic steps to ensure that schools and teachers do their jobs. Candidates regularly spar over such proposals as requiring annual tests and high school exit exams for students; report cards for schools; teacher testing; bonuses for good schools and sanctions for bad ones, and closing down schools that consistently fail to meet basic standards.

"You didn't hear this kind of talk about accountability, performance standards, flexibility and creativity four years ago," Pennsylvania Education Secretary Eugene W. Hickok, chairman of the Education Leaders Council, a group of education officials who advocate local control over schooling policies, said in an Oct. 4 interview. "Now that is part of the discussion on education everywhere you go."

Regardless of whether lawmakers will be working with a President Al Gore or a President George W. Bush, "the next Congress is going to be the busiest Congress in terms of education since the Great Society," said Vic Klatt, vice president of the lobbying firm of Van Scoyoc Associates Inc. and a former GOP staffer at the House Education and the Workforce Committee. "There will be no part of education that's left untouched."

In reality, there are limits to what Bush or Gore can do. The federal government provides only about 7 cents of every education dollar, and the political price can be high for anyone who tries to usurp what has been a state and local responsibility. The compromise has been to leverage the federal investment into local change; the 1994 reauthorization of ESEA required states to install performance standards and ways to measure student progress in order to get Title I funds for disadvantaged students. That helped get the accountability movement going — the question now is how to put more teeth in it. (*1994 Almanac, p. 383*)

Voters want to make sure their children will be ready for jobs in an increasingly high-tech economy, and they do not like what they see. While 58 percent of Americans said they had confidence in the public schools in 1973, only 36 percent did in 1999, according to Public Agenda, a nonpartisan, nonprofit public policy research group based in New York.

Parents read about studies such as a September report by the National Commission on Mathematics and Science Teaching for the 21st Century — called the "Glenn Commission" in honor of its chairman, former Ohio Democratic Sen. John Glenn (1974-99) — that ranked the math skills of American high school seniors "almost last" among the nations surveyed.

They hear about an "achievement gap" between the test scores of minority students and their peers, which was starting to close in the 1970s and 1980s and then basically flattened out in the 1990s, according to Education Trust, a nonprofit group that advocates tougher education standards.

Test scores are not actually falling. Since 1990, math scores on the National Assessment of Education Progress have risen an average of 1 percentage point a year, according to a July study by RAND, a nonprofit public policy research organization. That does not mean students' skills are strong, though; employers and college professors say they are unimpressed by young adults' math and writing abilities.

The road to higher standards and accountability has been paved for the next president by state governors, who are beginning to get results. Bush has not been shy about playing up progress in Texas, though he did not initiate many of the state programs. In an Oct. 5 survey by Public Agenda, more than eight out of 10 parents approved of efforts under way in their local schools to raise performance.

It is not unqualified support; parents say they need to be reassured that their children's entire future will not depend on a single test. But despite well-publicized controversies over standardized testing in some states — such as Virginia, where complaints have become an issue in a U.S. Senate race — Public Agenda found little danger of a national backlash.

So all the next president has to do is strengthen the "standards movement" and expand it . . . right?

Think again.

No Sure Thing

Whoever wins in November will walk into a political environment as polarized as any in recent years. Public support for the general idea of a wholesale education overhaul is one thing, but navigating the maze of partisan maneuvering in Congress and interest groups is another.

This is, after all, the year in which Congress — for the first time in the law's 35-year history — could not reauthorize ESEA, the main federal education aid program. Efforts fell apart because of ideological differences over everything from the channeling of federal dollars to proposals for gun control measures in public schools. (*2000 CQ Weekly, pp. 1105, 972*)

The danger of overreaching is very real. Ask President Clinton. Despite public support, he had to abandon a 1997 plan for voluntary national reading and math tests. The idea died in a barrage of criticism from Republicans and conservative groups, who feared it would lead to a national curricu-

lum. (*1997 CQ Almanac, p. 9-50*)

Since then, Clinton has done best with less controversial ideas, such as fixing aging schools and reducing class size in the early grades by hiring 100,000 new teachers. Both have broad support, but neither raises expectations for schools or teachers — and Clinton was unable to sell Congress on a 1999 plan to require teacher tests and new management for underperforming schools. (*1999 CQ Weekly, p. 176*)

Each nominee has unique strengths that could allow him to challenge interest groups' resistance to big changes — a modern-day equivalent of President Richard M. Nixon going to China. The stakes are high, though, and the next president could easily lose political latitude on the issue.

The Political Limits

Gore can talk about testing teachers to make sure they know their subjects without immediately provoking the wrath of powerful teachers' unions, such as the National Education Association. The rest of his agenda is so in synch with theirs, they have an interest in making sure he wins.

By talking about teacher testing and peer review for poorly performing educators, Gore "has shown a willingness to do his own thing," Andrew Rotherham, director of education policy at the Progressive Policy Institute and a former Clinton education adviser, said in an Oct. 3 interview.

Gore adds an important qualification, though: He talks about testing *new* teachers. He also sweetens his proposal with talk of pay raises for all teachers and professional development for those who agree to teach in poor districts. Such a balance has been crucial to winning union support for testing and tougher licensing requirements in such states as North Carolina — but it also makes critics suspect that Gore could back down on testing, pushing just the sweeteners.

Likewise, Bush must be careful not to alienate conservative groups as he advocates an increased federal role. He raised some eyebrows by suggesting during an Oct. 3 presidential debate that the federal government should require annual testing, even though states could choose the exam. "There are a whole lot of House Republicans who would shake their heads at that," said Klatt.

Then there are the social issues that get pulled into any education debate. The next president would likely face a repeat of this year's aborted Senate showdown over gun control. Democrats insist that school safety is a valid education issue; Republicans, most of whom oppose new gun control measures, call such amendments a distraction.

These are not just side issues. Parents have a wide range of concerns, and accountability is only one of them. In a 1999 survey by ICR Survey Research Group, lack of parental involvement, drug use, disruptive students, overcrowded classrooms and violence rounded out the list. "There's nothing in this that says, 'Full speed ahead, damn the torpedoes,' " said Public Agenda President Deborah Wadsworth. "It needs to be handled well and handled carefully."

What to Expect

The education debate is well defined, so the next president should not be surprised by the tough political obstacles.

• **Student testing.** Whether it is an annual test or a high school exit exam, students and parents may complain that assessments are unreasonably hard, as in Virginia. Officials in Texas and North Carolina — the two states that have had the most success with standards-based overhauls, according

to a RAND study — have eased resistance by making sure tests are tied directly to the state curriculum. In other words, students are tested on what they are actually taught.

• **Teacher testing.** To make requirements go over more smoothly, North Carolina included pay raises in the same package with its new rules, which included subject-area tests for beginning teachers and peer reviews for teachers who wanted to extend their licenses. If anything, the resistance came from school administrators, according to Karen Garr, an adviser to Democratic Gov. James B. Hunt Jr.; they worried they would have a tough time attracting good teachers.

• **School report cards.** Both Gore and Bush would require states to issue school report cards, which have been successful in Texas and North Carolina. When Texas began its accountability program in 1994, school districts were "very resistant" to the annual ratings, according to Criss Cloudt, the Texas Education Agency official who runs the program. Now, she said, everyone chases after good ratings.

• **Closing bad schools.** Gore would close underperforming schools, fire the principals and find "fair ways" to remove the worst teachers. Texas allows schools to be closed, Cloudt said, but in practice that does not happen because the state cannot afford to lose any; there are simply too many students. Instead, both Texas and North Carolina have replaced principals, though it is not a common occurrence.

• **Going outside the system.** As a last resort, Bush would let parents take their children out of failing public schools, using their share of Title I funds to switch to private or religious schools. The proposal has raised the same political arguments as school vouchers, with Democrats and educators arguing that needed funds should not be drained from the public schools. Instead, both parties and most interest groups have been more open to public school choice.

Finally, there is the issue of money. Texas and North Carolina have not raised their test scores merely because of standards and accountability measures. They have also spent money to help minority and disadvantaged students. "It takes both resources and standards-based reform. The two go together," said David Grissmer, lead author of the RAND study.

With all of the surpluses the next president will have to play with, that part, at least, should not be a problem.

PROGRESS ISN'T ELEMENTARY

■ Projected enrollment in public and private elementary and secondary education schools, 2008: 54.3 million. Increase from 1996: 6 percent.

■ Nations with average fourth-grade science scores lower than the U.S.: 19.

■ High school teachers who say most or all students have the skills to succeed in the workplace: 63 percent. Employers who say high school graduates lack the skills to succeed: 58 percent.

Health Care Costs Poised To Surge Again

Containment efforts could focus on reducing fraud, waste and medical errors

When it comes to health care coverage, nobody likes to be told "no." That simple fact explains why efforts to put the brakes on health care spending over the last decade have been so unpopular — and why the next president is not likely to turn that situation around.

Those who have tried to set limits, whether in the private-sector world of health plans and employers or in the political world of presidents and lawmakers, have done so at their peril.

The basic trade-off hasn't changed since President Clinton tried and failed to push his plan for universal health care through Congress in 1993-94. Expanding health insurance to Americans without it, and controlling costs, requires restricting benefits to those who already have coverage. Even proposals that fall far short of universal care, such as reducing growth in Medicare, raise the same basic dilemma. Congress tightened Medicare spending in 1997 only to be met with screams of protests by provider groups. Lawmakers are now writing legislation to "give back" about $30 billion in cuts. (*1994 CQ Almanac p. 319, Story, 2000 CQ Weekly, p. 2414*)

Clinton is not the only politician burned by the health care issue. In 1995, congressional Republicans tried unsuccessfully to turn Medicaid from an open-ended entitlement to a block grant program with spending caps. The managed-care industry, meanwhile, tried to cut down on medical spending in the private sector. All became hugely, painfully unpopular in the process. (*1995 CQ Almanac p. 7-16*)

Given those realities, and a burgeoning federal surplus, it is not surprising that the current political drive is to expand benefits — including proposals for a Medicare prescription drug coverage and giving patients more rights in managed-care plans — while largely ignoring warning signs of resurgent health care inflation.

"Cost containment is very unpleasant," said Robert J. Blendon, a professor of health policy at Harvard University. "The containment is in the future, and the pain is in the present. It's very difficult to do unless there's a crisis."

The focus on a Medicare drug benefit may work for Democratic candidate Vice President Al Gore and Texas GOP Gov. George W. Bush in the campaign, but it is not a strategy designed for the challenges of the next four years.

In 1998, the latest year for which official figures were available, the United States spent $1.1 trillion on health care. By 2008, that figure is expected to double as health care gobbles up an ever-increasing share of the nation's economy. After several years of hovering at around 13.5 percent of the gross domestic product, health care costs are expected to swell to 16.2 percent by 2008.

That kind of growth is likely to have consequences. When health care gets too expensive, employers may cut back on their workers' coverage or even drop it, and Medicare and Medicaid — the entitlement programs for the elderly and the poor — will become less stable.

Health care spending is not the ravenous beast it was when Clinton took office in 1993. At that time, annual insurance premiums were increasing at nearly double-digit rates and Medicare and Medicaid were growing at even more alarming speed. Double-digit growth rates are long gone, but the entitlement programs are far from under control — and private health insurance premiums are climbing again.

In 2000, the monthly premiums for employer-sponsored health insurance have grown by an average of 8.3 percent — the largest increase since 1993, according to a survey of employers released in September by the Henry J. Kaiser Family Foundation and the Health Research and Educational Trust. By comparison, average premiums rose only 4.8 percent in 1999.

Those are not the kinds of numbers that bode well for the health care system, since nearly two out of three Americans are insured through the workplace. "We're not quite back to the runaway inflation of the '80s and early '90s, but we're getting close," said Larry Levitt, director of the Kaiser Family Foundation's Changing Healthcare Marketplace Project.

All signs point to even greater costs in the coming years, analysts say. Newer, more expensive drugs and innovative medical technologies are being introduced all the time. That coincides with the aging of the Baby Boom generation. Boomers will need more care — and they will want the best.

"We're going to be an older society 10, 20 years from now. We're going to use more health care, even if it's the same health care," said Edward F. Howard, executive vice president of the Alliance for Health Reform, a nonpartisan organization. "But it's not going to be the same health care. It's going to be better, more sophisticated, more expensive health care."

The New Target: Prescription Drugs

So what can the next president do to control costs and help those who need coverage?

The biggest factor in the latest premium increases, employers say, is prescription drug spending. The Kaiser Family Foundation estimates that spending for prescription drugs shot up 15 percent between 1997 and 1998 — making it one of the fastest growing elements of the nation's health care expenditures. Prescription drug costs alone accounted for 40 percent of employers' premium increases between 1998 and 1999.

If rising drug prices were the only cause of the higher spending, the next president would at least have a target to aim at. It is not that simple, though. Most of the spending increases are happening not because all prescription drugs are more expensive, but because people are using them more and favoring the newest, most costly brand-names. Most people want the latest and the best, and it is unlikely the next president can say or do anything to change that.

The story of the managed-care industry should help the next president put from his mind any thoughts of trimming benefits. The rise of managed care was fueled by employers

who wanted a private-sector tool to reduce costs by setting limits on their workers' prescriptions and procedures. In practice, patients balked at the new restrictions. The proposed "Patients' Bill of Rights," which would ease some of the restrictions and give patients more leverage to appeal when a health plan denied coverage, is one of the most hotly debated health care issues in Congress. (*2000 CQ Weekly, p. 508*)

Workers have also voted with their feet. Enrollment in health maintenance organizations, the most restrictive form of managed care, has stagnated in recent years, while preferred provider organizations — which allow patients to see out-of-network doctors for an extra charge — have become the most popular managed-care plans.

That is why the centerpiece proposals of both the Gore and Bush health care plans — new prescription drug assistance for seniors who do not have drug coverage under Medicare — are more than just election-year politics. They may be the only realistic way to deal with a real need to purchase life-saving drugs. But instead of helping to control costs, such a plan will increase federal spending. While many advocates say that drug coverage is long overdue, the Medicare proposals only help those who already have coverage, and do not address the problem of the uninsured.

There is another reason cost containment is not on the next president's immediate health care agenda. For years, rising costs trickled down to Americans in a chain reaction: Higher premiums led employers to drop coverage or scale it back, which led to ever-increasing numbers of uninsured Americans. Lately, however, that has changed.

A Drop in the Uninsured

On Sept. 28, the Census Bureau announced that both the number of uninsured Americans and the percentage without health insurance dropped last year for the first time since 1987. The number of uninsured Americans fell from 44.3 million to 42.6 million and the uninsured rate dropped from 16.3 percent of all Americans to 15.5 percent.

The reason: More employers are giving health coverage to their workers. Even with premiums on the rise again, 62.8 percent of all Americans had health insurance through their workplace in 1999 — up from 62 percent in 1998, according to the Census Bureau.

While premiums are going up, many employers are not passing the full increases on to their workers. According to the Kaiser/HRET survey, employees have paid about the same share of the premiums for family coverage — an average of 27 percent — since 1996. With a strong economy and a tight labor market, analysts say, employers do not want to risk losing trained workers. So they simply absorb the rise.

There are still more uninsured people than when Clinton took office — 38 million at the time — but the first drop in years may make the problem seem less urgent for the next president, especially when politicians and the public cannot agree on what to do about it anyway.

Business groups regularly warn that they can only absorb so many health care cost increases and eventually will have to pass them on to workers. Even now, consumer advocates say it is too early to rejoice about the lower numbers of uninsured. "The real question is, with the economy being so strong, why did it take this long? And what should ever happen if we have a recession?" said Gail Shearer, director of health policy analysis at Consumers Union.

Deceptive Numbers

For the first time in its 35-year history, Medicare spending has actually dropped: It fell from $211 billion in fiscal 1998 to $209.3 billion in fiscal 1999, according to the Congressional Budget Office. That figure is likely to prove deceptive, however. Analysts say much of the decrease is due to the provider cuts Congress enacted in the 1997 Balanced Budget Act (PL 105-33) — which lawmakers are hurrying to undo. (*Background, 2000 CQ Weekly, p. 1879*)

And while Medicaid spending growth fell from 11.8 percent in fiscal 1993 to 3.9 percent in fiscal 1997, some of that was driven by a development no one wanted: Former welfare recipients who went to work lost their Medicaid coverage even when they were still eligible. Both Medicare and Medicaid spending growth are expected to pick up again in the coming years. (*2000 CQ Weekly, p. 2066*)

What approach is politically possible for the next president? Here are some of the options:

• **Fund initiatives to reduce medical errors.** This is hard to do, since provider groups fiercely oppose tough proposals such as mandatory reporting of mistakes, but policymakers and business groups see real potential for reducing costs. "Nobody wants to pay for treatments that cause complications. They want the treatment to cure the patient," said Paul W. Dennett, vice president for health policy at the American Benefits Council, representing corporate benefit plans.

• **Encourage research on what medical practices work best.** This can be done by increasing funding for the Agency for Healthcare Research and Quality, the focal point for government efforts to coordinate such research. The payoff, however, could be a long time in coming.

• **Cut waste, fraud and abuse.** It may sound like an easy out, but the Clinton administration has won praise for cracking down on fraud and abuse in Medicare. Analysts say the initiatives are responsible for some recent savings.

Only if these strategies fail, White House health care adviser Chris Jennings believes, would future presidents and lawmakers consider stronger steps to contain health costs — and only with the advance blessing of business. These options may be the softer side of cost containment, but they may be the only tools the next president will have left.

HEALTH SPENDING CLIMBS STEADILY

■ Medicare spending has increased from $148.7 billion in 1993 to a projected $244.5 billion in 2000, an estimated growth rate of 6.3 percent.

■ Federal, state and local Medicaid spending has increased from $121.7 billion in 1993 to a projected $193.4 billion in 2000. Its estimated rate of growth is 6.2 percent.

■ Private health insurance premiums increased an average of 8.5 percent in 1993 and rose 8.3 percent between spring 1999 and spring 2000.

Defining, Asserting the National Interest

Overseas missions, force modernization, missile defense make a demanding agenda

Despite an unmatched blend of economic power and military might, Congress and the White House have not been able to consistently define and assert U.S. interests abroad.

U.S. dominance has evolved relatively rapidly in the decade since the Soviet Union's collapse ended the Cold War. Although the situation is unlikely to change, the great fluidity with which the rest of the world is evolving has some experts convinced that the next president must develop a plan for capitalizing on the country's status, rather than simply reacting to events.

"The United States is more likely to succeed if it makes the task of preserving its preeminence a matter of conscious strategy, rather than leaving the matter to chance or to the usual array of ad hoc, reactive decisions by which it habitually makes foreign policy," Peter W. Rodman, director of national security programs at the Nixon Center, a foreign policy think tank in Washington, wrote in a recent report.

Meanwhile, many of the world's powers — including some American allies — chafe under U.S. hegemony. As Karsten D. Voigt, the German government's coordinator of U.S.-German cooperation, dryly observed in a speech in March: "Never before has American self-esteem had less reason to use benchmarks other than its own as the guiding principle for worldwide action."

National security questions that have been raised and are expected to continue over the next decade include: What criteria should the country use for sending military forces overseas? How long can troops stay abroad without the military becoming overextended? What is the correct balance between keeping the current military forces ready to fight and spending to modernize aging weapons? Should the United States try to build a national anti-missile shield, and who are the nation's potential enemies?

The new global scene still harbors residual effects of the Cold War. Many of the ethnic hatreds and conflicts that had been largely frozen in the competition between the United States and Soviet Union have thawed over the past 10 years, creating uprisings in Africa, the Balkans and other areas. At the same time, quarrelsome regimes such as that in Iraq are continually seeking new ways to exploit U.S. weaknesses.

"The fact that we are arguably the world's most powerful nation does not bestow invulnerability," Director of Central Intelligence George J. Tenet told the Senate Foreign Relations Committee in March. "In fact, it may make us a larger target for those who don't share our interests, values or beliefs."

Tenet and other foreign-policy observers say the growing perception of U.S. hegemony has created considerable resentment in the rest of the world. Relations among all of the world's major powers are more fragile now than they were in the years immediately following the end of the Cold War. As that has occurred, demands on the United States for humanitarian intervention and other assistance, such as fighting drug traffic in Colombia, continue to mount.

"What this adds up to," said Richard N. Haass, director of foreign policy studies at the Brookings Institution, a Washington think tank, "is an unbelievably diverse and demanding foreign policy agenda."

Keeping the Peace

If recent events are any indication, Congress and the next president will be hard-pressed to arrive at a consensus on when U.S. troops should be sent abroad. Some leading Republicans, such as Senate Armed Services Committee Chairman John W. Warner, R-Va., contend that the United States has overcommitted itself in such trouble spots as the Yugoslavian province of Kosovo, and they are likely to continue to sound alarm bells about overseas deployments in the future. *(Background, 2000 CQ Weekly, p. 114)*

Like many congressional Republicans, Warner also has shied away from reimbursing other countries that employ their troops in U.N. peacekeeping operations. GOP leaders argue that such troops lack sufficient military expertise for the missions. After a hiatus following U.N. failures in such countries as Somalia in the early 1990s, the size, number and expense of U.N. peacekeeping missions has risen sharply in the twilight days of the Clinton administration. That has led to a fight with Congress, which has been reluctant to help finance the new operations, especially when it is still haggling with the United Nations over about $1 billion the United States still owes the organization. Those debts were largely accumulated in the early 1990s, when the United States refused to pay some of its assessed share of U.N. operations in Bosnia and Somalia. Congress now has said it would pay the money only if the United Nations cuts its future dues. *(2000 CQ Weekly, p. 2031)*

The next president also will have to cope with questions that bedeviled his predecessors regarding the conduct of peacekeeping operations, such as whether they should be left strictly to regional organizations like NATO. The two major party presidential nominees, Vice President Al Gore and Texas Gov. George W. Bush, most likely would continue the internationalist stance of intervening in limited missions overseas. But the similarities appear to end there.

Republicans are more wary of straining military resources, a key issue in the presidential campaign. Defense policymakers are particularly interested in knowing how much more money the Defense Department will need for future tasks. Pentagon officials are expected to provide a starting point for that debate next year, when they conduct a second quadrennial assessment of military resources.

Despite recent increases in defense spending, military leaders say they lack infrastructure improvements and equipment. The shortfalls have left some Republicans concerned that the military will not be able to meet the current strategic requirement of being able to fight two regional wars almost simultaneously. Military leaders say that the risk of taking on

a second war would be high. Still, they have not called for abandoning the strategy, despite protests from some critics of increased defense spending who argue that the military is mired in a Cold War-era mindset. Those critics suggest, for example, that the broader question of the Navy's global mission should be re-thought before Congress decides to substantially increase shipbuilding. (*2000 CQ Weekly, p. 876*)

Missile Defenses

Of all the defense and foreign policy issues awaiting the next administration, none is as potentially volatile as the debate over what mix of high-tech weapons and old-fashioned diplomacy will best protect the country from long-range ballistic missiles. The next battle in this three-decade dispute between Republicans and Democrats will come next year, when the new president unveils his formula for balancing two goals: blunting the threat posed by hostile nations that might have a handful of ballistic missiles while not alienating Russia, which has thousands of missiles and remains committed to the 1972 Anti-Ballistic Missile (ABM) Treaty prohibiting anti-missile defenses.

Both Gore and Bush back a combination of limited anti-missile defenses and negotiations with Russia to make room for such a limited defense within the ABM Treaty. But the specifics of their proposals mirror the partisan divisions over the issue. Since party majorities are expected to remain thin in both the House and Senate, either man is likely to face an uphill fight to carry out his program.

To the dismay of some Democrats who remain skeptical of anti-missile defenses, Gore's approach mirrors President Clinton's. Both men advocate securing Moscow's agreement to changing the ABM Treaty for a limited defense — similar to the anti-missile systems allowed under the treaty now — and linking that deal with an agreement to reduce the Russian and U.S. arsenals by 1,000 nuclear warheads apiece. Most Republicans dismiss Clinton's proposed system as too feeble and contend that his proposed changes in the treaty would not give future presidents enough freedom to deploy the most effective anti-missile shield. If Gore cut the deal with Moscow that he seeks, he would need the support of roughly two out of every five Senate Republicans in order to amend the treaty.

The partisan obstacles facing Bush would be more subtle but potentially just as serious. In echoing the anti-missile defense position that has become congressional GOP orthodoxy, Bush calls for exploring all available approaches — including the use of sea-based and space-based systems banned under the ABM Treaty — to devise a system that could protect not only the United States but U.S. forces abroad from such unfriendly states as North Korea, Iran and Iraq.

Such a move would require a more sweeping revision of the treaty than Clinton has proposed. Bush, however, has made it clear that if the Russians would not budge, he would abrogate the treaty. And to fund whatever system he wanted to deploy, Bush would need the support of at least six to 10 Senate Democrats to get the 60 votes needed to break a filibuster. Given how sharply party lines have been drawn on the issue, that task would not be easy.

U.S. dealings with Russia do not end with missile defense. The country remains stuck between its former communist history and the capitalist democracy that U.S. policymakers are seeking, while fighting corruption and ethnic uprisings in Chechnya. The new president and Congress will have to build a relationship with Russian President Vladimir

V. Putin at a time when Putin is seeking to rebuild his nation's power abroad and limit dissent from within.

China Tradeoffs

As with Russia, U.S. relations with China have become considerably less predictable and more challenging. Experts believe China — the world's fastest rising power — poses the single greatest problem to a smooth U.S. foreign policy, largely because of the many facets of the relationship between the two countries: trade, human rights, nuclear nonproliferation and Taiwan. Chinese leaders are likely to see any development of a missile defense system as a threat to their own nuclear deterrent.

At the same time, Beijing is sensitive over its technological gap with the West and wary of any international encroachment on its dialogue with Taiwan, which it considers a renegade province. Some experts warn that the greatest potential for a war between two major powers in the next 15 years is between the United States and China over Taiwan.

In seeking to avoid such conflicts, Bush and Gore are expected to follow similar courses in continuing to engage China economically. Having normalized trade with China this fall, Congress gave up its annual debate on China policy, but lawmakers are expected to continue to make their concerns known. (*China trade, 2000 CQ Weekly, p. 2223*)

In southern Asia, the next president faces the challenge of continuing to improve relations with India, another emerging world power, while easing tensions between India and Pakistan. One solution Gore has proposed is to ratify the Comprehensive Test Ban Treaty (Treaty Doc 105-28), something many Republicans remain unwilling to do after the Senate rejected it last year. (*1999 Almanac, p. 9-40*)

With so many challenging relationships abroad, some lawmakers say they must make another attempt at solving the growing public apathy toward foreign affairs. "We can bemoan the public's skepticism and disengagement and wish that it didn't exist," said Sen. Max Cleland, D-Ga. "But it is a fact which impacts on all major foreign and defense policy issues facing the Congress."

THE STORY IN NUMBERS

■ In the 17 years since President Ronald Reagan proposed an anti-missile defense system, the United States has spent about $60 billion on the idea, historian Frances Fitzgerald estimates.

■ The U.S. trade deficit with China increased from $6.2 billion in 1989 to $68.7 billion in 1999, according to the Congressional Research Service.

■ The size of the U.S. military has been declining since its post-Vietnam peak of 2,174,217 in 1987, according to Pentagon figures. The total at the end of 1999 was 1,385,703.

Politics and Public Policy

The term *public policy making* refers to action taken by the government to address issues on the public agenda; it also refers to the method by which a decision to act on policy is reached. The work of Congress, the president and the federal bureaucracy, and the judiciary is to make, implement, and rule on policy decisions. Articles in this section discuss major policy issues that came before the federal government in 2000, many of which are likely to remain unresolved into 2001.

The first article discusses the gridlock that characterized the last few months of the second session of the 106th Congress. With a national election upon them, many Republicans and Democrats focused on casting their opponents on the wrong side of the issue rather than on resolving important legislative initiatives.

One of the most contentious issues to come before Congress in 2000 was whether to add prescription drug coverage to Medicare. While Republicans preferred a private-market approach, Democrats fought for a government-run prescription drug plan. Although the GOP plan passed the House, President Clinton vowed to veto the bill should it reach his desk. Even though the Senate did not take action on the GOP plan this session, prescription drug coverage will most likely be on top of the agenda for the 107th Congress, which convenes in January 2001.

Other issues that captured lawmakers' attention during the second session of the 106th Congress concern the budget surplus, tax cuts, immigration, and airline regulation. How will the new president use the estimated budget surplus? Will Congress pass business tax legislation that benefits businesses? Should the United States increase the number of visas granted to highly skilled workers needed in the high-tech sector? What are the dangers of airline mergers, and what will be the effect of these mergers on airline competition?

The issue of violence in entertainment continued to keep the attention of lawmakers. Spurred by a Federal Trade Commission (FTC) report on the improper marketing of violent movies, video games, and recordings, Sen. John McCain, R-Ariz., arranged a hearing to address some of the report's findings. The FTC report found that some entertainment companies have routinely targeted children for products that were inappropriate for minors. Although Congress did not pass legislation to deal with media violence, McCain warned that he would return to the issue during the 107th Congress.

Rounding out the section are discussions of other important public policy topics: requiring the auto industry to provide the government with more data on potential product defects, making permanent China's standing as a normal trading partner of the United States, and deciding to build a national anti-missile defense system.

These complex issues are clearly explained in the articles that follow. Because many of the topics discussed here will remain at the top of Congress's agenda in the months ahead, the reports are valuable as issue studies, predictors of legislative outcomes, and primers on the policy-making process.

Widely supported initiatives went nowhere as lawmaking ran a poor second to politics

Symbolism and Stalemate Closing Out 106th Congress

The 106th Congress stumbled toward adjournment with its last-minute battles overshadowed by a hotly contested national election. For a Congress that never was consumed with lawmaking as much as politics, this seems a fitting end.

This was a Congress forged by impeachment, embroiled in partisanship from the first day of the session to the hours approaching its last. A narrow and fragile House majority confronted with a Democratic minority united with President Clinton all but guaranteed gridlock in the 106th Congress.

"It's difficult to say that this has been an extremely productive Congress," George Edwards, director of the Center for Presidential Studies at Texas A&M University, observed with a chuckle. "The essential reasons are the reasons that caused the problem in the first place. You've got a highly polarized situation in the legislature. You've got divided government. You've got divisions among Republicans. And there's a strong overlay of hatred. It's not a good environ-

ment for accomplishing things."

Instead, lawmakers of both parties spent an inordinate amount of time trying to outmaneuver their rivals. Less effort was devoted to resolving important legislative initiatives that both sides claimed to support than in trying to cast one another as being on the wrong side of the issue. Often, the real motivation behind a debate seemed to be to force one's adversaries to cast politically tough votes or to inoculate one's party from being portrayed as on the wrong side of an issue.

On paper, Republicans and Democrats agreed on so many things. Overhauling Medicare and Social Security might have been expected to hold for the next administration, but other initiatives, such as getting rid of the so-called marriage penalty in the tax code, giving consumers a "patient's bill of rights," raising the minimum wage and cutting inheritance taxes, had sweeping support.

None of them, it appears, will become law, which is where the story of the 106th might say something about the future of the 107th. The lack of achievement on even those issues most everyone wanted leaves a record of mutual dis-

CQ PHOTOS/ SCOTT J. FERRELL

At left, Lott and Hastert confer at a rally though members in both chambers say their lack of coordination has contributed to adjournment delays. Above, Rep. Rosa DeLauro, D-Conn., and Sen. Richard J. Durbin, D-Ill., say the GOP is hanging Americans out to dry.

trust and a mountain of unfinished business.

"The 106th Congress was, from day one, about the 2000 elections," said Rep. Jim McDermott, D-Wash. "Everything was crafted on their side to win the election. And everything we tried to do was [to] derail them from winning the election . . . . It was the most unproductive public policy year[s] I've spent in my life."

Now that the election is nearly here, the tight polls in races across the country leave open the very real possibility that the dynamics of the next Congress may differ little from the dynamics of this one. Regardless of who wins the November elections, the incoming president will almost certainly inherit a narrowly divided and difficult to control 107th Congress.

Texas Gov. George W. Bush, the Republican presidential nominee, has claimed an ability to work across party lines. Even if Bush takes the White House and the GOP holds its majorities in both the House and Senate, the margins are likely to be thin, and Republicans won't have the luxury of ignoring the Democrats. Senate Majority Leader Trent Lott, R-Miss., has his doubts about prospects for bipartisanship under Bush.

"I think [Bush] is going to find out pretty quick that Democrats in Washington are a whole lot different than Democrats in Texas," Lott said.

While Democratic Vice President Al Gore and Bush are campaigning principally on major issues such as Social Security, Medicare and taxes, the unfinished business of the 106th Congress is sure to return. Bush, for example, would

have to confront a Democratic drive to let consumers sue their health maintenance organizations (HMOs) for unfair denials of treatment and to overhaul campaign finance laws. Gore and his Democratic allies, who appear to have an outside chance of reclaiming Congress, would likely face a renewed GOP push to ban so-called partial birth abortions.

Still Not Over

The 106th will soon be over, but not as soon as its leaders had hoped. Now it is clear that the earliest the Congress can adjourn sine die is the week of Oct 30, well past the Oct. 6 deadline and ominously close to Election Day, Nov. 7. Late election year adjournments have a history of working against the party in control of Congress. Republicans lost the Senate in 1986 after staying in session until Oct. 18; Democrats yielded both House and Senate in 1994 after an Oct. 8 preelection departure.

"You know, my attitude is we're going to stay here. We're going to do this thing right. I'm not going to be bum-rushed out of town with a bad deal," House Speaker J. Dennis Hastert (R-Ill.) told the Associated Press. "I'll stay 'til the election if I have to."

The slow crawl to adjournment has featured numerous concessions to Clinton on appropriations bills, but these losses, Republicans hope, may have been obscured as the public focused on the presidential campaign.

From the start of the 106th, Republicans tended to their all-important political "base," which had been dispirited in the 1998 election cycle: The GOP faithful were unhappy

Insurers' Queasiness About Costs Helped Sink GOP Prescription Drug Bill

Encouraging the private sector to do more so government can do less is a deeply held Republican ideal.

In practice, however, the philosophy has not always worked. Dozens of managed-care companies, which were supposed to move Medicare toward the open market, have left the program, citing low payments and burdensome rules. And few insurers offer tax-exempt medical savings accounts, even though many Republicans and some Democrats believe such accounts could reduce the ranks of the uninsured. (*Medicare+Choice, 2000 CQ Weekly, p. 1183*)

Despite that spotty record, House Republicans this year looked once again to the private sector on the politically charged issue of whether to add prescription drug coverage to Medicare. The GOP developed legislation that called on private insurers to set up drug-only policies for Medicare recipients. The party figured that insurers, longtime GOP allies, would come to the table to help derail President Clinton's government-run prescription drug plan.

They didn't. Nor did the AARP, the powerful seniors' lobbying group, due to fears that the monthly premiums for the proposed coverage would be too costly for many elderly.

"We were stepping off a cliff but we didn't have everyone together when we were jumping," said Rep. Mark Foley, R-Fla.

Perhaps most damaging to the GOP's prescription drug quest was the perception that the party was moving legislation solely for political cover. A GOP pollster, in an assessment later obtained by the press, asserted that passing some plan — any plan — was a "political imperative" for the party. "It is more important to communicate that you have a plan as it is to communicate what is in the plan," read the document presented to the House Republican Conference. (*2000 CQ Weekly, p. 1436*)

Clinton and Democrats honed in on what they perceived to be the weaknesses of the House initiative and pounced quickly to kill any momentum. On June 29, one day after the House legislation (HR 4680) squeaked through on a 217-214 vote, Clinton announced he would veto the bill should it reach his desk.

"The insurance companies themselves have said . . . this will not work, these policies will not be affordable [and] most seniors will not be able to take advantage of this bill," Clinton said.

Rep. Pete Stark of California, the ranking Democrat on the Ways and Means Health Subcommittee, called the GOP plan "a political placebo, not a real prescription drug benefit."

Ways and Means Health Subcommittee Chairman Bill Thomas, R-Calif., the chief architect of the GOP drug plan, dismissed such comments as "hogwash." But the criticisms stuck. House passage achieved Speaker J. Dennis Hastert's (R-Ill.) goal of acting on a drug bill, but was not a solution for getting a measure to Clinton's desk.

The Senate took no action, not even a committee markup, despite the fact that Finance Committee Chairman William V. Roth Jr., R-Del., facing a tight re-election race, proposed two different plans.

With little chance for enactment, the issue quickly became a political dividing line in the fall elections, with Republicans sticking to a private-market approach and Democrats preferring government oversight. (*Background, 2000 CQ Weekly, pp. 1896, 1729, 1521*)

Industry Opposition

The strongest attack on the House Republican plan came from Chip Kahn, president of the Health Insurance Association of America, the powerful insurers group.

Kahn, a former Ways and Means Health Subcommittee staffer, had worked closely with Thomas on issues such as the 1997 balanced-budget act (PL 105-33), which made some of the most significant changes to Medicare and Medicaid since they were created in 1965. (*Kahn profile, 1999 CQ Weekly, p. 132*)

This time, however, Kahn sided with his membership, insurers who feared the policies Thomas envisioned would be too costly to maintain.

"The pressures of ever-increasing drug costs, the predictability of drug expenses, and the likelihood that the people most likely to purchase this coverage will be the people anticipating the highest drug claims would make drug-only coverage virtually impossible for insurers to offer at an affordable premium," Kahn said in a statement issued June 13.

While the House Republican plan would have helped insurers pay the drug bills of higher-cost beneficiaries, insurers fretted over the smaller, yet steadier, expenses of millions of seniors who take drugs on a daily basis. As those costs increased, insurers would want to raise premiums, but lawmakers, eager to keep Medicare expenses under control, would probably try to limit such premium hikes.

Thomas said that if his plan became law, plenty of insurers would step up. "When you tell somebody you don't need them and, in fact, it's going to succeed without them, you'll be amazed at how some people will come around the back door and want to be part of it," Thomas said.

Although the House GOP plan did not become law, some lawmakers viewed it as a foundation for action in the 107th Congress.

"I don't think the president will sign a [drug] bill we come up with," Rep. Charlie Norwood, R-Ga., said in June. "But it will give a good start for next year when we can really do it."

with the 1998 "omnibus" spending plan that gave a scandal-tarred Clinton a big win, and, amid the furor over impeachment, Republicans got little boost for their role in the 1997 balanced-budget deal. *(1998 CQ Almanac, p. 1-3)*

For this Congress, that meant any serious compromises with Clinton were off the table. "The thing we learned in '98 was the base doesn't like it when we work with Clinton," said a senior Senate Republican aide.

Instead, Republicans sent Clinton a series of tax bills — including popular measures to ease the marriage penalty (HR 4810) and to phase out the estate tax (HR 8) — that he vetoed. As one of their last acts, Republicans prepared late the week of Oct. 23 to send Clinton a bill (HR 2614) consisting of an amalgam of tax provisions, coupled with a minimum wage increase and about $30 billion over five years to restore cuts in Medicare made three years ago as part of the 1997 balanced-budget law. But Clinton vowed yet another veto, chiefly over the details of the Medicare "give-back."

From the start, Democrats made it clear they were not interested in seeing Republicans deliver popular legislation to the voters. They signaled little willingness to compromise on signature bills such as the patients' bill of rights.

"The Democratic agenda had been, first, to stop the most radical parts of their proposals, to hopefully negotiate with them on some more modest things," said Rep. Edward J. Markey, D-Mass. "And then, at the end of the day, not accept their relatively modest concessions because we could wait until we might have control."

"We've entered into a pattern of blaming each other for failure," said Democratic Sen. John B. Breaux of Louisiana. "People were actually in some cases afraid to compromise because they would lose the issue. On both sides."

Breaux, who co-chaired the National Bipartisan Commission on the Future of Medicare, cited Democrats' rejection of his plan, backed by Republicans, to overhaul Medicare as an area where Democrats preferred to retain an issue for the voters.

But Breaux also blamed Republicans on taxes: "I'm sure [Republicans] discussed, 'Can you imagine what it looks like having Al Gore helping to sign a tax cut for the American people.'"

While on many issues this Congress

Lott leaves a briefing with reporters as Republican leaders prepared to send Clinton last-minute tax and appropriations bills the president said he would veto.

came up mostly empty, there have been some significant new laws made. A common element of the 106th Congress' success stories is that each issue advanced with bipartisan support and each had little resonance with voters and therefore little political value to members. They included:

• **China trade.** Last month, Clinton signed a bill (HR 4444 — PL 106-286) to expand trade with China by permanently extending normal trade status to China, which will be formalized when that nation joins the World Trade Organization. The bill advanced with the help of free-trade supporters in the GOP and pro-business and agriculture state Democrats. *(2000 CQ Weekly, p. 2223)*

• **Banking law.** Last year, Congress passed a historic overhaul of Depression-era banking laws (PL 106-102) to make it easier for banks, securities firms and insurance companies to enter each others' traditional lines of business. It had long been supported on both sides of the aisle, but the measure finally became law only after regulatory decisions and marketplace advances had largely eroded the barriers. *(1999 Almanac, p. 5-3)*

• **Defense.** Republicans tout their annual effort to boost the defense budget. The 2001 defense authorization bill (HR 4205) not only would add $4.6 billion to Clinton's already generous budget increase, but contains a 3.7 per-

cent pay raise and a 10-year, $60 billion new health care plan for military retirees. *(Defense, p. 62)*

• **Appropriations.** A panoply of popular initiatives has been advanced as lawmakers near resolution of the fiscal 2001 appropriations cycle. Trade sanctions on Cuba have been eased, rules banning the reimportation of prescription drugs have been curbed, some of the world's poorest countries have been provided debt relief, and a major new anti-drug program has been approved for Colombia.

On the other hand, the stalemate over the patient's bill of rights, gun control and education has given Democrats plenty of ammo to fire charges of a "do-nothing" Congress.

"Republicans killed a patients' bill of rights, a prescription drug benefit under Medicare, hate crimes legislation, gun safety laws, middle-class tax cuts," Gephardt said at an Oct. 26 news conference. "This has been the best Congress that special interests can buy."

Countered Lott at a competing Oct. 26 event to herald the Republicans' end-of-session tax bill: "At the conclusion of this session, we will have succeeded in our goal of putting 90 percent of the surplus into paying down the debt, which is the most important thing we can do for future generations. . . . But also we're going to have 10 percent that we can use for

Coalition of Interests, Budget Surplus Won New Benefits for Military Retirees

The expansion of medical benefits for military retirees — a new entitlement expected to cost $60 billion over 10 years — is a politically popular policy highlight of the 106th Congress.

It cannot be claimed as a victory solely by Republicans, for it was pushed into law by a formidable coalition that included retirees, the Joint Chiefs of Staff and members of both parties. And it would not have happened without forecasts of a growing budget surplus.

The health care initiative was cleared as part of the fiscal 2001 defense authorization bill (HR 4205). It will allow military retirees — those who serve at least 20 years on active duty — and their dependents to remain in the Pentagon's medical care and insurance system for life, rather than having to rely on Medicare after they turn 65. It also would allow most retirees to buy prescription drugs through a military system. (2000 CQ Weekly, p. 2423)

Medical care for retirees was authorized by law in 1956, but the government's legal obligation became defined as allowing retirees to use military hospitals and clinics on a space-available basis or else to obtain care from private health care providers who would accept reimbursement from a Pentagon-run insurance program. Once they turned 65, the retirees were to rely on Medicare.

Retirees complained for years that recruiters promised that career service members and their dependents would get free medical care for life. Their grumbling got louder during the 1990s, as many military bases and their hospitals were closed, making access more difficult for retirees even as health care costs were climbing and the number of Medicare-eligible retirees and dependents was growing to a current total of nearly 1.4 million.

By 1997, leaders of the armed services were warning that the issue of medical care was affecting recruitment and retention. That year, Congress authorized several pilot programs to test ways of offering retirees more satisfactory medical care options. But they were not enough.

President Clinton's fiscal 2001 budget request included $80 million to address some problems in the Pentagon's medical insurance program. But the administration turned down proposals by the Joint Chiefs of Staff to offer retirees mail-order pharmacy service and "medi-gap" insurance already available to civilian federal employees to cover the difference between the cost of medical treatment and what Medicare pays.

By February, it was clear that the House and Senate Armed Services committees, supported by many members not on those panels, would join the retirees' associations and the Joint Chiefs in trying to improve retirees' medical care. (2000 CQ Weekly, p. 979)

House Speaker J. Dennis Hastert, R-Ill., helped House Armed Services members ensure that the budget resolution (H Con Res 290) included enough funds to pay for a mail-order pharmacy benefit. The committee then wrote the pharmacy benefit into its version of the defense authorization bill, along with other provisions that would expand the existing pilot health care programs.

Projections of a growing surplus allowed the Senate Armed Services panel to write its version of the authorization bill with a grant to retirees of permanent, lifetime access to the Pentagon's medical insurance coverage. But Senate rules permit a point of order to block any bill that spends more than the budget caps allow, unless the point is waived by a 60-vote majority. Leery of that risk, Armed Services Chairman John W. Warner, R-Va., amended the bill on the floor to limit the program to two years' duration.

In conference, House Armed Services personnel subcommittee Chairman Steve Buyer, R-Ind., argued that a permanent entitlement had gathered enough political steam to roll over any opposition. Armed Services member Tillie Fowler, R-Fla., vice chairman of the GOP Conference, had secured Hastert's personal support.

Buyer likened the situation to a rare astronomical phenomenon: "We have a syzygy. . . . All the planets are aligned."

Breaking with the longstanding Armed Services tradition of keeping conference negotiations confidential, Buyer briefed several retirees' organizations and reporters on his proposal in hopes of putting pressure on the Senate. During a Sept. 27 hearing, he got the Joint Chiefs to endorse his proposal.

In a letter written the same day, Warner outlined to Senate Majority Leader Trent Lott, R-Miss., his concern that the House proposal risked losing a point of order that could jeopardize the whole defense bill. At a meeting in Lott's office a few days later, Hastert made a strong pitch for Buyer's proposal, saying that in return he would accept a Senate proposal for compensating nuclear weapons workers who had been exposed to hazardous substances.

Lott assured Warner he would help him round up the 60 votes needed to fend off a challenge from deficit hawks. Warner promptly accepted the House proposal and, in a news conference with senior Armed Services Democrat Carl Levin, D-Mich., predicted the budget challenge would fail.

The Senate took up the conference report on Oct. 12, hours after a terrorist bomb attack on the destroyer USS *Cole* killed 17 sailors. Warner, lauding the medical care provisions as a promise kept to America's military, offered a motion to waive the budget point of order.

It was agreed to, 84-9.

important priorities, like education and health legislation, but some tax relief for working Americans."

Never a Chance

At the beginning of the 106th Congress, one school of thought held that an impeached president and his enemies in the GOP had a common interest in cooperating. Clinton needed a legacy to cleanse him of the taint of impeachment; Republicans needed to repair their party's image with the public, which disapproved of their zeal to oust Clinton from office.

"The Republicans and the president had a common vested interest . . . in putting impeachment behind. That is, the president could show he could govern and Congress could show it could cooperate," said GOP Rep. Jim Leach of Iowa.

It was not to be. Instead, it soon became evident that Republicans, particularly in the Senate, were not of a mind to work with Clinton and Democrats.

"They could not have gone into a two-year cycle here saying they were going to be pals with Bill Clinton. That was an unacceptable option," said a top aide to House Minority Leader Richard A. Gephardt, D-Mo. "Impeachment radicalized their grass roots, but that of course tied their hands in trying to work with him."

At the same time, Clinton allied himself closely with his Democratic friends in the House and Senate, who had stood by him during his impeachment and trial in the Senate. Clinton had distanced himself from congressional Democrats as he ran for re-election in 1996, and the 1997 budget deal had divided the party. (*1997 Almanac, p. 2-18*)

But through this Congress, with exceptions such as the China trade bill, Clinton and his Democratic allies on Capitol Hill marched in lockstep. One high-profile example came on taxes, where Democrats blocked what they said was a too-generous GOP bill to curb the marriage penalty. Republican predictions that Clinton would ultimately acquiesce were wrong.

"I think [Hastert] was surprised by the president's veto of the marriage penalty," said Hastert press secretary John P. Feehery. "And I think that was because Dick Gephardt didn't want us to have a big victory."

It is striking to note that after Clinton vetoed the marriage penalty bill

and then the proposed phase-out of the estate tax cut, Republicans did not rework the bills to try to get them signed. Some House Republicans had pushed to revisit those issues, especially the estate tax. But the Senate remained adamant that they would not approach taxes on Clinton's terms.

"There's a time when you draw a line and say beyond this point you really won't go, that having the issue is by far a stronger position than a watered-down policy," said Sen. Larry E. Craig, R-Idaho. "Maybe it wasn't a time to craft good tax policy until we got [a president] who was willing to work with us to do it. That was always a part of it."

Countered Rep. Doug Bereuter, R-Neb.: "I think that the great percentage of Republicans in the House wanted to have a tax cut . . . even if the president got the credit, because we had our stamp on those issues."

Strategy Trouble

Beyond the political forces that guided the 106th Congress toward gridlock, a set of logistical problems beset GOP leaders from the start.

First, in the House, the narrow majority hamstrung efforts to quickly advance their agenda, and it gave Democrats an opportunity to successfully press issues such as the patient's bill of rights and campaign finance reform to the floor. At the same time, passing the 13 annual appropriations bills — often relying almost exclusively on GOP votes — proved an enormous headache for Republicans.

"You come into a body with a six- or seven-vote margin and you have to develop a strategy to adapt," said the Gephardt aide. "They chose a Republican-only strategy. Everything flows out of that."

One issue Hastert pushed hard to resolve was the patients' rights measure. The House last year gave a big vote to a bill written by Charlie Norwood, R-Ga., and John D. Dingell, D-Mich., that would give patients broad rights to sue their health maintenance organizations (HMOs) in state court if they believe they were wrongly denied care. But GOP House leaders opposed the bill, and Senate Republicans insisted they could not support such a broadly written measure. Senate leaders said privately that the issue did not have the kind of resonance with the voters it had earlier. (*1998 Almanac, p. 14-3*)

"I'm convinced we would have had HMO reform if the polls showed that was damaging [Republicans]," said Rep. Thomas M. Barrett, D-Wis. "My suspicion is that the polls showed it wasn't damaging them."

Hastert did permit votes on other Democrat-driven issues, including overhauling campaign finance laws and tinkering with gun control laws, but only after pressure from the public and from GOP moderates. But the Senate often didn't follow.

In the Senate, Lott often seemed more concerned about protecting his vulnerable incumbents from having to cast politically difficult votes than with getting legislation passed. Democrats were always poised to take advantage of Senate rules that permit them to offer virtually any of their favorite bills as amendments to anything Lott would bring up under normal procedures. Lott typically brought bills up in ways that blocked Democrats from offering amendments. Democrats concluded they had little option but to employ delaying tactics. A lot of bills ended up getting killed or pulled from the floor in the process. One example was the reauthorization of the Elementary and Secondary Education Act, which Lott pulled earlier this year.

The logistical forces favoring gridlock were buttressed by the divide between House and Senate Republicans over the central question of the 106th Congress: Get legislation signed into law, or thrust and parry and let voters decide? House Republicans, who entered the Congress down in the polls because of impeachment, said they favored passing bills.

"The Speaker's view from the start is you're better off getting accomplishments. Good policy makes good politics," Feehery said. "The Senate has a different philosophy, and we had to deal with that."

Bereuter said there is "a lot of dissatisfaction on the part of House Republicans with the Senate's inability to move legislation that we sent over there."

Sen. Gordon H. Smith, R-Ore., responding to the question of whether the House was more eager to pass legislation than the Senate, said: "I think that is a natural consequence of only one-third of our members being up for re-election and 100 percent of them being up for re-election." ◆

House leaders say failing to act soon could hand key election issue to Democrats

GOP's Prescription Drug Bill: A 'Political Imperative'?

Thomas, left, and Rep. Ben Cardin, D-Md., testify June 13 before the House Ways and Means Committee hearing to discuss adding a prescription drug benefit for Medicare recipients. Republicans say private sector participation is crucial to passing their plan.

Speaker J. Dennis Hastert is determined to push legislation through the House in the next few weeks that would, for the first time, cover prescription drug bills for tens of millions of seniors enrolled in Medicare.

The Illinois Republican's sense of urgency is not based on any likelihood that legislation will become law this year. Efforts to add drug coverage to Medicare have failed since President Lyndon Johnson created the program in 1965 as part of his Great Society. President Clinton and Democrats have sharply condemned the new House GOP plan, prescription drug coverage is not a legislative priority for Senate Republicans and House conservatives are balking at its $40 billion price tag.

Instead, as the speaker's staff readily admits, the planned floor vote is preventive medicine for House Republicans who are guarding a slight six-vote majority and see health care emerging as an issue in the districts of vulnerable members. (*Story, p. 67*)

Legislation to give consumers greater rights in managed-care plans, which the GOP had hoped could be a banner health care issue, is bogged down in a conference with the Senate. And new voter surveys give Democratic candidates a slight edge in the November election — a Gallup poll taken June 6-7 among likely voters in House races shows Democrats

leading Republicans 48 percent to 46 percent.

So it is not surprising that GOP pollster Glen Bolger told the House Republican Conference June 8 that it is a "political imperative" that they pass a prescription drug bill this year.

"You can't stop something that is as politically enticing as providing prescription drugs for seniors," conservative Rep. Mark Sanford, R-S.C., said in a June 13 interview. "Politics always come first around this place."

Two months after Hastert and other House Republican leaders unveiled a set of principles for Medicare prescription drug coverage, details of that proposal were made public the week of June 13. The Ways and Means Committee is tentatively scheduled to mark up the bill June 21, and the House could vote on it the week of June 26. (*Background, 2000 CQ Weekly, p. 900*)

Among its provisions, the GOP proposal would offer voluntary drug coverage to all seniors beginning in fiscal 2003, provide subsidies to help low-income seniors afford monthly premiums and deductibles, and pick up all medication costs for seniors whose annual drug bills were $6,000 or higher. The plan would look to the private sector to develop the benefits policies and mandate that seniors have at least two different choices for coverage. If private insurers did not offer coverage in a particular area, the federal government would. (*Chart, p. 66*)

Democrats, pollster Bolger said, see the issue as part of

their "four corner" strategy to win back the House, along with health care, education and Social Security, and they are perceived as the party best able to provide drugs to seniors.

Bolger, of the firm Public Opinion Strategies, told House Republicans they could gain ground simply by saying they have a plan. "It is more important to communicate that you have a plan than it is to communicate what is in the plan," reads a document that was prepared by Bolger's firm and obtained by CQ.

Hastert spokesman John P. Feehery acknowledged that politics is playing a large role in the timing of the prescription drug legislation.

"The quicker we get this done, the less chance it has to become embroiled in end-of-the-year politics," Feehery said in a June 14 interview. "It's important for our members to point to this as an accomplishment."

Since the beginning of the year, the GOP strategy has been to stay "on the offensive," Feehery said, "moving issues that are important to our voters, on our terms."

Part of that strategy has been to take up a series of small, targeted tax bills this year, in contrast to past years, when Republicans brought out one broad tax package that never garnered enough bipartisan support for passage.

Among the small bills that the House has been able to pass this year are measures to eliminate the "marriage penalty" (HR 6), estate and gift taxes (HR 8) and the Social Security earnings test, and to impose a five-year moratorium on Internet-specific taxes (HR 3709). *(2000 CQ Weekly, pp. 1377, 1116, 990, 290)*

Though the prescription drugs measure may not pass in the Senate, House Republicans say they can capitalize politically from their own action.

'A Good Start for Next Year'

"I don't think the president will sign a [drug] bill we come up with," Charlie Norwood, R-Ga., cosponsor of the managed-care bill (HR 2990) that passed the House in October, said in a June 14 interview. "But it will give a good start for next year when we can really do it."

He added that House Republicans must act this year for political reasons. "If we don't pass something, [Democrats] will say we hate senior citizens and that we don't want them to have medication. I can hear it all now."

The White House is already drumming up opposition to the Republican bill. It held three media events on prescription drugs the week of June 12 and used each occasion to blast the GOP plan.

"We have grave concerns because the Republican plan relies on a trickle-down scheme that would provide a subsidy for insurers and not a single-dollar of direct premium assistance for middle-class seniors," President Clinton said June 14.

With Senate Republican leaders hesitant to move on the drug issue, passing a House bill may be the only political cover House Republicans have on health care this year. Senate Republican leaders have said they prefer to add prescription drugs in the context of an overhaul of the 35-year-old Medicare program rather than consider a stand-alone measure.

There were some signs of Senate movement during the week of June 12 — such as a Health, Education, Labor and Pensions Committee hearing June 13 on drug safety and pricing and a private meeting June 15 of Senate Finance Committee members to discuss Medicare modernization and prescription drugs — but it is unclear whether they will produce legislation.

Some Republican senators whose fall election opponents are making prescription drugs a key issue, such as Spencer Abraham of Michigan and Conrad Burns of Montana, may only be able to cosponsor a measure rather than cast votes for one. *(Story, p. 67)*

Assistant Senate Majority Leader Don Nickles, R-Okla., who has had trouble finding consensus in the managed-care conference he heads, told reporters June 13 that Senate Republicans were "working on" a prescription drug plan, but he gave no details. Senate Republican Policy Committee Chairman Larry E. Craig of Idaho said in a June 13 interview that the party has not yet developed a strategy on the prescription drug issue, and it may take time to do so. "My guess is we won't get that consensus right away," Craig said.

Testifying before the full Ways and Means panel June 13, Health Subcommittee Chairman Bill Thomas, R-Calif., the chief GOP proponent of the drug plan, stressed repeatedly that the proposal was a bipartisan one because it had garnered the support of two Democrats — Collin C. Peterson of Minnesota and Ralph M. Hall of Texas.

Hall and Peterson are hardly typical Democrats. In a 1999 CQ study, Hall voted against his party's position 70 percent of the time, including three "yes" votes on four impeachment articles against Clinton. The same study found that Peterson voted against the Democratic position 49 percent of the time. At a June 13 news conference, Hall said presumptive GOP presidential nominee George W. Bush might be more open to signing a prescription drug benefit into law. "Maybe in late January, we'll have a president that . . . I can talk to," Hall said. *(Vote study, 1999 CQ Weekly, p. 2996)*

Looking to the Private Sector

The House GOP plan would look to the private sector to create drug policies for seniors and would provide "subsidies" to encourage insurers to participate, although industry officials have said it would be difficult to offer affordable policies. Federal reimbursements to insurers would increase on a sliding scale. The government would pay insurers 30 percent for drug costs between $1,250 and $1,350, rising to 90 percent once a beneficiary's yearly bill reached $6,000 or more.

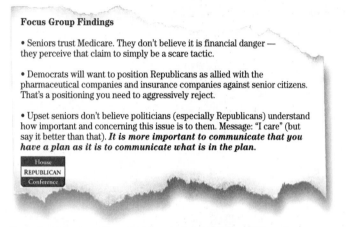

Focus Group Findings

• Seniors trust Medicare. They don't believe it is financial danger — they perceive that claim to simply be a scare tactic.

• Democrats will want to position Republicans as allied with the pharmaceutical companies and insurance companies against senior citizens. That's a positioning you need to aggressively reject.

• Upset seniors don't believe politicians (especially Republicans) understand how important and concerning this issue is to them. Message: "I care" (but say it better than that). *It is more important to communicate that you have a plan as it is to communicate what is in the plan.*

House
REPUBLICAN
Conference

Part of a drug benefit analysis made for the House GOP conference.

Drug Benefit Programs Compared

In 1996, the latest year for which statistics are available, nearly one-third of Medicare beneficiaries — more than 11 million people — lacked prescription drug coverage. President Clinton and House Republicans are offering competing plans to close that gap by proposing a Medicare prescription drug benefit for the elderly. Though their plans differ, both sides cite these statistics to make their point:

• The elderly make up 13 percent of the population but account for more than one-third of the nation's annual drug expenditures — estimated to reach $112 billion in 2000.

• In 1968, seniors spent an average of $64 annually on prescription drugs. By 1998, average expenditures had risen to $848.

• The average amount Medicare beneficiaries spent on drugs increased from 2.4 percent of their income in 1968 to 4.1 percent in 1998.

• In 1999, about half of Medicare beneficiaries spent less than $500 annually for drugs; 45 percent spent $500 to $3,000 and 6 percent spent $3,000 or more.

Issue	House GOP plan would:	President's plan would:
Premiums and Deductibles	Charge $40 in monthly premiums on average in fiscal 2003, the first year of the plan. Require beneficiaries to pay the first $250 in yearly drug costs, then cover half of prescription drug costs up to $2,100.	Assess monthly premiums of about $24 in fiscal 2003, rising to about $51 by fiscal 2010. Cover half of beneficiaries' yearly drug costs up to $2,000 in fiscal 2003, rising to half of $5,000 in fiscal 2009. There would be no yearly deductible.
Choice of Plans	Offer Medicare beneficiaries a choice of at least two plans for drug coverage. The federal government would only offer coverage in areas where private insurers did not. Beneficiary participation would be voluntary.	Cover all fee-for-service Medicare beneficiaries under the same plan. Medicare+Choice plans could continue to offer different packages. Beneficiary participation would be voluntary.
Catastrophic Coverage	Offer catastrophic coverage, beginning in fiscal 2003, once seniors' annual out-of-pocket drug costs reach $6,000. At that point, the government would pay 90 percent and the insurer 10 percent.	Set aside another $35 billion of the federal budget surplus from fiscal 2006 through fiscal 2010 to help cover catastrophic drug costs. No details have been released.
Effective Date	Begin in fiscal 2003.	Begin in fiscal 2003, excluding catastrophic coverage.
Cost	Approximately $40 billion over five years, including catastrophic coverage.	Approximately $38 billion over five years, excluding catastrophic coverage.
Method of Implementation	Be run by a new agency — the Medicare Benefits Administration — within the Department of Health and Human Services. Participating plans could use pharmaceutical benefit managers — companies that specialize in running insurers' drug benefit programs.	Be run by pharmaceutical benefits managers and supervised by the Health Care Financing Administration.

SOURCES: Medicare Payment Advisory Commission June 2000 Report to Congress, Congressional Budget Office, Health Care Financing Administration, Kaiser Family Foundation, House Republican plan.

Seniors would be required to pay the first $250 of drug costs each year, then half of their expenses would be covered up to $2,100. Medicare recipients whose drug bills were higher than $2,350 would be responsible for that amount until their annual out-of-pocket costs reached $6,000. At that point, so-called catastrophic coverage would begin, with insurers and the federal government paying all costs.

Under the GOP plan, catastrophic coverage begins in fiscal 2003. In Clinton's prescription drug proposal, it would not begin until fiscal 2006, and White House officials have provided few details. Thomas and other supporters stress this distinction as a key one, and it will be used to offset another difference between the two plans.

The GOP bill requires that beneficiaries, except those who qualify for low-income subsidies, pay monthly premiums — which would likely average $40 a month — plus a $250 deductible for a total of $730 in fiscal 2003. Clinton's plan would cost beneficiaries $288 in premiums with no deductible.

Thomas told the Ways and Means Committee on June 13 that the bill would include a "lockbox" that would return any Medicare-generated surpluses to the program rather than to

Florida District Is One Front In Medicare Benefits War

Medicare prescription drug benefits are a hot topic in Florida's 22nd Congressional District, where thousands of seniors have flocked to the beaches and condominiums that dominate a 91-mile strip of land running from Palm Beach County to Miami Beach.

The issue — which was simmering long before rival proposals were introduced by President Clinton and House Republicans — could present problems for Republican Rep. E. Clay Shaw Jr., who has successfully navigated the 22nd's centrist currents since his district was redrawn in 1992. It is also figuring in a handful of other competitive House and Senate races from Montana to Michigan.

Although Clinton carried Shaw's district in 1996 with 54 percent of the vote, Democrats did not bother to challenge the former Fort Lauderdale mayor in 1998, in part because of his popularity among elderly residents. This year, however, state Rep. Elaine Bloom has made Medicare coverage for prescription drugs one of the leading issues in her campaign to unseat the 10-term incumbent.

"It's probably one of the most important issues of this campaign," Bloom said in a telephone interview on June 13. "We have a very large population of senior citizens, and they are well aware . . . that this is a program whose time has come."

Bloom and Shaw agree that a Medicare prescription drug benefit is necessary, but they disagree on the details. Bloom favors a proposal outlined by Clinton, while Shaw backs the House Republican bill sponsored by Rep. Bill Thomas of California. (*Chart, p. 66*)

Shaw hopes congressional action on the House GOP bill will remove prescription drug benefits from November's political landscape. "If it passes, there's no issue," he said in a June 15 interview.

Some experts think the issue could favor Bloom this fall if the House fails to pass a bill. "That's a

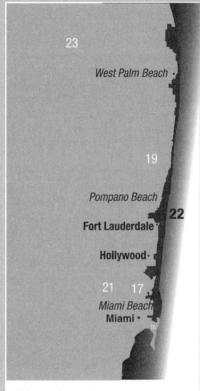

Florida 22

- **31** percent of residents 65 or older.
- **94** percent white.
- **67** percent of workers in white-collar jobs.
- Tourism and health care are the biggest industries.
- Not more than 3 miles wide at any point.

SOURCE: CQ's Politics in America

good issue for [her]," Dario Moreno, an associate professor of political science at Florida International University in Miami, said in a June 14 interview. "In that district, she can make a real impact."

Democrats have adroitly used Medicare and Social Security issues in past Florida campaigns, leaving Republicans to decry their "Mediscare" tactics. During the bitter 1994 gubernatorial race pitting Republican Jeb Bush against incumbent Democrat Lawton Chiles,

many seniors received telephone calls charging that Bush's running mate wanted to cut Social Security and Medicare funds. Bush lost that election, and Chiles' staff aides later admitted orchestrating the telephone campaign.

In Montana, Democratic challenger Brian Schweitzer is using more public tactics in an effort to unseat incumbent GOP Sen. Conrad Burns. Schweitzer takes busloads of seniors across the border to Canada — where pharmaceuticals are usually less expensive — to buy prescription drugs.

That tactic has attracted the attention of a pharmaceutical industry-backed group called Citizens for Better Medicare, which has aired television advertisements since March criticizing Canada's nationalized health care system and Schweitzer's bus trips.

Prescription drug prices are also an issue in Michigan and Washington state, where incumbent Republican senators are facing strong Democratic opposition.

In Michigan, Democratic Rep. Debbie Stabenow, who is challenging first-term GOP Sen. Spencer Abraham, solicits copies of prescription drug bills via her campaign Web site, where she posts letters complaining about high drug prices.

In Washington state, GOP Sen. Slade Gorton and his two Democratic opponents have been hearing from elderly residents for months about prescription drug prices.

Gorton is sponsoring a measure (S2464) that would require U.S. drug manufacturers to charge international wholesalers the same prices they charge American wholesalers, while State Insurance Commissioner Deborah Senn — who is running against former Rep. Maria Cantwell (1993-95) for the Democratic nomination — set up a task force on the issue two years ago.

the general treasury, which is the current practice. The provision was discussed again at a June 15 briefing for reporters but was not included in the drug bill's legislative language.

Rather, the Medicare "lockbox" may move as a separate piece of legislation. If approved, it would allow lawmakers to use Medicare savings to increase payments to doctors, hospitals, managed-care plans and other Medicare providers, which were cut in the 1997 balanced-budget law (PL 105-33).

Although Congress passed legislation (PL 106-113) last year to give those providers an additional $16 billion, they say that was not enough and are pressing for more money this year. (*Background, 1999 CQ Weekly, p. 2775*)

"Members should view Medicare as pork — it's just as important as a highway or an appropriations bill," said Fred Graefe, a health care lobbyist representing hospitals and manufacturers. "It's important for members to show that in an era of surplus they can return Medicare dollars to their districts, which benefits both beneficiaries and providers."

Karen Ignagni, president and chief executive officer of the American Association of Health Plans, which represents managed-care companies, said that since her members provide prescription drug coverage to millions of seniors, it is critical for Congress to give managed-care plans more money.

"Building on that success . . . is the first significant step we can make to answering the Medicare prescription drug challenge," Ignagni said June 13 in testimony before the Ways and Means Committee.

Thomas predicted that his plan will receive strong Democratic backing on the House floor even if it emerges from Ways and Means with only Republican support. "That will be more than enough evidence that this bill is bipartisan," Thomas said at the hearing.

Ways and Means Democrats and other critics of the Thomas plan said its reliance on private insurers could hurt seniors if the plans decided to alter benefits or leave a particular market. Allowing a variety of insurers to negotiate with drug companies would also divide the Medicare beneficiary pool into many segments, weakening the ability to get deep discounts based

on volume, critics say.

'A Complicated Scheme'

Charles B. Rangel, the panel's ranking Democrat, said at the Ways and Means hearing that the GOP plan was "not a true Medicare prescription drug benefit, but a complicated scheme designed to sell expensive, inadequate private insurance plans."

Ways and Means member Sander M. Levin, D-Mich., said few Democrats would sign on: "There may be some Democratic votes on the floor — a small minority — but it won't become law."

Thomas' plan must overcome more than just the ire of Democrats and Clinton. Insurance industry representatives have said they do not want to write the policies because they cannot make a profit doing so. Seniors with high drug bills would sign up in large numbers for the policies and file claims, which would drive up costs, increase premiums and make coverage unaffordable, insurers say.

"The pressures of ever-increasing drug costs, the predictability of drug expenses and the likelihood that the people most likely to purchase this coverage will be the people anticipating the highest drug claims would make drug-only coverage virtually impossible for insurers to offer at an affordable premium," Health Insurance Association of America President Chip Kahn said in a statement issued June 13.

Thomas believes there would be plenty of private insurers who would offer drug benefits to seniors.

"When you tell somebody you don't need them and, in fact, it's going to succeed without them, you'll be amazed at how some people will come around the back door and want to be part of it," Thomas told reporters June 13.

Peterson was confident that insurers would participate. "If you don't believe in the marketplace, you don't believe in this plan," he told reporters June 15.

A $2.5 Billion Criticism

Democrats also criticized Thomas' proposal to give roughly $2.5 billion of the $40 billion drug package to managed-care plans over the next five years and provide additional incentives to lure managed care to rural areas.

Such funding may persuade plans to

stay in Medicare+Choice, which was created in the 1997 balanced-budget law (PL 105-33) to encourage more managed-care insurers to offer coverage to beneficiaries. In each of the past two years, 99 plans have reduced services or left the program altogether. More plans are expected to announce by July 3, the federal deadline for plans to apply for participation in Medicare+Choice next year, that they will not be back. (*Background, 2000 CQ Weekly, p. 1183*)

"Why would we prop up [Medicare+Choice plans] . . . when they are continually pulling out of these counties?" said Ways and Means member Karen L. Thurman, D-Fla.

While the prescription drug debate is being fought mostly in the political arena, policy implications loom large for any benefit that becomes law.

The Republican proposal and the president's plan focus on providing a drug benefit for the short term, but if either became law, drug coverage would likely become a permanent part of Medicare. That would make lawmakers reluctant to scale back or eliminate drug coverage for the elderly, even if the current era of bountiful budget surpluses fades.

The Boomer Problem

Rep. Sanford said expanding Medicare to cover prescription drugs is "starting a new program which requires annual cuttings, which there won't be," because lawmakers will be reluctant to do something that could hurt them politically. Medicare is expected to be further taxed when millions of Baby Boomers begin to qualify for Medicare beginning in 2010. (*Medicare solvency, 2000 CQ Weekly, p. 769*)

Richard M. Burr of North Carolina, one of the plan's GOP cosponsors, said that the legislation would give Congress "a vision of where we need to be 15 to 20 years down the road," with Medicare, rather than creating more problems for the program.

There are no guarantees that any prescription plan that passes the House will become law, but Sanford is not so sure it will be added to the Senate's casualty list.

"It's like the boy in Holland who put his finger in the dike. One senator may be able to do it for a while, but over time the water comes over the dam," Sanford said. ◆

Leaders' quandary: focus on party-defining positions or modest but doable fixes?

Business Pushes for Top Spot On Republican Tax Agenda

Emboldened by a soaring surplus and strong poll numbers for their presidential candidate, Republican congressional leaders are returning from the July Fourth recess with their tax agenda coming into focus: Pressure a lame duck president who is eager to bolster his legacy into signing a populist tax cut — or be content to have another issue for the campaign trail if he does not.

The recent GOP fixation with moving tax bills for the masses has forced some of the party's most loyal allies to take a back seat. Businesses of all stripes are anxious for their own tax breaks and are beginning to pressure the Republicans, whose campaign coffers they have helped to swell, to pay more attention to advancing their cause.

"It is our feeling that the economy is being driven by business overall, and businesses contribute substantially to the surplus," said William T. Sinclaire, director of tax policy for the U.S. Chamber of Commerce. "If you look at it from that point of view, there should be a return."

Most are looking beyond the first tax bill afforded protection under the budget resolution — to alleviate the so-called marriage penalty — and hungrily toward the second such reconciliation measure, which is supposed to begin moving after Labor Day.

Even that, many say, is a long shot.

Despite a reverence for the economic virtues of a tax cut, the Republicans, now nearing the end of their sixth year in control of the Capitol, have not won the enactment of many of the tax cuts that businesses, particularly large corporations, expected for themselves. Instead, the GOP has focused its energies — and spent substantial political capital — on trying to ratchet down individual taxes through targeted fixes and working to address complaints with the tax code lodged by small businesses. (*Box, p. 72*)

To be sure, in the eyes of many business lobbyists, it is President Clinton who should shoulder most of the blame for neither proposing a substantial tax overhaul of his own nor signing much of the legislation the Republican Congress has sent him. But the GOP has also tended, particularly in the months before the midterm election of 1998 and the coming election in November, to view tax bills as political documents rather than as vehicles for overhauling the IRS code.

"Frustration is often expressed," said former Rep. Guy Vander Jagt of Michigan (1966-93), a lobbyist with a dozen corporate clients at the Washington law firm of Baker and Hostetler. The GOP takeover of Congress, he said, "certainly wasn't the bonanza that [businesses] thought it was going to be, and there is grumbling that it doesn't make much difference which party is in power."

Because it is given certain procedural advantages — first and foremost, a shield from Senate filibusters — the preferred vehicle for making both political statements about tax policy and for delivering "rifle shot" business tax breaks is a reconciliation measure. The name derives from its official purpose: to reconcile tax and spending policies with the revenue and outlay targets of the annual budget resolution. Generally, Congress considered one tax reconciliation bill a year, but the budget resolution governing fiscal 2001 (H Con Res 290) calls for two such measures. (*2000 CQ Weekly, p. 885*)

Larger firms benefited in 1997 from some tax changes enacted under the most recent reconciliation package to become law (PL 105-34) and from the tax package combined with a minimum wage increase (PL 104-188) the year before. But some who represent those interests complain that their generosity to Republican candidates has not been reciprocated in the setting of GOP tax policy. Further frustrating some large business, particularly retailers, has been their need to combat a new GOP tax-cutting campaign — to restrict sales taxes on Internet purchases. The focus of this debate is on legislation (HR 3709) the House passed in May.

It is these frustrations that have led some business lobbyists to press Republicans to reject the idea of focusing both reconciliation bills on highly politicized proposals, each of which appeared likely to draw a Clinton veto.

Shaping the Political Debate

The first reconciliation measure is expected to be debated on both sides of the Capitol the week of July 10. The House is expected to vote on a measure similar to one (HR 6) it passed in February. The Senate will consider a bill approved by the Finance Committee on June 28. Both are designed to alleviate the tax code's "marriage penalty" — a quirk that causes some married couples to owe more taxes than they would if they had remained single. (*2000 CQ Weekly, p. 1592*)

On June 27, House Majority Leader Dick Armey, R-Texas, said the second reconciliation measure would likely include only one or two other items in addition to a restatement of legislation (HR 8) the House passed in June to repeal taxes on estates, gifts and trust funds and only one or two other items. (*2000 CQ Weekly, p. 1377*)

Majority Leader Trent Lott, R-Miss., has vowed to try to pass such a bill in the Senate the week of July 10, which would require him to muster 60 votes to limit debate and amendments. If that move fails, the estate tax repeal will become the centerpiece of the Senate's second reconciliation bill, as well. Lott has said that measure might also include some debt reduction provisions and legislation (HR 3916) to repeal the century-old federal excise tax on telephone calls. (*2000 CQ Weekly, p. 1465*)

The scenario of moving the estate tax and marriage penalty measures as the core of the two reconciliation bills is designed to dare the president to reject politically attractive

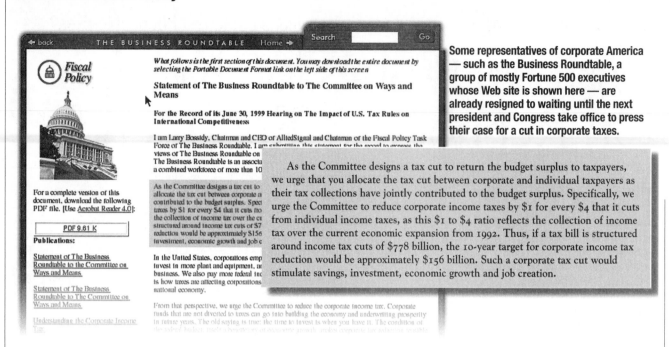

Fiscal Policy

What follows is the first section of this document. You may download the entire document by selecting the Portable Document Format link on the left side of this screen

Statement of The Business Roundtable to The Committee on Ways and Means

For the Record of its June 30, 1999 Hearing on The Impact of U.S. Tax Rules on International Competitiveness

I am Larry Bossidy, Chairman and CEO of AlliedSignal and Chairman of the Fiscal Policy Task Force of The Business Roundtable. I am submitting this statement for the record to express the views of The Business Roundtable on...
The Business Roundtable is an association...
a combined workforce of more than 10...

For a complete version of this document, download the following PDF file. [Use Acrobat Reader 4.0]:

PDF 9.61 K

Publications:

Statement of The Business Roundtable to the Committee on Ways and Means

Statement of The Business Roundtable to The Committee on Ways and Means

Understanding the Corporate Income Tax

As the Committee designs a tax cut to return the budget surplus to taxpayers, we urge that you allocate the tax cut between corporate and individual taxpayers as their tax collections have jointly contributed to the budget surplus. Specifically, we urge the Committee to reduce corporate income taxes by $1 for every $4 that it cuts from individual income taxes, as this $1 to $4 ratio reflects the collection of income tax over the current economic expansion from 1992. Thus, if a tax bill is structured around income tax cuts of $778 billion, the 10-year target for corporate income tax reduction would be approximately $156 billion. Such a corporate tax cut would stimulate savings, investment, economic growth and job creation.

Some representatives of corporate America — such as the Business Roundtable, a group of mostly Fortune 500 executives whose Web site is shown here — are already resigned to waiting until the next president and Congress take office to press their case for a cut in corporate taxes.

measures that the presumptive GOP presidential nominee, Texas Gov. George W. Bush, would likely sign. Such an in-your-face strategy would presumably preclude a compromise between the president and Congress on either reconciliation bill, unless Democrats conclude that it is politically unwise to oppose tax cuts at a time when the available budget surplus is forecast at $1.9 trillion over 10 years.

Senate Minority Leader Tom Daschle, D-S.D., signaled a willingness to deal at a news conference June 30. "There's no doubt that there is room for additional tax reduction, so long as we keep our balance," he said.

GOP leaders spurned Clinton's first compromise offer — to sign their marriage penalty bill if they moved his plan to cover prescription drugs for Medicare recipients. They said it was not thought through, but also signaled that they are reluctant to horse-trade with a president who has historically won the upper hand in such situations. And, they said, it is probably in their best interests to wait to seriously negotiate tax relief until next year — in the belief that the GOP will keep control of Congress and that Bush will defeat Vice President Al Gore, the presumed Democratic nominee.

Too Much of a Gamble?

Some lobbyists view that as a dangerous strategy, especially since many businesses have been aiding the effort of the top Democrat on the Ways and Means Committee, Charles B. Rangel of New York, to raise millions of dollars for his party's campaign to retake the House. Many of those contributions appear to have been made largely in order to curry favor with a potential chairman of the tax-writing committee and not out of fealty to the Democratic campaign agenda.

"What you want to do is push at every opportunity for the kind of tax provisions that will ensure this growth continues," Martin A. Regalia, the U.S. Chamber's chief economist, said in a June 27 interview. "You don't want to forgo dealing with the current because you're always looking and hoping for a better venue in the future."

Others representing corporate America — including leaders of the Business Roundtable, a group of mostly Fortune 500 company executives — say they are prepared to

wait until the next president takes office to push their agenda of cuts in corporate income tax rates.

Groups with a narrower focus are also waiting to launch a major effort. The National Beer Wholesalers Association, for instance, is working to cut the federal excise tax on the beverages it sells but has dedicated its campaign this year to "trying to build cosponsors," according to its president, David K. Rehr. A more concerted push this summer would be pointless, he suggested, because "it looks like the clock is running against us."

Orphaned Ideas

The main argument of lobbyists seeking corporate tax cuts is that Washington should return something to the businesses driving the booming economy — and whose income tax payments, as a result, are expected to grow by 10 percent during fiscal 2000, to $202.7 billion, according to the most recent Office of Management and Budget (OMB) figures.

When Clinton on June 26 unveiled the OMB report predicting new, more optimistic surplus figures, he said that a main use for the money should be retiring the $3.5 trillion national debt by 2012, a year ahead of his previous schedule. "By paying down the debt, we can keep interest rates lower and free up more capital for private sector investment, creating more jobs and economic growth for years and years to come."

Many businesses would just as soon keep some of the money for themselves. While some believe their chances of receiving tax cuts this year — in either of the reconciliation bills or an omnibus fiscal 2001 appropriations package — are slim, many are still getting in line in case such breaks are forthcoming. And, some think they have a reasonable shot at winning inclusion of their provisions in some moving vehicle.

"We're cautiously optimistic," said J. Leon Peace Jr., a lobbyist for the American Bankers Association. "There are so many tax provisions that need to be done, and Congress has shown some willingness to pass some legislation that can be signed. . . . I haven't given up hope."

Peace is not alone. Some members of the Ways and Means Committee are pushing leaders to move a bill that can address some of what have been termed "orphan tax ideas" by com-

mittee member Phil English, R-Pa. Examples, according to English, are proposals to increase the federal income tax credits that states may distribute to the developers of low-income housing — a measure that could move on an emerging community renewal bill — and other provisions that are specific concerns for particular industries.

"With surpluses of the dimension we're looking at, some of these things should be possible," English said.

Another panel member, Dave Camp, R-Mich., said he was open to considering varying strategies for the second reconciliation bill. "I certainly would like to see more tax relief rather than less," he said. "And I'd like to see us do something that could be enacted."

But Mark Foley, R-Fla., who also serves on the committee, said Republicans should be cautious about adding tax breaks for businesses. "We've got to be very careful that we don't cloud our own message," he said, arguing that the strategy of advancing single-issue tax bills has been successful in raising public awareness of the GOP tax agenda, even if only one of the measures (HR 5 — PL 106-182) has been enacted: to end the Social Security earnings limit for many seniors.

Foley said he feared that if Republicans loaded up the reconciliation bills with too many business tax breaks, Clinton and congressional Democrats would paint them as giving "tax cuts to big business and the rich, and the little guys get nothing."

Packwood's Prediction

It is also not clear what the Senate wants. The desire of businesses to use the second reconciliation bill as a venue for tax breaks appears likely to be shared by Finance Committee Chairman William V. Roth Jr., R-Del., who faces a tough race for re-election and could benefit from an opportunity to help out home-state companies and others with a strong economic presence in his state. Roth is also expected to try to add to his legacy of encouraging retirement savings through tax-deferred contributions to Individual Retirement Accounts.

Majority Whip Don Nickles, R-

Okla., like Lott a member of the Finance Committee, said June 27 that it was too early to tell what the second reconciliation bill would entail.

With the surplus ballooning and Clinton eager to burnish his legacy, some members and lobbyists say the time for a tax agreement could be ripe.

"What we're trying to weigh is how serious Mr. Clinton is," said English. "We think there's some wiggle room."

Former Senate Finance Chairman Bob Packwood, R-Ore. (1969-95), who

The GOP takeover of Congress "certainly wasn't the bonanza that [businesses] thought it was going to be, and there is grumbling that it doesn't make much difference which party is in power."

— Corporate lobbyist and former Rep. Guy Vander Jagt

now represents corporate clients such as Marriott International and Northwest Airlines, said that the "overall philosophical case" against tax cuts "gets harder and harder for Democrats as the surplus gets bigger and bigger."

It could be possible, he said, for the GOP to get a tax cut as big as the 10-year, $792 billion package (HR 2488) vetoed last year and for Democrats to meet their spending goals. "That's why I think there would be room for compromise," he said.

But Packwood and other observers believe that the prospects for an agreement will remain unclear until later this month, when the Congressional Budget Office releases its midyear surplus projections, and possibly until after presidential race polling at Labor Day, the traditional benchmark for the fall campaign. If Bush's lead remains substantial, Packwood said, "Republicans would be advisable just to wait" until next year, when they would be more likely to be able to enact their tax agenda intact.

Business Not a Monolith

Some lobbyists say that even the start of a Bush presidency and continued GOP majorities in Congress would not guarantee corporate America everything it wants.

Robert A. Rusbuldt, a lobbyist for the Independent Insurance Agents of America, noted that Bush's proposal to

cut taxes by $483 billion over five years does not include some items that business seeks, such as a cut in the tax rates for capital gains, although it does address other priorities, such as cutting corporate income tax rates. Bush "will set the agenda on taxes and it will not be everything that business wants, but it will be a lot better for the economy and the private sector" than under a Gore administration, he said.

The next president may also find it challenging at times to decipher what "business" wants. Lobbyists point out that businesses do not speak with one voice on tax questions. Small and large companies often have different priorities.

For instance, the National Federation of Independent Business (NFIB), a small-business trade association credited with raising the profile of Main Street on the Hill, lists as one of its major goals the repeal of a provision in last year's law (PL 106-170) extending some tax credits. The change would allow business owners who use the accrual accounting method — generally service providers such as architects — to sell their businesses over several years and spread the capital gains on that sale over the same number of years. Last year's change required the entire capital gain to be paid in the first year of the sale.

The provision would cost $2.1 billion over 10 years and is a high priority for a host of groups, including the U.S. Chamber of Commerce and the National Association of Manufacturers, which count small business owners as members. Most in Congress support the change and are simply looking for a vehicle to move it.

Another provision being pushed by a different coalition would carry a much larger price tag, likely more than $20 billion over five years.

Rep. Jerry Weller, R-Ill., has sponsored a bill (HR 4279) to allow businesses to write off the purchase of personal computers in the year in which the purchase occurs. Currently, businesses must depreciate the cost of computers over five years. Weller said that the average business replaces comput-

Business Tax Legislation
In the GOP-Controlled Congress

Republicans have pushed a host of tax proposals since taking control of Congress five years ago. The few that have become law have focused on cutting rates for individuals and small businesses and on revamping the IRS — not on making big changes to the taxation of corporate America.

1995

• In December, President Clinton vetoed a bill, which House Republicans called the "crowning jewel" of their "Contract With America" campaign platform of the year before, to cut a variety of taxes by $245 billion over seven years. The main provision was a per-child tax credit for families, beginning at $400 and rising to $500. It also would have cut the capital gains rate on corporate profits from the sale of assets to 28 percent from 35 percent; phased out the corporate alternative minimum tax; and allowed the first $1 million in proceeds from the sale of a family-owned business or farm to be exempted from estate taxes. Republicans would have offset the lost revenue by erasing 27 corporate tax benefits worth $30.2 billion and significantly restructuring the earned-income tax credit (EITC), which enhanced or provided refunds to the working poor. (1995 CQ Almanac, pp. 2-66, 2-71)

• In April, Clinton signed a measure (PL 104-7) making permanent a provision increasing to 30 percent from 25 percent the amount of health care premiums that the self-employed may deduct from their taxes. The bill was a major priority of small businesses. Its $2.96 billion cost over six years was offset by ending a tax break for companies that sold broadcast properties to minority investors and by tightening EITC rules. (1995 Almanac, p. 2-74)

• In December, Congress cleared a bill, which Clinton signed in January 1996 (PL 104-95), barring states from imposing taxes on the retirement income of former residents. Some Democrats argued it allowed wealthy corporate executives to shield their pensions from higher income-tax states. (1995 Almanac, p. 2-77)

1996

• Yielding to pressure from Democrats and moderate Republicans to increase the minimum wage, GOP leaders combined a 90-cent increase in the minimum (to $5.15) with a package of tax sweeteners worth $20 billion over 10 years — targeted mostly at the small business community, which was most likely to be affected by the higher minimum wage. The law Clinton signed (PL 104-188) in August provided greater expensing of new equipment; tax incentives to create pension plans; and looser requirements for creating S Corporations, which have a limited number of stockholders and are not subject to corporate income tax. Bigger businesses won the relaxation of limits on the size of tax-deferred retirement plans available to higher-paid workers and repeal of a tax on some foreign-held assets. (1996 Almanac, p. 2-38)

1997

• Republicans finally pushed many of their priorities — including the per-child tax credit — through on the only tax reconciliation measure (PL 105-34) that has won Clinton's signature since the GOP took control of the Capitol. At a cost of $275 billion over 10 years, the measure Clinton signed that August provided the deepest tax cut since the Reagan administration. Its array of benefits for individuals included credits for college education, tax-deferred savings for education, a lower tax rate for individual capital gains and a new type of Individual Retirement Account, which was named for its sponsor, Senate Finance Committee Chairman William V. Roth Jr., R-Del.

For businesses, the law changed the way depreciation is addressed under the corporate alternative minimum tax to allow greater tax write-offs; exempted more estates from taxes; extended tax breaks, such as the credit for the makers of unprofitable drugs and the research and development tax credit, important to some corporations; allowed large retailers, manufacturers and other businesses to discount their taxable inventories for breakage and theft based on physical estimates; made workers' compensation payments tax exempt; increased deductions for business meals; and allowed more companies to qualify as controlled foreign corporations that could defer some of their taxes. It altered the means of calculating taxes on certain business activities to offset part of the bill's cost. (1997 Almanac, p. 2-30)

1998

• Republican leaders began the year by pitching a $100 billion tax cut over five years, but they had to settle for $9.2 billion because the House and Senate GOP could not reach agreement on a broader bill. Leaders eventually inserted a tax package, including extensions of corporate tax credits and accelerated health insurance deductions for the self-employed, in the omnibus fiscal 1999 spending law (PL 105-277), which Clinton signed in October. (1998 Almanac, p. 21-14)

1999

• With GOP leaders in both chambers in agreement this time, Republicans pushed a big tax break: $792 billion over a decade. But Clinton vetoed the measure (HR 2488) in September. The bill included corporate priorities, such as greatly cutting the alternative minimum tax. The GOP again was forced to settle for a narrower bill to extend tax credits, although for longer periods of time. A credit for research was extended for five years, while other provisions won 18-month approvals. Clinton signed that bill (PL 106-170) in December. (1999 CQ Weekly, p. 2888)

By the time a tax bill is formally considered in the grandiose Ways and Means hearing room, shown here at a February markup, most of the dealmaking is done. In recent years, corporate America has not benefited from those negotiations as much as it expected from the GOP.

ers every 14 to 18 months and that the tax code should not discourage businesses from using modern technology.

While the provision is supported by high-technology firms and other businesses, some industries are trying to expand its application. The Printing Industries of America Inc., Chicago-based printer R.R. Donnelley & Sons Co. and the NFIB are working with Weller to see if the tax code's definition of computers can be updated to expressly include computerized printing equipment and the robots used in tool and dye manufacturing.

In addition, a variety of industries including companies large and small would like to see the reconciliation package shorten depreciation schedules for other property.

Ways and Means Committee Chairman Bill Archer, R-Texas, has said that he will push to move a bipartisan overhaul of depreciation schedules once the Treasury Department issues a report on the current system. But that document was due in March and has still not been released.

Other issues larger corporations would like to see tackled — likely not this year — are an overhaul of interna-

tional tax rules and reductions in corporate tax rates or corporate capital gains. But all businesses do not list such changes as priorities. Even within one trade association different companies have varying, and sometimes conflicting, desires.

The Independent Insurance Agents of America, for instance, includes thousands of small agencies as well as a few large firms. The smaller concerns, most of whom are organized as S Corporations, are generally focused on cutting individual tax rates, because their stockholders pay income tax on capital gains from the company while the firm's bottom line is not subject to corporate income tax. Larger companies, which are not organized in such a way, want a corporate rate cut.

The American Bankers Association faces similar issues. Small banks, known as community banks, are working to clarify a 1997 change to S Corporation rules that allowed banks to organize in that fashion. Larger banks are more interested in ensuring that Congress and the president work out a settlement with the European Union to find another way to help exporters, now that the

World Trade Organization (WTO) has ruled that the United States' foreign sales corporation provisions violate world trade rules. Such language is expected to be moved in a bill separate from budget reconciliation, but under the WTO ruling, the United States is required to change its laws by Oct. 1. (*Background, 2000 CQ Weekly, p. 1038*)

Small businesses have not generally been actively involved in those efforts, chiefly because many would not see as much benefit from them as corporations would. While small businesses, whose lobbying is led by the NFIB and a handful of other groups, have won a greater share of the provisions in tax law enacted since the GOP took over in 1995, corporate America's bottom line has generally grown quickly under the economic expansion.

William G. Gale, a Brookings Institution senior fellow, said large corporations are right in arguing that they have not been the focus of many tax debates. "There have been fewer provisions for large business than for individuals and small business," he said. "I don't know if that justifies whining." ◆

As GOP works on H-1B visa bill, Hispanics seek action on residency, guest workers

Juggling Business' Agenda And Immigrants' Interests

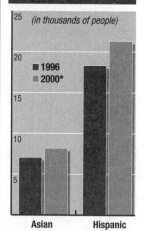

Datafile

(in thousands of people)

■ 1996
■ 2000*

Asian   Hispanic

*Projection

Voting Age Minorities

The surge in the voting age population of Asians and Hispanics is making them ever more powerful politically, which makes immigration law changes ever more perilous to Congress. Although Census Bureau figures for 1996 and 2000 include some immigrants not eligible to vote, both ethnic groups are growing far faster than all others.

Section 245(i) of the Immigration and Nationality Act let some illegal immigrants seek permanent residency. Immigrants lined up in 1997 as the law expired, and now Democrats want to bring it back.

It should have been a slam dunk. Virtually every major business group, the vast majority of both Republicans and Democrats in Congress, and the Clinton administration all agreed earlier this year to support proposals for increasing visas for temporary, highly skilled workers coming to the United States to help feed the high-tech community's voracious need for more workers.

Even organized labor has not opposed the visa increases this time, though it fought them bitterly in 1998.

But by mid-September, H-1B visa bills in both the House and the Senate were stalled (HR 4227, HR 3983, S 2045), not so much because of controversy over the bills, but over a host of other immigration issues advocates want added to the popular measures. (*Proposals, p. 75*)

Several proposals are in play as additions to H-1B, including a bill that would make it easier for immigrants in the United States to become permanent residents. And some Republicans are pushing to change the agriculture guest worker program, which could force the party to choose between satisfying business interests and alienating voting blocs like Hispanics who have grown to critical importance in states such as Florida and California.

"Immigration issues are white hot," said Judith Golub, a lobbyist for the American Immigration Lawyers Association. "They are important for the election."

No one believes the H-1B visa issue will be allowed to die. Even though few immigration issues have been formally considered by Congress, pressure from outside groups is building, and Democrats and the White House seem likely to get some of their issues in a final package that carries business' top priority: H-1B visas. Some form of that proposal is almost certain to travel on a year-end spending bill, the new way for immigration issues to become law.

Indeed, in what has become an annual tradition since Republicans won control of Congress in 1994, many of the most serious immigration issues likely to become law will be added quietly to an end-of-session bill, with little or no floor debate in either chamber.

It wasn't always this way. Republicans passed a stand-alone bill cracking down on illegal immigration in 1996 (PL 104-208) and included provisions restricting immigrant access to government benefits in the welfare overhaul that year (PL 104-193). (*1996 CQ Almanac, p. 5-3, 6-3*)

But those measures proved tremendously problematic for Republicans, opening fissures within the party and generating a backlash,

CQ Weekly Sept. 23, 2000

Drive for H-1B Visas Could Provide Vehicle for Other Immigration Bills

The H-1B visa proposal could be the engine for several other immigration measures at the end of the session. The measures include:

■ **H-1B Visas:** Proposals to increase the number of these temporary, highly skilled worker visas are central to all discussion of immigration bills in these final weeks. An H-1B visa allows foreign workers to come to the United States for up to six years to fill specialized jobs for which companies say they cannot find qualified U.S. workers. Under a 1998 law (PL 105-277), there will be 107,500 H-1B visas issued in fiscal 2001, which begins Oct. 1, down from 115,000 authorized in fiscal 2000. The allotment for fiscal 2000 was filled in March, and the business community — in particular the increasingly powerful high-tech segment — has been agitating for an increase. The House and Senate Judiciary committees approved legislation to increase visa levels (S 2045, HR 4227), but other requirements in the House bill soured the business community, and it seems unlikely to be part of a final deal. Even with Senate floor action on S 2045 the week of Sept. 18, an H-1B bill is not likely to move on its own. (*2000 CQ Weekly, p. 1186*)

Outlook: A virtual lock. Some kind of increase will be enacted before the lights go out on the 106th Congress, though it probably will be part of an omnibus spending bill.

■ **H-2A Visas:** Despite overwhelming opposition from Hispanic groups and the Clinton administration, Republicans hope to attach revisions in the H-2A farm-worker program to any H-1B visa bill. The farm worker program provides temporary visas that allow migrant workers to come into the United States to pick crops. Agricultural interests long have said that the program is too cumbersome and makes it too hard to bring workers in. A bill (HR 4548), approved by the House

Judiciary Committee on Sept. 20 and scheduled for a floor vote the week of Sept. 25, would create a three-year pilot program that would let farmers pay migrant workers lower wages than are currently required. In addition, farmers could give workers housing stipends instead of actually locating housing for them.

Outlook: Enactment seems unlikely. Hispanic groups say the Clinton administration is firmly opposed to the proposal and would veto it. Despite strong support on the part of some Republicans, it seems unlikely to get further than the House floor.

■ **Amnesty:** Perhaps the most controversial immigration bill, this would allow some illegal immigrants who have lived in the United States continuously for a significant number of years to apply to become legal residents. Supporters say this has become routine, done roughly every 14 years; opponents say it rewards illegal immigration. Currently, immigrants who have lived illegally in the U.S. since 1972 and can show "good moral character" can apply for legal residency. The proposal would change the date to 1986. Supporters say this would help many immigrants who were eligible to become permanent residents under a 1986 law (PL 99-603) but were denied the chance to apply by problems the Immigration and Naturalization Service had in implementing that law. (1986 Almanac, p. 62)

Outlook: Toss-up. The Clinton administration and Democrats are pushing to package this with the H-1B measure, with the support of Hispanic and pro-immigration lobbying groups. The GOP congressional leadership opposes the proposal. The U.S. Chamber of Commerce recently joined the Essential Worker Immigration Coalition, an umbrella group that includes dozens of business groups supporting this change, and some Republicans in swing districts are concerned

about alienating Latino voters.

■ **245(i):** Another of the proposals seeking to hitch a ride on any H-1B bill, this would restore a provision of U.S. immigration law that expired in 1997. The issue is where immigrants must be living when they apply to become permanent residents. The proposal would allow immigrants in line for permanent residency (a green card) to apply from the United States, even if their visa has expired. Currently, if an immigrant's visa expires, he or she must leave the country to apply for legal residency. In an immigration catch-22, a 1996 law (PL 104-208) imposes a penalty on illegal immigrants who leave and then attempt to return.

Outlook: Enactment likely. The provision is in the Senate version of the Commerce, Justice, State appropriations bill (HR 4690). Appropriators like it because it raises revenue — the fee for applying in the United States is $1,000. But House Judiciary Immigration Subcommittee Chairman Lamar Smith, R-Texas, and other GOP members vehemently oppose it. (*2000 CQ Weekly, p. 1805*)

■ **NACARA parity:** The 1996 immigration law made it more difficult for many immigrants from Central America and the former Soviet bloc countries to apply for permanent residency by setting time limits for applications. Congress has enacted legislation (PL 105-100, PL 105-277) that would help Nicaraguans, Cubans, Haitians and, to a lesser extent, El Salvadorans and Guatemalans, deal with this problem. Left out of the fix were Hondurans. The proposal would make it easier for anyone in those categories to apply for permanent residency.

Outlook: Toss-up. Less politically explosive, the proposal also affects fewer people. It seems likely to share the fate of the amnesty proposal.

especially from the Hispanic community. Many of the most dramatic revisions have since been reversed; the fixes tucked into year-end spending bills.

This year, the piecemeal strategy continues as Republicans try to accommodate the wishes of business leaders without giving ground on immigration issues important to Hispanics. In fact, with the presidential campaign of GOP Texas Gov. George W. Bush reaching out to Hispanic voters, there is pressure on congressional Republicans not to rock the boat with Latinos.

High-tech lobbyists want to see their visa bill stand for a floor vote, and the Hispanic community hopes to take advantage of the political atmosphere to push proposals that would make it easier for some immigrants to become permanent legal residents.

"The community is watching very closely," said Cecilia Muñoz, vice president of the office of research, advocacy and legislation for the National Council of La Raza, a civil rights group. "This is where the rubber meets the road."

One measure the Hispanic community does not want to see enacted is the bill (HR 4548) that would lower minimum wages for temporary farm workers and ease other hiring rules. "It's poison for all of us," said Muñoz.

With the bill, Republicans are "planting the seeds for national Latino opposition to the Republican Party," said Howard L. Berman, D-Calif.

Senate Shuffle

The H-1B proposal is at the heart of the debate. The intense lobbying campaign by the computer industry and other high-tech sectors for the additional workers has made the visa increase a must-pass this Congress. No one wants to be blamed for its failure.

The visas allow highly skilled foreign workers to come to the United States for up to six years. While the majority of the visas are used by the high-tech community, others go to a variety of occupations including nurses and physical therapists.

Neither chamber has debated the proposals on the floor. The Senate on Sept. 19 voted 97-1 to proceed to the bill (S 2045) that had been approved by the Judiciary Committee on March 9.

The House Judiciary Committee approved a vastly different measure (HR 4227) on May 17.

Under a 1998 law (PL 105-277), the number of H-1B visas authorized to be issued will drop to 107,500 in fiscal 2001, which begins Oct. 1. In fiscal 2000, 115,000 visas were permitted, but the supply was exhausted by the end of March. (*1998 Almanac, p. 17-3*)

The Senate version would increase the visa allocation to 195,000 each year for three years, but the cap excludes a large number of visas for those graduating from or working for universities.

Republicans argue that Democrats have blocked the bill by demanding votes on unrelated immigration issues. Democrats respond that the GOP is afraid to cast votes on politically touchy issues.

The Sept. 19 vote served two purposes for Republicans. It removed one procedural obstacle, and, more importantly, gave a strong signal to the increasingly nervous high-tech community that senators support the bill.

"We are pleased that both Republican and Democratic leaders in the Senate have acknowledged the need to act on the H-1B visa bill before Congress adjourns this year and applaud today's action," said Sandra Boyd, who chairs an umbrella group of businesses known as the American Businesses for Legal Immigration.

An H-1B increase "is very important to our country, to the need for high-tech workers," Senate Majority Leader Trent Lott, R-Miss., said Sept. 19. "And this is not just a large corporation issue; small businesses, businesses all across America need these additional high-tech workers."

Democrats want to offer amendments that would make it easier for longtime illegal immigrants to gain permanent legal residency, extend deadlines for residency applications for immigrants from some Central American countries, and restore a law that allowed immigrants to stay in the country beyond their visa if an application for residency was pending.

At their luncheon before the cloture vote on Sept. 19, Senate Democrats were briefed by members of the House Hispanic Caucus on the value of those proposals. Vice Chairman of the House Democratic Caucus Robert Menendez, of New Jersey, said the issue is fairness for Hispanics. He said if Republicans block the Democrats' amendment package, the GOP will be telling Hispanics "we'll do immigration issues for businesses, but we won't do immigration issues for families who want to be reunited."

The Senate may hold another cloture vote Sept. 26, this time to limit debate, but it is not clear whether Democrats will support this second motion. Democrats expect their amendments to be ruled out of order as non-germane if the Senate ever considers the H-1B bill, though that will not end the battle. "We're not going to give up on them just because we can't get a vote," said a top Democratic staffer.

House Problems

The difficulties in the House are similar but more extensive. House leaders have been reluctant to bring an H-1B visa bill to the floor because of concerns about the immigration provisions Democrats want to debate. Though House rules would allow the GOP to preclude amendments, Democrats could use parliamentary tools to get symbolic votes.

In addition, Republicans have not decided which version of the H-1B bill to bring to the floor.

The House Judiciary Committee approved a bill (HR 4227) in May that was largely authored by Immigration and Claims Subcommittee Chairman Lamar Smith, R-Texas. Though it would remove any cap on H-1B visas for three years, the business community intensely dislikes a provision that would require companies seeking H-1B workers to pay them at least $40,000 a year. Those companies would have to show an increase in the median wage paid to U.S. workers from year to year.

House Rules Committee Chairman David Dreier, R-Calif., and Zoe Lofgren, D-Calif., introduced legislation (HR 3983) far more to the industry's liking. It would raise the cap to 200,000 annually for three years, with no new conditions for employers.

Lobbyists thought the House leadership was planning to bring the Dreier-Lofgren bill to the floor in place of the Smith bill, but the two sponsors appear to have had a falling out over Lofgren's support of the other immigration proposals, and theirs has gone nowhere.

Agriculture Workers

A bill that might reach the House floor is the one (HR 4548) most strongly opposed by Hispanics, that was approved 16-11 by the House Judiciary Committee on Sept. 20.

The bill would create a three-year pilot program that would require all

U.S. farm workers to be listed in a state registry to make them easier for employers to locate. It also would allow growers to pay lower wages and in some cases give workers a housing stipend instead of housing.

The measure was pushed through the committee at the behest of House Speaker J. Dennis Hastert, R-Ill., according to Judiciary Committee Chairman Henry J. Hyde, R-Ill. Hyde voted against the measure, calling it "a bad bill . . . I thought it was unfair to workers."

John P. Feehery, a spokesman for Hastert, said the bill was intended to ease a farm worker shortage. "We need to help our farmers," he said.

The measure could be on the floor as soon as the week of Sept. 25.

Hispanic groups have vowed all-out war against the bill, even if it is packaged with the other immigration provisions they want. "[I]f anyone in Congress is flirting with the notion of adding the farm worker bill as the 'price' for other immigration legislation, I would like to state, clearly and unequivocally, that the National Council of La Raza will never agree to sacrifice our farm worker brothers and sisters for the sake of any legislation," La Raza president and chief executive officer Raul Yzaguirre said in a statement Sept. 12.

Democrats said Clinton likely would veto the bill, but some groups were clearly uneasy that it had gone as far as being marked up. "We're nervous," said Bruce Goldstein, a lobbyist for the Farmworker Justice Fund.

Much of the debate during the two days of the committee markup centered on wages and housing for farmworkers. Under current law, an employer must provide housing for temporary workers.

The bill as approved by the Immigration and Claims Subcommittee would have allowed employers to charge farmworkers for maintenance and utilities and collect a security deposit. It also would have let employers pay workers a "reasonable housing allowance," in lieu of actually providing housing.

Democrats attacked the idea that farmworkers could compete for apart-

"None of these proposals would add a single person to the population of the United States."

— Cecilia Muñoz,
National Council of La Raza

ments in such a tight housing market with a relatively small allowance. Berman did some calculations, based on an annual average salary for most workers of $7,500, and said: "If you think that a weekly allowance of $27 is going to get somebody an apartment . . . you're dreaming."

Republicans responded that their plan would take some of the burden off employers. "This is more than fair, considering this is in addition to the wages they are being paid," Smith said. "It's not fair to make them landlords."

The issue was the subject of two competing amendments during the markup. On Sept. 19, the committee adopted, 14-13, an amendment by Sheila Jackson-Lee, D-Texas, that stripped the new housing provision and replaced it with current law.

The vote succeeded, in part, because three Republicans, Hyde, F. James Sensenbrenner Jr., Wis., and Elton Gallegly, Calif., joined the Democrats.

But just before the committee concluded its work for the day on Sept. 19, Gallegly said he had changed his mind and called for a revote on the amendment. Democrats managed to postpone it until the next morning.

By that time, Gallegly had changed his plan. Instead of re-voting on the first amendment, he offered a second provision. That amendment, adopted 17-14 on Sept. 20 after an equally intense debate, would allow growers to pay workers a subsidy for housing if the governor of the state certified that housing was available.

Democrats did win on another Jackson-Lee amendment. The committee adopted, 15-13, her provision that would restore something called the "three-quarters" rule.

Under current law, employers are required to pay workers for at least three-quarters of the time for which they were promised work (barring an Act of God such as weather). So, if a grower promised eight weeks of work, he must pay at least six weeks wages.

The bill would have lifted that requirement. Smith argued that it had "long been a burdensome requirement" on employers. He said workers "know going into the program they will have work only as long as there is work to do."

Jackson-Lee responded, "It's not unfair to simply ask [employers] to keep their word."

The committee rejected, by voice vote, an amendment by Berman that would have limited the number of foreign guest workers allowed into the country to 100,000 per year.

Smith argued that the cap was "not nearly enough to meet demand — estimated at nearly one million."

In the Senate, Republican Policy Chairman Larry E. Craig of Idaho has been pushing similar legislation and has said for months he wanted to attach it to the H-1B bill. But he acknowledged Sept. 19 that a deal seemed unlikely and H-1B visas are too important to risk.

"I will offer it if we can get to a compromise," he said. "We may not get there this year." ◆

Lawmakers Wary of Unfriendly Skies Weigh Revisiting Airline Regulation

Critics say consolidation trend could leave U.S. with just a few mega-carriers, decry withering of competition as country is parceled into 'fortress hubs'

After two grueling weeks of congressional grilling about the largest proposed airline merger in U.S. history, James Goodwin looked like a man eager to get on a plane and get out of town.

The chairman and CEO of United Airlines, Goodwin had just faced a roomful of skeptical lawmakers during a House Judiciary Committee hearing — his fourth public browbeating in two weeks. Beside him at the witness table were his partners in the merger: U.S. Airways Chairman Stephen Wolf and Robert Johnson, chairman and CEO of D.C. Air, a new airline that would begin operations as the child of the union.

Lawmakers at the June 23 hearing peppered the businessmen with tough questions about details of the $11.6 billion deal, announced just one month before: How could it be anything but disastrous for consumers? Would other major airlines have to merge to compete? Would D.C. Air become a true low-fare carrier or just a high-cost United subcontractor?

Even Committee Chairman Henry J. Hyde of Illinois, a conservative Republican whose district includes United's home base at O'Hare International Airport, spoke about collusion and monopolistic behavior.

"I can't understand why the country seems to be geographically divided up [by the airlines]," Hyde said. "Everybody's got their backyard. They dominate and others stay out."

The executives countered that the bigger United got, the better it could serve its customers. "If fear of consolidation stops this merger, it will stop the creation of the first truly national airline," Goodwin said. "It will stop more than 90 new flights."

Goodwin, Wolf and Johnson must have felt relieved that Congress does not have to vote on their merger. Rep. Ray LaHood, R-Ill., who could not be construed as a crusading trust-buster,

Goodwin, chairman of United Airlines; Johnson, chairman of D.C. Air; and Wolf, chairman of U.S. Airways testify at the House Transportation Committee.

said the House would reject it if it could.

But they and other airline executives might want to worry about broader legislative issues ahead.

Congress thought it had finished with aviation issues for some time in March, when it completed two years of painstaking work on a Federal Aviation Administration (FAA) reauthorization (HR 1000 — PL 106-181) that was supposed to address one of the driving causes of declining airline service: lack of direct competition among major airlines. (2000 CQ Weekly, p. 595)

A growing number of lawmakers now say, reluctantly, that rapid consolidation of the industry may leave them with no choice but to reopen the debate and, eventually, to impose tougher restrictions on airlines. The industry was deregulated in 1978 (PL 95-504) under the leadership of President Jimmy Carter, part of an effort to stimulate the economy by cutting government red tape. (History, p. 80; 1978 CQ Almanac, p. 496)

"One of the concerns is that this merger would undo all of the good work we did in AIR-21," said John E. Sween-

ey, R-N.Y., using congressional shorthand for the FAA law. "Nobody wants to talk about the nasty R-word, but the reality is it may have to happen," Sweeney said, referring to re-regulation.

The merger of the largest and sixth-largest U.S. carriers would create a behemoth nearly twice as big as its nearest U.S. rival, American Airlines. In the weeks following the United-U.S. Airways announcement, all the major airlines were engaged in intense merger discussions. Industry experts say that in order to compete, American will look to merge with another competitor, perhaps Northwest. Delta and Continental have had their own discussions. TWA has been talking to low-cost Air-Tran.

In a very short time, the country could be down to three mega-airlines, experts said. Very few on Capitol Hill are ready to bless that kind of result.

House Transportation and Infrastructure ranking Democrat James L. Oberstar of Minnesota, one of a handful of remaining House members who voted to deregulate the airlines in 1978, summed up the thoughts of many at a June 13 meeting of his committee.

The merger "could do more to determine the future of the airline industry than anything that has happened in the 22 years since deregulation," Oberstar said. "In short, the pending merger places at risk the consumer benefits of airline deregulation."

Slow Congress, Fast Economy

The debate shows how difficult it is for a slow-moving, deliberate Congress to keep pace with a fast-moving industry.

The new aviation law passed only after wrangling on several contentious issues, such as whether cities are entitled to federal funding for their airports and how many flights should be squeezed into busy hubs. Even supporters felt the bill did too little on some issues, like modernizing the nation's strained air-traffic control system.

The law aimed at lowering the barriers for entry for new airlines, mostly through a construction boom that should lead to bigger airports and new gates and by phasing out "slot" restrictions at Chicago's O'Hare International and New York's John F. Kennedy and LaGuardia airports.

The FAA law authorized a more than 60 percent increase for the Airport Improvement Program in fiscal 2001 and protected that funding level with special parliamentary points of order. Appropriators provided $3.2 billion in versions of the Transportation appropriations bill (HR 4475) passed by the House and Senate. It also contained grants to make service to small communities more attractive to airlines. But the bill was designed for a country with seven big airlines, not three.

Oberstar said in an interview that consolidation would result in regional private-sector monopolies without government controls. He would be ready to look at re-regulation. "They're not going to compete with each other. They won't go head to head," Oberstar said. "With only three carriers, we'd have to treat them as a utility."

Deregulation = Consolidation?

Oberstar and other lawmakers are especially wary of the airlines' plans in light of what has happened to other deregulated industries. "More and more in this country we have less and less," said Sen. John B. Breaux, D-La.

Freight railroads have become so consolidated after a wave of mergers that the Surface Transportation Board imposed a 15-month moratorium on any new deals. Shipping has undergone a similar wave.

"I predict in a few years mergers and consolidations will be a burning issue in American politics," said Sen. Paul Wellstone, D-Minn. "Somebody eventually has to say somewhere, somehow, enough is enough."

Even before the United-U.S. Airways merger announcement, airlines were not among the most popular industries on Capitol Hill.

Consumers are frustrated by confusing and often expensive fares. Leisure passengers say it is hard to know if they are being quoted the lowest price. Business travelers who must fly on short notice can be forced to pay thousands of dollars for seats that cost others a few hundred.

Complaints about deteriorating service are on the rise, more than doubling in the past year according to the Transportation Department. Airports and airplanes are crowded. Flight delays are on the rise, even after record numbers of delays last summer.

Congress may act in several areas to address the concerns. The most immediate is customer service, an issue where lawmakers, among the nation's most frequent fliers, have firsthand experience.

Last year, Congress backed off several bills that would have enshrined in law passenger "rights" such as being quoted the lowest available fare and larger awards for lost baggage. Instead, lawmakers opted to give the industry a chance to make voluntary changes.

The voluntary plans are still being implemented, but many of the lawmakers who negotiated the deal worry that changes are not coming fast enough.

A June 28 report by Department of Transportation Inspector General Kenneth M. Mead gave the airlines mixed results on implementing an industry-wide "customer service commitment."

Mead said airlines are making a greater effort to communicate with customers about delays and cancellations, but frequently give erroneous information. Their pledge to locate lost baggage within 24 hours is suffering be-

A U.S. Airways plane taxis past a United Airlines aircraft at Ronald Reagan Washington National Airport. Lawmakers fear a proposed merger of carriers would stifle competition.

cause some airlines do not start the clock until a lost bag arrives at the destination airport. Mead acknowledged progress on airlines' pledge to hold customer reservations free for 24 hours or cancel a paid reservation without a penalty for up to 24 hours.

He was quick to point out that some problems that most vex consumers — such as weather-related flight delays — are often not the fault of airlines. Federal funding has failed to keep pace with needs, especially in terms of airport expansion and air-traffic control. The FAA employs about the same number of air traffic controllers today as in 1981, even though traffic has nearly doubled in that span, to about 650 million passengers a year.

Most Senate Commerce Committee members at a June 28 hearing urged the airlines to step up their efforts.

Lawmakers Over the Years Chip Away At Transportation Regulation

Soon after his election in 1976, President Jimmy Carter promised to "free the American people from the burden of overregulation" by looking "industry by industry" for harmful effects of stifled competition. The first sector of the economy singled out for deregulation was the airline industry, which had operated under federal economic and safety restrictions since its earliest days.

1926 — The Air Commerce Act of 1926 was the central legislation in the history of airline regulation. The law gave the Department of Commerce the authority to regulate air commerce, air traffic and air safety.

1938 — The Civil Aeronautics Act transferred regulation of the nation's airways to an independent agency, the Civil Aeronautics Authority. It also gave the new agency power to regulate airline fares and set the routes that airline carriers could serve.

1940 — Regulatory authority was split between two agencies — the Civil Aeronautics Administration and the Civil Aeronautics Board. The CAA regulated air traffic and air safety enforcement. Responsibility for setting safety rules, investigating accidents and regulating economics went to the CAB.

1958 — The Federal Aviation Agency was created. Safety rule-making and the other responsibilities of the CAA were transferred to the new agency, which was renamed the Federal Aviation Administration in 1967.

1961 — The Federal Maritime Commission was established to regulate overseas shipping. It replaced the depression-era Federal Maritime Board and investigated the practices of ocean carriers and freight operators. *(1961 almanac p. 365)*

1967 — Oversight of the two regulatory agencies was transferred to the new Department of Transportation and accident investigation was transferred to the National Transportation Safety Board.

1976 — The Railroad Revitalization and Regulatory Reform Act (PL 94-210) created the Consolidated Rail Corporation (Conrail). *(1976 Almanac, p. 637)*

1977 — Consumer advocates, with support from members of Congress, argued that regulation of the airline industry elevated fares and harmed consumers. Deregulation was opposed by representatives of the airline industry and airline employees' unions. Congress began hearings on the issue. *(1977 Almanac, p. 554)*

1978 — Carter signed the Airline Deregulation Act (PL 95-504) on Oct. 24. The law instructed the CAB, the agency that regulated airline service, routes and fares, to stress competition in its regulatory decisions, preserve service to small communities and prevent anti-competitive airline practices. It created an automatic market entry program that allowed airlines to enter into their competitors' markets and an essential air service program that was supposed to protect small routes. It also required the CAB to be shut down by Jan. 1, 1985. *(1978 Almanac, p. 496)*

1980 — Congress deregulated the trucking industry (PL 96-296) in the last days of Carter's presidency. *(1980 Almanac, p. 242)*

Congress also deregulated rail service (PL 96-448). The law, known as the Staggers Act, removed antitrust immunity for discussions and votes on rates. It allowed railroads to change rates without government interference. *(1980 Almanac, p. 248)*.

1984 — The CAB's consumer protection powers were transferred to the Department of Transportation. Legislation gave the department power to approve consolidations, mergers and antitrust exemptions, to police anti-competitive practices in the airline industry and to issue rules on smoking on flights, baggage damage and the bumping of passengers. *(1984 Almanac, p. 281)*

In the Shipping Act of 1984 (PL 98-237) Congress extended the antitrust immunity of ocean liner companies that join cartels that fix prices or otherwise limit competition. The immunity dated from 1916.

1990 — Congress cleared legislation that would have forced President George Bush to set up an emergency panel to recommend a settlement to the Eastern Airlines strike. Bush vetoed the measure and the House voted to sustain the veto.

In 1989, five days after its employees went on strike, Eastern Airlines filed for Chapter 11 bankruptcy. Critics of Eastern Airlines charged that the bankruptcy declaration was a ploy to bust the unions. House Democrats argued that Eastern's demise would spur concentration in the airline industry, lead to higher fares and dampen incentives for airlines to offer high-quality service. *(CQ Weekly, March 18, 1989 and 1990 Almanac, p 369)*

1998 — On the 20th anniversary of airline deregulation, Transportation Secretary Rodney Slater called it "an overwhelming success." Former CAB head Alfred E. Kahn, a leading advocate of deregulation, criticized predatory pricing among airlines. Richard Branson, chairman of Virgin Group Ltd., sought a relaxation of a requirement that U.S. citizens hold at least 75 percent of the voting stock in a domestic airline.

"If the airlines' voluntary effort falls short, I am committed to moving forward on additional, enforceable passenger fairness legislation," said committee Chairman John McCain, R-Ariz.

Some senators went further, excoriating airline executives for not letting consumers who contact the companies by telephone know that lower fares were available over the Internet.

Ron Wyden, D-Ore., said he grudgingly went along with the airlines' voluntary plans last year. Now he thinks the airlines have blown their chance.

"This illustrates the consumer is part of a shell game," Wyden said. "It shows the airlines are not committed even to their limited plans."

Hub and Spoke

Another area of criticism and possible action is the hub-and-spoke system that has developed since deregulation. Few cities serve as the hub for more than one airline, which in effect carves up the country into little monopolies.

"We have this system of fortress hubs whereby seven airlines have carved up the nation's aviation market like apple pie," said Sen. Peter G. Fitzgerald, R-Ill., as a witness before House Judiciary on June 14.

"The question we need to ask is, when the airlines talk about the friendly skies, are they talking about being friendly to each other or being friendly to consumers? Have the friendly skies become a little too cozy as far as competition is concerned?" he said.

In "fortress hubs" such as Pittsburgh, Cincinnati and Charlotte, N.C., the dominant airline carries about 90 percent of passengers; in Minneapolis, Memphis, Atlanta, Detroit and Houston, the figure is about 80 percent. Three other airports meet the Transportation Department's 70 percent standard for monopoly status.

Fares to and from such hubs average 20 to 40 percent higher than comparable cities where airlines compete. At the same time, many cities work to make their airports attractive enough to become a hub, because area businesses and travelers then enjoy a huge number of direct flights. Airlines often bargain for and get a say in airport governance, which can mean a veto over expansion or redistribution of gates to competitors.

Meanwhile, residents of small and midsize "spoke" cities often find themselves with the choice of a single airline, with monopoly prices, or a long drive to another airport. Lawmakers representing such areas, such as Republican Sens. Susan Collins and Olympia J. Snowe of Maine and Rep. Louise M. Slaughter, D-N.Y., have become outspoken airline critics.

Sen. Ernest F. Hollings, D-S.C., a supporter of the 1978 deregulation, has had second thoughts as service to Charleston has withered in the intervening years. Hollings told Wolf he had a problem with his explanation that U.S. Airways needed to merge, because the only way to survive was to become bigger. He warned that such a move would only make Charleston's bad situation worse.

"You're saying the only way to get more competitive is to get more monopolistic," Hollings said.

In an interview a few days later, Hollings said he routinely pays $700 for a round trip to Washington, with U.S. Airways as his only option. In 1978, four airlines flew the route. "By next year we're going to look at some kind of control of these hubs," Hollings said.

Big airlines have also been accused of using their economic resources to crush low-cost competitors. Upstarts often are faced with an established carrier slashing its fares and increasing service, losing money to keep market share, until the upstart is forced out of business. When market share is re-established, the dominant airline usually raises fares to a level higher than they were before the competition began, according to consumer groups.

That is what happened in Minneapolis when low-fare carriers Republic and later Sun Country tried to compete head-on with Northwest. It happened at Washington's Dulles International Airport, when United crushed an attempt by U.S. Airways to expand its service there in early 1999.

A Jan. 6, 1999, letter that U.S. Airways sent to Transportation Secretary Rodney Slater outlined its concerns about United's action. Chairman Wolf wrote that United had increased its service by 60 percent as U.S. Airways was expanding.

"The unrelenting attempts of the major trunk carriers to undermine the operations and expansion of smaller carriers," Wolf wrote, "is a clear and present danger to free market competition."

"Most successful, recent new entrant carriers acknowledge that they will not enter the majors' hub markets because they cannot survive in a head-to-head battle," said McCain at a June 21 hearing. "Additional consolidation would only make it worse."

Whither the Merger

United and U.S. Airways tried to make the case on Capitol Hill that they are uniquely compatible. United is strong mostly on East-West routes, with hubs in Washington, Chicago, Los Angeles, Denver and San Francisco. U.S. Airways is concentrated in the East, with North-South routes.

The combination will create the first truly national air carrier, Goodwin and Wolf said, giving consumers the benefit of new, seamless connections.

Without the merger, Wolf said, U.S. Airways would have a hard time getting out from under its high cost structure. Its costs, the highest in the industry, are a result of several previous mergers and labor agreements, he said.

To allay fears of federal regulators, the airlines proposed creating D.C. Air. The new airline would compete, from Ronald Reagan Washington National Airport, with United's Dulles operation.

Without the new airline, the expanded United would control 62 percent of flights at Dulles, 39 percent at National and 35 percent at Baltimore-Washington International Airport.

D.C. Air President Johnson, who is also chief executive of the $2.5 billion Black Entertainment Network, labored to assure lawmakers that D.C. Air would become a vigorous competitor. Most were skeptical, noting that the newcomer would begin operation by leasing equipment and employees from high-cost U.S. Airways.

The Justice Department must review the proposed deal for compliance with antitrust law, a process expected to take several months. If the department finds that the merger would reduce competition, it can file suit to block it. It can also approve the plan subject to modifications. The Transportation Department helps Justice analyze the competitive effect on specific routes.

"Any transaction of this size that touches so many people in an industry that means so much to them is going to generate a lot of interest," said United's Goodwin as he prepared to leave Washington. "They [lawmakers] want to learn about this transaction. We're working hard . . . to provide the kind of information they need to make a value judgment." ◆

Bill would require manufacturers to provide more extensive data on defects

Hill Clears Auto Safety Measure With Some Concessions to Industry

Quick Contents

Barely a month after its first hearing on the Firestone tire recall, Congress cleared legislation that would require the auto industry to give the government more data on possible product defects. The bill also would require government rollover tests of new cars and light trucks.

Congress sent landmark auto safety legislation to President Clinton on Oct. 11, having overcome strong objections from business groups. The bill would require the auto industry to share with the government a broad range of data on possible defects in their products. Those who hide information or mislead regulators could get 15 years in prison.

The Senate cleared the bill (HR 5164) Oct. 11 after the House passed it early the same day, both by voice vote. The Senate had been considering similar legislation (S 3059). Clinton is expected to sign the bill.

The legislation, a direct response to this summer's recall of 6.5 million Firestone tires, promises to alter the political landscape for the auto industry in Washington. After years of blocking increases in fuel economy standards, more stringent air bag tests and public disclosure of the risk that vehicles might roll over, the industry now will be more closely monitored by the National Highway Traffic Safety Administration (NHTSA) and a coalition of consumer groups energized by the Firestone case.

During a flurry of hearings in the weeks following the August recess, lawmakers heard repeated testimony that Bridgestone/Fire-

CQ Weekly Oct. 14, 2000

stone Inc. and Ford Motor Co. had extensive knowledge of tread separation on Firestone's ATX and Wilderness AT tires causing Ford Explorer sport utility vehicles to spin out of control. Federal investigators are looking into 101 deaths and more than 400 injuries linked to the tires. Almost all of the accidents occurred on the Explorer, the country's best-selling SUV.

Final passage of the auto safety bill came barely one month after the first hearings on the tire issue.

"The last time there was such a massive tire recall was in the '70s, and Congress did nothing to fix the problem," said Fred Upton, R-Mich., sponsor of the House bill. "As a result, our tire standards haven't been updated in some 30 years. Tonight we changed that trend."

Many of those involved in highway safety issues hailed the bill as much more than the minimum Congress could have done after hearings exposed gaping holes in the system for reporting auto safety problems.

Instead of settling on a simple bill to close one or two loopholes, Upton and W.J. "Billy" Tauzin, R-La., wrote a comprehensive measure that will result in broad new data collection efforts and fines of up to $15 million and possible prison terms for those who try to evade the requirements.

Rating Risks

The bill also broke a logjam on other contentious auto safety issues. For instance, it would require new tests to determine the propensity of cars and light trucks to roll over. Rollover accidents account for more than 9,000 deaths annually, but efforts to create a government rollover test and ratings have been stymied for years. A much more modest government proposal on rollover tests had been blocked most of this year on the fiscal 2001 transportation appropriations bill (HR 4475) until conferees removed the provision the week of Oct. 2. (*2000 CQ Weekly, p. 2345*)

The auto safety bill would also update a 30-year-old safety standard for tires, requiring a low-tire-pressure warning system for new cars, and launch a program that aims to improve children's car seats.

"This is some of the best work we have

Bridgestone/Firestone Chairman and CEO Masatoshi Ono, here testifying before the Senate Commerce Committee Sept. 12, announced his retirement Oct. 10.

ever seen Congress do," said David Snyder of the American Insurance Association. "It usually takes years to get these things done."

Before the measure cleared, it was in danger of falling victim to complex Senate procedures. Commerce Committee Chairman John McCain, R-Ariz., was blocked several times in trying to bring up his own auto safety bill (S 3059) and the House bill with amendments. In most cases, a fellow senator exercised an anonymous "hold" on the legislation.

The delay made McCain apoplectic. But his scoldings on the Senate floor did little to sway opponents of his bill, which contained stiffer criminal penalties than the House measure and was strongly opposed by the auto industry and business groups.

"I will tell you, in straight talk, what this is all about," McCain said. "Trial lawyers do not want it because . . . they want to be able to sue anybody for anything under any circumstances. And the automotive industry wants this thing killed, figuring that the publicity surrounding these accidents and these tragedies that are taking place will die out and they will be able to kill off this legislation next year."

McCain settled for moving the House bill without any amendments. That measure had drawn support from the Alliance of Automobile Manufacturers and the U.S. Chamber of Commerce.

"The reality we face in the remaining days of Congress because of these tactics is that we pass the House bill or we pass nothing," McCain complained.

Judiciary Committee Chairman Orrin G. Hatch, R-Utah, said earlier on Oct. 11 that he was concerned about the speed with which the measure was being considered. He also said his committee should have had a hand in writing the Senate bill's criminal penalties but had not been contacted.

"These are very difficult issues," Hatch said. "We don't want to play politics. I don't think enough hearings have been held."

Unresolved Issues

When Congress returns next year, it will be looking to fine-tune the auto safety initiatives. The authorization for NHTSA is scheduled to expire, and the reauthorization bill could become a new battleground for the controversies McCain was seeking to debate. McCain's Commerce, Science and Transportation Committee will have jurisdiction over that bill.

Sen. Ernest F. Hollings, D-S.C., wants to look at whether the auto industry should have to supply the government with more information about warranty claims and warranty lawsuits, according to Hollings spokesman Andy Davis. The industry has been unwilling to take that step.

Consumer groups vowed to return to fight what they described as loopholes created by the House bill, another concern of Hollings'.

Public Citizen, an interest group founded by Green Party presidential candidate Ralph Nader, criticized concessions made to the industry on keeping vast portions of the new collected data secret. Auto companies had lobbied hard on this issue, claiming it was necessary to protect proprietary information.

Under the bill, the new data will be made public only if the Transportation secretary deems it in the public interest. Currently, NHTSA information is made public unless the secretary makes an affirmative decision to block the release, after industry states a specific objection. Consumer groups fear that the new restrictions will curtail the flow of information.

Auto lobbyists said that the relevant information will still be available under the Freedom of Information Act, but that it will not be as easy for consumer groups and others to fish for auto information.

Public Citizen had also urged lawmakers to strengthen penalty provisions and place more limitations on an escape clause, or "safe harbor," that would allow those who know of safety problems to avoid criminal penalties by coming clean and eventually reporting them.

"No one will be prosecuted under this bill," said Laura MacCleery, a lawyer with the group.

Consumer groups also will continue pushing for safety standards not included in the legislation, such as a manufacturing standard for preventing rollovers and a stronger standard for roofs to protect passengers in rollover crashes. Automakers have resisted these measures. ◆

Fast track, pacts with Jordan and Vietnam will revive labor, environment, human rights issues

After the China Bill: Fresh Start For the Trade Expansion Debate

Quick Contents

A stunning 83 senators cleared the measure to permanently make China a normal U.S. trading partner. That climaxed one of the most heavily lobbied battles of the 106th Congress, cemented Clinton's free-trade legacy and showed how bipartisan Washington can be when global economic growth is in the offing. Gore and Bush both favor more trade expansion. But plenty of issues — first among them, whether environmental and labor concerns should be a part of future trade accords — will make the next round of trade debates anything but simple.

Barshefsky, surrounded by reporters in the Capitol as the Senate cleared the China bill Sept. 19, said that Congress' growing involvement in trade may make obsolete the need to revive "fast track" procedures.

The overwhelming Senate vote to make permanent China's standing as a normal trading partner of the United States is more than a historic milestone in Sino-American relations and the finale in one of the most consequential debates of the 106th Congress. It also is a dramatic illustration of the breadth of support that trade expansion is capable of generating.

The 83-15 vote on Sept. 19 to clear the China trade legislation (HR 4444) is no guarantee, however, that the next Congress and the next president will face easy sledding when it comes to trade expansion. (*Vote 251, 2000 CQ Weekly, p. 2234*)

The questions on their collective trade plate during the next two years are wide-ranging: Whether to revive an expedited process for congressional debate of trade pacts; whether to embrace a bilateral trade deal with Vietnam reached this summer and another one about to be sealed with Jordan; what weight to give attempts to chip away at sanctions on countries unfriendly to the United States, especially Cuba and Iran; and how to tackle public concerns about international commerce, namely its effects on labor rights and environmental degradation.

Outside Congress, U.S. negotiators will continue to push trade expansion forward, by attempting to reduce trade barriers worldwide through the World Trade Organization (WTO) and trying to facilitate trade throughout the Western Hemisphere.

Debates on the benefits of most of those actions will not be as easy to sell to Congress — and the public — as the virtues of enhanced and stable trade with the world's most populous nation. The sales pitch for that bill was eased by the sheer number of cuts to tariffs, quotas and other trade barriers that the Chinese committed to make last fall in return for one change to U.S. law: ending the annual rite of the president and Congress reviewing China's behavior before granting its imports another year of low tariffs. (*Primer, p. 86*)

The bill's enactment promises that billions of dollars in economic benefits will come to American business. They will come despite continued complaints that a country with a poor labor and human rights history is not worthy of the same low-tariff treatment most other countries get. Still, the issue has received scant debate outside Washington or on the campaign trail.

Both Vice President Al Gore, the Democratic nominee, and Gov. George W. Bush of Texas, the Republican nominee, supported

CQ Weekly Sept. 23, 2000

the bill. Both also espouse the importance of continuing the expansion of trade — particularly within the Western Hemisphere — that has been one of the foreign policy hallmarks of the Clinton administration.

The candidates' similar views, and the splits trade creates in both major political parties, has forced trade expansion into the background on the campaign trail. When it does come up, it is usually in the stump speeches of the two most prominent minor party candidates — Reform nominee Pat Buchanan and Green nominee Ralph Nader. Although from the right and left edges of the American political spectrum, they share an opposition to trade expansion, contending that it is wrong to give potential boosts to corporate profits priority over national security, in Buchanan's view, or the well-being of people worldwide, in Nader's.

A similar political pattern was evident in the Senate's vote Sept. 19, in which the smaller-than-expected minority was formed by five of the more liberal Democrats, five of the most conservative Republicans, three GOP senators with pro-union leanings and two Democrats from import sensitive states in voting against the bill. (The Senate's 83 percent show of support dwarfed the 54 percent House majority that passed the bill May 24.)

Fast track authority

If either Bush or Gore is to achieve his goal of expanding trade, the path would be eased by the renewal of "fast track" trade negotiating authority, granted to each president since Gerald R. Ford but allowed to lapse at the end of 1994. The procedure allows the administration to negotiate a trade agreement without fear that Congress will amend the pact. Instead, when a president submits a bill to Congress to implement a trade agreement, Congress has 90 days to endorse it or reject it, but may not alter it.

Two years ago, the House defeated Clinton's request to revive this procedure. (*1998 CQ Almanac, p. 23-3*)

The next president will be under great pressure, particularly if Democrats control all or part of Congress, to alter the fast track procedure of the past to ensure that trade's effects on laborers' rights and environmental degradation are taken into account.

That debate could be joined on some trade agreements that will be put before

the 107th Congress, including those with Vietnam and Jordan. The pending deal with Jordan will contain language on labor and the environment, according to U.S. Trade Representative Charlene Barshefsky, and could serve as a test case for tackling such concerns overall. (*Vietnam, 2000 CQ Weekly, p. 1902*)

Bush would likely seek to revive the previous fast track terms, and would probably get his wish if Republicans retain control of Congress. If Democrats take back the House their insistence on addressing labor and environmental matters could polarize the debate anew, straining trade's longstanding tradition — so clearly echoed in the Senate vote — of being a non-partisan issue.

Gore has already said that if elected he would ensure that future trade pacts address labor rights and environmental quality. How strongly he would push would be paramount to his success in winning concessions in those areas, on which many nations say the United States has no business butting in. So his promise could bog down progress on trade expansion.

It is also not clear that Gore would seek to revive fast track. Barshefsky, in a Sept. 20 interview, said that Congress' growing involvement in trade matters may make the need for fast track obsolete.

"We need to think very carefully about whether to pursue fast track," said Barshefsky, whose views are likely to carry weight even though she is unlikely to be a part of a Gore administration. "The question has to be considered anew in a very dispassionate way and not blinded by old thinking."

Scaling the Great Wall

Those on both sides of the trade debate agree on one thing: Making permanent the U.S. trade relationship with China — and making possible billions of dollars in projected benefits for U.S. industries — was a much easier sell than a somewhat fuzzy trade procedure such as fast track will be.

As part of its effort to join the WTO later this year, China committed in November to significant cuts in tariffs and other trade barriers on U.S.-made products. The United States has similarly cut tariffs on Chinese-made products since 1980, a year after leaders in Beijing signed a trade pact with President Jimmy Carter. Since 1989, Congress has annually voted to uphold that trade status. (*1980 Almanac, p. 356*)

Big business poured millions into lobbying for a permanent trade relationship with China, and smaller organizations, such as farm groups, put grass-roots pressure on lawmakers. The high-technology industry cut its fledgling lobbying teeth on the bill.

Enactment of the bill had also been one of the few top-tier priorities for Clinton during his last year in the White House. His signature will provide the coda on a presidency that will be marked as one under which international trade was greatly expanded. He opened his first term by pushing through a hesitant Congress the North American Free Trade Agreement (PL 103-182), which had been negotiated by his predecessor, George Bush. The next year, just before his fast-track power lapsed, he pushed Congress to send him a measure (PL 103-465) to implement a new General Agreement on Tariffs and Trade, the sweeping changes to the world trade system under which the WTO was created. (*1993 Almanac, p. 171; 1994 Almanac p. 123*)

"The China debate became a debate on the overall course of the China relationship," said Myron A. Brilliant, a lobbyist for the U.S. Chamber of Commerce, which has led lobbying campaigns for trade expansion. "On trade agreements and on fast track, it centers much more on the role of labor and environmental issues."

Daniel A. Seligman, director of the Sierra Club's Responsible Trade Campaign, said that "if the debate is around a country, the issue often gets reduced to whether or not you like that particular country. Having a debate around a trade agreement or trade negotiating authority, then it's easier to conduct the debate on a level of principle."

The principles Seligman would like debated focus on preventing world trade rules from tying the hands of governments that want to set their own environmental and labor laws. Environmentalists say that in the name of creating a level playing field for businesses, the WTO has essentially overridden local regulations.

Some in Congress see the China debate as an example of how they might deal with some constituent worries about the global marketplace.

Despite months of ardent lobbying, success for the China bill was not assured until a week before the House vote, when its supporters agreed to add on creation of an executive branch-congres-

Trade With China: The Next Steps

Q: What will happen under the bill the Senate cleared Sept. 19?

A: The measure (HR 4444) would allow the president to permanently extend normal, non-discriminatory treatment to Chinese goods once China is accepted into the World Trade Organization (WTO). It would do this by permanently exempting China from the requirements of the Jackson-Vanik amendment to the 1974 Trade Act (93-618). Under that law, this normal trade relations status — known as NTR — may be extended to some countries for only one year at a time. The law was designed to punish communist nations that made it difficult for citizens to leave. (2000 CQ Weekly, p. 1164; 1974 Almanac, p. 553)

Q: How will this enhance trade between the United States and China?

A: Before permanent NTR for China may take effect, the president must certify to Congress that the terms for China's entry into the WTO are as rigorous as those agreed to under a bilateral trade agreement signed Nov. 15 by U.S. Trade Representative Charlene Barshefsky and Chinese Premier Zhu Rongji. In that deal, Beijing promised to phase out its import quotas and make steep cuts during the next four years in its tariffs on U.S.-made goods.

Q: What is the WTO, and who belongs to it?

A: The Geneva-based body governs world trade, ruling on disputes between countries and otherwise monitoring international commerce. It was created as part of the Uruguay Round of the General Agreement on Tariffs and Trade, which Congress agreed to implement through a law (PL 103-465) enacted six years ago. (1994 Almanac, p. 123) Albania became the 138th member on Sept. 8. China is among 30 other nations that are attempting to join. Another such nation is Vietnam; as with China, its push to join the WTO was enhanced when it signed a trade agreement with the United States. That pact was reached in July. (2000 CQ Weekly, p. 1902)

Q: What else must China do before it may join the WTO?

A: The world's most populous nation still must firm up negotiations with the WTO over the protocol for its membership. This will focus largely on deadlines for implementing changes in China required by WTO rules, such as moving away from state ownership of industries. Finalization of this language and of the details of trade agreements with any other WTO members will probably come either late this year or early next year.

Q: What other countries are likely to join the WTO, and how will Congress be involved?

A: Taiwan has been waiting for years to join and is expected to be allowed in the WTO shortly after China. Although China considers Taiwan a renegade province, U.S. leaders believe that will not prevent Taiwan from joining. Russia is the next major country likely to join, or accede. While officials there have recently announced their intent to speed the process of winning membership, it looks to be years away. Russia does not have permanent NTR, which means Congress would have to take a vote on Russia's trade status, such as it just has on China. But if the United States were to sign a trade agreement with Russia, which would be a likely precursor to WTO membership, Congress would have a vote on that if it changed any U.S. laws.

Q: What other nations have an irregular trade relationship with the United States?

A: Seven countries do not have any form of NTR: Afghanistan, Cuba, Laos, North Korea, Vietnam, Serbia and Montenegro. President Clinton has waived Vietnam's compliance with Jackson-Vanik, but the country still needs its trade pact approved by Congress to be eligible for normal trade status. Thirteen other nations have NTR conditionally, so long as they allow free emigration. Clinton has certified every six months that Russia and 10 other former states of the Soviet Union — Armenia, Azerbaijan, Georgia, Kazakhstan, Kyrgyzstan, Moldova, Russia, Tajikistan, Turkmenistan, Ukraine and Uzbekistan — along with Albania are complying fully with Jackson-Vanik. He has granted a waiver of Jackson-Vanik requirements to the former Soviet republic of Belarus.

sional commission to review China's record on labor and human rights, the environment and other issues. Any legislation it recommended would receive expedited consideration in Congress. (Provisions, 2000 CQ Weekly, p. 1246)

"If fast track did take into consideration those issues on the same basis the China trade bill does, it would be a worthy compromise," Charles E. Grassley, R-Iowa, chairman of the Senate Finance International Trade Subcommittee, told reporters Sept. 19.

"In my judgment, there's no choice but to tackle these issues; they won't go away," said Rep. Sander M. Levin, D-Mich., a sponsor of the additional language, which has been derided by unions and other opponents of the China bill as no more than a "fig leaf" to cover Congress' failure to take steps guaranteeing that the Chinese will see their lives improved along with expanded trade.

Some pro-trade Democrats such as Rep. Robert T. Matsui of California, who led the administration's campaign for passage of the China bill, say it will be necessary in future deals to take such steps. Without them, said Rep. Sherrod Brown, D-Ohio, a leading opponent of recent trade expansion legislation, fast track will remain a dead letter. "If Bill Clinton couldn't do it . . . no president will be able to do it," he said in an interview Sept. 19.

PAC Man Bites Back

The PAC man giveth, and giveth again. The PAC man may also taketh away.

Advocates on both sides said election year pressures — and the influence of campaign contributions — shaped the debate about whether to create permanent normal trade relations with China. Current Federal Election Commission records do not reflect recent gifts to senators, who cleared the bill (HR 4444) Sept. 19. But reports of House members, who passed the bill May 24, give some indication about the role of campaign cash in the debate.

Promoters of China trade pressed the Senate not to alter the bill and thereby force its return to the House because, they feared, leverage from unions might turn some "yes" votes of spring into "no" votes closer to Election Day. Evidence of such leverage was provided by Martin Frost of Texas, among the last House Democrats to end his public indecision. After he cast his "yes" vote, he said in an interview Sept. 20, he received a call from the International Association of Machinists and Aerospace Workers asking for the return of a $5,000 political action committee donation delivered seven weeks before. "It's their right to ask for it back," said Frost, who returned the money.

But the use of corporate money to reward and punish waverers may have been just as strong. David L. Hobson of Ohio, among the last of the undeclared Republicans, received $500 on March 28 from Boeing Co., one of the biggest business promoters of the China deal. Two weeks after Hobson cast his "yes" vote, the aircraft giant's PAC sent him another $1,000. Frost received $1,000 from Boeing on Feb. 25 and another $1,000 on June 20.

Boeing was not so generous to members who voted against it. Several lawmakers who were late in leaving the undecided camp — Robert B. Aderholt, R-Ala.; John Baldacci, D-Maine; Karen McCarthy, D-Mo.; James L. Oberstar, D-Minn.; and Ed Pastor, D-Ariz. — all received PAC checks in the spring; none received anything more after they voted against the bill.

Some of the most pro-trade members in both parties, however, see such steps as unnecessary. Congress would "build the support we need for fast track," Sen. Phil Gramm, R-Texas, said in an interview Sept. 19, if there was "a president that we trust." Former Rep. David K. McCurdy, D-Okla., (1981-95), president of the pro-trade Electronics Industries Alliance, said, "There's no reason to qualify it [fast track] right now."

The Long Term

For the loose coalition of environmental, labor, religious, consumer and other groups that lost the hard-fought battle over China trade, the last year has still presented some bright spots. They pressed their cause to the forefront of national awareness with their protests at the WTO session in Seattle last year, and they see the lingering attention as offering hope for future success. (*1999 CQ Weekly, p. 2924*)

While she termed the China loss "a pretty big blow," Thea Lee, the AFL-CIO's assistant director of public policy, said that "there's a long-term struggle that we have made progress on."

Seligman was less circumspect. "I think Seattle knocked Humpty Dumpty off the wall in a way that the victory on China will not be able to put him back together," he said.

While some believe the China vote showed that the anti-globalization forces are not as strong as thought, it is increasingly unlikely that Seligman's group and others will be shut out of the arenas in which trade policy is made.

Much of their focus in coming years will not be on Congress. A dialogue with the nations of Latin America, initiated in the Reagan and Bush administrations and known as the Free Trade Area of the Americas, is considered a prime spot to address trade's affects on environment and culture. The talks have a 2005 deadline, although Barshefsky said a new president could speed their conclusion. While Congress would not have a vote on the process until a trade agreement was completed, members have provided input to U.S. negotiators and are expected to be consulted more often as the process zeroes in on controversial issues.

This proposal would essentially extend NAFTA throughout the Western Hemisphere, but the next president may aim to give some nations a head start. For instance, GOP nominee Bush's father promised to work for Chile's inclusion in 1992. (The Clinton administration has done little to advance that proposal.) In addition, some Republicans, such as Gramm, want to see Great Britain admitted to NAFTA. And members will also push for a one-year exemption from some textile quotas for Colombia, Ecuador, Peru and Bolivia, if that proposal does not find its way into an end-of-the-session bill this year. (*2000 CQ Weekly, p. 2089*)

Separate negotiations will also probably be ongoing within the WTO on a new round of talks to reduce trade barriers across a spectrum of industries.

Although the Seattle meeting failed to launch a new round as had been anticipated, some observers believe the election of a new U.S. president may jump start world-wide trade talks. Such discussions usually take three to five years to be completed.

Because Clinton, as a lame duck, could not see through any negotiations he launched, his status has been an obstacle to beginning new trade projects. Many in Congress look forward to returning to full strength next year.

"It may be on the back burner in the campaign — all foreign policy issues seem to be — but it will very much be on the front burner" in 2001, Levin said. ◆

U.S. decision will affect not only Russia and China but also actions of aspiring nuclear powers

The International Fallout Of an Anti-Missile System

CQ PHOTO / EMILY BARNES

Quick Contents

The United States soon may have missiles able to knock down at least a few incoming nuclear warheads. The question that will face the next president and Congress is whether such a system should be deployed. Supporters say it is long overdue and could help stabilize the world. Opponents say it will touch off a new nuclear arms race. Russia is adamantly against the system and China is preparing to increase its nuclear arms production in response.

Cohen, right, told members of the Senate Armed Services Committee on July 25: "This is an ambitious program, but I do not believe it's excessively so." Later he delayed a recommendation to the president.

If the United States builds a national anti-missile defense system, would it protect the country and help stabilize international relations, or would it lead to a worldwide nuclear arms race and a greater threat of war? That is the central defense and foreign policy question of the presidential campaign and a key decision for the next chief executive and Congress.

The Clinton administration, which only reluctantly adopted the idea of building a limited missile defense system, is leaving the crucial decisions for Clinton's successor.

Defense Secretary William S. Cohen is putting off until September his recommendation to President Clinton on whether a missile defense system is feasible and affordable enough to warrant preliminary construction of a radar site in the Aleutians. Development problems could delay the 2005 target date for fielding a system. (*Story, p. 89*)

Most attention has focused on the technology of knocking down incoming ballistic missiles, which is far from proven even after almost 20 years and an estimated $60 billion in research and experimentation.

The most vital assessment that the next president and Congress must make, however, deals more with geopolitics than with missile guidance.

"This is a very heavy-lifting diplomatic project as well as a technical project, and not nearly enough of that has been done," said Richard G. Lugar, R-Ind., a senior member of the Senate Foreign Relations Committee.

Pro and Con

Opponents of missile defense, in Washington and abroad, argue that such a system would undermine the policy of mutual deterrence — embodied in the 1972 Anti-Ballistic Missile (ABM) Treaty — that helped the world survive the Cold War face-off between the United States and the Soviet Union without a single nuclear weapon being fired.

Building a missile defense system, they say, would encourage current and future nuclear powers to build as many offensive weapons as possible to overcome or evade any U.S. defenses.

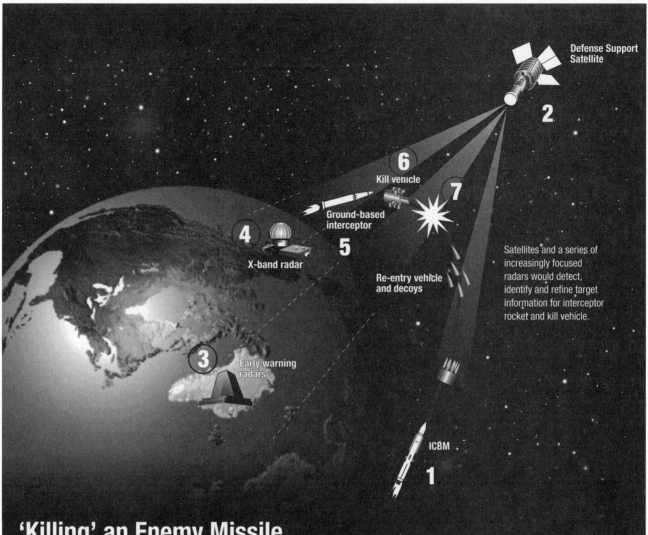

Defense Support Satellite **2**

6 Kill vehicle

7

Ground-based interceptor

4 **5**

X-band radar

Re-entry vehicle and decoys

Satellites and a series of increasingly focused radars would detect, identify and refine target information for interceptor rocket and kill vehicle.

3 Early warning radars

ICBM **1**

'Killing' an Enemy Missile

The U.S. anti-missile defense system is designed to block a very limited attack. After an intercontinental ballistic missile (ICBM) **(1)** is fired from another country, a defense support satellite **(2)** estimates the impact point and alerts military headquarters. Early warning radar sites **(3)** and X-band radar **(4)** provide an increasingly sophisticated picture of the incoming warheads and any decoys and help guide the high-speed interceptor missile **(5)** that already has been launched. Multiple sensors in the kill vehicle **(6)** take over for the intercept **(7)**.

■ **1946-69**
The United States and the Soviet Union developed and deployed limited anti-missile systems using explosive warheads. The U.S. weapons were dismantled in 1969; the Soviets kept theirs to defend Moscow.

■ **1972**
The United States and the Soviet Union signed the Anti-Ballistic Missile (ABM) Treaty restricting each nation to two sites of 100 interceptors, later cut to one site.

■ **1983-84**
President Ronald Reagan launched a Strategic Defense Initiative (SDI) to explore land-based and space-based missile de-fense systems. Critics dubbed the program "Star Wars."

■ **1987**
U.S. scientists began work on "Brilliant Pebbles," a plan to sow thousands of miniature satellite/interceptors in Earth orbit to be activated in case of attack. The program was later absorbed into broader research.

■ **1991**
President George Bush changed the focus of SDI to defense against limited missile attacks, such as a mistaken launch.

■ **1993**
The Clinton administration puts more em-phasis on military theater missile defense than national missile defense.

■ **1998**
A special commission reports that North Korea, Iran and Iraq could have a missile that would threaten the U.S. mainland within five years, sooner than expected. North Korea tests a medium-range missile over the Pacific.

■ **1999**
Congress passed and President Clinton signed legislation (PL 106-38) declaring U.S. policy to deploy a national anti-missile defense system as soon as technologically feasible.

A classified U.S. intelligence report disclosed Aug. 9 predicts that China would accelerate its nuclear weapons buildup if the United States deploys a national missile defense system. That could, in turn, speed up the nuclear arms race between India and Pakistan and solidify cooperation between potential U.S. foes who fear the new system.

Both Russia and China have strongly opposed even the most limited U.S. defense system as a potential threat to their own security. "The main international problem today," Russian President Vladimir V. Putin said July 25, "is the plan to destroy the strategic balance in the world."

Some U.S. lawmakers, such as Joseph R. Biden Jr. of Delaware, ranking Democrat on the Senate Foreign Relations Committee, are disheartened by what they see as a fortress mentality among missile defense advocates.

"A decade ago, even conservatives saw hope for a world in transformation, a world transformed," Biden said at a national defense symposium in June. "Now that vision has been discarded, and their hope is put instead in better weapons.

"I think we still have an opportunity to build a more stable world," Biden said. "But . . . I fear that acting upon our worst fears will only make those fears come true."

Those who want to build a missile defense system contend that the end of the Cold War already has eroded the value of mutual deterrence between the United States and Russia. Weapons and technology, they say, are spreading to North Korea, Iran, Iraq and Libya and could go farther.

As Peter Huessy, a senior associate at the National Defense University Foundation, put it, "The very things that arms controllers warn us about that will happen if the United States, God forbid, protects itself with a missile defense, are already happening."

In that environment, supporters of missile defense say, the United States and its allies could be blackmailed by just the threat of a nuclear attack.

Senate Armed Services Committee Chairman John W. Warner, R-Va., said that U.S. defense strategy must shed "outdated arguments, including the argument that strategic defenses are inconsistent with strategic stability, nuclear deterrence and arms control.

"Such arguments make sense only if one believes that we should perpetuate mutually assured destruction as the basis of our strategic policy," Warner said at a July 25 hearing. "I think mutual assured destruction must be replaced by a more pragmatic and realistic policy."

It was the long-standing conservative distrust of mutually assured destruction and the ABM Treaty that led President Ronald Reagan to propose his strategic defense initiative in 1983.

The ambitious plan for space-based battle stations, which critics ridiculed as "Star Wars," never got off the drawing board. Subsequent Republican efforts to make missile defense a political

Air Force Lt. Gen. Ronald T. Kadish, director of the Ballistic Missile Defense Organization, testifies before the House Armed Services subcommittee on military research June 22.

issue met with public indifference. Clinton promised only to continue developing a defense system that one day might be deployed.

Emerging Threats

Two events in 1998 changed the calculus. A panel of experts led by former Defense Secretary Donald H. Rumsfeld warned that North Korea and Iran could have missiles within five years capable of reaching the U.S. mainland. And North Korea tested a medium-range missile far over the Pacific. (*1998 CQ Almanac p. 8-17*)

The following year, Congress passed and Clinton signed legislation (PL 106-38) declaring it U.S. policy to deploy a national missile defense system as soon as technologically feasible.

Yet Clinton worried about the international consequences of the law. His administration had opposed deployment and had not tried to persuade

skeptical allies and potential adversaries it was necessary.

At Clinton's insistence, Congress added a provision to the law that any deployment decision must take into account the system's cost and impact on U.S. foreign relations.

Clinton's strategy has been to develop a system to protect the United States from a small number of missiles that might be fired by mistake or by a "rogue" state, but that would not be effective against a massive Russian attack. At the same time, he wanted to negotiate with Russia for changes in the ABM Treaty that would allow either country to have such a small-scale defense.

Vice President Al Gore, campaigning to succeed Clinton, has supported the same approach.

Texas Gov. George W. Bush, the Republican presidential nominee, argues that Clinton's approach hamstrings the ability of the United States to build a truly effective missile defense system.

Condoleeza Rice, Bush's senior foreign policy adviser, questions the value of amending the ABM Treaty.

"This is a treaty that was intended to keep you away from national missile defense," she said in a recent interview. "It's going to be hard to get you out of the box."

Neither Republicans in Congress nor Russian leaders in Moscow have been interested in negotiating with Clinton in the twilight of his adminis-

tration. (*2000 CQ Weekly, p. 999*)

Despite Clinton's assurances, Russian officials argue that the basic components of any limited U.S. missile defense system easily could be upgraded to defend against a full-scale attack.

The U.S. plan provokes a visceral reaction among many Russians, said Anthony H. Cordesman, senior fellow for strategic assessment at the Center for Strategic and International Studies.

"At a minimum," Cordesman wrote in a recent paper, "U.S. deployment of a [national missile defense] system threatens Russian prestige. At a maximum, it threatens Russia with American hegemony at a time Russia feels that U.S. and Western intervention in Kosovo has shown that it cannot trust its partnership with the West."

Russian officials also worry that although on paper they have a nuclear arsenal that could overwhelm any defense, many of those weapons are aging, and Moscow does not have the money to replace them. According to Russian defense officials, the factory warranty has expired on nearly three-quarters of their nuclear inventory.

At a June summit with Clinton, Putin acknowledged that the two countries could be threatened by the proliferation of weapons of mass destruction, but he resisted calls for altering the ABM Treaty. Russian officials have generally downplayed the risks of proliferation and said they are better addressed through diplomacy and deterrence than missile defense.

"We propose creation of a political umbrella by joint efforts on the political front among the United States, Russia, and other nations to fend off missile threats," Russian Defense Minister Igor Sergeyev said in June. Such agreements, he said, would be based on joint threat assessments and include "mutual agreements and mutual obligations under tight control."

Moscow Moves

Putin, in his first year in office, also has tried to raise the diplomatic cost to Clinton of deploying a missile defense and to offer U.S. allies a credible alternative to missile defense.

The U.S. push for a defense system comes as Putin is being forced to choose between a proposal by his top leaders to downplay the role of land-based nuclear missiles in favor of conventional forces and an effort by Sergeyev to maintain the status quo.

A Slipping Timetable

Even if technology and diplomacy cooperate, it could be six years and likely longer before the United States could field a system for shooting down any ballistic missiles.

The Defense Department had theorized about deploying a national missile defense in 2003, then last year pushed the target date back to 2005, at an estimated additional cost of $20.3 billion through 2007. Even then, some experts warned that the timetable was too risky.

The Pentagon now has acknowledged that the deployment date could slip by as much as two years.

Accumulating delays, problems with developing a faster booster rocket and glitches from a failed test on July 8 using an older booster have put the 2005 date into doubt, Pentagon spokesman Kenneth H. Bacon said Aug. 8.

The date is the basis for a detailed schedule of decisions great and small that could eventually commit the country to a missile defense system.

Defense Secretary William S. Cohen, on the basis of a "deployment readiness review," was supposed to send President Clinton a recommendation this month on whether the system is technologically feasible and affordable.

On that basis, Clinton was supposed to decide this fall whether to begin the groundwork next spring for a radar station on the remote Aleutian island of Shemya, where fog and rain limit construction to a few months a year.

Clinton already had delayed his decision from summer to fall. Since Cohen has now put off his recommendation until September, Clinton's decision could come in the winter, if at all.

"A number of difficult issues remain to be resolved," Cohen said in an Aug. 7 statement.

As the delays have mounted, a number of lawmakers from both parties have asked Clinton to leave all decisions to his successor.

More than 90 congressional Democrats, including 33 senators, have called for Clinton to delay a deployment decision. (*2000 CQ Weekly, p. 1903*)

"If the 2005 deployment date is no longer realistic, that date should no longer drive the president's decision this year," Carl Levin of Michigan, ranking Democrat on the Senate Armed Services Committee, said during a July 25 hearing. "President Clinton should adopt what I call the 3-D policy for the remainder of his time in office: develop, discuss and defer."

Like many Republicans, Chuck Hagel of Nebraska contends that Clinton only set up a decision on missile defense this year to insulate Vice President Al Gore, the Democratic Party standard-bearer, from charges that the administration was weak on defense. Indeed, the Pentagon announcement of problems with the deployment schedule only came after Gore chose a key Democratic supporter of the missile defense system, Sen. Joseph I. Lieberman of Connecticut, as his running mate.

"I just don't buy this that we've got to pour concrete right away or North Korea in five years will send a missile over," said Hagel in a recent interview. "I'm not sure how you go ahead and pour concrete based on some design when you're still testing the options."

Cohen has resisted slowing the timetable. But the technical problems may have become too serious for him to proceed with the compressed time frame. Pentagon officials said they involve problems with the integration of three separate rocket motors as well as the computer link that tells the "kill vehicle" — the small interceptor packed with sensors that is designed to collide with an incoming warhead — when and how to separate from the booster rockets. Under the Pentagon's plan, 20 of these interceptors would be in place in Alaska by 2005.

Cohen talks on with Warner, right, and Levin, who recommended that Clinton "develop, discuss and defer" decisions on national missile defense until his successor takes office.

His recent moves indicate that Putin favors the calls for change, but he is first trying to score some diplomatic points.

His first move came earlier this year when the Russian parliament, after years of delay, approved two separate arms control measures: the 1993 Strategic Arms Reduction Treaty (START II) and the Comprehensive Test Ban Treaty.

In an effort to put the United States on the diplomatic defensive, the parliament said several conditions would have to be fulfilled before Russia would consider the treaties legally binding:

• The United States would have to maintain adherence to the ABM Treaty.

• Congress would have to ratify amendments to the ABM Treaty that Clinton negotiated with Russian leaders in 1997 to distinguish between national missile defense and those designed to protect troops in the field and to extend the treaty to three other former Soviet states. These agreements have not been submitted to the Senate because Clinton fears they would be rejected, much as the test ban treaty was last year. (*1999 CQ Weekly, p. 2435*)

Many U.S. foreign policy analysts, such as Rice, say that the United States should call Russia's bluff, noting that Russia's financial situation leaves it little choice but to comply with the treaties on a de facto basis.

A recent analysis of the trends in Russian strategic forces carried out by Alexander A. Pikayev of the Carnegie Endowment for International Peace concluded that no matter what the U.S. does, Russian strategic forces are destined to shrink drastically by 2010 anyway.

Other arms control authorities worry that Russia might retaliate by stepping up, rather than controlling, the spread of weapons technology to other countries.

"An uncontrollable arms race could result, characterized by small, unstable players that would gain in stature by leveraging their newly acquired nuclear capability," warned Ellen O. Tauscher, D-Calif., a member of the House Armed Services Committee, in a March column in the Los Angeles Times.

Trouble Among Friends

European leaders worry that by building a missile defense system, the United States would be retreating from the NATO alliance, protecting itself while leaving its friends vulnerable.

Clinton has even met resistance from Britain, traditionally America's closest ally. The cabinet of Prime Minister Tony Blair is split on the issue — the defense ministry supports the concept of missile defense and the foreign ministry opposes it. European support is crucial, partly because advanced radar units would be based in Britain and Greenland, which is owned by Denmark.

Foreign ministers preparing for July's summit of the wealthy nations — which included many NATO allies and Japan — agreed to a statement that they were "deeply concerned" that the U.S. missile defense system would undermine anti-proliferation efforts and urged "preserving and strengthening" the ABM treaty.

"There are so many other ways we could be pursuing stability," Canadian Foreign Minister Lloyd Axworthy said. "We have expressed very strong concerns that any movement of the national missile defense that abrogates the ABM Treaty would be wrong. We don't like anything that would further expand acceleration of missile capacity."

At the July 25 Armed Services Committee hearing, Cohen said allied support was "critical" to building a successful system.

"The allies, in my judgment, will support [national missile defense] if there is agreement on the part of the Russians," Cohen said. "But unless the allies remain behind us, then the Russians are unlikely to agree."

Kremlin officials have tried to increase European unease. Russian military spokesmen have said that if the United States deploys a missile defense system, Russia might withdraw from the 1987 Intermediate Nuclear Forces Treaty, which bans U.S. and Soviet nuclear weapons in Europe that have a range of between 1,000 kilometers and 5,500 kilometers. (*1987 CQ Almanac, p. 135*)

Playing the good cop, Putin traveled to Europe soon after his summit with Clinton to propose that Russia and NATO jointly develop a system that could defend Europe against missile threats, but still comply with the ABM Treaty.

The system, according to Russian officials, would use boost-phase intercept technology — destroying a missile soon after launch — to protect all of Europe.

Some lawmakers say the proposal is worth pursuing. "A cooperative missile defense would knit Russia into a Western defense framework," Biden said in his CATO Institute speech. "It would also, theoretically at least, transform Russia's role in the world. It might just pave the way for a world-wide shift from pure deterrence to an agreed mix of offense and defense."

Clinton administration officials are skeptical. "It is my judgment that such a system cannot be a substitute for defenses against the emerging threat of

ballistic missiles that could strike the United States," Cohen told the Senate Armed Services Committee July 25. "Such a system would leave much of NATO defenseless when attacked by a long range missile that could be launched from Iran."

But Cohen and other administration officials have expressed an interest in working with Russia to jointly develop boost phase technology rather than waiting for it to sow warheads in the outer atmosphere.

China Skeptics

Putin's diplomacy, meanwhile, has ranged beyond Europe. In July, he joined Chinese President Jiang Zemin in a harsh criticism of the U.S. missile defense plan.

China also used last month's annual meeting of the Association of Southeast Asian Nations to stir further diplomatic opposition to the U.S. move.

"We believe this idea of the United States will inevitably support a new round of arms races and will compromise international peace and security," said Chinese Foreign Minister Tang Jiaxuan. "The issue is by no means a dispute between China and the United States, but between the United States and the international community."

After Russia, China is the next largest nuclear power that could threaten the United States.

Yet its strategic nuclear arsenal is so small — only a couple of dozen missiles capable of reaching the United States — that Chinese officials fear a successful missile defense system could allow the United States to launch a nuclear strike without fear of retaliation. Such an imbalance, Chinese officials worry, could tip the scales in a potential Sino-American conflict over Taiwan.

John D. Holum, the State Department's top arms control negotiator, said it is a "hard argument" to convince skeptical Chinese of U.S. intentions.

"They can say, 'Yes, but we have to focus on capabilities, not intentions. It looks like you are building 100 interceptors and we have far fewer than that ICBMs,'" Holum said.

U.S. assurances also are undermined, Holum said, by missile defense proponents who talk about blunting China's missile threat.

Senate Foreign Relations Committee Chairman Jesse Helms, R-N.C., said earlier this year, "After issuing nuclear threat after nuclear threat, China now has the nerve to complain that a U.S. missile defense is a threat to their security. To the contrary, leaving the American people vulnerable to Beijing's nuclear blackmail is a threat to U.S. national security."

If a system is deployed, Chinese officials have threatened to respond by deploying enough offensive missiles to ensure their security. Most U.S. officials and analysts say that China is likely to increase its force in any case, although they disagree on the potential speed, scope and sophistication of its strategic modernization.

Korean Overtures

Meanwhile, China's Jiang and Russia's Putin have both sought to meet U.S. concerns by persuading erstwhile ally North Korea to drop its program to develop long-range missiles and nuclear weapons. The latest wrinkle came during the G-8 summit in July, when Putin told world leaders that North Korea's Kim Jong Il had offered to convert his missile program to peaceful satellite launches.

Administration officials worried initially that Moscow might help Pyongyang launch satellites from North Korean territory. Since rocket technology is very similar to missile technology, U.S. officials fretted that the satellite launchings would accelerate Pyongyang's missile program.

"That would have been the opposite of helpful," said Deputy Secretary of State Strobe Talbott. "It would have contributed to the problem, not the solution."

In a recent exchange of letters with Putin, North Korea's Kim said his government was willing to drop its intercontinental ballistic missile program if other countries would launch two or three satellites a year for Pyongyang at their expense.

Yet North Korea has failed to make clear to U.S. officials if that is the path it would indeed pursue. An attempt by Secretary of State Madeleine K. Albright to clarify the offer during a July 28 meeting with North Korea's Foreign Minister, Paek Nam Sun, made little headway.

The meeting came at a time that North Korea appears to be opening up to the world following a June summit between the leaders of North and South Korea. In recent months, it has established diplomatic relations with almost half-a-dozen U.S. allies: Australia, New Zealand, Italy, Canada, and the Philippines. And it will be holding talks on normalizing relations with Japan.

U.S. officials have said they would only consider normalizing relations if North Korea halts its nuclear and missile programs. North Korea has suspended long range missile tests. (2000 CQ Weekly, p. 1508)

After her meeting with Paek, Albright said she was "somewhat more hopeful than before for the long-term stability on the Korean peninsula." But the administration remains wary.

"One summit doesn't change a tiger into a domestic cat," Cohen told the Armed Services Committee. "We have to, in fact, see whether or not the North Koreans are going to continue to follow through with their relationship with the South, whether they are in fact serious about some of the statements that were related secondhand to President Clinton about their desire to possibly give up their missile capacity."

Similar questions surround the future of other unfriendly states such as Iran, Iraq and Libya.

But according to Michael Krepon, president of the Henry L. Stimson Center and an expert on proliferation issues, "the arms competition to watch is in Asia," where the fallout from deployment of a U.S. missile defense system could further stir up longstanding rivalries between China and India, and between India and Pakistan.

"Ambitious U.S. national missile defense plans will drive up China's deployments, which, in turn, can have adverse repercussions on the fledgling nuclear and missile programs in India and Pakistan," Krepon wrote. "New Delhi is now seriously debating how much of a nuclear deterrent to acquire. Growing Chinese nuclear capabilities can drive up Indian force levels, and Pakistan has always referenced its security requirements against India's arsenal."

As Joseph Cirincione, director of the non-proliferation project at the Carnegie Endowment for International Peace, wrote earlier this year, the "political firewalls" that slowed or prevented nuclear proliferation are "now crumbling in much of the world, particularly in Asia, where declining faith in arms control is prompting advanced and developing countries alike to contemplate the acquisition or development of nuclear weapons." ◆

Hollywood's 'Culture of Carnage' Blasted by Lawmakers, Candidates

Demand for action peaks after FTC study shows entertainment companies' tepid enforcement of age-based restrictions

Lynne Cheney, former chairman of the National Endowment for the Humanities and wife of GOP vice presidential nominee Dick Cheney, testifies at a Senate Commerce hearing.

The entertainment industry came under blistering attack on Capitol Hill the week of Sept. 11, after the Federal Trade Commission (FTC) released a study on improper marketing of violent movies, video games and recordings.

The study's conclusion — that entertainment companies "routinely target" children as the audience for products that they themselves deem appropriate only for adults — unleashed a torrent of criticism in Congress and on the presidential campaign trail.

GOP presidential nominee George W. Bush accused the industry of "polluting our children's minds" but eschewed further government regulation. Democratic vice presidential nominee Sen. Joseph I. Lieberman of Connecticut, in congressional testimony Sept. 13, decried a "culture of carnage." Lieberman and presidential nominee Al Gore said Congress should rein in industry marketing practices, if, after six months, voluntary self-policing does not work.

Some influential lawmakers are not willing to wait that long.

Senate Commerce, Science and Transportation Committee Chairman John McCain, R-Ariz., scheduled a markup during the week of Sept. 18 on a long-stalled bill (S 876), sponsored by Ernest F. Hollings of South Carolina, the panel's ranking Democrat, to limit the hours when violent television programming can be shown.

The bill is expected to be approved by the committee, but it has little chance of reaching the Senate floor because of strong opposition from critics who argue that it would inhibit free speech and potentially force broadcasters to cut back on both news and entertainment programs.

McCain's New Hearing

Angered by the refusal of top entertainment executives to appear at his hastily assembled Sept. 13 hearing, McCain scheduled another hearing the week of Sept. 25 and insisted on attendance by industry leaders.

McCain said executives who declined an invitation to his first hearing had provided a "sad commentary on corporate responsibility."

GOP leaders in both chambers said

legislation to restrict violence in the media would have strong support among social conservatives, but added that there was simply not enough time remaining in the 106th Congress to develop a compromise that would also satisfy concerns from guardians of free speech.

"I'm not going to make a knee-jerk reaction. We'll take a look at it next year," said House Speaker J. Dennis Hastert, R-Ill.

Senate Majority Leader Trent Lott, R-Miss., said Sept. 12 that Republicans wanted to bring the issue of violent entertainment to the floor before the session ends, but added that there was no agreement on specific legislation.

"Violence is something we're going to have to deal with. Industry has not done the job. I don't think we ought to wait six months," Lott said.

While legislation may not be enacted this year, McCain's plan to continue oversight is certain to keep the issue on the front burner and set the stage for possible action in the next session.

Possible participants in the upcoming hearing include Gerald Levin, chairman and chief executive officer of Time Warner Inc., and Michael Eisner, chairman and chief executive officer of Walt Disney Co.

Along with legislation, McCain is pushing the entertainment industry to take voluntary action to restrict marketing and sales. As an example, he cites efforts by major retailers to limit the sale of violent video games. Target Corp., Kmart Corp. and Wal-Mart Stores Inc. announced in early September that they would begin requiring buyers of mature-rated video games to provide proof that they are 17 or older. Other chains, including Sears Roebuck and Co., have stopped carrying mature video games.

Disney reacted to the FTC study by announcing on Sept. 12 that it would curb promotion of movies containing violence and sex. It said the company's ABC television network would no longer accept advertising for R-rated

PRESSLINK PHOTO / CHUCK KENNEDY

movies during prime-time hours before 9 p.m., and promised not to target advertising for such movies to children under age 17.

President Clinton asked the FTC to study violence in the media after the April 20, 1999 massacre at Columbine High School in Colorado. Officials and lawmakers were concerned that the two students who went on a shooting spree were spurred on, in part, by violent images in music, television and video games.

"The extent, and in some instances the brazenness, of marketing to children . . . is striking," Federal Trade Commission Chairman Robert Pitofsky told the Commerce Committee on Sept. 13.

The FTC study found that movie theaters and other retailers do little to enforce age-based restrictions. One internal industry document cited in the report found that a company's target-market for video games that were ranked for mature audiences included boys ages 12 to 17.

In his testimony, Lieberman argued for what would amount to a brief moratorium to give industry time to take action before Congress moves. He said that if industry fails to police itself, Congress should consider "narrowly tailored legislation to augment the FTC's authority." Lieberman did not specifically mention a bill (S 2497) he has sponsored with McCain to crack down on violent entertainment.

That bill would encourage the industry to develop a voluntary plan for labeling violent content. Within a year of enactment, it would require the FTC to develop its own mandatory labeling requirements and age restrictions for the sale of video games, recordings and movies that feature violence.

Lynne Cheney, former chairman of the National Endowment for the Humanities and the wife of the GOP nominee for vice president, former Rep. Dick Cheney, R-Wyo. (1979-1989), also testified. She agreed with Lieberman that legislation was not needed in the current Congress. Cheney sharply criticized the Gore campaign for not offering more of what she said would be a quick antidote to the problem: personal pleas to prominent media executives.

Cheney singled out Harvey Weinstein, the co-chairman of Disney's Miramax Films, and a prominent Gore supporter. Weinstein declined to testify, citing scheduling conflicts. Cheney and other Republicans were quick to point out, however, that he had time to organize a Sept. 14 fundraiser for the Gore campaign.

"I suggest Sen. Lieberman and Vice President Gore would ask Mr. Weinstein when they see him . . . to be accountable," Cheney said.

Cheney's criticism was echoed by other Republicans, who complained that Democrats were playing both sides of the issue: seeking campaign donations from the industry while talking tough on violence.

"Everybody that's making accusations just took money from everybody in Hollywood," Hastert said.

Some Senate Republicans, including Rick Santorum of Pennsylvania, said they were considering strategies for forcing a floor vote on McCain's bill, thereby requiring Lieberman to take a stand on the measure.

"I'd love to take the bill up. But I'm sure there will be objections," McCain said. He criticized the influence of Hollywood and its campaign donors on both parties.

A study by the Center for Responsive Politics, a campaign finance watchdog group, found that the entertainment industry has given more than $22 million to candidates and political action committees of both parties, with 61 percent going to Democrats and 39 percent to Republicans, in the 2000 election cycle.

V-Chip's Mixed Success

The debate on violent entertainment comes in the midst of an examination of a 1996 telecommunications overhaul (PL 104-104) that mandated new technology to help parents restrict programming. *(1996 CQ Almanac, p. 3-43)*

The measure, which was championed by Lieberman, required the entertainment industry to help develop an electronic device known as the "v-chip," implanted in television sets, that could be used to block unwanted programs based on ratings for violence, sex and offensive language.

The v-chip became widely available this year and has been required in virtually all new television sets since July 1.

A recent study by the Henry J. Kaiser Family Foundation, a nonprofit research group, found that nearly one in 10 parents of children ages 2 to 17 owned a television with a v-chip, but only a third of that group had programmed the chip to block television programs.

Advocates of stronger legislation, including Hollings, argued at the Sept. 13 hearing that the study showed the v-chip was not the solution to the violence in the media. He said parents found the ratings system used by the television industry hard to understand and did not have time to monitor their children's viewing habits.

Defenders of the v-chip opposed changing the ratings system without further evidence.

"It would be premature to pass legislation that would make changes in the v-chip and the rating system," said Rep. Edward J. Markey, D-Mass., a champion of the 1996 law.

"I would argue that the v-chip is working. It is being used by families with small children. Not every family has to use the v-chip," he said.

Industry officials have argued strongly in favor of self-regulation, combined with parental discretion. They have threatened to challenge in court any mandatory limits on distribution and marketing of their products as a violation of the First Amendment guarantee of free speech.

The prospect of a daunting legal battle has made both parties wary of embracing legislation.

Action Next Year?

Critics of the industry from both parties said McCain's next hearing could set the stage for action in 2001 and predicted that Congress will be more willing to risk a legal battle after the election.

House Judiciary Committee Chairman Henry J. Hyde, R-Ill., said he hopes there would be a strong push next year. "There is no legislation because of the power of Hollywood. The money. The clout," he said.

Hyde faces dissent in his own caucus. Mark Foley, R-Fla., chairman of the 21-member House GOP entertainment industry task force, said he would continue a campaign begun by the group's founder, the late Rep. Sonny Bono, R-Calif. (1995-98), to compete more aggressively with Democrats for Hollywood campaign donations.

He said he would oppose legislation to impose restrictions on the industry.

"The problem is not the National Rifle Association, and it's not Hollywood. We have a problem in our society," Foley said. ◆

Senators Pan Entertainment Industry's Plan to Shield Children From Violence

Movie executives at Sept. 27 hearing. From left, Walter Parkes, co-head of DreamWorks; Mel Harris of Sony; Jack Valenti, president of the Motion Picture Association of America; Stacy Snider of Universal Pictures; Alan Horn of Warner Bros.; and Roger Iger of Disney.

In an effort to head off possible legislation restricting the sale of movies, recordings and video games with gory themes, eight entertainment industry executives traveled to Capitol Hill the week of Sept. 25 carrying a voluntary plan to curb the exposure of children to violent entertainment.

Lawmakers made it clear during a showdown Senate Commerce, Science and Transportation Committee hearing on Sept. 27, however, that they did not think the industry had gone far enough to police itself. They suggested that the companies fire employees who peddle violent material to children and urged executives to develop public service announcements on violence similar to anti-tobacco and anti-drug advertising.

"If you don't try to make this really work, then you are going to see some kind of legislation because parents are throwing up their hands," said Kay Bailey Hutchison, R-Texas.

Many — but not all — lawmakers

stopped well short of pushing for immediate Senate action on legislation, even though the committee on Sept. 20 marked up a bill (S 876) that could lead to a ban on violent television programs during the early evening hours. (2000 CQ Weekly, p. 2216)

Commerce Committee Chairman John McCain, R-Ariz., said after the hearing that he remained skeptical of the industry's voluntary efforts.

At the same time, he said he doubted Congress would pass legislation to deal with the issue of media violence in the waning weeks of the session. McCain warned that he would return to the issue next year.

"I look forward to working with you collectively and individually," he told the executives.

Others said there was a chance still this year that Congress might enact a bill to give entertainment companies a limited exemption from antitrust laws so they could accelerate their efforts and develop a broader code of conduct that would have teeth.

"It's clear the industry does not want a tough code of conduct," said Mike DeWine, R-Ohio, chairman of the Senate Judiciary Antitrust, Business Rights and Competition Subcommittee said Sept. 27. "If we can provide this exemption, it will take that issue off the table. They will have no more excuses."

Industry officials said after the hearing that they opposed an antitrust bill (S 2127) sponsored by Sam Brownback, R-Kan.

"I'm not sure we need an antitrust exemption," said Robert Iger, president and chief operations officer for The Walt Disney Co., who met privately with the senator.

Despite the cool reaction, Brownback said he would try to offer his bill as a rider to an appropriations bill. Senate Judiciary Committee Chairman Orrin G. Hatch, R-Utah, has backed a similar measure.

"We should do this. There is bipartisan support," Brownback said. He added, however, that he had no commitments from GOP leaders.

Donation or Denunciation?

The uncertainty in Congress about how far to push the issue underscores the political pitfalls in dealing with Hollywood violence.

Congressional probes into media violence and its possible effects on children have a rich history that dates back to the 1950s. The Senate in 1953 launched the first of a series of high-profile hearings that investigated connections between juvenile delinquency and violent depictions in comic books and radio and television programs. (1954 CQ Almanac, p. 211)

While the hearings have long been a tradition, so has Congress' reluctance to legislate. Lawmakers have generally given the entertainment industry wide leeway to set standards for itself.

For example, in the 1980s, Tipper Gore, the wife of Vice President Al Gore, who was then a Democratic senator from Tennessee (1985-93), helped

lead a crusade against violent lyrics in popular songs. Lawmakers threatened to restrict the sale of violent music to children, but relented when recording companies agreed to police themselves and to put warning labels on albums that contained graphic lyrics about sex and violence.

In the wake of the mass murder by two students at Columbine High School near Denver on April 20, 1999, lawmakers launched a new set of inquiries into the effect of violence in the media. The rampage was blamed partly on the students' exposure to violent recordings and video games, and led to a Federal Trade Commission (FTC) study of violence in media.

Criticism of the entertainment industry escalated Sept. 11 when the FTC released its report stating that some companies targeted children with advertising for graphic movies, video games and recordings that were inappropriate for minors.

While lawmakers want to respond to voter concerns about excessive violence in media, members of both parties are wary of enacting mandatory restrictions on marketing practices that could be hard to implement and subject to legal challenges as a potential violation of the constitutional protection of free speech.

On the presidential campaign trail, Democratic nominee Gore has said he would consider mandatory restrictions if, within six months, the industry failed to curb marketing for movies with violent themes aimed at children. Texas Gov. George W. Bush, the Republican nominee, also has been critical of Hollywood violence. But like Gore, he and other Republicans have shied away from embracing immediate legislation.

Instead, the GOP has questioned Gore's sincerity about fighting Hollywood violence, pointing to his efforts to raise campaign donations from the entertainment industry.

At a news conference Sept. 27, Lynne Cheney, wife of former Rep. Dick Cheney, R-Wyo. (1979-89), Bush's running mate, accused Gore of criticizing Hollywood violence with a "wink and a nudge" while holding a series of fundraising events that target contributions from Hollywood.

"We are trying to make the point that Democrats are not consistent on this issue," said Rick Santorum, R-Pa. "They want to stop Hollywood vio-

lence, but then they take all of this money from Hollywood."

Faced with the prospect of further attacks by McCain and other lawmakers, the Motion Picture Association of America, the trade group representing movie companies, unveiled a voluntary plan Sept. 26 for addressing problems revealed by the FTC study.

But the group said it would only support self-policing measures, and expressed strong doubts about legislation.

"The freedom of expression is terribly, terribly important," said Alan Horn, president and chief operating officer of Warner Brothers. "There's a Pandora's box issue that is related to any kind of government intervention."

In lieu of legislation, the group said it would take steps to strengthen enforcement of its current system for rating movies.

Under that system, G-rated movies are deemed suitable for children, R-rated movies may be viewed by children accompanied by their parents, and movies with the PG-13 rating are suitable for older children, but contain material that may be inappropriate for those under the age of 13.

Ratings Not Enforced

The FTC study alleged that the rating system was not well enforced in theaters and concluded that industry officials had often allowed underage children to take part in marketing studies for R-rated movies.

As part of their voluntary plan, the companies pledged to stop using children in marketing studies for such movies unless they were accompanied by parents. They said they would ask theater owners to tighten enforcement of the ratings and to stop showing clips or trailers of R-rated movies during movies that are G-rated.

The companies also promised not to "inappropriately" target children as the audience for R-rated movies.

McCain said he believed the industry's plan gave too much discretion to industry, but he did not plan to push this year for a bill (S 2497) he sponsored that would require the FTC to develop a new, uniform system for labeling and setting age restrictions on the sale of video games, recordings and movies that feature violence. That bill would effectively merge different rating systems used by different mediums into one system that could be more easily understood by parents.

Most executives at the hearing balked at McCain's bill, but some said they would consider a voluntary universal rating system.

"We believe that a universal system would represent a significant step toward helping parents make informed decisions about the entertainment their children see and hear," Iger said.

'Safe Harbor' Ban

During the hearing, Ernest F. Hollings, D-S.C., and other lawmakers argued that the industry's past attempts to police itself had failed.

Hollings tried unsuccessfully to recruit supporters among the witnesses for his committee-approved bill (S 876) to direct the Federal Communications Commission (FCC), pending completion of a study of violent television programs, to take action to limit the hours when violent programs could be aired.

He argued that the current rating system for television programs was ineffective and that parents were not using a television device called a "v-chip" that allows viewers to block programs that are appropriate only for mature viewers. The 1996 telecommunications overhaul (PL 104-104) required the v-chip to be installed in all new televisions starting July 1. (*2000 CQ Weekly, p. 2135*)

Hollings said legislation was needed because the industry was sharply divided on whether to voluntarily restrict violent programming and advertising in the early evening hours when many children are watching television.

He noted that Disney had adopted a "safe harbor" ban on advertising for R-rated movies between the hours of 8 p.m. and 9 p.m. Hollings said he had been informed by Disney that other companies had refused to follow its lead.

In light of such disagreement, Hollings pressed Iger to explain why Disney did not support his bill. Iger said he opposed the bill because it went beyond advertising and applied to television programming, including heavily edited R-rated movies that are sometimes shown before 9 p.m. He said it would be wrong for government to make "programming decisions for us."

Some executives said they would match a Fox Entertainment proposal to stop advertising R-rated movies on TV and Internet websites, if people under age 17 made up at least 35 percent of the audience. Others disagreed. ◆

Foundations of American Government

The U.S. Constitution performs several functions: it guarantees individual liberties from encroachment by the government; it sets forth the jurisdiction and powers of the three branches of government and regulates relations between the branches; and it sets boundaries between the jurisdictions of the federal government and the states.

The first article in this section looks at the tone that marked the 1999 Supreme Court term: confidence in its role as the ultimate arbiter of power at all levels of government. The Supreme Court covered a variety of important social issues this term such as gay rights, abortion, pornography, and violence against women. The common theme throughout all these decisions was the importance of the separation of powers.

In *United States v. Playboy Entertainment Group Inc.* the Court held that restrictions on the broadcasting of adult material placed an undue burden on free speech. The ruling declared unconstitutional a section of the 1996 telecommunications law (PL 104-104). The Court found that Congress had overstepped its authority when it required cable operators to scramble signals from adult entertainment channels.

The final article in this section discusses the Court's willingness to draw boundaries for state governments as well. In *Stenberg v. Carhart* the Court struck down a Nebraska law banning what abortion opponents call "partial birth abortion." The Court found that the law was too broadly drawn and placed an "undue burden" on a woman seeking to end a pregnancy. The ruling, which limits the authority of thirty other states with similar statutes, could also make it difficult for abortion opponents in Congress to continue their battle to outlaw the controversial procedure.

Supreme Court Term Dominated By Confident Rulings Limiting Scope Of Federal and State Governments

Quick Contents

In its 1999 term, the Supreme Court expressed supreme confidence in its role as the ultimate arbiter of power at all levels of government. It continued efforts to rein in congressional power but also asserted its authority to set boundaries for the executive branch and state governments.

In its 1999 term, the Supreme Court ruled on a wide variety of passionately fought social issues such as gay rights and abortion. Perhaps even more important than any decision was the tone that marked the court's opinions across the board: absolute confidence in its role as the ultimate arbiter of power at all levels of government.

Not since the court took on the administration of Franklin D. Roosevelt in the 1930s have the justices been so willing to stake out the structure of the federal system as has the Rehnquist court over the last several years. While none of the 74 signed opinions issued this term is likely to be viewed by itself as a blockbuster, they add up to a strong statement on the separation of powers.

"I can't remember any time when the court has been more assertive, more aware of its own prerogatives, more willing to delineate where Congress' power ends," said A. E. Dick Howard, a law professor at the University of Virginia. The curbs on Congress' reach were specific and somewhat narrow in each case. But they were written in a way that will make it difficult for Congress to rewrite the legislation in question to make it pass constitutional muster — at least under the current court, which was split 5-4 in many cases.

The Supreme Court has been equally willing to draw boundaries for state and local governments, ruling this term, for example, that Massachusetts could not pursue sanctions against the government of Myanmar, formerly Burma. Foreign policy, a unanimous court held in *Crosby v. National Foreign Trade Council*, is the territory of the federal government. (*2000 CQ Weekly, p. 1549*)

The Politics of One Vote

One of the most controversial of the 5-4 decisions was in *Stenberg v. Carhart*. In that case, the court struck down a Nebraska law that aimed to ban a procedure that abortion opponents call "partial birth" abortion. In a ruling that limited not only Nebraska's power but also that of the 30 other states with similar statutes, the court held that the law was unconstitutionally broad and did not contain an exemption to protect the health of the woman. (*2000 CQ Weekly, p. 1612*)

The court also ruled 5-4 that Congress overstepped its authority when it attempted to regulate adult entertainment on cable television. The court had more 5-4 decisions this term than any time in the last decade. (*Close decisions, p. 101*)

The significance of that was not lost on presidential front-runners George W. Bush or Al Gore, or those cheering from the sidelines. The next president may appoint two to four Supreme Court justices, President Clinton told members of the Democratic Senatorial Campaign Committee on July 3. "So whichever one of them gets elected, it's going to change the balance of the Supreme Court," he said.

Except for the Nebraska abortion ruling, conservatives were generally pleased with the court. They also recognize its split nature. "There are a lot of things that would go completely the other way . . . if Al Gore becomes president," Senate Judiciary Committee Chairman Orrin G. Hatch, R-Utah, said July 2 on NBC News' "Meet the Press."

It is not clear how many — if any — high court seats will come open during the next four years. Jimmy Carter is the only president to serve a complete, four-year term without having a chance to nominate a justice. George Bush had two nominations in four years; Clinton had two in eight years.

The oldest member of the court, John Paul Stevens, is frequently mentioned as a possible retiree. At 80, he is the leader of the loyal opposition. No one dissented this year more than he. But age is not always a good guide: Justice Oliver Wendell Holmes retired at 90. Antonin Scalia, the justice with the most biting dissents, has been rumored to be dissatisfied with his job. But he might not want to relinquish his seat to a Gore nominee.

The two female justices, Sandra Day O'Connor and Ruth Bader Ginsburg, have both had health problems. But O'Connor, who was appointed by Ronald Reagan in 1981, seems to be hitting her stride — she was a key vote on the court this term, dissenting in just four decisions, the least of any justice.

The New Federalism

In its decisions the court curbed Congress' power in several areas but also struck down attempts by the executive branch or state and local governments to encroach on Congress' territory. Many have called this a return to a more federalist court, with greater

deference given to states.

Howard argues that it is more than federalism. "It's federalism coupled with separation of powers, coupled with judicial review," he said. Others argue that the fundamental issue before the court is how to interpret congressional powers in the Constitution.

Said Thomas E. Baker, a professor at Drake University Law School: "There are two very different visions of Article 1 on the two sides of First Street N.E. On the court side, it's an 18th century, 19th century idea of Congress having enumerated powers; on the Congress side, the operative constitutional vision of members of Congress, Republicans and Democrats, is kind of a postmodern, post-New Deal attitude that 'we're going to decide what's good for the country.' "

This dichotomy was clear in the court's rebuke to Congress over the 1994 Violence Against Women Act (PL 103-322) in *United States v. Morrison*. Members had created a private right of action that allowed women to sue their attackers, in part because so many women seemed unable to find justice in the system.

But the court said that despite mountains of evidence provided by Congress aimed at showing a link between the violence and women's economic activity, the legislature's constitutional power to regulate interstate commerce could not be stretched that far.

It was one of 24 federal laws struck down by the court over the last five years, according to Walter E. Dellinger, a Washington lawyer. Dellinger said it shows "a court whose relative inclination to strike down federal statutes seems to be at a very, very high level."

The court nullified two other federal laws this year on constitutional grounds. In *Dickerson v. United States*, the court threw out a 1968 law (PL 90-351) allowing "voluntary"confessions with the aim of overturning the court's 1966 decision in *Miranda v. Arizona*. In a 7-2 ruling, the court said its requirement that suspects be informed of their rights was a "constitutional rule" and could not be changed by Congress.

But the court also protected congressional territory. For example, it upheld the primacy of federal laws on oil tankers in *United States v. Locke*, striking down a state law that imposed different rules. And in *Geier v. American Honda Motor Co.*, the court invalidated a state law that allowed a plaintiff to sue an automobile maker for not including an airbag when federal law required none.

The court seemed to be protecting what it saw as an overreach by the executive branch in *FDA v. Brown and Williamson Tobacco Corp.* The court ruled, 5-4, that the Food and Drug Administration could not regulate tobacco without a specific authorization from Congress. (*2000 CQ Weekly,* p. 661)

"The court is willing to let Congress have generous power where the court believes that power is properly exercised," Howard said. ◆

Close Rulings by Court

Cases include several hot-button issues

Of the 74 signed decisions issued by the Supreme Court this session, 21 were decided completely or in part in rulings of 5-4, on issues such as abortion rights, gay rights and criminal procedures. The following are key split decisions.

Case	Ruling
Kimel v. Florida Board of Regents	The court held that federal anti-discrimination laws regarding age could not be applied to state employees. (*2000 CQ Weekly,* p. 80)
Illinois v. Wardlow	Fleeing from police can sometimes be considered suspicious behavior that justifies a search, the court ruled.
FDA v. Brown and Williamson Tobacco Corp.	The court ruled that the Food and Drug Administration does not have the authority to regulate tobacco without a more specific authorization from Congress. (*Ruling, 2000 CQ Weekly,* p. 661)
United States v. Morrison	The majority found that Congress exceeded its authority when it allowed women who were victims of violence to sue their attackers in federal court. (*2000 CQ Weekly,* p. 1188)
United States v. Playboy Entertainment Group Inc.	The majority said that restrictions on the broadcasting of adult material, enacted by Congress in the 1996 telecommunications law (PL 104-104), placed an undue burden on free speech. (*2000 CQ Weekly,* p. 1279; *1996 CQ Almanac,* p. 3-43)
Apprendi v. New Jersey	On hate crimes, the court ruled that the Constitution requires that juries — not judges — determine whether a crime was motivated by bias. A jury must determine that a crime was motivated by bias beyond a reasonable doubt in order for a more severe sentence to be imposed.
Boy Scouts of America v. Dale	The majority found that requiring the Boy Scouts to admit homosexuals violated the group's free association rights.
Stenberg v. Carhart	A narrow majority said a Nebraska law banning what abortion opponents call "partial-birth" abortions was too broadly drawn and presented an undue burden on a woman seeking an abortion. The court also said it was unconstitutional because it did not contain an exception to protect the health of the woman. (*2000 CQ Weekly,* p. 1612)

High Court Says Some Curbs On Adult Cable TV Channels Violate the First Amendment

Congress is not likely to try to rewrite a 1996 law that was designed to keep children from inadvertently seeing or hearing adult programming on cable television channels, a prime sponsor said after the Supreme Court ruled May 22 that it placed an undue burden on free speech.

Sen. Dianne Feinstein, D-Calif., who co-authored the set of restrictions thrown out by the court, said the decision "struck a blow against the ability of Congress to protect our children from sexually explicit material."

But Feinstein acknowledged that it would be difficult to craft another provision that would pass muster. "The measure was narrowly tailored, and no equally effective alternative exists," she said.

By a 5-4 vote, the court struck down part of the 1996 telecommunications overhaul (PL 104-104) that required cable operators to completely scramble signals from adult entertainment channels, such as Playboy Television or Spice. If the scrambling was not complete, cable operators were allowed to broadcast only late at night. (*1996 CQ Almanac, p. 3-43*)

Writing for the majority in *United States v. Playboy Entertainment Group Inc.*, Justice Anthony M. Kennedy found that when a law places a burden on free speech, "it must be narrowly tailored to promote a compelling government interest. If a less restrictive alternative would serve the government's purpose, the legislature must use that alternative."

Kennedy found that another section of the law — which requires cable companies to install blocking equipment to kill the signal for adult channels at each individual household that requested it — would accomplish the goal of protecting children without interfering with the First Amendment.

The court's decision is the second time a section of the 1996 telecommunications law has been declared unconstitutional. In 1997, the court struck down the section of the law designed to bar "indecent" material on the Internet. (*1997 Almanac, p. 5-25*)

'Signal Bleed'

Cable companies use scrambling to make sure that only those who pay for certain channels have access to them. Most scrambling techniques are not completely successful; a certain amount of the picture or sound comes through in what is known as "signal bleed."

In the 1996 law, Congress said that if a company could not "fully scramble or otherwise fully block" sexually explicit channels, the companies would be allowed to broadcast only from 10 p.m. until 6 a.m.

Most cable companies began obeying the late-night broadcasting restriction, which cut into the revenues of the adult entertainment channels.

Playboy Entertainment, owner of Playboy Television and Spice, challenged the law in U.S. District Court in Delaware. In March 1998, the District Court concluded that the law was unconstitutional because Congress had not imposed the least restrictive way to regulate the speech.

The trial judges found that the section of the law mandating installation of individual blocking devices, if sufficiently publicized, could meet the government's goal and would impose less of a burden on the free speech rights of Playboy. Key to the decision was the fact that the government was not alleging that the material distributed by Playboy was obscene. If the material had been found to be obscene, it would not have been entitled to the First Amendment protections given it, first by the District Court and later by the Supreme Court.

"As this case has been litigated, it is not alleged to be obscene; adults have a constitutional right to view it," wrote Kennedy.

Kennedy said that when the government seeks to regulate speech based on its content, the government has a high burden of proof to show that the benefit outweighs the constitutionally protected right. "It is rare that a regulation restricting speech because of its content will ever be permissible," he wrote.

He said the government failed to show how widespread the problem of signal bleed is and, given that, it failed to meet its burden. "The First Amendment requires a more careful assessment and characterization of an evil in order to justify a regulation as sweeping as this," he wrote.

Kennedy closed: "We cannot be influenced, moreover, by the perception that the regulation in question is not a major one because the speech is not very important. The history of the law of free expression is one of vindication in cases involving speech that many citizens may find shabby, offensive or even ugly."

Joining Kennedy in the majority were Justices John Paul Stevens, David H. Souter, Ruth Bader Ginsburg and Clarence Thomas. Thomas, in his own opinion, said he thought the material could have been classified as obscene (thus giving it no protection), but because the government did not raise that point, the Supreme Court could not reach back and change the court record.

'Vanishing Point'

Justice Steven G. Breyer wrote the dissent, which was supported by Chief Justice William H. Rehnquist and Justices Sandra Day O'Connor and Antonin Scalia.

Breyer argued that the government had made its case for the need to protect children, and he found that the alternative scheme embraced by the majority would not be as effective in keeping the material away from children. "By finding 'adequate alternatives' where there are none, the Court reduces Congress' protective power to the vanishing point," Breyer wrote. "That is not what the First Amendment demands." ◆

Supreme Court Abortion Ruling Complicates GOP Efforts To Craft 'Partial Birth' Ban

The Supreme Court's June 28 decision striking down a late-term abortion ban in Nebraska appears to make it very difficult for the Republican majority in Congress to continue its battle to outlaw the procedure that opponents call "partial birth abortion."

In a 5-4 decision, the court ruled that the Nebraska law was unconstitutional because it did not include an exception to protect the health of the woman and because the language defining the procedure was too broad. It presented the woman seeking to end her pregnancy with an "undue burden" on her right to choose abortion, the majority said.

Congress has twice cleared legislation to outlaw the procedure; both times President Clinton vetoed it. The House and Senate have passed similar versions of the ban this Congress (HR 3660, S 1692). (2000 CQ Weekly, p. 839; 1999 CQ Weekly, p. 2857; 1997 CQ Almanac, p. 6-12; 1996 Almanac, p. 6-43)

While the language in the House and Senate bills defining the controversial procedure is far more specific than the Nebraska law, neither bill includes an exception for the health of the woman — an exception its supporters say would gut the bill.

Clinton said again on June 28 that he would sign the bill if it contained a health exception.

Though anti-abortion lawmakers roundly criticized the ruling in Stenberg v. Carhart, none articulated any way that Congress could get around the health issue. Rep. Charles T. Canady, R-Fla., and Sen. Rick Santorum, R-Pa., sponsors of the two bills, were slated to meet to discuss their options, according to a staff aide.

The only solution to their problem might be the one advocated by House GOP Conference Chairman J.C. Watts Jr., R-Okla. — a new Supreme Court. The issue is being debated in the presidential race.

"I look forward to the day when a Republican president will replace retiring liberals with justices who will truthfully interpret the Constitution rather than impose their activist views against states and the people," Watts said in a statement.

The *Casey* Case

The majority and minority opinions in Stenberg relied on their interpretation of the court's 1992 abortion decision, Planned Parenthood of Southeastern Pennsylvania v. Casey.

In that case, also settled by a narrow 5-4 majority, the court held that the 1973 Supreme Court decision, Roe v. Wade — which effectively gave women the right to have an abortion before the fetus becomes viable after 21 to 24 weeks — did not prohibit states from regulating abortions.

But, under Casey, the state could only do so if the regulation did not impose an "undue burden" on women seeking to have an abortion before fetal viability. As for later abortions, the court held the state could ban them, except when it was "necessary, in appropriate medical judgement, for the preservation of the life or health of the mother." (1992 Almanac, p. 398)

At issue in the Stenberg decision was a 1997 Nebraska law that defined the abortion procedure in question as "partially deliver[ing] vaginally a living unborn child before killing the unborn child and completing the delivery."

The law prohibited "deliberately and intentionally delivering into the vagina a living unborn child or a substantial portion thereof, for the purpose of performing a procedure that the person performing such procedure knows will kill the unborn child and does kill the unborn child."

LeRoy H. Carhart, a Nebraska doctor who performs third-trimester abortions, sued, and the 8th U.S. Circuit Court of Appeals, based in St. Louis, Mo., struck down the Nebraska law.

The Supreme Court, in an opinion written by the newest member of the court, Stephen G. Breyer, held that Casey required a health exception. "[T]his court has made it clear that a state may promote but not endanger a woman's health when it regulates the methods of abortion. . . . A risk to a woman's health is the same whether it happens to arise from regulating a particular method of abortion, or from barring abortion entirely," he wrote.

The court also found the description of the abortion procedure in the Nebraska law to be too vague. The majority found that because it did not specify the one kind of abortion opponents said they were trying to ban — the dilation and extraction, or D&X method — it could also ban another, far more common kind of abortion for pre-viable fetuses, called a D&E, or dilation and evacuation.

"All those who perform abortion procedures using that [D&E] method must fear prosecution, conviction, and imprisonment. The result is an undue burden upon a woman's right to make an abortion decision," Breyer wrote.

Joining Breyer in the majority were Justices John Paul Stevens, Sandra Day O'Connor, David H. Souter and Ruth Bader Ginsburg. Dissenting were Chief Justice William H. Rehnquist and Justices Antonin Scalia, Anthony M. Kennedy and Clarence Thomas.

"Ignoring substantial medical and ethical opinion, the court substitutes its own judgement for the judgement of Nebraska and some 30 other states and sweeps the law away," Kennedy wrote in his own dissent. "The court's holding stems from misunderstanding the record, misinterpretation of Casey, outright refusal to respect the law of a state and statutory construction in conflict with settled rules."

Thomas, writing for the other three dissenters, argued that the decision, rather than resting on the Casey decision, obliterated the Casey decision: "The rule set forth by the majority . . . dramatically expands our prior abortion cases and threatens to undo any state regulation of abortion procedures." ◆

Appendix

Senate, House, Gubernatorial Results

Following are preliminary, unofficial results from the Nov. 7 elections. It could take weeks to certify the final vote tallies in most states. For the most up-to-date results, check Congressional Quarterly's election partner: *washingtonpost.com* at *washingtonpost.com/onpolitics*.

Symbols:

Incumbent	•
Winner without opposition	x
At-large district	AL
2000 new member	#

	Vote Total	%
ALABAMA		
House		
1 • Sonny Callahan (R)	151,024	91.5
Richard M. "Dick" Coffee (LIBERT)	14,032	8.5
2 • Terry Everett (R)	154,785	68.3
Charles Woods (D)	67,624	29.8
Wallace McGahan (LIBERT)	4,214	1.9
3 • Bob Riley (R)	152,585	87.5
John P. Sophocleus (LIBERT)	21,770	12.5
4 • Robert B. Aderholt (R)	139,915	60.9
Marsha Folsom (D)	86,338	37.6
Craig Goodrich (LIBERT)	3,387	1.5
5 • Robert E. "Bud" Cramer (D)	178,792	89.3
Alan Fulton Barksdale (LIBERT)	21,334	10.7
6 • Spencer Bachus (R)	208,084	88.2
Terry Reagin Sr. (LIBERT)	27,787	11.8
7 • Earl F. Hilliard (D)	147,415	74.8
Ed Martin (R)	45,905	23.3
Kennon Harding "Ken" Hager (LIBERT)	3,806	1.9
ALASKA		
AL • Don Young (R)	157,671	70.2
Clifford Mark Greene (D)	36,828	16.4
Anna C. Young (GREEN)	17,857	8.0
Jim Dore (AKI)	7,903	3.5
Leonard J. "Len" Karpinski (LIBERT)	3,825	1.7
write-ins	642	.3
ARIZONA		
Senate		
• Jon Kyl (R)	966,370	78.8
William Toel (I)	98,213	8.0
Vance Hansen (GREEN)	97,428	8.0

	Vote Total	%
Barry Hess (LIBERT)	63,892	5.2
House		
1 # Jeff Flake (R)	100,122	52.6
David Mendoza (D)	82,559	43.4
Jon Burroughs (LIBERT)	7,752	4.1
2 • Ed Pastor (D)	77,844	68.2
Bill Barenholtz (R)	31,080	27.2
Geoffrey Weber (LIBERT)	2,937	2.6
Barbara Shelor (NL)	2,219	2.0
3 • Bob Stump (R)	170,622	65.4
Gene Scharer (D)	83,786	31.0
Edward R. Carlson (LIBERT)	7,929	3.6
4 • John Shadegg (R)	116,615	63.2
Ben Jankowski (D)	61,614	33.4
Ernest Hancock (LIBERT)	6,222	3.4
5 • Jim Kolbe (R)	162,278	60.0
George Cunningham (D)	95,840	35.5
Michael Jay Green (GR)	8,335	3.1
Aage Nost (LIBERT)	3,764	1.4
6 • J.D. Hayworth (R)	161,862	60.3
Larry Nelson (D)	98,681	36.8
Rick Duncan (LIBERT)	7,985	3.0
ARKANSAS		
1 • Marion Berry (D)	110,498	59.2
Susan Myshka (R)	76,150	40.8
write-in	19	—
2 • Vic Snyder (D)	123,825	57.5
Bob Thomas (R)	91,664	42.5
3 • Asa Hutchinson (R)	x	x
4 # Mike Ross (D)	105,494	50.9
• Jay Dickey (R)	101,921	49.1
CALIFORNIA		
Senate		
• Dianne Feinstein (D)	5,313,355	56.0
Tom Campbell (R)	3,449,647	36.4

	Vote Total	%
Medea Susan Benjamin (GREEN)	291,395	3.1
Gail Lightfoot (LIBERT)	168,636	1.8
Diane Beall Templin (AMI)	120,340	1.3
Jose Luis "Joe" Camahort (REF)	87,196	.9
Brian Rees (NL)	52,612	.6
House		
1 • Mike Thompson (D)	141,876	65.2
Russell J. "Jim" Chase (R)	60,381	27.8
Cheryl Kreier (NL)	6,614	3.0
Emil Rossi (LIBERT)	5,857	2.7
Pamela Elizondo (REF)	2,889	1.3
2 • Wally Herger (R)	156,581	65.7
Stan Morgan (D)	67,351	28.3
John McDermott (NL)	8,283	3.5
Charles Martin (LIBERT)	6,083	2.5
3 • Doug Ose (R)	120,943	56.1
Bob Kent (D)	87,304	40.5
Douglas Tuma (LIBERT)	4,908	2.3
Channing Jones (NL)	2,437	1.1
4 • John T. Doolittle (R)	171,453	62.4
Mark Norberg (D)	88,752	32.3
William Frey (LIBERT)	8,576	3.1
Robert Ray (NL)	5,790	2.1
5 • Robert T. Matsui (D)	134,242	68.6
Ken Payne (R)	51,355	26.3
Ken Adams (GREEN)	5,625	2.9
Cullene Lang (LIBERT)	2,644	1.4
Charles Kersey (NL)	1,777	.9
6 • Lynn Woolsey (D)	168,603	64.3
Ken McAuliffe (R)	74,337	28.4
Justin "Justo" Moscoso (GREEN)	12,261	4.7
Richard Barton (LIBERT)	4,328	1.6
Alan Barreca (NL)	2,675	1.0
7 • George Miller (D)	137,989	76.6
Christopher Hoffman (R)	37,763	21.0
Martin Sproul (NL)	4,355	2.4
8 • Nancy Pelosi (D)	152,479	84.6

Abbreviations for Party Designations

AC	— American Constitution	GR	— Grassroots	LU	— Liberty Union	PRO	— Progressive
AKI	— Alaskan Independence	GREEN	— Green	MOUNT	— Mountain	R	— Republican
AMI	— American Independent	I	— Independent	NJC	— New Jersey Conservative	REF	— Reform
C	— Conservative	IA	— Independent American	Party		RTL	— Right to Life
CC	— Concerned Citizens	INDC	— Independence	NJI	— New Jersey Independents	S	— Socialist
CITFIRST	— Citizens First	IP	— Independent Party	NL	— Natural Law	SW	— Socialist Workers
CNSTP	— Constitution	L	— Liberal	POPDEM	— Popular Democratic	USTAX	— U.S. Taxpayers
CONSTL	— Constitutional	LIBERT	— Libertarian	PRI	— Puerto Rican Indepen-	VG	— Vermont Grassroots
D	— Democratic	LMP	— Legalize Marijuana	dence		WFM	— Working Families

	Vote Total	%
Adam Sparks (R)	20,703	11.5
Erik Bauman (LIBERT)	4,834	2.7
David Smithstein (NL)	2,271	1.3
9 • Barbara Lee (D)	157,514	85.1
Arneze Washington (R)	17,659	9.5
Fred Foldvary (LIBERT)	6,124	3.3
Ellen Jefferds (NL)	3,725	2.0
10 • Ellen O. Tauscher (D)	135,595	52.7
Claude B. Hutchison Jr. (R)	113,355	44.1
Valerie Janlois (NL)	8,234	3.2
11 • Richard W. Pombo (R)	110,361	57.9
Tom Santos (D)	72,581	38.1
Kathryn Russow (LIBERT)	4,624	2.4
Jon Kurey (NL)	3,099	1.6
12 • Tom Lantos (D)	135,056	74.4
Mike Garza (R)	37,874	20.9
Barbara Less (LIBERT)	5,615	3.1
Rifkin Young (NL)	3,087	1.7
13 • Pete Stark (D)	113,277	70.7
James Goetz (R)	38,402	23.9
Howard Mora (LIBERT)	4,124	2.6
Tim Hoehner (NL)	2,370	1.5
Don Grundmann (AMI)	2,137	1.3
14 • Anna G. Eshoo (D)	139,863	70.3
Bill Quraishi (R)	51,021	25.6
Joseph W. Dehn III (LIBERT)	4,097	2.1
John H. Black (NL)	3,938	2.0
15 # Mike Honda (D)	116,693	54.5
Jim Cunneen (R)	89,937	42.0
Ed Wimmers (LIBERT)	4,312	2.0
Douglas Gorney (NL)	3,212	1.5
16 • Zoe Lofgren (D)	100,139	72.5
Horace Thayn (R)	31,636	22.9
Dennis Michael Umphress (LIBERT)	4,127	3.0
Edward Klein (NL)	2,285	1.6
17 • Sam Farr (D)	127,127	68.5
Clint Engler (R)	45,996	24.8
E. Craig Coffin (GREEN)	7,288	3.9
Rick Garrett (LIBERT)	2,232	1.2
Lawrence Fenton (REF)	2,008	1.1
Scott Hartley (NL)	881	.5
18 • Gary A. Condit (D)	105,420	67.2
Steve Wilson (R)	49,005	31.2
Page Roth Riskin (NL)	2,521	1.6
19 • George P. Radanovich (R)	129,278	64.8
Daniel Rosenberg (D)	63,497	31.8
Elizabeth Taylor (LIBERT)	3,857	1.9
Robert Miller (NL)	1,793	.9
Edmon V. Kaiser (AMI)	1,144	.6
20 • Cal Dooley (D)	58,017	52.6
Rich Rodriguez (R)	49,916	45.3
Walter Ruehlig (NL)	1,224	1.1
Arnold Kriegbaum (LIBERT)	1,160	1.1
21 • Bill Thomas (R)	131,647	71.6
Pedro Martinez (D)	45,560	24.8
James Manion (LIBERT)	6,646	3.6
22 • Lois Capps (D)	113,636	52.8
Mike Stoker (R)	96,103	44.6
Richard D. "Dick" Porter (REF)	2,163	1.0
Joe Furcinite (LIBERT)	1,767	.8
J. Carlos Aguirre (NL)	1,610	.8
23 • Elton Gallegly (R)	96,054	53.4
Michael Case (D)	74,101	41.2
Cary Savitch (REF)	5,239	2.9
Roger Peebles (LIBERT)	3,105	1.7
Stephen Hospodar (NL)	1,252	.7
24 • Brad Sherman (D)	142,398	66.4

	Vote Total	%
Jerry Doyle (R)	63,040	29.4
Juan Ros (LIBERT)	6,371	3.0
Michael Cuddehe (NL)	2,657	1.2
25 • Howard P. "Buck" McKeon (R)	128,149	62.2
Sid Gold (D)	68,501	33.2
Bruce Acker (LIBERT)	6,682	3.2
Mews Small (NL)	2,748	1.3
26 • Howard L. Berman (D)	90,739	84.1
Bill Farley (LIBERT)	12,290	11.4
David Cossak (NL)	4,909	4.5
27 # Adam Schiff (D)	106,063	52.8
• James E. Rogan (R)	87,972	43.8
Miriam Hospodar (NL)	3,579	1.8
Ted Brown (LIBERT)	3,430	1.7
28 • David Dreier (R)	109,624	56.8
Janice M. Nelson (D)	76,974	39.9
Randall Weissbuch (LIBERT)	2,653	1.4
M. Lawrence Allison (NL)	1,952	1.0
Joe Haytas (AMI)	1,831	.9
29 • Henry A. Waxman (D)	167,056	75.8
Jim Scileppi (R)	42,298	19.2
J. C. "Jack" Anderson (LIBERT)	7,329	3.3
Bruce Currivan (NL)	3,815	1.7
30 • Xavier Becerra (D)	77,935	83.3
Tony Goss (R)	11,057	11.8
Jason Heath (LIBERT)	2,660	2.8
Gary Hearne (NL)	1,907	2.0
31 # Hilda Solis (D)	84,513	79.6
Krista Lieberg-Wong (GREEN)	9,457	8.9
Michael McGuire (LIBERT)	6,694	6.3
Richard Griffin (NL)	5,525	5.2
32 • Julian C. Dixon (D)	127,926	83.6
Kathy Williamson (R)	18,514	12.1
Bob Weber (LIBERT)	3,641	2.4
Rashied Jibri (NL)	3,006	2.0
33 • Lucille Roybal-Allard (D)	57,270	84.6
Wayne Miller (R)	7,781	11.5
Nathan Craddock (LIBERT)	1,511	2.2
William Harpur (NL)	1,130	1.7
34 • Grace F. Napolitano (D)	99,752	71.2
Robert Arthur Canales (R)	31,567	22.5
Julia F. Simon (NL)	8,702	6.2
35 • Maxine Waters (D)	94,948	86.5
Carl McGill (R)	11,914	10.9
Gordon Michael Mego (AMI)	1,794	1.6
Rick Dunstan (NL)	1,081	1.0
36 # Jane Harman (D)	106,975	48.4
• Steven T. Kuykendall (R)	103,142	46.6
Daniel Sherman (LIBERT)	5,615	2.5
John Konopka (REF)	3,297	1.5
Matt Ornati (NL)	2,078	.9
37 • Juanita Millender-McDonald (D)	88,324	82.4
Vernon Van (R)	12,077	11.3
Margaret Glazer (NL)	3,858	3.6
Herb Peters (LIBERT)	2,988	2.8
38 • Steve Horn (R)	81,446	48.4
Gerrie Schipske (D)	79,830	47.5
Karen Blasdell-Wilkinson (NL)	3,486	2.1
Jack Neglia (LIBERT)	3,375	2.0
39 • Ed Royce (R)	116,559	62.4
Gill G. Kanel (D)	59,458	31.8
Ron Jevning (NL)	5,982	3.2
Keith Gann (LIBERT)	4,799	2.6
40 • Jerry Lewis (R)	140,954	79.8
Frank Schmit (NL)	17,878	10.1
Jay Lindberg (LIBERT)	17,686	10.0
41 • Gary G. Miller (R)	96,133	58.6
Rodolfo "Rudy" Favila (D)	61,927	37.7

	Vote Total	%
David F. Kramer (NL)	6,115	3.7
42 • Joe Baca (D)	85,405	60.0
Elia Pirozzi (R)	49,727	34.9
John "Scott" Ballard (LIBERT)	3,823	2.7
Gwyn Hartley (NL)	3,452	2.4
43 • Ken Calvert (R)	129,095	73.6
Bill Reed (LIBERT)	27,543	15.7
Nathaniel Adam (NL)	18,703	10.7
44 • Mary Bono (R)	113,971	59.0
Ron Oden (D)	73,444	38.0
Gene Smith (REF)	3,784	2.0
Jim Meuer (NL)	1,829	.9
45 • Dana Rohrabacher (R)	119,219	61.8
Ted Crisell (D)	62,973	32.6
Don Hull (LIBERT)	7,511	3.9
Constance Betton (NL)	3,226	1.7
46 • Loretta Sanchez (D)	59,100	59.4
Gloria Matta Tuchman (R)	35,397	35.6
Richard Benjamin Boddie (LIBERT)	2,756	2.8
Larry G. Engwall (NL)	2,174	2.2
47 • Christopher Cox (R)	153,819	65.3
John L. Graham (D)	71,342	30.3
David Nolan (LIBERT)	7,067	3.0
Iris Adam (NL)	3,283	1.4
48 # Darrell Issa (R)	135,228	61.0
Peter Kouvelis (D)	63,482	28.6
Eddie Rose (REF)	9,685	4.4
Sharon K. Miles (NL)	7,110	3.2
Joe Cobb (LIBERT)	6,278	2.8
49 # Susan A. Davis (D)	95,167	49.8
• Brian P. Bilbray (R)	87,890	46.0
Doris Ball (LIBERT)	5,494	2.9
Tahir Bhatti (NL)	2,588	1.4
50 • Bob Filner (D)	80,821	68.8
Bob Divine (R)	31,738	27.0
David Willoughby (LIBERT)	2,968	2.5
Leeann Kendall (NL)	1,940	1.6
51 • Randy "Duke" Cunningham (R)	141,159	63.8
George "Jorge" Barraza (D)	68,131	30.8
Daniel L. Muhe (LIBERT)	5,923	2.7
Eric Hunter Bourdette (NL)	5,922	2.7
52 • Duncan Hunter (R)	109,123	64.2
Craig B. Barkacs (D)	54,090	31.8
Michael Benoit (LIBERT)	5,099	3.0
Robert Sherman (NL)	1,787	1.1

COLORADO

	Vote Total	%
1 • Diana DeGette (D)	140,230	68.8
Jesse L. Thomas (R)	55,278	27.1
Richard Combs (LIBERT)	5,804	2.9
Lyle L. Nasser (REF)	2,422	1.2
2 • Mark Udall (D)	146,229	55.2
Carolyn Cox (R)	101,042	38.1
Ron Forthofer (GREEN)	12,256	4.6
David Baker (LIBERT)	5,454	2.1
3 • Scott McInnis (R)	192,705	65.9
Curtis Imrie (D)	85,285	29.2
Drew Sakson (LIBERT)	9,349	3.2
Victor A. Good (REF)	5,172	1.8
4 • Bob Schaffer (R)	204,439	81.0
Dan Sewell Ward (NL)	19,342	7.7
Kordon Baker (LIBERT)	19,287	7.6
Leslie Hanks (AC)	9,402	3.7
5 • Joel Hefley (R)	253,130	82.7
Kerry Kantor (LIBERT)	37,720	12.3
Randy MacKenzie (NL)	15,269	5.0

		Vote Total	%
6 •	Tom Tancredo (R)	141,053	54.0
	Ken Toltz (D)	110,291	42.2
	Adam D. Katz (LIBERT)	6,551	2.5
	John Heckman (COPP)	3,408	1.3

CONNECTICUT

Senate

		Vote Total	%
•	Joseph I. Lieberman (D)	807,429	63.3
	Philip A. Giordano (R)	438,441	34.4
	William Kozak (CC)	21,756	1.7
	Wildey J. Moore (LIBERT)	8,181	.6

House

		Vote Total	%
1 •	John B. Larson (D)	146,704	71.4
	Bob Backlund (R)	58,707	28.6
2 #	Rob Simmons (R)	114,215	50.6
•	Sam Gejdenson (D)	111,395	49.4
3 •	Rosa DeLauro (D)	149,577	72.0
	June Gold (R)	57,179	27.5
	Gail J. Dalby (NL)	1,073	.5
4 •	Christopher Shays (R)	118,278	57.6
	Stephanie Sanchez (D)	84,295	41.1
	Daniel Gislao (LIBERT)	1,786	.9
	Frank M. Don (INDC)	963	.5
5 •	Jim Maloney (D)	117,694	53.5
	Mark D. Nielsen (R)	97,612	44.4
	Joseph A. Zdonczyk (CC)	4,578	2.1
	write-in	7	—
6 •	Nancy L. Johnson (R)	136,854	63.0
	Paul Vincent Valenti (D)	71,354	32.8
	Audrey A. Cole (GREEN)	6,468	3.0
	Timothy A. Knibbs (CC)	2,719	1.3

DELAWARE

Governor

		Vote Total	%
#	Ruth Ann Minner (D)	191,484	59.3
	John Burris (R)	128,436	39.7
	Floyd E. McDowell Sr. (IP)	3,263	1.0

Senate

		Vote Total	%
#	Thomas R. Carper (D)	181,387	55.5
•	William V. Roth Jr. (R)	142,683	43.7
	J. Burke Morrison (LIBERT)	1,103	.3
	Mark E. Dankof (CNSTP)	1,041	.3
	Robert Mattson (NL)	389	.1

House

		Vote Total	%
AL •	Michael N. Castle (R)	211,546	67.6
	Mike Miller (D)	96,538	30.9
	James P. Webster (CNSTP)	2,486	.8
	Brad C. Thomas (LIBERT)	2,346	.8

FLORIDA

Senate

		Vote Total	%
#	Bill Nelson (D)	2,981,667	51.0
	Bill McCollum (R)	2,698,770	46.2
	Willie Logan (I)	80,541	1.4
	Joe Simonetta (NL)	26,004	.5
	Darrell L. McCormick (I)	21,578	.4
	Joel Deckard (REF)	17,253	.3
	Andy Martin (I)	15,830	.3

House

		Vote Total	%
1 •	Joe Scarborough (R)	x	x
2 •	Allen Boyd (D)	185,351	72.2
	Doug Dodd (R)	71,539	27.9
3 •	Corrine Brown (D)	102,062	57.6
	Jennifer Carroll (R)	75,089	42.4
4 #	Ander Crenshaw (R)	202,890	67.0
	Tom Sullivan (D)	94,501	31.2
	Deborah Katz Pueschel (I)	5,598	1.9
5 •	Karen L. Thurman (D)	180,157	64.3
	Peter C.K. "Pete" Enwall (R)	100,108	35.7
6 •	Cliff Stearns (R)	x	x
7 •	John L. Mica (R)	170,690	63.2
	Daniel Vaughen (D)	99,394	36.8
8 #	Richard "Ric" Keller (R)	125,211	50.9
	Linda Chapin (D)	121,032	49.1
9 •	Michael Bilirakis (R)	209,586	81.9
	Jon Scott Duffey (REF)	46,385	18.1
10 •	C.W. Bill Young (R)	146,135	75.7
	Josette Green (NL)	26,751	13.9
	Randy Heine (NP)	20,220	10.5
11 •	Jim Davis (D)	149,433	84.6
	Charlie Westlake (LIBERT)	27,194	15.4
12 #	Adam Putnam (R)	125,071	57.0
	Michael Stedem (D)	94,349	43.0
13 •	Dan Miller (R)	175,841	63.9
	Daniel E. Dunn (D)	99,514	36.1
14 •	Porter J. Goss (R)	242,560	85.3
	Sam Farling (NL)	41,975	14.8
15 •	Dave Weldon (R)	176,112	58.8
	Patsy Ann Kurth (D)	117,477	39.3
	Gerry Newby (I)	5,742	1.9
16 •	Mark Foley (R)	176,058	60.3
	Jean Elliott Brown (D)	108,317	37.1
	John Michael McGuire (REF)	7,546	2.6
17 •	Carrie P. Meek (D)	x	x
18 •	Ileana Ros-Lehtinen (R)	x	x
19 •	Robert Wexler (D)	170,873	71.6
	Morris Kent Thompson (R)	67,696	28.4
20 •	Peter Deutsch (D)	x	x
22 •	E. Clay Shaw Jr. (R)	105,611	50.2
	Elaine Bloom (D)	104,974	49.8
21 •	Lincoln Diaz-Balart (R)	x	x
23 •	Alcee L. Hastings (D)	89,080	76.3
	Bill Lambert (R)	27,609	23.7

GEORGIA

Senate

		Vote Total	%
•	Zell Miller (D)	1,112,328	55.9
	Mack Mattingly (R)	800,428	40.2
	Paul Robert MacGregor (LIBERT)	21,361	1.1
	Ben Ballenger (R)	19,206	1.0
	Jeff Gates (GREEN)	16,507	.8
	Bobby Rudolph Wood (R)	10,512	.5
	Winnie Walsh (I)	9,150	.5

House

		Vote Total	%
1 •	Jack Kingston (R)	127,150	69.3
	Joyce Marie Griggs (D)	56,183	30.6
2 •	Sanford D. Bishop Jr. (D)	92,426	52.9
	Dylan Glenn (R)	82,164	47.1
3 •	Mac Collins (R)	146,668	63.8
	Gail Notti (D)	83,348	36.2
4 •	Cynthia A. McKinney (D)	139,240	60.9
	Sunny Warren (R)	89,535	39.1
5 •	John Lewis (D)	56,248	75.2
	Hank Schwab (R)	18,534	24.8
6 •	Johnny Isakson (R)	221,841	74.5
	Brett DeHart (D)	76,091	25.5
7 •	Bob Barr (R)	110,600	54.0
	Roger Kahn (D)	94,327	46.0
8 •	Saxby Chambliss (R)	110,007	58.5
	Jim Marshall (D)	78,049	41.5
9 •	Nathan Deal (R)	158,189	76.0
	James Harrington (D)	50,067	24.0
10 •	Charlie Norwood (R)	121,992	63.2
	Marion Spencer "Denise" Freeman (D)	71,011	36.8
11 •	John Linder (R)	x	x

HAWAII

Senate

		Vote Total	%
•	Daniel K. Akaka (D)	251,174	72.7
	John S. Carroll (R)	84,677	24.5
	Lauri A. Clegg (NL)	4,218	1.2
	Lloyd Jeffery Mallan (LIBERT)	3,126	.9
	David Porter (CNSTP)	2,360	.7

House

		Vote Total	%
1 •	Neil Abercrombie (D)	108,504	69.0
	Philip L. Meyers (R)	44,947	28.6
	Gerard Murphy (LIBERT)	3,688	2.4
2 •	Patsy T. Mink (D)	112,832	61.6
	Russell R. Francis (R)	65,878	36.0
	Lawrence Duquesne (LIBERT)	4,468	2.4

IDAHO

		Vote Total	%
1 #	C. L. "Butch" Otter (R)	149,727	65.1
	Linda Pall (D)	71,343	31.0
	Ronald G. Wittig (LIBERT)	5,290	2.3
	Kevin Philip Hambsch (REF)	3,607	1.6
2 •	Mike Simpson (R)	144,869	71.3
	Craig Williams (D)	51,700	25.4
	Donovan Bramwell (LIBERT)	6,737	3.3

ILLINOIS

		Vote Total	%
1 •	Bobby L. Rush (D)	168,934	87.7
	Raymond G. Wardingley (R)	23,640	12.3
2 •	Jesse L. Jackson Jr. (D)	172,723	89.8
	Robert Gordon III (R)	19,523	10.2
3 •	William O. Lipinski (D)	143,022	75.4
	Karl Groth (R)	46,581	24.6
4 •	Luis V. Gutierrez (D)	87,269	88.7
	Stephanie Sailor (LIBERT)	11,124	11.3
5 •	Rod R. Blagojevich (D)	139,881	87.3
	Matthew Joseph Beauchamp (LIBERT)	20,361	12.7
6 •	Henry J. Hyde (R)	133,137	59.0
	Brent Christensen (D)	92,646	41.0
7 •	Danny K. Davis (D)	160,558	85.9
	Robert Dallas (R)	26,284	14.1
8 •	Philip M. Crane (R)	141,101	61.0
	Lance Pressl (D)	90,104	39.0
9 •	Jan Schakowsky (D)	144,814	76.3
	Dennis J. Driscoll (R)	44,886	23.7
10 #	Mark Steven Kirk (R)	120,431	51.1
	Lauren Beth Gash (D)	115,004	48.9
11 •	Jerry Weller (R)	132,347	56.4
	James P. Stevenson (D)	102,410	43.6
12 •	Jerry F. Costello (D)	x	x
13 •	Judy Biggert (R)	192,705	66.2
	Thomas Mason (D)	98,336	33.8
14 •	J. Dennis Hastert (R)	188,189	74.0
	Vern Deljonson (D)	66,096	26.0
15 #	Timothy V. Johnson (R)	125,328	53.2
	Mike Kelleher (D)	110,158	46.8
16 •	Donald Manzullo (R)	178,174	66.7
	Charles W. Hendrickson (D)	88,781	33.3
17 •	Lane Evans (D)	132,467	54.9
	Mark Baker (R)	108,844	45.1

		Vote Total	%
18 •	Ray LaHood (R)	166,994	66.8
	Joyce Harant (D)	82,944	33.2
19 •	David D. Phelps (D)	153,391	64.5
	James E. "Jim" Eatherly (R)	84,253	35.5
20 •	John Shimkus (R)	161,393	63.1
	Jeffrey Cooper (D)	94,382	36.9

INDIANA

Governor
•	Frank L. O'Bannon (D)	1,216,285	56.6
	David M. McIntosh (R)	858,802	40.0
	Andrew Horning (LIBERT)	71,898	3.4

Senate
•	Richard G. Lugar (R)	1,407,732	66.5
	David L. Johnson (D)	674,764	31.9
	Paul Hager (LIBERT)	34,408	1.6

House
1 •	Peter J. Visclosky (D)	135,531	72.1
	Jack Reynolds (R)	49,832	26.5
	Christopher Nelson (LIBERT)	2,546	1.4
2 #	Mike Pence (R)	106,023	50.9
	Bob Rock (D)	80,885	38.8
	William G. Frazier (I)	19,077	9.2
	Michael Anderson (LIBERT)	2,420	1.2
3 •	Tim Roemer (D)	107,427	51.6
	Chris Chocola (R)	98,817	47.4
	Scott C. Baker (LIBERT)	2,050	1.0
4 •	Mark Souder (R)	126,421	62.2
	Mike Foster (D)	72,199	35.5
	Michael Donlan (LIBERT)	4,722	2.3
5 •	Steve Buyer (R)	130,911	60.9
	Greg Goodnight (D)	80,456	37.5
	Scott Benson (LIBERT)	3,473	1.6
6 •	Dan Burton (R)	198,326	70.3
	Darin Patrick Griesey (D)	74,261	26.3
	Joe Hauptmann (LIBERT)	9,414	3.3
7 #	Brian D. Kerns (R)	131,562	64.6
	Michael Graf (D)	65,174	32.0
	Bob Thayer (LIBERT)	6,871	3.4
8 •	John Hostettler (R)	116,860	52.7
	Paul Perry (D)	100,461	45.3
	Thomas Tindle (LIBERT)	4,240	1.9
9 •	Baron P. Hill (D)	125,978	54.2
	Michael Everett Bailey (R)	101,790	43.8
	Sara Chambers (LIBERT)	4,634	2.0
10 •	Julia Carson (D)	91,300	58.5
	Marvin B. Scott (R)	61,818	39.6
	Na'llah Ali (LIBERT)	2,852	1.8

IOWA

1 •	Jim Leach (R)	163,580	61.9
	Bob Simpson (D)	95,392	36.1
	Russ Madden (LIBERT)	5,527	2.1
2 •	Jim Nussle (R)	139,196	55.4
	Donna L. Smith (D)	109,732	43.7
	Albert W. Schoeman (LIBERT)	2,294	.9
3 •	Leonard L. Boswell (D)	153,847	63.0
	Jay B. Marcus (R)	81,936	33.5
	Sue Atkinson (INDC)	5,495	2.3
	Joe Seehusen (LIBERT)	2,240	.9
	Jim Hennager (EF)	881	.4
4 •	Greg Ganske (R)	168,097	61.5
	Michael L. Huston (D)	100,277	36.7
	Steve Zimmerman (LIBERT)	4,359	1.6
	Edwin B. Fruit (SW)	592	.2
5 •	Tom Latham (R)	158,023	68.8

		Vote Total	%
	Mike Palecek (D)	66,815	29.1
	Ben L. Olson (LIBERT)	2,830	1.2
	Ray Holtorf (I)	1,916	.8

KANSAS

1 •	Jerry Moran (R)	216,953	89.3
	Jack W. Warner (LIBERT)	26,012	10.7
2 •	Jim Ryun (R)	163,151	67.4
	Stanley Wiles (D)	70,925	29.3
	Ira Dennis "Dennis" Hawver (LIBERT)	7,994	3.3
3 •	Dennis Moore (D)	154,157	50.2
	Phill Kline (R)	143,538	46.8
	Chris Mina (LIBERT)	9,360	3.0
4 •	Todd Tiahrt (R)	128,737	54.5
	Carlos Nolla (D)	99,283	42.0
	Steven A. Rosile (LIBERT)	8,405	3.6

KENTUCKY

1 •	Edward Whitfield (R)	130,818	57.9
	Brian Roy (D)	95,178	42.1
2 •	Ron Lewis (R)	160,628	67.7
	Brian Pedigo (D)	74,429	31.4
	Michael A. Kirkman (LIBERT)	2,120	.9
3 •	Anne M. Northup (R)	142,106	52.9
	Eleanor Jordan (D)	118,785	44.2
	Donna Walker Mancini (LIBERT)	7,804	2.9
4 •	Ken Lucas (D)	126,704	54.2
	Don Bell (R)	101,934	43.6
	Ken Sain (GR)	3,675	1.6
	Alan Handleman (LIBERT)	1,494	.6
5 •	Harold Rogers (R)	144,608	73.4
	Sidney "Jane" Bailey-Bamer (D)	52,455	26.6
6 •	Ernie Fletcher (R)	142,971	52.8
	Scotty Baesler (D)	94,167	34.8
	Gatewood Galbraith (I)	32,436	12.0
	Joseph Novak (LIBERT)	1,229	.5

LOUISIANA

1 •	David Vitter (R)	190,657	80.5
	Michael A. Armato (D)	29,858	12.6
	Cary J. Deaton (D)	10,929	4.6
	Martin A. Rosenthal (NL)	3,126	1.3
	John Paul "Jack" Simanonok (LIBERT)	2,380	1.0
2 •	William J. Jefferson (D)	x	x
3 •	W.J. "Billy" Tauzin (R)	142,156	77.9
	Edwin J. "Eddie" Albares (I)	16,797	9.2
	Anita Rosenthal (NL)	13,377	7.3
	Dion Bourque (LIBERT)	10,073	5.5
4 •	Jim McCrery (R)	122,481	70.5
	Phillip R. Green (D)	43,558	25.1
	Michael "Mike" Taylor (I)	4,053	2.3
	James Ronals Skains (I)	3,625	2.1
5 •	John Cooksey (R)	123,722	69.0
	Roger Beall (D)	42,900	23.9
	Sam Houston Melton Jr. (D)	7,201	4.0
	Raymond A. "Chuck" Dumas (LIBERT)	5,346	3.0
6 •	Richard H. Baker (R)	165,388	68.0
	Kathy J. Rogillio (D)	71,979	29.6
	Michael S. Wolf (LIBERT)	5,708	2.4
7 •	Chris John (D)	152,798	83.3
	Michael P. Harris (LIBERT)	30,708	16.7

MAINE

		Vote Total	%

Senate
•	Olympia J. Snowe (R)	402,829	68.5
	Mark Lawrence (D)	185,100	31.5

House
1 •	Tom Allen (D)	181,516	59.8
	Jane Amero (R)	110,733	36.5
	J. Frederic Staples (I)	11,162	3.7
2 •	John Baldacci (D)	209,423	73.3
	Richard Campbell (R)	76,361	26.7

MARYLAND

Senate
•	Paul S. Sarbanes (D)	1,171,091	63.3
	Paul Rappaport (R)	678,376	36.6
	write-ins	1,282	.1

House
1 •	Wayne T. Gilchrest (R)	154,732	64.6
	Bennett Bozman (D)	84,956	35.4
2 •	Robert L. Ehrlich Jr. (R)	152,135	69.2
	Kenneth T. Bosley (D)	67,606	30.8
3 •	Benjamin L. Cardin (D)	139,343	75.7
	Colin Harby (R)	44,641	24.3
4 •	Albert R. Wynn (D)	160,534	87.4
	John B. Kimble (R)	23,101	12.6
5 •	Steny H. Hoyer (D)	158,458	65.3
	Thomas E. "Tim" Hutchins (R)	84,326	34.7
6 •	Roscoe G. Bartlett (R)	159,959	60.7
	Donald DeArmon (D)	103,759	39.3
7 •	Elijah E. Cummings (D)	130,253	87.4
	Kenneth Kondner (R)	18,807	12.6
8 •	Constance A. Morella (R)	144,659	51.9
	Terry Lierman (D)	127,479	45.7
	Brian D. Saunders (CNSTP)	6,528	2.3
	write-ins	344	.1

MASSACHUSETTS

Senate
•	Edward M. Kennedy (D)	1,752,772	72.5
	Jack E. Robinson (R)	317,666	13.1
	Carla Howell (LIBERT)	292,721	12.1
	Philip Lawler (CNSTP)	40,680	1.7
	Dale E. Friedgen (I)	12,900	.5

House
1 •	John W. Olver (D)	157,181	67.2
	Pete Abair (R)	71,574	30.6
	Robert Potvin (I)	4,991	2.1
2 •	Richard E. Neal (D)	x	x
3 •	Jim McGovern (D)	x	x
4 •	Barney Frank (D)	188,214	75.1
	Martin D. Travis (R)	52,736	21.1
	David J. Euchner (LIBERT)	9,537	3.8
5 •	Martin T. Meehan (D)	x	x
6 •	John F. Tierney (D)	186,958	71.0
	Paul McCarthy (R)	76,329	29.0
7 •	Edward J. Markey (D)	x	x
8 •	Michael E. Capuano (D)	x	x
9 •	Joe Moakley (D)	160,500	76.3
	Janet E. Jeghelian (R)	43,978	20.9
	David Rosa (I)	5,971	2.8
10 •	Bill Delahunt (D)	210,828	74.6
	Eric V. Bleichen (R)	71,644	25.4

		Vote Total	%

MICHIGAN

Senate

		Vote Total	%
#	Debbie Stabenow (D)	2,035,521	49.2
•	Spencer Abraham (R)	1,992,561	48.1
	Matthew R. Abel (GREEN)	37,334	.9
	Michael R. Corliss (LIBERT)	29,552	.7
	Mark Forton (REF)	26,203	.6
	John Mangopoulos (USTAX)	11,547	.3
	William Quarton (NL)	5,817	.1

House

		Vote Total	%
1 •	Bart Stupak (D)	169,888	58.4
	Chuck Yob (R)	116,856	40.1
	John W. Loosemore (LIBERT)	2,455	.8
	Wendy Conway (NL)	1,837	.6
2 •	Peter Hoekstra (R)	186,825	64.4
	Bob Shrauger (D)	96,331	33.2
	Susan J. Goldberg (NL)	2,705	.9
	Bruce A. Smith (LIBERT)	2,638	.9
	Ronald E. Graeser (USTAX)	1,448	.5
3 •	Vernon J. Ehlers (R)	179,542	65.0
	Tim Steele (D)	91,314	33.0
	Erwin J. Haas (LIBERT)	2,403	.9
	Tom Grego (USTAX)	1,093	.4
	Kenneth L. Lowndes (REF)	1,053	.4
	Jerry Berta (NL)	861	.3
4 •	Dave Camp (R)	181,948	68.0
	Lawrence D. Hollenbeck (D)	78,022	29.1
	Alan Gamble (GREEN)	3,793	1.4
	Richard Whitelock (LIBERT)	2,118	.8
	John Emerick (USTAX)	974	.4
	Stuart J. Goldberg (NL)	787	.3
5 •	James A. Barcia (D)	186,056	74.5
	Ronald G. Actis (R)	59,266	23.7
	Clint Foster (LIBERT)	3,067	1.2
	Brian D. Ellison (NL)	1,345	.5
6 •	Fred Upton (R)	159,237	67.9
	James Bupp (D)	68,457	29.2
	William Bradley (LIBERT)	3,564	1.5
	Richard M. Overton (REF)	1,859	.8
	Dennis C. James (USTAX)	1,281	.6
7 •	Nick Smith (R)	147,756	61.0
	Jennie Crittenden (D)	87,020	35.9
	Perry Spencer (REF)	2,376	1.0
	Robert F. Broda Jr. (LIBERT)	2,144	.9
	Steve Cousino (USTAX)	1,949	.8
	Gail A. Petrosoff (NL)	1,188	.5
8 #	Mike Rogers (R)	145,164	48.8
	Dianne Byrum (D)	145,012	48.7
	Bonnie Bucqueroux (GREEN)	3,484	1.2
	James P. Eyster (LIBERT)	2,442	.8
	Patricia Rayfield Allen (NL)	713	.2
	Francisco R. Gualdoni (USTAX)	695	.2
9 •	Dale E. Kildee (D)	158,162	61.1
	Grant Garrett (R)	92,907	35.9
	Laurie M. Martin (LIBERT)	5,336	2.1
	Terry R. Haines (USTAX)	1,656	.6
	Alaya Bouche (NL)	823	.3
10 •	David E. Bonior (D)	180,281	64.2
	Thomas Turner (R)	93,878	33.4
	Richard Friend (LIBERT)	4,399	1.6
	Joseph M. Pilchak (USTAX)	2,302	.8
11 •	Joe Knollenberg (R)	170,785	55.8
	Matthew Frumin (D)	124,061	40.5
	Marilyn MacDermaid (GREEN)	4,191	1.4
	Dick Gach (LIBERT)	3,371	1.1
	Joseph A. Ditzhazy Jr. (REF)	1,425	.5
	Daniel E. Malone (USTAX)	1,244	.4
	Bonnie Hixson (NL)	1,229	.4
12 •	Sander M. Levin (D)	157,613	64.3
	Bart Baron (R)	78,792	32.1
	Thomas Ness (GREEN)	4,127	1.7
	Andrew Le Cureaux (LIBERT)	3,630	1.5
	Fred D. Rosenberg (NL)	887	.4
13 •	Lynn Rivers (D)	160,148	64.7
	Carl F. Barry (R)	79,450	32.1
	Karin R. Corliss (LIBERT)	4,580	1.9
	Harold H. Dunn (USTAX)	2,110	.8
	David Arndt (NL)	1,304	.5
14 •	John Conyers Jr. (D)	164,493	89.4
	William A. Ashe (R)	16,496	9.0
	Constance J. Catalfio (LIBERT)	2,034	1.1
	Richard R. Miller (NL)	1,011	.6
15 •	Carolyn Cheeks Kilpatrick (D)	132,695	88.3
	Chrysanthea D. Boyd-Fields (R)	13,849	9.2
	Raymond H. Warner (LIBERT)	1,632	1.1
	Robert L. Thomas (USTAX)	1,353	.9
	Gregory F. Smith (NL)	755	.5
16 •	John D. Dingell (D)	163,416	70.8
	William Morse (R)	61,074	26.5
	Edward Hlavac (LIBERT)	3,185	1.4
	Ken Larkin (USTAX)	2,185	.9
	Noha F. Hamze (NL)	932	.4

MINNESOTA

Senate

		Vote Total	%
#	Mark Dayton (D)	1,176,438	48.7
•	Rod Grams (R)	1,043,814	43.2
	James Gibson (INDC)	141,363	5.9
	David Daniels (GR)	22,004	.9
	Rebecca Ellis (SW)	13,665	.6
	David Swan (CNSTP)	9,306	.4
	Erik D. Pakieser (LIBERT)	7,507	.3

House

		Vote Total	%
1 •	Gil Gutknecht (R)	159,804	56.4
	Mary Rieder (D)	117,934	41.6
	Rich Osness (LIBERT)	5,438	1.9
2 #	Mark Kennedy (R)	138,939	48.1
•	David Minge (D)	138,789	48.1
	Gerald W. Brekke (INDC)	7,872	2.7
	Ron Helwig (LIBERT)	1,929	.7
	Dennis A. Burda (CNSTP)	1,337	.5
3 •	Jim Ramstad (R)	220,625	67.6
	Sue Shuff (D)	96,852	29.7
	Bob Odden (LIBERT)	5,806	1.8
	Arne Niska (CNSTP)	3,154	1.0
4 #	Betty McCollum (D)	130,374	48.0
	Linda Runbeck (R)	83,836	30.9
	Tom Foley (INDC)	55,894	20.6
	Nicholas Skrivanek (CNSTP)	1,285	.5
5 •	Martin Olav Sabo (D)	176,998	68.8
	Frank Taylor (R)	58,697	22.8
	Rob Tomich (INDC)	11,837	4.6
	Chuck P. Charnstrom (LIBERT)	4,836	1.9
	Renee Lavoi (CNSTP)	4,829	1.9
6 •	Bill Luther (D)	176,340	49.6
	John Kline (R)	170,900	48.0
	Ralph A. Hubbard (CNSTP)	8,584	2.4
7 •	Collin C. Peterson (D)	180,991	66.6
	Glen Menze (R)	85,588	31.5
	Owen Sivertson (CNSTP)	5,356	2.0
8 •	James L. Oberstar (D)	207,811	67.9
	Robert Lemen (R)	79,942	26.1
	Mike Darling (I)	18,143	5.9

MISSISSIPPI

Senate

		Vote Total	%
•	Trent Lott (R)	129,020	63.4
	Troy Brown (D)	69,152	34.0
	Jim Giles (I)	1,928	.9
	Lewis Napper (LIBERT)	1,786	.9
	Shawn O'Hara (REF)	1,477	.7

House

		Vote Total	%
1 •	Roger Wicker (R)	56,292	67.3
	Joey Grist (D)	26,021	31.1
	Christopher N. "Chris" Lawrence (LIBERT)	1,332	1.6
2 •	Bennie Thompson (D)	109,086	64.7
	Hardy Caraway (R)	52,871	31.4
	William G. "Will" Chipman (LIBERT)	4,426	2.6
	Lee F. Dilworth (REF)	2,126	1.3
3 •	Charles W. "Chip" Pickering Jr. (R)	57,573	72.4
	William Clay Thrash (D)	21,027	26.4
	Jonathan R. Golden (LIBERT)	929	1.2
4 •	Ronnie Shows (D)	52,272	62.3
	Dunn Lampton (R)	29,903	35.6
	Ernie John Hopkins (LIBERT)	1,197	1.4
	Betty Pharr (REF)	565	.7
5 •	Gene Taylor (D)	57,096	79.3
	Randy McDonnell (R)	12,719	17.7
	Wayne Parker (LIBERT)	1,115	1.6
	Katie Perrone (REF)	1,039	1.4

MISSOURI

Governor

		Vote Total	%
#	Bob Holden (D)	1,152,211	49.1
	James M. Talent (R)	1,130,963	48.2
	Larry Rice (I)	34,439	1.5
	John M. Swenson (LIBERT)	11,268	.5
	Lavoy "Zaki Baruti" Reed (GREEN)	9,010	.4
	Richard A. Kline (REF)	4,906	.2
	Richard L. Smith (CNSTP)	3,140	.1

Senate

		Vote Total	%
#	Mel Carnahan (D)	1,191,423	50.5
•	John Ashcroft (R)	1,142,512	48.4
	Evaline Taylor (GREEN)	10,609	.5
	Grant Samuel Stauffer (LIBERT)	10,194	.4
	Hugh Foley (REF)	4,164	.2
	Charles Dockins (NL)	1,930	.1

House

		Vote Total	%
1 #	William Lacy Clay Jr. (D)	138,208	74.3
	Zellner Dwight Billingsly (R)	41,751	22.4
	Brenda "Ziah" Reddick (GREEN)	2,939	1.6
	Tamara A. Millay (LIBERT)	2,138	1.1
	Robert Penningroth (REF)	1,074	.6
2 #	Todd Akin (R)	164,926	55.3
	Ted House (D)	126,441	42.4
	Mike Odell (GREEN)	2,907	1.0
	James "Jim" Higgins (LIBERT)	2,524	.8
	Richard J. Gimpelson (REF)	1,264	.4
3 •	Richard A. Gephardt (D)	147,225	57.8
	William J. Federer (R)	100,965	39.7
	Mary Maroney (GREEN)	3,266	1.3
	Michael H. Crist (LIBERT)	2,245	.9
	Anthony J. "Tony" Windisch (REF)	839	.3
4 •	Ike Skelton (D)	174,480	67.1
	James A. Noland Jr. (R)	80,688	31.0

		Vote Total	%
	Thomas L. Knapp (LIBERT)	2,855	1.1
	James Edward Rinehart (REF)	1,910	.7
5 •	Karen McCarthy (D)	159,481	68.8
	Steve Gordon (R)	66,270	28.6
	Charles Reitz (GREEN)	2,554	1.1
	Allen Newberry (LIBERT)	2,346	1.0
	Dennis M. Carriger (REF)	974	.4
6 #	Sam Graves (R)	138,896	50.9
	Steve Danner (D)	127,757	46.8
	James "Jimmy" Dykes (LIBERT)	3,694	1.4
	Marie Richey (NL)	2,790	1.0
7 •	Roy Blunt (R)	202,305	73.8
	Charles Christrup (D)	65,510	23.9
	Doug Burlison (LIBERT)	2,960	1.1
	Sharalyn Harris (NL)	2,169	.8
	Ron Lapham (REF)	987	.4
8 •	Jo Ann Emerson (R)	162,228	69.3
	Bob Camp (D)	67,759	28.9
	John B. Hendricks Jr. (LIBERT)	2,328	1.0
	Tom Sager (GREEN)	1,739	.7
9 •	Kenny Hulshof (R)	172,785	59.3
	Steven R. Carroll (D)	111,660	38.3
	Robert Hoffman (LIBERT)	3,608	1.2
	Devin M. Scherubel (GREEN)	2,388	.8
	Steven D. Dotson (REF)	1,165	.4

MONTANA

Governor

		Vote Total	%
#	Judy Martz (R)	209,127	51.0
	Mark O'Keefe (D)	193,338	47.1
	Stan Jones (LIBERT)	7,926	1.9

Senate

•	Conrad Burns (R)	207,500	50.5
	Brian Schweitzer (D)	194,003	47.3
	Gary Lee (REF)	9,064	2.2

House

AL #	Denny Rehberg (R)	210,400	51.4
	Nancy Keenan (D)	189,199	46.2
	James J. Tikalsky (LIBERT)	9,995	2.4

NEBRASKA

Senate

		Vote Total	%
#	Ben Nelson (D)	329,914	50.9
	Don Stenberg (R)	317,863	49.1

House

1 •	Doug Bereuter (R)	148,790	66.4
	Alan Jacobsen (D)	69,454	31.0
	David Oenbring (LIBERT)	5,776	2.6
2 •	Lee Terry (R)	133,423	66.1
	Shelley Kiel (D)	62,173	30.8
	John J. Graziano (LIBERT)	6,248	3.1
3 #	Tom Osborne (R)	157,593	80.4
	Rollie Reynolds (D)	33,775	17.2
	Jerry Hickman (LIBERT)	4,738	2.4

NEVADA

Senate

		Vote Total	%
#	John Ensign (R)	321,769	56.1
	Ed Bernstein (D)	232,936	40.6
	Kathryn Rusco (GREEN)	9,990	1.7
	J.J. Johnson (LIBERT)	5,192	.9
	Ernie Berghof (IA)	2,461	.4
	Bill Grutzmacher (CITFIRST)	1,514	.3

House

		Vote Total	%
1 •	Shelley Berkley (D)	118,469	51.7
	Jon Porter (R)	101,276	44.2
	Charles Schneider (LIBERT)	4,011	1.8
	Christopher Hansen (IA)	3,933	1.7
	Swannie Swenson (CITFIRST)	1,546	.7
2 •	Jim Gibbons (R)	218,936	64.5
	Tierney Cahill (D)	101,766	30.0
	Dan Hansen (IA)	5,354	1.6
	A. Charles Laws (GREEN)	5,287	1.6
	Terry C. Savage (LIBERT)	5,047	1.5
	Ken Brenneman (CITFIRST)	2,199	.7
	Robert Winquist (NL)	1,084	.3

NEW HAMPSHIRE

Governor

		Vote Total	%
•	Jeanne Shaheen (D)	275,019	48.8
	Gordon Humphrey (R)	246,780	43.7
	Mary Brown (I)	35,904	6.4
	John Babiarz (LIBERT)	6,446	1.1

House

1 •	John E. Sununu (R)	150,037	53.2
	Martha Fuller Clark (D)	126,480	44.8
	Bob Bevill (I)	5,540	2.0
2 •	Charles Bass (R)	152,474	56.3
	Barney Brannen (D)	110,307	40.7
	Brian Christeson (LIBERT)	6,012	2.2
	Roy Kendel (CA)	2,131	.8

NEW JERSEY

Senate

		Vote Total	%
#	Jon Corzine (D)	1,363,094	50.7
	Bob Franks (R)	1,251,404	46.5
	Bruce Afran (I)	28,914	1.1
	Pat DiNizio (I)	16,524	.6
	Emerson Ellett (I)	6,376	.2
	Dennis A. Breen (I)	5,412	.2
	J.M. Carter (I)	5,153	.2
	Lorraine LaNeve (I)	3,310	.1
	Gregory Pason (I)	3,298	.1
	Nancy Rosenstock (I)	2,649	.1
	George Gostigian (I)	2,418	.1

House

1 •	Robert E. Andrews (D)	109,315	77.7
	Charlene Cathcart (R)	27,831	19.8
	Catherine L. Parrish (I)	1,737	1.2
	Edward Forchion (I)	1,303	.9
	Joseph A. Patalivo (I)	470	.3
2 •	Frank A. LoBiondo (R)	114,244	67.4
	Edward G. Janosik (D)	52,519	31.0
	Robert Gabrielsky (I)	1,802	1.1
	Constantino Rozzo (I)	995	.6
3 •	H. James Saxton (R)	90,391	56.1
	Susan Bass Levin (D)	68,641	42.6
	Aaron M. Kromash (I)	1,226	.8
	Norman E. Wahner (I)	513	.3
	Ken Feduniewicz (I)	255	.2
4 •	Christopher H. Smith (R)	87,055	61.2
	Reed Gusciora (D)	52,553	37.0
	Stuart Chaifetz (I)	2,093	1.5
	Paul D. Teel (I)	495	.3
5 •	Marge Roukema (R)	166,665	65.3
	Linda Mercurio (D)	77,945	30.5
	Michael "MJ" King (I)	5,093	2.0
	Robert J. McCafferty (I)	3,945	1.5
	Ira W. Goodman (I)	1,300	.5

		Vote Total	%
	Helen Hamilton (I)	455	.2
6 •	Frank Pallone Jr. (D)	139,854	67.4
	Brian T. Kennedy (R)	61,795	29.8
	Earl Gray (I)	4,156	2.0
	Karen Zaletel (I)	1,275	.6
	Sylvia Kuzmak (I)	323	.2
7 #	Mike Ferguson (R)	115,422	49.5
	Maryanne S. Connelly (D)	109,801	47.1
	Jerry L. Coleman (I)	6,433	2.8
	Darren Young (I)	931	.4
	Shawn Gianella (I)	360	.1
	Mary T. Johnson (I)	271	.1
8 •	Bill Pascrell Jr. (D)	126,535	67.4
	Anthony Fusco Jr. (R)	55,949	29.8
	Joseph A. Fortunato (I)	4,230	2.3
	Viji Sargis (I)	935	.5
9 •	Steven R. Rothman (D)	132,753	67.8
	Joseph Tedeschi (R)	58,896	30.1
	Lewis Pell (I)	2,117	1.1
	Michael Perrone Jr. (I)	1,019	.5
	Robert Corriston (I)	944	.4
10 •	Donald M. Payne (D)	126,111	87.5
	Dirk B. Weber (R)	17,606	12.2
	Maurice Williams (I)	430	.3
11 •	Rodney Frelinghuysen (R)	184,386	68.0
	John P. Scollo (D)	79,973	29.5
	John Pickarski (I)	5,130	1.9
	James E. Spinosa (I)	1,517	.6
12	Dick Zimmer (R)	143,291	48.7
•	Rush D. Holt (D)	142,920	48.6
	Carl J. Mayer (I)	5,691	1.9
	John P. Desmond (I)	1,216	.4
	Worth Winslow (I)	1,138	.4
13 •	Robert Menendez (D)	113,661	78.4
	Theresa de Leon (R)	27,325	18.9
	Claudette C. Meliere (I)	2,632	1.8
	Dick Hester (I)	566	.4
	Herbert H. Shaw (I)	347	.2
	Alina Lydia Fonteboa (I)	227	.2
	Kari Sachs (I)	157	.1

NEW MEXICO

Senate

		Vote Total	%
•	Jeff Bingaman (D)	326,386	62.9
	Bill Redmond (R)	192,440	37.1
	Orlin G. Cole — write-in	313	.1

House

1 •	Heather A. Wilson (R)	70,179	47.0
	John Kelly (D)	68,108	45.6
	Daniel Kerlinsky (GREEN)	11,152	7.5
2 •	Joe Skeen (R)	100,585	58.1
	Michael A. Montoya (D)	72,622	41.9
3 •	Tom Udall (D)	132,162	67.8
	Lisa L. Lutz (R)	62,720	32.2

NEW YORK

Senate

		Vote Total	%
#	Hillary Rodham Clinton (D, L, WFM)	3,422,027	55.0
	Rick A. Lazio (R, C)	2,681,221	43.1
	Jeff Graham (INDC)	42,308	.7
	Mark Dunau (GREEN)	37,455	.6
	John Adefope (RTL)	20,700	.3
	John Clifton (LIBERT)	5,032	.1
	Louis P. Wein (CNSTP)	4,683	.1
	Jacob Perasso (SW)	4,103	.1

		Vote Total	%
House			
1 #	Felix J. Grucci Jr. (R, INDC, C, RTL)	124,063	55.9
	Regina Seltzer (D)	89,247	40.2
•	Michael P. Forbes (WFM)	5,872	2.6
	William G. Holst (GREEN)	2,811	1.3
2 #	Steven Israel (D)	84,477	47.7
	Joan B. Johnson (R)	61,032	34.4
	Robert T. Walsh Sr. (RTL)	10,860	6.1
	Richard Thompson (C)	10,473	5.9
	David Bishop (INDC, GREEN, WFM)	10,346	5.8
3 •	Peter T. King (R, INDC, C, RTL)	135,328	59.6
	Dal LaMagna (D, GREEN, WFM)	90,290	39.8
	Selma Olchin (L)	1,378	.6
4 •	Carolyn McCarthy (D, INDC, WFM)	128,484	60.3
	Greg R. Becker (R, C, RTL)	83,469	39.2
	Barbara Vitanza (L)	1,109	.5
5 •	Gary L. Ackerman (D, INDC, L, WFM)	128,327	67.6
	Edward Elkowitz (R, C)	57,903	30.5
	Anne T. Robinson (RTL)	3,569	1.9
6 •	Gregory W. Meeks (D, WFM)	x	x
7 •	Joseph Crowley (D)	70,403	70.5
	Rose Robles Birtley (R)	22,838	22.9
	Robert E. Hurley (C)	3,467	3.5
	Paul Gilman (GREEN)	1,943	2.0
	Garafalia Christea (RTL)	1,191	1.2
8 •	Jerrold Nadler (D, L, WFM)	134,532	80.0
	Marian S. Henry (R)	26,157	15.6
	Dan Wentzel (GREEN)	4,675	2.8
	Anthony A. LaBella (C)	1,760	1.1
	Harry Kresky (INDC)	928	.6
9 •	Anthony Weiner (D, L)	90,136	67.7
	Noach Dear (R, C)	43,014	32.3
10 •	Edolphus Towns (D, L)	104,301	89.8
	Ernestine M. Brown (R)	6,222	5.4
	Barry Ford (WFM)	4,850	4.2
	Ernest Johnson (C)	750	.7
11 •	Major R. Owens (D, WFM)	101,338	87.5
	Susan Cleary (R)	7,200	6.2
	Una Clarke (D, L)	6,689	5.8
	Cartrell Gore (C)	563	.5
12 •	Nydia M. Velazquez (D, WFM)	75,423	85.2
	Rosemary Markgraf (R)	9,836	11.1
	Paul Pederson (SW)	1,271	1.4
	Caesar Estevez (C)	1,034	1.2
	Mildred Rosario (RTL)	935	1.1
13 •	Vito J. Fossella (R, C, RTL)	102,475	64.5
	Katina M. Johnstone (D, WFM)	53,812	33.9
	Anita Lerman (INDC, GREEN)	2,471	1.6
14 •	Carolyn B. Maloney (D, L)	133,420	73.2
	Carla Rhodes (R)	41,603	22.8
	Sandra Stevens (GREEN)	5,193	2.9
	Frederick D. Newman (INDC)	2,157	1.2
15 •	Charles B. Rangel (D, L, WFM)	116,183	90.9
	Jose A. Suero (R)	7,509	5.9
	Dean Loren (GREEN)	1,997	1.6
	Jessie Fields (INDC)	1,054	.8
	Frank D. Valle (C)	563	.4
	Scott Jeffrey (LIBERT)	458	.4
16 •	Jose E. Serrano (D, L)	92,404	95.4
	Richard Retcho (C)	3,925	4.0
	Aaron Justice (R)	519	.5
17 •	Eliot L. Engel (D, L)	100,871	89.1
	Patrick McManus (C, R)	12,361	10.9
18 •	Nita M. Lowey (D)	105,868	66.7

		Vote Total	%
	John G. Vonglis (R, C)	49,912	31.4
	Florence T. O'Grady (RTL)	3,003	1.9
19 •	Sue W. Kelly (R, C)	132,411	63.1
	Larry Otis Graham (D, L, WFM)	70,974	33.8
	Frank X. Lloyd (RTL)	3,491	1.7
	Mark R. Jacobs (GREEN)	3,084	1.5
20 •	Benjamin A. Gilman (R)	132,304	57.4
	Paul J. Feiner (D, L, GREEN, WFM)	93,145	40.4
	Christine M Tighe (RTL)	4,934	2.1
21 •	Michael R. McNulty (D, INDC, C)	159,214	73.9
	Thomas G. Pillsworth (R)	56,102	26.1
22 •	John E. Sweeney (R, C)	153,592	68.2
	Kenneth F. McCallion (D, GREEN, WFM)	71,533	31.8
23 •	Sherwood Boehlert (R, INDC)	111,263	59.9
	David Vickers (C, RTL)	39,148	21.1
	Richard W. Englebrecht (D)	35,361	19.0
24 •	John M. McHugh (R, C)	126,444	74.3
	Neil P. Tallon (D)	39,048	22.9
	Willard E. Smith (INDC, GREEN)	4,719	2.8
25 •	James T. Walsh (R, INDC, C)	139,877	68.9
	Francis J. Gavin (D)	59,530	29.3
	Howie Hawkins (GREEN)	3,478	1.7
26 •	Maurice D. Hinchey (D, INDC, WFM, L)	126,785	61.8
	Bob Moppert (R, C)	76,321	37.2
	Paul J. Laux (RTL)	2,166	1.1
27 •	Thomas M. Reynolds (R, C)	141,061	69.7
	Thomas W. Pecoraro (D)	61,439	30.3
28 •	Louise M. Slaughter (D)	141,367	65.5
	Mark C. Johns (R, C)	71,017	32.9
	Eve Hawkins (GREEN)	2,123	1.0
	Stephen Healey (LIBERT)	1,457	.7
29 •	John J. LaFalce (D, INDC, L)	118,504	61.1
	Brett M. Sommer (R, C, RTL)	75,308	38.9
30 •	Jack Quinn (R, C, INDC)	126,970	67.0
	John Fee (D, L, WFM)	62,656	33.0
31 •	Amo Houghton (R, C)	140,756	77.0
	Kisun J. Peters (D)	42,005	23.0

NORTH CAROLINA

		Vote Total	%
Governor			
#	Mike Easley (D)	1,492,170	51.9
	Richard Vinroot (R)	1,335,862	46.4
	Barbara J. Howe (LIBERT)	40,409	1.4
	Douglas Schell (REF)	8,458	.3
House			
1 •	Eva Clayton (D)	107,885	65.5
	Duane E. Kratzer Jr. (R)	53,545	32.5
	Christopher Sean Delaney (LIBERT)	3,173	1.9
2 •	Bob Etheridge (D)	137,106	57.9
	Doug Haynes (R)	97,638	41.3
	Mark D. Jackson (LIBERT)	1,953	.8
3 •	Walter B. Jones Jr. (R)	94,359	60.3
	Leigh Harvey McNairy (D)	60,160	38.4
	David F. Russell (LIBERT)	2,060	1.3
4 •	David E. Price (D)	196,705	61.7
	Jess Ward (R)	116,631	36.6
	C. Brian Towey (LIBERT)	5,424	1.7
5 •	Richard M. Burr (R)	169,899	92.8
	Steven Francis LeBoeuf (LIBERT)	13,140	7.2
6 •	Howard Coble (R)	187,913	91.1
	Jeffrey D. Bentley (LIBERT)	18,273	8.9

		Vote Total	%
7 •	Mike McIntyre (D)	152,993	69.3
	James Adams (R)	64,847	29.4
	Bob Burns (LIBERT)	2,943	1.3
8 •	Robin Hayes (R)	109,588	55.4
	Mike Taylor (D)	86,230	43.6
	Jack Schwartz (LIBERT)	1,968	1.0
9 •	Sue Myrick (R)	144,798	68.2
	Ed McGuire (D)	64,323	30.3
	Christopher S. Cole (LIBERT)	2,057	1.0
	James M. Cahaney (REF)	1,065	.5
10 •	Cass Ballenger (R)	162,054	68.2
	Delmas Parker (D)	70,020	29.5
	Deborah Garrett Eddins (LIBERT)	5,510	2.3
11 •	Charles H. Taylor (R)	143,220	54.9
	Sam Neill (D)	110,321	42.3
	C. Barry Williams (LIBERT)	7,205	2.8
12 •	Melvin Watt (D)	119,702	64.9
	Joshua "Chad" Mitchell (R)	61,190	33.2
	Anna Lyon (LIBERT)	3,573	1.9

NORTH DAKOTA

		Vote Total	%
Governor			
#	John Hoeven (R)	157,809	55.0
	Heidi Heitkamp (D)	129,107	45.0
	write-ins	9	—
Senate			
•	Kent Conrad (D)	175,181	61.4
	Duane Sand (R)	110,057	38.6
House			
AL •	Earl Pomeroy (D)	150,018	53.0
	John Dorso (R)	126,195	44.5
	Jan Shelver (I)	4,630	1.6
	Kenneth R. Loughead (I)	2,430	.9
	Dana Paul Brandenburg — write-in	11	—

OHIO

		Vote Total	%
Senate			
•	Mike DeWine (R)	2,599,392	60.1
	Ted Celeste (D)	1,545,723	35.7
	John R. McAlister (LIBERT)	113,854	2.6
	John A. Eastman (NL)	69,148	1.6
	Patrick Allen Flower — write-in	62	—
	Michael Fitzsimmons — write-in	23	—
House			
1 •	Steve Chabot (R)	112,449	53.5
	John Cranley (D)	92,874	44.1
	David A. Groshoff (LIBERT)	3,266	1.6
	Richard L. Stevenson (NL)	1,811	.9
2 •	Rob Portman (R)	198,688	73.7
	Charles W. Sanders (D)	62,142	23.0
	Robert E. Bidwell (LIBERT)	8,961	3.3
3 •	Tony P. Hall (D)	172,686	82.9
	Regina Burch (NL)	35,713	17.1
4 •	Michael G. Oxley (R)	152,288	67.4
	Daniel L. Dickman (D)	65,571	29.0
	Ralph Mullinger (LIBERT)	8,030	3.5
5 •	Paul E. Gillmor (R)	166,665	69.9
	Dannie Edmon (D)	60,801	25.5
	David J. Schaffer (NL)	5,717	2.4
	John F. Green (LIBERT)	5,306	2.2
6 •	Ted Strickland (D)	134,913	57.6
	Michael Azinger (R)	94,600	40.4
	Kenneth R. MacCutcheon (LIBERT)	4,539	1.9
7 •	David L. Hobson (R)	159,941	67.7
	Donald E. Minor Jr. (D)	58,941	25.0

		Vote Total	%
	John R. Mitchel (I)	13,552	5.7
	Jack Null (LIBERT)	3,670	1.6
8 •	John A. Boehner (R)	174,808	71.0
	John G. Parks (D)	64,421	26.2
	David R. Shock (LIBERT)	7,033	2.9
9 •	Marcy Kaptur (D)	163,309	74.4
	Dwight E. Bryan (R)	48,608	22.1
	Galen Fries (LIBERT)	4,266	1.9
	Dennis Slotnick (NL)	3,414	1.6
10 •	Dennis J. Kucinich (D)	160,901	74.9
	Bill Smith (R)	47,304	22.0
	Ron Petrie (LIBERT)	6,551	3.0
11 •	Stephanie Tubbs Jones (D)	157,691	84.6
	James Sykora (R)	21,499	11.5
	Joel C. Turner (LIBERT)	4,068	2.2
	Sonja K. Glavina (NL)	3,234	1.7
12 #	Pat Tiberi (R)	136,107	53.0
	Maryellen O'Shaughnessy (D)	112,301	43.7
	Lawrence N. Hogan (LIBERT)	4,412	1.7
	Gregory B. Richey (NL)	2,531	1.0
	Charles "ED" Jordan (I)	1,523	.6
13 •	Sherrod Brown (D)	166,663	64.5
	Rick H. Jeric (R)	82,771	32.1
	Michael A. Chmura (LIBERT)	5,751	2.2
	David Kluter (NL)	3,022	1.2
14 •	Tom Sawyer (D)	145,167	64.8
	Rick Wood (R)	69,772	31.1
	William C. McDaniel Jr. (LIBERT)	5,432	2.4
	Walter P. Keith (NL)	3,762	1.7
15 •	Deborah Pryce (R)	153,046	67.6
	Bill Buckel (D)	63,006	27.8
	Scott T. Smith (LIBERT)	10,389	4.6
16 •	Ralph Regula (R)	158,628	69.3
	William Smith (D)	61,176	26.7
	Richard L. Shetler (LIBERT)	5,999	2.6
	Brad Graef (NL)	3,129	1.4
17 •	James A. Traficant Jr. (D)	118,226	50.0
	Paul Alberty (R)	53,911	22.8
	Randy D. Walter (I)	50,849	21.5
	Lou D'Apolito (I)	9,405	4.0
	Carol Ann McCoy (NL)	3,062	1.3
	M. Ross Norris (LIBERT)	1,242	.5
18 •	Bob Ney (R)	149,377	64.7
	Marc D. Guthrie (D)	76,772	33.2
	John R. Bargar Sr. (LIBERT)	4,820	2.1
19 •	Steven C. LaTourette (R)	167,976	69.4
	Dale Virgil Blanchard (D)	67,254	27.8
	Sid Stone (LIBERT)	6,667	2.8

OKLAHOMA

House

		Vote Total	%
1 •	Steve Largent (R)	138,528	69.3
	Dan Lowe (D)	58,493	29.3
	Michael Clem (LIBERT)	2,984	1.5
2 #	Brad Carson (D)	107,273	54.9
	Andy Ewing (R)	81,672	41.8
	Neil Mavis (LIBERT)	6,467	3.3
3 •	Wes Watkins (R)	137,815	86.6
	Argus W. Yandell Jr. (I)	14,660	9.2
	R.C. Sevier White (LIBERT)	6,730	4.2
4 •	J.C. Watts Jr. (R)	114,000	64.9
	Larry Weatherford (D)	54,808	31.2
	Susan Ducey (REF)	4,897	2.8
	Keith B. Johnson (LIBERT)	1,979	1.1
5 •	Ernest Istook (R)	133,997	68.5
	Garland McWatters (D)	53,168	27.2
	Bill Maguire (I)	5,922	3.0

		Vote Total	%
	Robert T. Murphy (LIBERT)	2,651	1.4
6 •	Frank D. Lucas (R)	95,635	59.3
	Randy Beutler (D)	63,106	39.1
	Joseph V. Cristiano (LIBERT)	2,435	1.5

OREGON

		Vote Total	%
1 •	David Wu (D)	127,078	57.4
	Charles Starr (R)	87,372	39.4
	Beth King (LIBERT)	7,111	3.2
2 •	Greg Walden (R)	165,697	74.7
	Walter A. Ponsford (D)	56,160	25.3
3 •	Earl Blumenauer (D)	122,187	67.3
	Jeffrey L. Pollock (R)	45,056	24.8
	Tre Arrow (GREEN)	8,581	4.7
	Bruce Alexander Knight (LIBERT)	2,996	1.6
	Walter F. "Walt" Brown (S)	2,696	1.5
4 •	Peter A. DeFazio (D)	174,315	67.9
	John Lindsey (R)	79,374	30.9
	David G. Duemler (S)	2,889	1.1
5 •	Darlene Hooley (D)	134,320	56.5
	Brian Boquist (R)	103,398	43.5

PENNSYLVANIA

Senate

		Vote Total	%
•	Rick Santorum (R)	2,462,881	52.4
	Ron Klink (D)	2,133,834	45.4
	John J. Featherman (LIBERT)	47,041	1.0
	Lester B. Searer (CNSTP)	28,639	.6
	Robert E. Domske (REF)	23,911	.5

House

		Vote Total	%
1 •	Robert A. Brady (D)	147,959	84.0
	Steven N. Kush (R)	28,082	15.9
2 •	Chaka Fattah (D)	179,555	98.2
	Ken V. Krawchuk (LIBERT)	3,307	1.8
3 •	Robert A. Borski (D)	129,038	68.7
	Charles F. Dougherty (R)	58,712	31.3
4 #	Melissa Hart (R)	145,297	59.0
	Terry Van Horne (D)	100,904	41.0
5 •	John E. Peterson (R)	147,303	85.6
	William M. Belitskus (GREEN)	13,785	8.0
	Thomas A. Martin (LIBERT)	10,992	6.4
6 •	Tim Holden (D)	136,663	66.6
	Thomas G. Kopel (R)	68,468	33.4
7 •	Curt Weldon (R)	171,670	64.7
	Peter A. Lennon (D)	93,655	35.3
8 •	James C. Greenwood (R)	153,785	59.2
	Ron Strouse (D)	100,520	38.7
	Philip C. Holmen (REF)	5,377	2.1
9 •	Bud Shuster (R)	x	x
10 •	Donald L. Sherwood (R)	124,151	52.6
	Patrick Casey (D)	111,879	47.4
11 •	Paul E. Kanjorski (D)	130,780	66.3
	Stephen A. Urban (R)	66,450	33.7
12 •	John P. Murtha (D)	144,880	70.8
	Bill Choby (R)	56,335	27.5
	James N. O'Neil (REF)	3,319	1.6
13 •	Joseph M. Hoeffel (D)	142,276	52.8
	Stewart Greenleaf (R)	122,931	45.6
	Ken Cavanaugh (LIBERT)	4,110	1.5
14 •	William J. Coyne (D)	x	x
15 •	Patrick J. Toomey (R)	118,427	53.4
	Ed O'Brien (D)	103,514	46.6
16 •	Joseph R. Pitts (R)	161,925	67.0
	Robert S. Yorczyk (D)	79,920	33.0
17 •	George W. Gekas (R)	165,013	71.6
	Leslye Hess Herrmann (D)	65,467	28.4

		Vote Total	%
18 •	Mike Doyle (D)	155,400	69.4
	Craig C. Stephens (R)	68,554	30.6
19 #	Todd Platts (R)	166,937	72.6
	Jeff Sanders (D)	60,861	26.5
	Michael L. Paoletta (CNSTP)	2,174	.9
20 •	Frank R. Mascara (D)	144,476	64.3
	Ronald J. Davis (R)	80,146	35.7
21 •	Phil English (R)	134,325	60.7
	Mark Flitter (D)	86,838	39.3

RHODE ISLAND

Senate

		Vote Total	%
•	Lincoln Chafee (R)	212,996	56.9
	Bob Weygand (D)	153,939	41.1
	Christopher Young (REF)	3,982	1.1
	Kenneth P. Proulx (I)	3,511	.9

House

		Vote Total	%
1 •	Patrick J. Kennedy (D)	117,447	66.7
	Steve Cabral (R)	58,681	33.3
2 #	Jim Langevin (D)	118,680	62.1
	Rodney D. Driver (I)	41,805	21.9
	Robert G. "Bob" Tingle (R)	26,275	13.8
	Dorman J. Hayes Jr. (I)	4,304	2.3

SOUTH CAROLINA

		Vote Total	%
1 #	Henry Brown (R)	128,304	59.9
	Andy Brack (D)	77,310	36.1
	Bill Woolsey (LIBERT)	5,680	2.6
	Bob Batchelder (REF)	3,028	1.4
	write-ins	55	—
2 •	Floyd D. Spence (R)	137,918	56.5
	Jane Frederick (D)	101,050	41.4
	Timothy Moultrie (LIBERT)	3,223	1.3
	George C. Taylor (NL)	2,042	.8
	write-ins	70	—
3 •	Lindsey Graham (R)	149,281	69.5
	George Brightharp (D, UC)	61,150	28.5
	Adrian Banks (LIBERT)	3,088	1.4
	LeRoy J. Klein (NL)	1,115	.5
	write-ins	31	—
4 •	Jim DeMint (R)	150,153	79.6
	Ted Adams (CNSTP)	16,495	8.7
	April Bishop (LIBERT)	12,731	6.8
	Peter J. Ashy (REF, UC)	6,192	3.3
	C. Faye Walters (NL)	2,627	1.4
	write-ins	451	.2
5 •	John M. Spratt Jr. (D)	126,865	58.8
	Carl Gullick (R)	85,134	39.5
	Tom Campbell (LIBERT)	3,664	1.7
	write-ins	24	—
6 •	James E. Clyburn (D)	142,833	72.0
	Vince Ellison (R)	51,097	25.8
	Dianne Nevins (NL)	2,338	1.2
	Lynwood Earl Hines (LIBERT)	2,064	1.0
	write-ins	58	—

SOUTH DAKOTA

		Vote Total	%
AL •	John Thune (R)	221,489	73.7
	Curt M. Hohn (D)	74,098	24.6
	Brian Lerohl (LIBERT)	5,158	1.7

TENNESSEE

Senate

		Vote Total	%
•	Bill Frist (R)	1,099,415	65.2

	Vote Total	%
Jeff Clark (D)	540,717	32.0
Tom Burrell (GREEN)	23,436	1.4
Charles F. Johnson (I)	9,019	.5
Robert O. Watson (I)	7,452	.4
David Jarrod Ownby (I)	4,252	.3
Joel Kinstle (I)	2,818	.2
write-ins	101	—

House

		Vote Total	%
1 •	Bill Jenkins (R)	157,181	100.0
	write-ins	5	—
2 •	John J. "Jimmy" Duncan Jr. (R)	186,840	89.3
	Kevin J. Rowland (LIBERT)	22,275	10.7
	write-ins	2	—
3 •	Zach Wamp (R)	136,281	64.0
	Will Callaway (D)	73,783	34.6
	Trudy A. Austin (LIBERT)	2,972	1.4
	write-ins	78	—
4 •	Van Hilleary (R)	133,660	65.9
	David H. Dunaway (D)	67,008	33.0
	J. Patrick Lyons (I)	2,260	1.1
	write-ins	3	—
5 •	Bob Clement (D)	145,953	72.7
	Stan Scott (R)	48,528	24.2
	David Carew (LIBERT)	6,158	3.1
6 •	Bart Gordon (D)	140,933	66.2
	David Charles (R)	68,275	32.1
	Jim Coffer (I)	3,698	1.7
	write-in	1	—
7 •	Ed Bryant (R)	125,906	67.5
	Richard P. Sims (D)	58,121	31.2
	Denis Solee (I)	2,505	1.3
	write-ins	21	—
8 •	John Tanner (D)	134,189	73.4
	Billy Yancy (R)	48,662	26.6
9 •	Harold E. Ford Jr. (D)	x	x

TEXAS

Senate

		Vote Total	%
•	Kay Bailey Hutchison (R)	4,075,109	65.1
	Gene Kelly (D)	2,022,574	32.3
	Douglas S. Sandage (GREEN)	91,225	1.5
	Mary Ruwart (LIBERT)	72,541	1.2

House

		Vote Total	%
1 •	Max Sandlin (D)	118,007	55.7
	Noble Willingham (R)	91,886	43.4
	Raymond Carr (LIBERT)	2,016	.9
2 •	Jim Turner (D)	161,414	91.1
	Gary Lyndon Dye (LIBERT)	15,740	8.9
3 •	Sam Johnson (R)	187,461	71.6
	Billy Wayne Zachary (D)	67,224	25.7
	Lance Flores (LIBERT)	7,174	2.7
4 •	Ralph M. Hall (D)	145,843	60.3
	Jon Newton (R)	91,556	37.9
	Joe Turner (LIBERT)	4,416	1.8
5 •	Pete Sessions (R)	100,510	54.0
	Regina Montoya Coggins (D)	82,685	44.5
	Ken Ashby (LIBERT)	2,842	1.5
6 •	Joe L. Barton (R)	222,634	88.1
	Frank Brady (LIBERT)	30,044	11.9
7 #	John Culberson (R)	182,140	73.9
	Jeff Sell (D)	60,180	24.4
	Drew Parks (LIBERT)	4,152	1.7
8 •	Kevin Brady (R)	233,043	91.6
	Gil Guillory (LIBERT)	21,305	8.4
9 •	Nick Lampson (D)	130,079	59.2
	Paul Williams (R)	87,049	39.6

		Vote Total	%
	Chuck Knipp (LIBERT)	2,505	1.1
10 •	Lloyd Doggett (D)	203,503	84.5
	Michael Davis (LIBERT)	37,189	15.4
11 •	Chet Edwards (D)	107,636	55.0
	Ramsey W. Farley (R)	86,478	44.2
	Mark Swanstrom (LIBERT)	1,595	.8
12 •	Kay Granger (R)	117,712	62.6
	Mark Greene (D)	67,598	36.0
	Rick L. Clay (LIBERT)	2,565	1.4
13 •	William M. "Mac" Thornberry (R)	117,975	67.6
	Curtis Clinesmith (D)	54,329	31.1
	Brad Clardy (LIBERT)	2,134	1.2
14 •	Ron Paul (R)	137,188	59.7
	Loy Sneary (D)	92,656	40.3
15 •	Ruben Hinojosa (D)	103,691	88.8
	Frank L. Jones (LIBERT)	13,035	11.2
16 •	Silvestre Reyes (D)	92,631	68.3
	Daniel Power (R)	40,904	30.2
	Dan Moser (LIBERT)	2,077	1.5
17 •	Charles W. Stenholm (D)	120,643	59.0
	Darrell Clements (R)	72,514	35.5
	Debra Monde (LIBERT)	11,179	5.5
18 •	Sheila Jackson-Lee (D)	130,746	76.6
	Bob Levy (R)	37,725	22.1
	Colin Nankervis (LIBERT)	2,308	1.4
19 •	Larry Combest (R)	172,031	91.6
	John M. Turnbow (LIBERT)	15,741	8.4
20 •	Charlie Gonzalez (D)	106,956	87.7
	Alejandro "Alex" DePena (LIBERT)	14,983	12.3
21 •	Lamar Smith (R)	249,693	75.9
	Jim Green (D)	72,938	22.2
	C. W. "Jinx" Steinbrecher (LIBERT)	6,481	2.0
22 •	Tom DeLay (R)	154,279	60.3
	Jo Ann Matranga (D)	92,488	36.2
	Bob Schneider (REF)	5,559	2.2
	Kent J. Probst (LIBERT)	3,376	1.3
23 •	Henry Bonilla (R)	118,361	59.6
	Isidro Garza Jr. (D)	76,621	38.5
	Jeffrey C. Blunt (LIBERT)	3,760	1.9
24 •	Martin Frost (D)	103,131	61.8
	Bryndan Wright (R)	61,222	36.7
	Robert T. Worthington (LIBERT)	2,560	1.5
25 •	Ken Bentsen (D)	105,826	59.9
	Phil Sudan (R)	68,511	38.8
	Clifford Lee Messina (LIBERT)	2,422	1.4
26 •	Dick Armey (R)	213,992	72.5
	Steve Love (D)	75,589	25.6
	Fred E. Badagnani (LIBERT)	5,645	1.9
27 •	Solomon P. Ortiz (D)	102,229	63.4
	Pat Ahumada (R)	54,601	33.9
	William Bunch (LIBERT)	4,323	2.7
28 •	Ciro D. Rodriguez (D)	121,926	89.1
	William A. "Bill" Stallknecht (LIBERT)	14,937	10.9
29 •	Gene Green (D)	84,117	73.4
	Joe Vu (R)	29,365	25.6
	Ray E. Dittmar (LIBERT)	1,186	1.0
30 •	Eddie Bernice Johnson (D)	109,158	91.8
	Kelly Rush (LIBERT)	9,796	8.2

UTAH

Governor

		Vote Total	%
•	Michael O. Leavitt (R)	422,359	55.8
	Bill Orton (D)	320,186	42.3

		Vote Total	%
	Jeremy Friedbaum (IA)	14,914	2.0

Senate

		Vote Total	%
•	Orrin G. Hatch (R)	501,928	65.6
	Scott N. Howell (D)	241,127	31.5
	Carlton Edward Bowen (AMI)	11,929	1.6
	Jim Dexter (LIBERT)	10,271	1.3

House

		Vote Total	%
1 •	James V. Hansen (R)	179,475	69.0
	Kathleen McConkie (D)	70,867	27.2
	Hartley D. Anderson (IA)	5,108	2.0
	Dave S. Seely (LIBERT)	3,125	1.2
	Matthew D. Frandsen (NL)	1,694	.7
2 #	Jim Matheson (D)	144,373	55.9
	Derek W. Smith (R)	106,565	41.3
	Bruce Bangerter (IA)	4,673	1.8
	Peter Pixon (LIBERT)	2,157	.8
	Steven A. Voris (X)	593	.2
3 •	Christopher B. Cannon (R)	138,125	58.6
	Donald Dunn (D)	87,868	37.3
	Michael J. Lehman (IA)	5,388	2.3
	Kitty K. Burton (LIBERT)	3,543	1.5
	Randall Tolpinrud (NL)	842	.4

VERMONT

Governor

		Vote Total	%
•	Howard Dean (D)	131,869	50.6
	Ruth Dwyer (R)	99,276	38.1
	Anthony Pollina (PRO)	24,843	9.5
	Phil Stannard Sr. (I)	1,782	.7
	Joel W. Williams (VG)	1,101	.4
	Marilyn "Mom" Verna Christian (I)	905	.3
	Hardy Macia (LIBERT)	567	.2
	Richard Gottlieb (LU)	298	.1

Senate

		Vote Total	%
•	James M. Jeffords (R)	188,070	65.7
	Ed Flanagan (D)	72,909	25.5
	Charles W. Russell (CNSTP)	9,816	3.4
	Rick Hubbard (I)	5,466	1.9
	Billy Greer (VG)	4,737	1.6
	Hugh Douglas (LIBERT)	3,798	1.3
	Jerry Levy (LU)	1,455	.5

House

		Vote Total	%
AL •	Bernard Sanders (I)	174,201	70.1
	Karen Kerin (R)	46,305	18.6
	Peter Diamondstone (D)	13,073	5.3
	Stewart Skrill (I)	8,949	3.6
	Jack "Buck" Rogers (VG)	3,809	1.5
	Daniel H. Krymkowski (LIBERT)	2,259	.9

VIRGINIA

Senate

		Vote Total	%
#	George F. Allen (R)	1,401,495	52.0
•	Charles S. Robb (D)	1,293,515	48.0
	write-ins	1,129	—

House

		Vote Total	%
1 #	Jo Ann Davis (R)	150,251	57.6
	Lawrence Davies (D)	96,075	36.8
	Sharon Wood (LIBERT)	9,907	3.8
	Josh Billings (I)	4,221	1.6
	write-ins	480	.2
2 #	Edward L. Schrock (R)	97,853	51.9
	Jody Wagner (D)	90,472	48.0
	write-ins	104	.1
3 •	Robert C. Scott (D)	134,600	98.2
	write-ins	2,441	1.8
4 •	Norman Sisisky (D)	181,477	99.5

		Vote Total	%
	write-ins	1,001	.6
5 •	Virgil H. Goode Jr. (I)	141,741	67.4
	John Boyd (D)	64,798	30.8
	Joseph S. Spence (I)	3,859	1.8
	write-ins	28	—
6 •	Robert W. Goodlatte (R)	153,412	99.4
	write-ins	919	.6
7 #	Eric I. Cantor (R)	191,037	66.8
	Warren A. Stewart (D)	94,737	33.1
	write-ins	282	.1
8 •	James P. Moran (D)	164,203	62.9
	Demaris Miller (R)	90,471	34.6
	Ron Crickenberger (I)	3,471	1.3
	Rick Herron (I)	2,781	1.1
	write-ins	295	.1
9 •	Rick Boucher (D)	134,878	69.1
	Michael D. "Oz" Osborne (R)	60,325	30.9
	write-ins	15	—
10 •	Frank R. Wolf (R)	234,461	84.0
	Brian M. Brown (LIBERT)	29,036	10.4
	Marc A. Rossi (I)	15,504	5.5
	write-ins	109	—
11 •	Thomas M. Davis III (R)	148,753	60.5
	Mike Corrigan (D)	88,233	35.9
	Robert McBride (LIBERT)	4,670	1.9
	C.W. "Levi" Levy (I)	3,992	1.6
	write-ins	52	—

WASHINGTON

Governor

		Vote Total	%
•	Gary Locke (D)	1,022,213	58.1
	John Carlson (R)	703,593	40.0
	Steve LePage (LIBERT)	33,032	1.9

Senate

		Vote Total	%
•	Slade Gorton (R)	937,487	49.1
	Maria Cantwell (D)	922,571	48.3
	Jeff Jared (LIBERT)	49,345	2.6

House

		Vote Total	%
1 •	Jay Inslee (D)	107,065	54.9
	Dan McDonald (R)	82,630	42.3
	Bruce Newman (LIBERT)	5,490	2.8
2 #	Rick Larsen (D)	115,508	50.3

		Vote Total	%
	John Koster (R)	105,337	45.8
	Stuart Andrews (LIBERT)	5,923	2.6
	Glen Johnson (NL)	3,052	1.3
3 •	Brian Baird (D)	128,772	56.4
	Trent Matson (R)	93,176	40.8
	Erne Lewis (LIBERT)	6,371	2.8
4 •	Richard "Doc" Hastings (R)	105,919	61.2
	Jim Davis (D)	63,974	37.0
	Fred Krauss (LIBERT)	3,159	1.8
5 •	George Nethercutt (R)	119,520	57.1
	Tom Keefe (D)	82,047	39.2
	Greg Holmes (LIBERT)	7,786	3.7
6 •	Norm Dicks (D)	110,633	64.9
	Bob Lawrence (R)	53,023	31.1
	John Bennett (LIBERT)	6,737	4.0
7 •	Jim McDermott (D)	129,938	72.9
	Joe Szwaja (GREEN)	35,105	19.7
	Joel Grus (LIBERT)	13,133	7.4
8 •	Jennifer Dunn (R)	119,533	62.0
	Heidi Behrens-Benedict (D)	68,876	35.7
	Bernard McIlroy (LIBERT)	4,437	2.3
9 •	Adam Smith (D)	92,558	61.9
	Chris Vance (R)	51,937	34.8
	Jonathan V. Wright (LIBERT)	4,939	3.3

WEST VIRGINIA

Governor

		Vote Total	%
#	Bob Wise (D)	320,430	50.1
•	Cecil H. Underwood (R)	301,370	47.1
	Denise Giardina (MOUNT)	10,114	1.6
	Bob Myers (LIBERT)	6,067	.9
	Randall B. Ashelman (NL)	1,488	.2

Senate

		Vote Total	%
•	Robert C. Byrd (D)	445,329	78.1
	David T. Gallaher (R)	112,840	19.8
	Joe Whelan (LIBERT)	11,918	2.1

House

		Vote Total	%
1 •	Alan B. Mollohan (D)	167,393	87.8
	Richard Kerr (LIBERT)	23,212	12.2
2 #	Shelley Moore Capito (R)	96,615	47.5
	Jim Humphreys (D)	94,802	46.6
	John Brown (LIBERT)	11,783	5.8

		Vote Total	%
3 •	Nick J. Rahall II (D)	140,920	91.5
	Jeff Robinson (LIBERT)	13,072	8.5

WISCONSIN

Senate

		Vote Total	%
•	Herb Kohl (D)	1,559,669	61.6
	John Gillespie (R)	939,186	37.1
	Tim Peterson (LIBERT)	21,120	.8
	Eugene A. Hem (I)	9,425	.4
	Robert R. Raymond (CNSTP)	4,229	.2

House

		Vote Total	%
1 •	Paul D. Ryan (R)	176,673	66.4
	Jeffrey C. Thomas (D)	89,253	33.6
2 •	Tammy Baldwin (D)	163,436	51.4
	John Sharpless (R)	154,502	48.6
3 •	Ron Kind (D)	173,267	64.0
	Susan Tully (R)	97,681	36.0
4 •	Gerald D. Kleczka (D)	162,939	60.8
	Tim Riener (R)	101,289	37.8
	Nikola Rajnovic (LIBERT)	3,692	1.4
5 •	Thomas M. Barrett (D)	171,504	78.2
	Jonathan Smith (R)	47,901	21.8
6 •	Tom Petri (R)	179,412	65.1
	Daniel Flaherty (D)	96,016	34.9
7 •	David R. Obey (D)	172,452	63.3
	Sean Cronin (R)	99,976	36.7
8 •	Mark Green (R)	211,167	74.7
	Dean Reich (D)	71,419	25.3
9 •	F. James Sensenbrenner Jr. (R)	239,130	74.1
	Mike Clawson (D)	83,634	25.9

WYOMING

Senate

		Vote Total	%
•	Craig Thomas (R)	153,815	73.4
	Mel Logan (D)	46,662	22.3
	Margaret Dawson (LIBERT)	8,954	4.3

House

		Vote Total	%
AL •	Barbara Cubin (R)	138,209	66.4
	Michael Allen Green (D)	60,098	28.9
	Lewis Stock (LIBERT)	6,335	3.0
	Victor Raymond (NL)	3,390	1.6

The Legislative Process in Brief

Note: Parliamentary terms used below are defined in the glossary.

Introduction of Bills

A House member (including the resident commissioner of Puerto Rico and non-voting delegates of the District of Columbia, Guam, the Virgin Islands and American Samoa) may introduce any one of several types of bills and resolutions by handing it to the clerk of the House or placing it in a box called the hopper. A senator first gains recognition of the presiding officer to announce the introduction of a bill. If objection is offered by any senator, the introduction of the bill is postponed until the following day.

As the next step in either the House or Senate, the bill is numbered, referred to the appropriate committee, labeled with the sponsor's name and sent to the Government Printing Office so that copies can be made for subsequent study and action. Senate bills may be jointly sponsored and carry several senators' names. Until 1978, the House limited the number of members who could cosponsor any one bill; the ceiling was eliminated at the beginning of the 96th Congress. A bill written in the executive branch and proposed as an administration measure usually is introduced by the chairman of the congressional committee that has jurisdiction.

Bills — Prefixed with HR in the House, S in the Senate, followed by a number. Used as the form for most legislation, whether general or special, public or private.

Joint Resolutions — Designated H J Res or S J Res. Subject to the same procedure as bills, with the exception of a joint resolution proposing an amendment to the Constitution. The latter must be approved by two-thirds of both houses and is thereupon sent directly to the administrator of general services for submission to the states for ratification instead of being presented to the president for his approval.

Concurrent Resolutions — Designated H Con Res or S Con Res. Used for matters affecting the operations of both houses. These resolutions do not become law.

Resolutions — Designated H Res or S Res. Used for a matter concerning the operation of either house alone and adopted only by the chamber in which it originates.

Committee Action

With few exceptions, bills are referred to the appropriate standing committees. The job of referral formally is the responsibility of the Speaker of the House and the presiding officer of the Senate, but this task usually is carried out on their behalf by the parliamentarians of the House and Senate. Precedent, statute and the jurisdictional mandates of the committees as set forth in the rules of the House and Senate determine which committees receive what kinds of bills. An exception is the referral of private bills, which are sent to whatever committee is designated by their sponsors. Bills are technically considered "read for the first time" when referred to House committees.

When a bill reaches a committee it is placed on the committee's calendar. At that time the bill comes under the sharpest congressional focus. Its chances for passage are quickly determined — and the great majority of bills falls by the legislative roadside. Failure of a committee to act on a bill is equivalent to killing it; the measure can be withdrawn from the committee's purview only by a discharge petition signed by a majority of the House membership on House bills, or by adoption of a special resolution in the Senate. Discharge attempts rarely succeed.

The first committee action taken on a bill usually is a request for comment on it by interested agencies of the government. The committee chairman may assign the bill to a subcommittee for study and hearings, or it may be considered by the full committee. Hearings may be public, closed (executive session) or both. A subcommittee, after considering a bill, reports to the full committee its recommendations for action and any proposed amendments.

The full committee then votes on its recommendation to the House or Senate. This procedure is called "ordering a bill reported." Occasionally a committee may order a bill reported unfavorably; most of the time a report, submitted by the chairman of the committee to the House or Senate, calls for favorable action on the measure since the committee can effectively "kill" a bill by simply failing to take any action.

After the bill is reported, the committee chairman instructs the staff to prepare a written report. The report describes the purposes and scope of the bill, explains the committee revisions, notes proposed changes in existing law and, usually, includes the views of the executive branch agencies consulted. Often committee members opposing a measure issue dissenting minority statements that are included in the report.

Usually, the committee "marks up" or proposes amendments to the bill. If they are substantial and the measure is complicated, the committee may order a "clean bill" introduced, which will embody the proposed amendments. The original bill then is put aside and the clean bill, with a new number, is reported to the floor.

The chamber must approve, alter or reject the committee amendments before the bill itself can be put to a vote.

Floor Action

After a bill is reported back to the house where it originated, it is placed on the calendar.

There are five legislative calendars in the House, issued in one cumulative calendar titled *Calendars of the United States House of Representatives and History of Legislation.* The House

How a Bill Becomes a Law

This graphic shows the most typical way in which proposed legislation is enacted into law. There are more complicated, as well as simpler, routes, and most bills never become law. The process is illustrated with two hypothetical bills, House bill No. 1 (HR 1) and Senate bill No. 2 (S 2). Bills must be passed by both houses in identical form before they can be sent to the president. The path of HR 1 is traced by a gray line, that of S 2 by a black line. In practice, most bills begin as similar proposals in both houses.

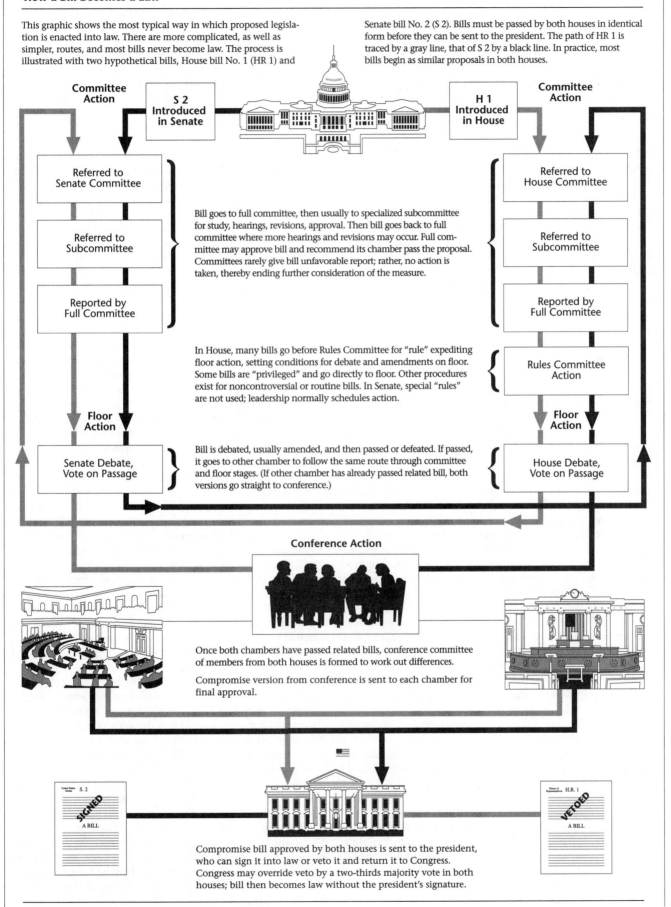

Committee Action

S 2 Introduced in Senate

H 1 Introduced in House

Committee Action

Referred to Senate Committee

Referred to Subcommittee

Reported by Full Committee

Referred to House Committee

Referred to Subcommittee

Reported by Full Committee

Bill goes to full committee, then usually to specialized subcommittee for study, hearings, revisions, approval. Then bill goes back to full committee where more hearings and revisions may occur. Full committee may approve bill and recommend its chamber pass the proposal. Committees rarely give bill unfavorable report; rather, no action is taken, thereby ending further consideration of the measure.

Rules Committee Action

In House, many bills go before Rules Committee for "rule" expediting floor action, setting conditions for debate and amendments on floor. Some bills are "privileged" and go directly to floor. Other procedures exist for noncontroversial or routine bills. In Senate, special "rules" are not used; leadership normally schedules action.

Floor Action

Floor Action

Senate Debate, Vote on Passage

Bill is debated, usually amended, and then passed or defeated. If passed, it goes to other chamber to follow the same route through committee and floor stages. (If other chamber has already passed related bill, both versions go straight to conference.)

House Debate, Vote on Passage

Conference Action

Once both chambers have passed related bills, conference committee of members from both houses is formed to work out differences.

Compromise version from conference is sent to each chamber for final approval.

S 2 — SIGNED — A BILL

H.R. 1 — VETOED — A BILL

Compromise bill approved by both houses is sent to the president, who can sign it into law or veto it and return it to Congress. Congress may override veto by a two-thirds majority vote in both houses; bill then becomes law without the president's signature.

calendars are:

The Union Calendar to which are referred bills raising revenues, general appropriations bills and any measures directly or indirectly appropriating money or property. It is the Calendar of the Committee of the Whole House on the State of the Union.

The House Calendar to which are referred bills of public character not raising revenue or appropriating money.

The Corrections Calendar to which are referred bills to repeal rules and regulations deemed excessive or unnecessary when the Corrections Calendar is called the second and fourth Tuesday of each month. (Instituted in the 104th Congress to replace the seldom-used Consent Calendar.) A three-fifths majority is required for passage.

The Private Calendar to which are referred bills for relief in the nature of claims against the United States or private immigration bills that are passed without debate when the Private Calendar is called the first and third Tuesdays of each month.

The Discharge Calendar to which are referred motions to discharge committees when the necessary signatures are signed to a discharge petition.

There is only one legislative calendar in the Senate and one "executive calendar" for treaties and nominations submitted to the Senate. When the Senate Calendar is called, each senator is limited to five minutes' debate on each bill.

Debate. A bill is brought to debate by varying procedures. If a routine measure, it may await the call of the calendar. If it is urgent or important, it can be taken up in the Senate either by unanimous consent or by a majority vote. The majority leader, in consultation with the minority leader and others, schedules the bills that will be taken up for debate.

In the House, precedence is granted if a special rule is obtained from the Rules Committee. A request for a special rule usually is made by the chairman of the committee that favorably reported the bill, supported by the bill's sponsor and other committee members. The request, considered by the Rules Committee in the same fashion that other committees consider legislative measures, is in the form of a resolution providing for immediate consideration of the bill. The Rules Committee reports the resolution to the House where it is debated and voted on in the same fashion as regular bills. If the Rules Committee fails to report a rule requested by a committee, there are several ways to bring the bill to the House floor — under suspension of the rules, on Calendar Wednesday or by a discharge motion.

The resolutions providing special rules are important because they specify how long the bill may be debated and whether it may be amended from the floor. If floor amendments are banned, the bill is considered under a "closed rule," which permits only members of the committee that first reported the measure to the House to alter its language, subject to chamber acceptance.

When a bill is debated under an "open rule," amendments may be offered from the floor. Committee amendments always are taken up first but may be changed, as may all amendments up to the second degree; that is, an amendment to an amendment to an amendment is not in order.

Duration of debate in the House depends on whether the bill is under discussion by the House proper or before the House when it is sitting as the Committee of the Whole House on the State of the Union. In the former, the amount of time for debate either is determined by special rule or is allocated with an hour for each member if the measure is under consideration without a rule. In the Committee of the Whole the amount of time agreed on for general debate is equally divided

between proponents and opponents. At the end of general discussion, the bill is read section by section for amendment. Debate on an amendment is limited to five minutes for each side; this is called the "five-minute rule." In practice, amendments regularly are debated more than ten minutes, with members gaining the floor by offering pro forma amendments or obtaining unanimous consent to speak longer than five minutes.

Senate debate usually is unlimited. It can be halted only by unanimous consent by "cloture," which requires a three-fifths majority of the entire Senate except for proposed changes in the Senate rules. The latter requires a two-thirds vote.

The House considers almost all important bills within a parliamentary framework known as the Committee of the Whole. It is not a committee as the word usually is understood; it is the full House meeting under another name for the purpose of speeding action on legislation. Technically, the House sits as the Committee of the Whole when it considers any tax measure or bill dealing with public appropriations. It also can resolve itself into the Committee of the Whole if a member moves to do so and the motion is carried. The Speaker appoints a member to serve as the chairman. The rules of the House permit the Committee of the Whole to meet when a quorum of 100 members is present on the floor and to amend and act on bills, within certain time limitations. When the Committee of the Whole has acted, it "rises," the Speaker returns as the presiding officer of the House and the member appointed chairman of the Committee of the Whole reports the action of the committee and its recommendations. The Committee of the Whole cannot pass a bill; instead it reports the measure to the full House with whatever changes it has approved. The full House then may pass or reject the bill — or, on occasion, recommit the bill to committee. Amendments adopted in the Committee of the Whole may be put to a second vote in the full House.

Votes. Voting on bills may occur repeatedly before they are finally approved or rejected. The House votes on the rule for the bill and on various amendments to the bill. Voting on amendments often is a more illuminating test of a bill's support than is the final tally. Sometimes members approve final passage of bills after vigorously supporting amendments that, if adopted, would have scuttled the legislation.

The Senate has three different methods of voting: an untabulated voice vote, a standing vote (called a division) and a recorded roll call to which members answer "yea" or "nay" when their names are called. The House also employs voice and standing votes, but since January 1973 yeas and nays have been recorded by an electronic voting device, eliminating the need for time-consuming roll calls.

Another method of voting, used in the House only, is the teller vote. Traditionally, members filed up the center aisle past counters; only vote totals were announced. Since 1971, one-fifth of a quorum can demand that the votes of individual members be recorded, thereby forcing them to take a public position on amendments to key bills. Electronic voting now is commonly used for this purpose.

After amendments to a bill have been voted upon, a vote may be taken on a motion to recommit the bill to committee. If carried, this vote removes the bill from the chamber's calendar and is usually a death blow to the bill. If the motion is unsuccessful, the bill then is "read for the third time." An actual reading usually is dispensed with. Until 1965, an opponent of a bill could delay this move by objecting and asking for a full reading of an engrossed (certified in final form) copy of the bill. After the "third reading," the vote on final passage is taken.

Examples of
Legislative Documents

The final vote may be followed by a motion to reconsider, and this motion may be followed by a move to lay the motion on the table. Usually, those voting for the bill's passage vote for the tabling motion, thus safeguarding the final passage action. With that, the bill has been formally passed by the chamber. While a motion to reconsider a Senate vote is pending on a bill, the measure cannot be sent to the House.

Action in Second House

After a bill is passed it is sent to the other chamber. This body may then take one of several steps. It may pass the bill as is — accepting the other chamber's language. It may send the bill to committee for scrutiny or alteration, or reject the entire bill, advising the other house of its actions. Or it simply may ignore the bill submitted while it continues work on its own version of the proposed legislation. Frequently, one chamber may approve a version of a bill that is greatly at variance with the version already passed by the other house, and then substitute its contents for the language of the other, retaining only the latter's bill number.

A provision of the Legislative Reorganization Act of 1970 permits a separate House vote on any non-germane amendment added by the Senate to a House-passed bill and requires a majority vote to retain the amendment. Previously the House was forced to act on the bill as a whole; the only way to defeat the non-germane amendment was to reject the entire bill.

Often the second chamber makes only minor changes. If these are readily agreed to by the other house, the bill then is routed to the president. However, if the opposite chamber significantly alters the bill submitted to it, the measure usually is "sent to conference." The chamber that has possession of the "papers" (engrossed bill, engrossed amendments, messages of transmittal) requests a conference and the other chamber must agree to it. If the second house does not agree, the bill dies.

Conference, Final Action

Conference. A conference works out conflicting House and Senate versions of a legislative bill. The conferees usually are senior members appointed by the presiding officers of the two houses, from the committees that managed the bills. Under this arrangement the conferees of one house have the duty of trying to maintain their chamber's position in the face of amending actions by the conferees (also referred to as "managers") of the other house.

The number of conferees from each chamber may vary, the range usually being from three to nine members in each group, depending upon the length or complexity of the bill involved. There may be five representatives and three senators on the conference committee, or the reverse. But a majority vote controls the action of each group so that a large representation does not give one chamber a voting advantage over the other chamber's conferees.

Theoretically, conferees are not allowed to write new legislation in reconciling the two versions before them, but this curb sometimes is bypassed. Many bills have been put into acceptable compromise form only after new language was provided by the conferees. The 1970 Reorganization Act attempted to tighten restrictions on conferees by forbidding them to introduce any language on a topic that neither chamber sent to conference or to modify any topic beyond the scope of the different House and Senate versions.

Frequently the ironing out of difficulties takes days or even weeks. Conferences on involved appropriations bills sometimes are particularly drawn out.

As a conference proceeds, conferees reconcile differences between the versions, but generally they grant concessions only insofar as they remain sure that the chamber they represent will accept the compromises. Occasionally, uncertainty over how either house will react, or the positive refusal of a chamber to back down on a disputed amendment, results in an impasse, and the bills die in conference even though each was approved by its sponsoring chamber.

Conferees sometimes go back to their respective chambers for further instructions, when they report certain portions in disagreement. Then the chamber concerned can either "recede and concur" in the amendment of the other house or "insist on its amendment."

When the conferees have reached agreement, they prepare a conference report embodying their recommendations (compromises). The report, in document form, must be submitted to each house.

The conference report must be approved by each house. Consequently, approval of the report is approval of the compromise bill. In the order of voting on conference reports, the chamber which asked for a conference yields to the other chamber the opportunity to vote first.

Final Steps. After a bill has been passed by both the House and Senate in identical form, all of the original papers are sent to the enrolling clerk of the chamber in which the bill originated. He then prepares an enrolled bill, which is printed on parchment paper. When this bill has been certified as correct by the secretary of the Senate or the clerk of the House, depending on which chamber originated the bill, it is signed first (no matter whether it originated in the Senate or House) by the Speaker of the House and then by the president of the Senate. It is next sent to the White House to await action.

If the president approves the bill, he signs it, dates it and usually writes the word "approved" on the document. If he does not sign it within 10 days (Sundays excepted) and Congress is in session, the bill becomes law without his signature.

However, should Congress adjourn before the 10 days expire, and the president has failed to sign the measure, it does not become law. This procedure is called the pocket veto.

A president vetoes a bill by refusing to sign it and, before the 10-day period expires, returning it to Congress with a message stating his reasons. The message is sent to the chamber that originated the bill. If no action is taken on the message, the bill dies. Congress, however, can attempt to override the president's veto and enact the bill, "the objections of the president to the contrary notwithstanding." Overriding a veto requires a two-thirds vote of those present, who must number a quorum and vote by roll call.

Debate can precede this vote, with motions permitted to lay the message on the table, postpone action on it or refer it to committee. If the president's veto is overridden by a two-thirds vote in both houses, the bill becomes law. Otherwise it is dead.

When bills are passed finally and signed, or passed over a veto, they are given law numbers in numerical order as they become law. There are two series of numbers, one for public and one for private laws, starting at the number "1" for each two-year term of Congress. They are then identified by law number and by Congress — for example, Private Law 21, 97th Congress; Public Law 250, 97th Congress (or PL 97–250).

The Budget Process in Brief

Through the budget process, the president and Congress decide how much to spend and tax during the upcoming fiscal year. More specifically, they decide how much to spend on each activity, ensure that the government spends no more and spends it only for that activity, and report on that spending at the end of each budget cycle.

The President's Budget

The law requires that, by the first Monday in February, the president submit to Congress his proposed federal budget for the next fiscal year, which begins on October 1. In order to accomplish this, the president establishes general budget and fiscal policy guidelines. Based on these guidelines, executive branch agencies make requests for funds and submit them to the White House's Office of Management and Budget (OMB) nearly a year prior to the start of a new fiscal year. The OMB, receiving direction from the president and administration official, reviews the agencies' requests and develops a detailed budget by December. From December to January the OMB prepares the budget documents, so that the president can deliver it to Congress in February.

The president's budget is the executive branch's plan for the next year — but it is just a proposal. After receiving it, Congress has its own budget process to follow from February to October. Only after Congress passes the required spending bills — and the president signs them — has the government created its actual budget.

Action in Congress

Congress first must pass a "budget resolution" — a framework within which the members of Congress will make their decisions about spending and taxes. It includes targets for total spending, total revenues, and the deficit, and allocations within the spending target for the two types of spending — discretionary and mandatory.

Discretionary spending, which currently accounts for about 33 percent of all federal spending, is what the president and Congress must decide to spend for the next year through the thirteen annual appropriations bills. It includes money for such activities as the FBI and the Coast Guard, for housing and education, for NASA and highway and bridge construction, and for defense and foreign aid.

Mandatory spending, which currently accounts for 67 percent of all spending, is authorized by laws that have already been passed. It includes entitlement spending — such as for Social Security, Medicare, veterans' benefits, and food stamps — through which individuals receive benefits because they are eligible based on their age, income, or other criteria. It also includes interest on the national debt, which the government pays to individuals and institutions that hold Treasury bonds and other government securities. The only way the president and Congress can change the spending on entitlement and other mandatory programs is if they change the laws that authorized the programs.

Currently, the law imposes a limit or "cap" through 1998 on total annual discretionary spending. Within the cap, however, the president and Congress can, and often do, change the spending levels from year to year for the thousands of individual federal programs.

In addition, the law requires that legislation that would raise mandatory spending or lower revenues — compared to existing law — be offset by spending cuts or revenue increases. This requirement, called "pay-as-you-go" is designed to prevent new legislation from increasing the deficit.

Once Congress passes the budget resolution, it turns its attention to passing the thirteen annual appropriations bills and, if it chooses, "authorizing" bills to change the laws governing mandatory spending and revenues.

Congress begins by examining the president's budget in detail. Scores of committees and subcommittees hold hearings on proposals under their jurisdiction. The House and Senate Armed Services Authorizing Committees, and the Defense and Military Construction Subcommittees of the Appropriations Committees, for instance, hold hearings on the president's defense budget. The White House budget director, cabinet officers, and other administration officials work with Congress as it accepts some of the president's proposals, rejects others, and changes still others. Congress can change funding levels, eliminate programs, or add programs not requested by the president. It can add or eliminate taxes and other sources of revenue, or make other changes that affect the amount of revenue collected. Congressional rules require that these committees and subcommittees take actions that reflect the congressional budget resolution.

The president's budget, the budget resolution, and the appropriations or authorizing bills measure spending in two ways — "budget authority" and "outlays." Budget authority is what the law authorizes the federal government to spend for certain programs, projects, or activities. What the government actually spends in a particular year, however, is an outlay. For example, when the government decides to build a space exploration system, the president and Congress may agree to appropriate $1 billion in budget authority. But the space system may take ten years to build. Thus, the government may spend $100 million in outlays in the first year to begin construction and the remaining $900 million during the next nine years as the construction continues.

Congress must provide budget authority before the federal agencies can obligate the government to make outlays. When Congress fails to complete action on one or more of the regular annual appropriations bills before the fiscal year begins on October 1, budget authority may be made on a temporary basis

through continuing resolutions. Continuing resolutions make budget authority available for limited periods of time, generally at rates related through some formula to the rate provided in the previous year's appropriation.

Monitoring the Budget

Once Congress passes and the president signs the federal appropriations bills or authorizing laws for the fiscal year, the government monitors the budget through (1) agency program managers and budget officials, including the Inspectors General, who report only to the agency head; (2) the Office of Management and Budget; (3) congressional committees; and (4) the General Accounting Office, an auditing arm of Congress.

This oversight is designed to (1) ensure that agencies comply with legal limits on spending, and that they use budget authority only for the purposes intended; (2) see that programs are operating consistently with legal requirements and existing policy; and (3) ensure that programs are well managed and achieving the intended results.

The president may withhold appropriated amounts from obligation only under certain limited circumstances — to provide for contingencies, to achieve savings made possible through changes in requirements or greater efficiency of operations, or as otherwise provided by law. The Impoundment Control Act of 1974 specifies the procedures that must be followed if funds are withheld. Congress can also cancel previous authorized budget authority by passing a rescissions bill — but it also must be signed by the president.

Glossary of Congressional Terms

Absolute Majority—A vote requiring approval by a majority of all members of a house rather than a majority of members present and voting. Also referred to as constitutional majority.

Act—(1) A bill passed in identical form by both houses of Congress and signed into law by the president or enacted over his veto. A bill also becomes an act without the president's signature if he does not return it to Congress within 10 days (Sundays excepted) and if Congress has not adjourned within that period. (2) Also, the technical term for a bill passed by at least one house and engrossed.

Adjourn for More Than Three Days—Under Article I, Section 5, of the Constitution, neither house may adjourn for more than three days without the approval of the other. The necessary approval is given in a concurrent resolution and agreed to by both houses, which may permit one or both to take such an adjournment.

Adjournment Sine Die—Final adjournment of an annual or two-year session of Congress; literally, adjournment without a day. The two houses must agree to a privileged concurrent resolution for such an adjournment. A sine die adjournment precludes Congress from meeting again until the next constitutionally fixed date of a session (January 3 of the following year) unless Congress determines otherwise by law or the president calls it into special session. Article II, Section 3, of the Constitution authorizes the president to adjourn both houses until such time as he thinks proper when the two houses cannot agree to a time of adjournment, but no president has ever exercised this authority.

Adjournment to a Day (and Time) Certain—An adjournment that fixes the next date and time of meeting for one or both houses. It does not end an annual session of Congress.

Advice and Consent—The Senate's constitutional role in consenting to or rejecting the president's nominations to executive branch and judicial offices and the treaties he submits. Confirmation of nominees requires a simple majority vote of the senators present and voting. Treaties must be approved by a two-thirds majority of senators present and voting.

Amendment—A formal proposal to alter the text of a bill, resolution, amendment, motion, treaty, or some other text. Technically, it is a motion. An amendment may strike out (eliminate) part of a text, insert new text, or strike out and insert—that is, replace all or part of the text with new text. The texts of amendments considered on the floor are printed in full in the *Congressional Record*.

Amendment in the Nature of a Substitute—Usually, an amendment to replace the entire text of a measure. It strikes out everything after the enacting clause and inserts a version that may be somewhat, substantially, or entirely different. When a committee adopts extensive amendments to a measure, it often incorporates them into such an amendment. Occasionally, the term is applied to an amendment that replaces a major portion of a measure's text.

Annual Authorization—Legislation that authorizes appropriations for a single fiscal year and usually for a specific amount. Under the rules of the authorization-appropriation process, an annually authorized agency or program must be reauthorized each year if it is to receive appropriations for that year. Sometimes Congress fails to enact the reauthorization but nevertheless provides appropriations to continue the program, circumventing the rules by one means or another.

Appeal—A member's formal challenge of a ruling or decision by the presiding officer. On appeal, a house or a committee may overturn the ruling by majority vote. The right of appeal ensures the body against arbitrary control by the chair. Appeals are rarely made in the House and are even more rarely successful. Rulings are more frequently appealed in the Senate and occasionally overturned, in part because its presiding officer is not the majority party's leader, as in the House.

Apportionment—The action, after each decennial census, of allocating the number of members in the House of Representatives to each state. By law, the total number of House members (not counting delegates and a resident commissioner) is fixed at 435. The number allotted to each state is based approximately on its proportion of the nation's total population. Since the Constitution guarantees each state one representative no matter how small its population, exact proportional distribution is virtually impossible. The mathematical formula currently used to determine the apportionment is called the Method of Equal Proportions. (*See Method of Equal Proportions.*)

Appropriation—(1) Legislative language that permits a federal agency to incur obligations and make payments from the Treasury for specified purposes, usually during a specified period of time. (2) The specific amount of money made available by such language. The Constitution prohibits payments from the Treasury except "in Consequence of Appropriations made by Law." With some exceptions, the rules of both houses forbid consideration of appropriations for purposes that are unauthorized in law or of appropriation amounts larger than those authorized in law. The House of Representatives claims the exclusive right to originate appropriation bills—a claim the Senate denies in theory but accepts in practice.

Authorization—(1) A statutory provision that establishes or continues a federal agency, activity or program for a fixed or indefinite period of time. It may also establish policies and restrictions and deal with organizational and administrative matters. (2) A statutory provision that authorizes appropriations for an agency, activity, or program. The appropriations may be authorized for one year, several years, or an indefinite period of time, and the authorization may be for a specific amount of money or an indefinite amount ("such sums as may be necessary"). Authorizations of specific amounts are construed as ceilings on the amounts that subsequently may be appropriated in an appropriation bill, but not as minimums; either house may appropriate lesser amounts or nothing at all.

Backdoor Spending Authority—Authority to incur obligations that evades the normal congressional appropriations process because it is provided in legislation other than appropriation acts. The most common forms are borrowing authority, contract authority, and entitlement authority.

Baseline—A projection of the levels of federal spending, revenues, and the resulting budgetary surpluses or deficits for the upcoming and subsequent fiscal years, taking into account laws enacted to date and assuming no new policy decisions. It provides a benchmark for measuring the budgetary effects of proposed changes in federal revenues or spending, assuming certain economic conditions.

Bill—The term for the chief vehicle Congress uses for enacting laws. Bills that originate in the House of Representatives are designated as H.R., those in the Senate as S., followed by a number assigned in the order in which they are introduced during a two-year Congress. A bill becomes a law if passed in identical language by both houses and signed by the president, or passed over his veto, or if the president fails to sign it within 10 days after he has received it while Congress is in session.

Bills and Resolutions Introduced—Members formally present measures to their respective houses by delivering them to a clerk in the chamber when their house is in session. Both houses permit any number of members to join in introducing a bill or resolution. The first member listed on the measure is the sponsor; the other members listed are its cosponsors.

Bills and Resolutions Referred—After a bill or resolution is introduced, it is normally sent to one or more committees that have jurisdiction over its subject, as defined by House and Senate rules and precedents. A Senate measure is usually referred to the committee with jurisdiction over the predominant subject of its text, but it may be sent to two or more committees by unanimous consent or on a motion offered jointly by the majority and minority leaders. In the House, a rule requires the Speaker to refer a measure to the committee that has primary jurisdiction. The Speaker is also authorized to refer measures sequentially to additional committees.

Borrowing Authority—Statutory authority permitting a federal agency, such as the Export-Import Bank, to borrow money from the public or the Treasury to finance its operations. It is a form of backdoor spending. To bring such spending under the control of the congressional appropriation process, the Congressional Budget Act requires that new borrowing authority shall be effective only to the extent and in such amounts as are provided in appropriations acts.

Budget—A detailed statement of actual or anticipated revenues and expenditures during an accounting period. For the national government, the period is the federal fiscal year (October 1–September 30). The budget usually refers to the president's budget submission to Congress early each calendar year. The president's budget estimates federal government income and spending for the upcoming fiscal year and contains detailed recommendations for appropriation, revenue, and other legislation. Congress is not required to accept or even vote directly on the president's proposals, and it often revises the president's budget extensively. *(See Fiscal Year.)*

Budget Act—Common name for the Congressional Budget and Impoundment Control Act of 1974, which established the basic procedures of the current congressional budget process; created the House and Senate Budget committees; and enacted procedures for reconciliation, deferrals, and rescissions. *(See Budget Process, Deferral, Impoundment, Reconciliation, Rescission. See also Gramm-Rudman-Hollings Act of 1985.)*

Budget and Accounting Act of 1921—The law that, for the first time, authorized the president to submit to Congress an annual budget for the entire federal government. Prior to the act, most federal agencies sent their budget requests to the appropriate congressional committees without review by the president.

Budget Authority—Generally, the amount of money that may be spent or obligated by a government agency or for a government program or activity. Technically, it is statutory authority to enter into obligations that normally result in outlays. The main forms of budget authority are appropriations, borrowing authority, and contract authority. It also includes authority to obligate and expend the proceeds of offsetting receipts and collections. Congress may make budget authority available for only one year, several years, or an indefinite period, and it may specify definite or indefinite amounts.

Budget Process—(1) In Congress, the procedural system it uses (a) to approve an annual concurrent resolution on the budget that sets goals for aggregate and functional categories of federal expenditures, revenues, and the surplus or deficit for an upcoming fiscal year; and (b) to implement those goals in spending, revenue, and, if necessary, reconciliation and debt-limit legislation. (2) In the executive branch, the process of formulating the president's annual budget, submitting it to Congress, defending it before congressional committees, implementing subsequent budget-related legislation, impounding or sequestering expenditures as permitted by law, auditing and evaluating programs, and compiling final budget data. The Budget and Accounting Act of 1921 and the Congressional Budget and Impoundment Control Act of 1974 established the basic elements of the current budget process. Major revisions were enacted in the Gramm-Rudman-Hollings Act of 1985 and the Budget Enforcement Act of 1990.

Budget Resolution—A concurrent resolution in which Congress establishes or revises its version of the federal budget's broad financial features for the upcoming fiscal year and several additional fiscal years. Like other concurrent resolutions, it does

not have the force of law, but it provides the framework within which Congress subsequently considers revenue, spending, and other budget-implementing legislation. The framework consists of two basic elements: (1) aggregate budget amounts (total revenues, new budget authority, outlays, loan obligations and loan guarantee commitments, deficit or surplus, and debt limit); and (2) subdivisions of the relevant aggregate amounts among the functional categories of the budget. Although it does not allocate funds to specific programs or accounts, the budget committees' reports accompanying the resolution often discuss the major program assumptions underlying its functional amounts. Unlike those amounts, however, the assumptions are not binding on Congress.

By Request—A designation indicating that a member has introduced a measure on behalf of the president, an executive agency, or a private individual or organization. Members often introduce such measures as a courtesy because neither the president nor any person other than a member of Congress can do so. The term, which appears next to the sponsor's name, implies that the member who introduced the measure does not necessarily endorse it. A House rule dealing with by-request introductions dates from 1888, but the practice goes back to the earliest history of Congress.

Calendar—A list of measures or other matters (most of them favorably reported by committees) that are eligible for floor consideration. The House has five calendars; the Senate has two. A place on a calendar does not guarantee consideration. Each house decides which measures and matters it will take up, when, and in what order, in accordance with its rules and practices.

Calendar Wednesday—A House procedure that on Wednesdays permits its committees to bring up for floor consideration nonprivileged measures they have reported. The procedure is so cumbersome and susceptible to dilatory tactics, however, that committees rarely use it.

Call of the Calendar—Senate bills that are not brought up for debate by a motion, unanimous consent, or a unanimous consent agreement are brought before the Senate for action when the calendar listing them is "called." Bills must be called in the order listed. Measures considered by this method usually are noncontroversial, and debate on the bill and any proposed amendments is limited to a total of five minutes for each senator.

Caucus—(1) A common term for the official organization of each party in each house. (2) The official title of the organization of House Democrats. House and Senate Republicans and Senate Democrats call their organizations "conferences." (3) A term for an informal group of members who share legislative interests, such as the Black Caucus, Hispanic Caucus, and Children's Caucus.

Censure—The strongest formal condemnation of a member for misconduct short of expulsion. A house usually adopts a resolution of censure to express its condemnation, after which the presiding officer reads its rebuke aloud to the member in the presence of his colleagues.

Chamber—The Capitol room in which a house of Congress normally holds its sessions. The chamber of the House of Representatives, officially called the Hall of the House, is considerably larger than that of the Senate because it must accommodate 435 representatives, four delegates, and one resident commissioner. Unlike the Senate chamber, members have no desks or assigned seats. In both chambers, the floor slopes downward to the well in front of the presiding officer's raised desk. A chamber is often referred to as "the floor," as when members are said to be on or going to the floor. Those expressions usually imply that the member's house is in session.

Christmas Tree Bill—Jargon for a bill adorned with amendments, many of them unrelated to the bill's subject, that provide benefits for interest groups, specific states, congressional districts, companies, and individuals.

Classes of Senators—A class consists of the 33 or 34 senators elected to a six-year term in the same general election. Since the terms of approximately one-third of the senators expire every two years, there are three classes.

Clean Bill—After a House committee extensively amends a bill, it often assembles its amendments and what is left of the bill into a new measure that one or more of its members introduces as a "clean bill." The revised measure is assigned a new number.

Clerk of the House—An officer of the House of Representatives responsible principally for administrative support of the legislative process in the House. The clerk is invariably the candidate of the majority party.

Cloture—A Senate procedure that limits further consideration of a pending proposal to 30 hours in order to end a filibuster. Sixteen senators must first sign and submit a cloture motion to the presiding officer. One hour after the Senate meets on the second calendar day thereafter, the chair puts the motion to a yea-and-nay vote following a live quorum call. If three-fifths of all senators (60 if there are no vacancies) vote for the motion, the Senate must take final action on the cloture proposal by the end of the 30 hours of consideration and may consider no other business until it takes that action. Cloture on a proposal to amend the Senate's standing rules requires approval by two-thirds of the senators present and voting.

Code of Official Conduct—A House rule that bans certain actions by House members, officers, and employees; requires them to conduct themselves in ways that "reflect creditably" on the House; and orders them to adhere to the spirit and the letter of House rules and those of its committees. The code's provisions govern the receipt of outside compensation, gifts, and honoraria, and the use of campaign funds; prohibit members from using their clerk-hire allowance to pay anyone who does not perform duties commensurate with that pay; forbids discrimination in members' hiring or treatment of employees on the grounds of race, color, religion, sex, handicap, age, or national origin; orders members convicted of a crime who might be punished by imprisonment of two or more years not to participate in committee business or vote on the floor until exonerated or reelected; and restricts employees' contact with federal agencies on matters in which they have a significant financial interest. The Senate's rules contain some similar prohibitions.

College of Cardinals—A popular term for the subcommittee chairmen of the appropriations committees, reflecting their influence over appropriation measures. The chairmen of

the full appropriations committees are sometimes referred to as popes.

Committee—A panel of members elected or appointed to perform some service or function for its parent body. Congress has four types of committees: standing, special or select, joint, and, in the House, a Committee of the Whole.

Committees conduct investigations, make studies, issue reports and recommendations, and, in the case of standing committees, review and prepare measures on their assigned subjects for action by their respective houses. Most committees divide their work among several subcommittees. With rare exceptions, the majority party in a house holds a majority of the seats on its committees, and their chairmen are also from that party.

Committee of the Whole—Common name of the Committee of the Whole House on the State of the Union, a committee consisting of all members of the House of Representatives. Measures from the union calendar must be considered in the Committee of the Whole before the House officially completes action on them; the committee often considers other major bills as well. A quorum of the committee is 100, and it meets in the House chamber under a chairman appointed by the Speaker. Procedures in the Committee of the Whole expedite consideration of legislation because of its smaller quorum requirement, its ban on certain motions, and its five-minute rule for debate on amendments. Those procedures usually permit more members to offer amendments and participate in the debate on a measure than is normally possible. The Senate no longer uses a Committee of the Whole.

Committee Veto—A procedure that requires an executive department or agency to submit certain proposed policies, programs, or action to designated committees for review before implementing them. Before 1983, when the Supreme Court declared that a legislative veto is unconstitutional, these provisions permitted committees to veto the proposals. They no longer do so, and the term is now something of a misnomer. Nevertheless, agencies usually take the pragmatic approach of trying to reach a consensus with the committees before carrying out their proposals, especially when an appropriations committee is involved.

Concurrent Resolution—A resolution that requires approval by both houses but is not sent to the president for his signature and therefore cannot have the force of law. Concurrent resolutions deal with the prerogatives or internal affairs of Congress as a whole. Designated H. Con. Res. in the House and S. Con. Res. in the Senate, they are numbered consecutively in each house in their order of introduction during a two-year Congress.

Conference—(1) A formal meeting or series of meetings between members representing each house to reconcile House and Senate differences on a measure (occasionally several measures). Since one house cannot require the other to agree to its proposals, the conference usually reaches agreement by compromise. When a conference completes action on a measure, or as much action as appears possible, it sends its recommendations to both houses in the form of a conference report, accompanied by an explanatory statement. (2) The official title of the organization of all Democrats or Republicans in the Senate and of all

Republicans in the House of Representatives. (*See Party Caucus.*)

Confirmations—(*See Nomination.*)

Congress—(1) The national legislature of the United States, consisting of the House of Representatives and the Senate. (2) The national legislature in office during a two-year period. Congresses are numbered sequentially; thus, the 1st Congress of 1789–1791 and the 102d Congress of 1991–1993. Before 1935, the two-year period began on the first Monday in December of odd-numbered years. Since then it has extended from January of an odd-numbered year through noon on January 3 of the next odd-numbered year. A Congress usually holds two annual sessions, but some have had three sessions and the 67th Congress had four. When a Congress expires, measures die if they have not yet been enacted.

Congressional Record—The daily, printed, and substantially verbatim account of proceedings in both the House and Senate chambers. Extraneous materials submitted by members appear in a section titled "Extensions of Remarks." A "Daily Digest" appendix contains highlights of the day's floor and committee action plus a list of committee meetings and floor agendas for the next day's session.

Although the official reporters of each house take down every word spoken during the proceedings, members are permitted to edit and "revise and extend" their remarks before they are printed. In the Senate section, all speeches, articles, and other material submitted by senators but not actually spoken or read on the floor are set off by large black dots, called bullets. However, bullets do not appear when a senator reads part of a speech and inserts the rest. In the House section, undelivered speeches and materials are printed in a distinctive typeface. The term "permanent *Record*" refers to the bound volumes of the daily *Record*s of an entire session of Congress.

Congressional Terms of Office—A term normally begins on January 3 of the year following a general election and runs two years for representatives and six years for senators. A representative chosen in a special election to fill a vacancy is sworn in for the remainder of his predecessor's term. An individual appointed to fill a Senate vacancy usually serves until the next general election or until the end of the predecessor's term, whichever comes first. Some states, however, require their governors to call a special election to fill a Senate vacancy shortly after an appointment has been made.

Continuing Resolution (CR)—A joint resolution that provides funds to continue the operation of federal agencies and programs at the beginning of a new fiscal year if their annual appropriation bills have not yet been enacted; also called continuing appropriations.

Contract Authority—Statutory authority permitting an agency to enter into contracts or incur other obligations even though it has not received an appropriation to pay for them. Congress must eventually fund them because the government is legally liable for such payments. The Congressional Budget Act of 1974 requires that new contract authority may not be used unless provided for in advance by an appropriation act, but it permits a few exceptions.

Controllable Expenditures—Federal spending that is permitted but not mandated by existing authorization law and therefore may be adjusted by congressional action in appropriation bills. (*See Appropriation.*)

Correcting Recorded Votes—The rules of both houses prohibit members from changing their votes after a vote result has been announced. Nevertheless, the Senate permits its members to withdraw or change their votes, by unanimous consent, immediately after the announcement. In rare instances, senators have been granted unanimous consent to change their votes several days or weeks after the announcement.

Votes tallied by the electronic voting system in the House may not be changed. But when a vote actually given is not recorded during an oral call of the roll, a member may demand a correction as a matter of right. On all other alleged errors in a recorded vote, the Speaker determines whether the circumstances justify a change. Occasionally, members merely announce that they were incorrectly recorded; announcements can occur hours, days, or even months after the vote and appear in the *Congressional Record.*

Corrections Calendar—Members of the House may place on this calendar bills reported favorably from committee that repeal rules and regulations considered excessive or unnecessary. Bills on the Corrections Calendar normally are called on the second and fourth Tuesday of each month at the discretion of the Speaker in consultation with the minority leader. A bill must be on the calendar for at least three legislative days before it can be brought up for floor consideration. Once on the floor, a bill is subject to one hour of debate equally divided between the chairman and ranking member of the committee of jurisdiction. A vote may be called on whether to recommit the bill to committee with or without instructions. To pass, a three-fifths majority, or 261 votes if all House members vote, is required.

Cosponsor—A member who has joined one or more other members to sponsor a measure. (*See Bills and Resolutions Introduced.*)

Current Services Estimates—Executive branch estimates of the anticipated costs of federal programs and operations for the next and future fiscal years at existing levels of service and assuming no new initiatives or changes in existing law. The president submits these estimates to Congress with his annual budget and includes an explanation of the underlying economic and policy assumptions on which they are based, such as anticipated rates of inflation, real economic growth, and unemployment, plus program caseloads and pay increases.

Custody of the Papers—Possession of an engrossed measure and certain related basic documents that the two houses produce as they try to resolve their differences over the measure.

Dance of the Swans and the Ducks—A whimsical description of the gestures some members use in connection with a request for a recorded vote, especially in the House. When a member wants his colleagues to stand in support of the request, he moves his hands and arms in a gentle upward motion resembling the beginning flight of a graceful swan. When he wants his colleagues to remain seated in order to avoid such a vote, he moves his hands and arms in a vigorous downward motion resembling a diving duck.

Dean—Within a state's delegation in the House of Representatives, the member with the longest continuous service.

Debt Limit—The maximum amount of outstanding federal public debt permitted by law. The limit (or ceiling) covers virtually all debt incurred by the government except agency debt. Each congressional budget resolution sets forth the new debt limit that may be required under its provisions.

Deferral—An impoundment of funds for a specific period of time that may not extend beyond the fiscal year in which it is proposed. Under the Impoundment Control Act of 1974, the president must notify Congress that he is deferring the spending or obligation of funds provided by law for a project or activity. Congress can disapprove the deferral by legislation.

Deficit—The amount by which the government's outlays exceed its budget receipts for a given fiscal year. Both the president's budget and the annual congressional budget resolution provide estimates of the deficit or surplus for the upcoming and several future fiscal years.

Degrees of Amendment—Designations that indicate the relationships of amendments to the text of a measure and to each other. In general, an amendment offered directly to the text of a measure is an amendment in the first degree, and an amendment to that amendment is an amendment in the second degree. Both houses normally prohibit amendments in the third degree—that is, an amendment to an amendment to an amendment.

Dilatory Tactics—Procedural actions intended to delay or prevent action by a house or a committee. They include, among others, offering numerous motions, demanding quorum calls and recorded votes at every opportunity, making numerous points of order and parliamentary inquiries, and speaking as long as the applicable rules permit. The Senate's rules permit a battery of dilatory tactics, especially lengthy speeches, except under cloture. In the House, possible dilatory tactics are more limited. Speeches are always subject to time limits and debate-ending motions. Moreover, a House rule instructs the Speaker not to entertain dilatory motions and lets the Speaker decide whether a motion is dilatory. However, the Speaker may not override the constitutional right of a member to demand the yeas and nays, and in practice usually waits for a point of order before exercising that authority. (*See Cloture.*)

Discharge a Committee—Remove a measure from a committee to which it has been referred in order to make it available for floor consideration. Noncontroversial measures are often discharged by unanimous consent. However, because congressional committees have no obligation to report measures referred to them, each house has procedures to extract controversial measures from recalcitrant committees. Six discharge procedures are available in the House of Representatives. The Senate uses a motion to discharge, which is usually converted into a discharge resolution.

Discharge Calendar—The House calendar to which motions to discharge committees are referred when they have the required number of signatures (218) and are awaiting floor action.

Discharge Petition—(*See Discharge a Committee.*)

Discharge Resolution—In the Senate, a special motion that any senator may introduce to relieve a committee from consideration of a bill before it. The resolution can be called up for Senate approval or disapproval in the same manner as any other Senate business. (*House procedure, see Discharge a Committee.*)

Division Vote—A vote in which the chair first counts those in favor of a proposition and then those opposed to it, with no record made of how each member votes. In the Senate, the chair may count raised hands or ask senators to stand, whereas the House requires members to stand; hence, often called a standing vote. Committees in both houses ordinarily use a show of hands. A division usually occurs after a voice vote and may be demanded by any member or ordered by the chair if there is any doubt about the outcome of the voice vote. The demand for a division can also come before a voice vote. In the Senate, the demand must come before the result of a voice vote is announced. It may be made after a voice vote announcement in the House, but only if no intervening business has transpired and only if the member was standing and seeking recognition at the time of the announcement. A demand for the yeas and nays or, in the House, for a recorded vote, takes precedence over a division vote.

Enacting Clause—The opening language of each bill, beginning "Be it enacted by the Senate and House of Representatives of the United States of America in Congress assembled..." This language gives legal force to measures approved by Congress and signed by the president or enacted over his veto. A successful motion to strike it from a bill kills the entire measure.

Engrossed Bill—The official copy of a bill or joint resolution as passed by one chamber, including the text as amended by floor action, and certified by the clerk of the House or the secretary of the Senate (as appropriate). Amendments by one house to a measure or amendments of the other also are engrossed. House engrossed documents are printed on blue paper; the Senate's are printed on white paper.

Enrolled Bill—The final official copy of a bill or joint resolution passed in identical form by both houses. An enrolled bill is printed on parchment. After it is certified by the chief officer of the house in which it originated and signed by the House Speaker and the Senate president pro tempore, the measure is sent to the president for his signature.

Entitlement Program—A federal program under which individuals, businesses, or units of government that meet the requirements or qualifications established by law are entitled to receive certain payments if they seek such payments. Major examples include Social Security, Medicare, Medicaid, unemployment insurance, and military and federal civilian pensions. Congress cannot control their expenditures by refusing to appropriate the sums necessary to fund them because the government is legally obligated to pay eligible recipients the amounts to which the law entitles them.

Executive Calendar—The Senate's calendar for committee reports on its executive business, namely treaties and nominations. The calendar numbers indicate the order in which items were referred to the calendar but have no bearing on when or if the Senate will consider them. The Senate, by motion or unanimous consent, resolves itself into executive session to consider them.

Executive Document—A document, usually a treaty, sent by the president to the Senate for approval. It is referred to a committee in the same manner as other measures. Resolutions to ratify treaties have their own "treaty document" numbers. For example, the first treaty submitted in the 106th Congress would be "Treaty Doc 106-1."

Executive Order—A unilateral proclamation by the president that has a policy-making or legislative impact. Members of Congress have challenged some executive orders on the grounds that they usurped the authority of the legislative branch. Although the Supreme Court has ruled that a particular order exceeded the president's authority, it has upheld others as falling within the president's general constitutional powers.

Executive Privilege—The assertion that presidents have the right to withhold certain information from Congress. Presidents have based their claim on: (1) the constitutional separation of powers; (2) the need for secrecy in military and diplomatic affairs; (3) the need to protect individuals from unfavorable publicity; (4) the need to safeguard the confidential exchange of ideas in the executive branch; and (5) the need to protect individuals who provide confidential advice to the president.

Executive Session—A meeting of a Senate or House committee (or occasionally of either chamber) that only its members may attend. Witnesses regularly appear at committee meetings in executive session — for example, Defense Department officials during presentations of classified defense information. Other members of Congress may be invited, but the public and press are not to attend.

Expenditures—The actual spending of money as distinguished from the appropriation of funds. Expenditures are made by the disbursing officers of the administration; appropriations are made only by Congress. The two are rarely identical in any fiscal year. In addition to some current budget authority, expenditures may represent budget authority made available one, two, or more years earlier.

Expulsion—A member's removal from office by a two-thirds vote of his house; the super majority is required by the Constitution. It is the most severe and most rarely used sanction a house can invoke against a member. Although the Constitution provides no explicit grounds for expulsion, the courts have ruled that it may be applied only for misconduct during a member's term of office, not for conduct before the member's election. Generally, neither house will consider expulsion of a member convicted of a crime until the judicial processes have been exhausted. At that stage, members sometimes resign rather than face expulsion. In 1977 the House adopted a rule urging members convicted of certain crimes to voluntarily abstain from voting or participating in other legislative business.

Federal Debt—The total amount of monies borrowed and not yet repaid by the federal government. Federal debt consists of public debt and agency debt. Public debt is the portion of the federal debt borrowed by the Treasury or the Federal Financing Bank directly from the public or from another federal fund or

account. For example, the Treasury regularly borrows money from the Social Security trust fund. Public debt accounts for about 99 percent of the federal debt. Agency debt refers to the debt incurred by federal agencies like the Export-Import Bank, but excluding the Treasury and the Federal Financing Bank, which are authorized by law to borrow funds from the public or from another government fund or account.

Filibuster—The use of obstructive and time-consuming parliamentary tactics by one member or a minority of members to delay, modify, or defeat proposed legislation or rules changes. Filibusters are also sometimes used to delay urgently needed measures in order to force the body to accept other legislation. The Senate's rules permitting unlimited debate and the extraordinary majority it requires to impose cloture make filibustering particularly effective in that chamber. Under the stricter rules of the House, filibusters in that body are short-lived and therefore ineffective and rarely attempted

Fiscal Year—The federal government's annual accounting period. It begins October 1 and ends on the following September 30. A fiscal year is designated by the calendar year in which it ends and is often referred to as FY. Thus, fiscal year 1999 began October 1, 1998, ended September 30, 1999, and is called FY99. In theory, Congress is supposed to complete action on all budgetary measures applying to a fiscal year before that year begins. It rarely does so.

Five-Minute Rule—In its most common usage, a House rule that limits debate on an amendment offered in Committee of the Whole to five minutes for its sponsor and five minutes for an opponent. In practice, the committee routinely permits longer debate by two devices: the offering of pro forma amendments, each debatable for five minutes, and unanimous consent for a member to speak longer than five minutes. Also a House rule that limits a committee member to five minutes when questioning a witness at a hearing until each member has had an opportunity to question that witness.

Floor Manager—A majority party member responsible for guiding a measure through its floor consideration in a house and for devising the political and procedural strategies that might be required to get the measure passed. The presiding officer gives the floor manager priority recognition to debate, offer amendments, oppose amendments, and make crucial procedural motions.

Frank—Informally, a member's legal right to send official mail postage free under his or her signature; often called the franking privilege. Technically, it is the autographic or facsimile signature used on envelopes instead of stamps that permits members and certain congressional officers to send their official mail free of charge. The franking privilege has been authorized by law since the first Congress, except for a few months in 1873. Congress reimburses the U.S. Postal Service for the franked mail it handles.

Function or Functional Category—A broad category of national need and spending of budgetary significance. A category provides an accounting method for allocating and keeping track of budgetary resources and expenditures for that function because it includes all budget accounts related to the functions subject or purpose such as agriculture, administration of justice, commerce and housing and energy. Functions do not necessarily correspond with appropriations acts or with the budgets of individual agencies.

Germane—Basically, on the same subject as the matter under consideration. A House rule requires that all amendments be germane. In the Senate, only amendments proposed to general appropriation bills and budget resolutions or under cloture must be germane. Germaneness rules can be evaded by suspension of the rules in both houses, by unanimous consent agreements in the Senate, and by special rules from the Rules Committee in the House.

Gerrymandering—The manipulation of legislative district boundaries to benefit a particular party, politician, or minority group. The term originated in 1812 when the Massachusetts legislature redrew the lines of state legislative districts to favor the party of Gov. Elbridge Gerry, and some critics said one district looked like a salamander.

Gramm-Rudman-Hollings Act of 1985—Common name for the Balanced Budget and Emergency Deficit Control Act of 1985, which established new budget procedures intended to balance the federal budget by fiscal year 1991. The timetable subsequently was extended and then deleted. The act's chief sponsors were senators Phil Gramm (R-Texas), Warren Rudman (R-N.H.), and Ernest Hollings (D-S.C.).

Grandfather Clause—A provision in a measure, law, or rule that exempts an individual, entity, or a defined category of individuals or entities from complying with a new policy or restriction. For example, a bill that would raise taxes on persons who reach the age of 65 after a certain date inherently grandfathers out those who are 65 before that date. Similarly, a Senate rule limiting senators to two major committee assignments also grandfathers some senators who were sitting on a third major committee prior to a specified date.

Grants-in-Aid—Payments by the federal government to state and local governments to help provide for assistance programs or public services.

Hearing—Committee or subcommittee meetings to receive testimony from witnesses on proposed legislation during investigations or for oversight purposes. Relatively few bills are important enough to justify formal hearings. Witnesses often include experts, government officials, spokespersons for interested groups, officials of the General Accounting Office, and members of Congress. Also, the printed transcripts of hearings.

Hold—A senator's request that his or her party leaders delay floor consideration of certain legislation or presidential nominations. The majority leader usually honors a hold for a reasonable period of time, especially if its purpose is to assure the senator that the matter will not be called up during his or her absence or to give the senator time to gather necessary information.

Hold-Harmless Clause—In legislation providing a new formula for allocating federal funds, a clause to ensure that recipients of those funds do not receive less in a future year than they did in the current year if the new formula would result in a reduction for them. Similar to a grandfather clause, it has been

used most frequently to soften the impact of sudden reductions in federal grants. (*See Grandfather Clause.*)

Hopper—A box on the clerk's desk in the House chamber into which members deposit bills and resolutions to introduce them. In House jargon, to drop a bill in the hopper is to introduce it.

Hour Rule—(1) A House rule that permits members, when recognized, to hold the floor in debate for no more than one hour each. The majority party member customarily yields one-half the time to a minority member. Although the hour rule applies to general debate in Committee of the Whole as well as in the House, special rules routinely vary the length of time for such debate and its control to fit the circumstances of particular measures.

House—The House of Representatives, as distinct from the Senate, although each body is a "house" of Congress.

House as in Committee of the Whole—A hybrid combination of procedures from the general rules of the House and from the rules of the Committee of the Whole, sometimes used to expedite consideration of a measure on the floor.

House Calendar—The calendar reserved for all public bills and resolutions that do not raise revenue or directly or indirectly appropriate money or property when they are favorably reported by House committees.

House Manual—A commonly used title for the handbook of the rules of the House of Representatives, published in each Congress. Its official title is *Constitution, Jefferson's Manual, and Rules of the House of Representatives*.

House of Representatives—The house of Congress in which states are represented roughly in proportion to their populations, but every state is guaranteed at least one representative. By law, the number of voting representatives is fixed at 435. Four delegates and one resident commissioner also serve in the House; they may vote in their committees but not on the House floor. Although the House and Senate have equal legislative power, the Constitution gives the House sole authority to originate revenue measures. The House also claims the right to originate appropriation measures, a claim the Senate disputes in theory but concedes in practice. The House has the sole power to impeach, and it elects the president when no candidate has received a majority of the electoral votes. It is sometimes referred to as the lower body.

Immunity—(1) Members' constitutional protection from lawsuits and arrest in connection with their legislative duties. They may not be tried for libel or slander for anything they say on the floor of a house or in committee. Nor may they be arrested while attending sessions of their houses or when traveling to or from sessions of Congress, except when charged with treason, a felony, or a breach of the peace. (2) In the case of a witness before a committee, a grant of protection from prosecution based on that person's testimony to the committee. It is used to compel witnesses to testify who would otherwise refuse to do so on the constitutional ground of possible self-incrimination. Under such a grant, none of a witness testimony may be used against him or her in a court proceeding except in a prosecution for perjury or for giving a false statement to Congress.

Impeachment—The first step to remove the president, vice president, or other federal civil officers from office and to disqualify them from any future federal office "of honor, Trust or Profit." An impeachment is a formal charge of treason, bribery, or "other high Crimes and Misdemeanors." The House has the sole power of impeachment and the Senate the sole power of trying the charges and convicting. The House impeaches by a simple majority vote; conviction requires a two-thirds vote of all senators present.

Impoundment—An executive branch action or inaction that delays or withholds the expenditure or obligation of budget authority provided by law. The Impoundment Control Act of 1974 classifies impoundments as either deferrals or rescissions, requires the president to notify Congress about all such actions, and gives Congress authority to approve or reject them. The Constitution is unclear on whether a president may refuse to spend appropriated money, but Congress usually expects the president to spend at least enough to achieve the purposes for which the money was provided whether or not he agrees with those purposes.

Joint Committee—A committee composed of members selected from each house. The functions of most joint committees involve investigation, research, or oversight of agencies closely related to Congress. Permanent joint committees, created by statute, are sometimes called standing joint committees. Once quite numerous, only four joint committees remained as of 1997: Joint Economic, Joint Taxation, Joint Library, and Joint Printing. No joint committee has authority to report legislation.

Joint Resolution—A legislative measure that Congress uses for purposes other than general legislation. Like a bill, it has the force of law when passed by both houses and either approved by the president or passed over the president's veto. Unlike a bill, a joint resolution enacted into law is not called an act; it retains its original title.

Most often, joint resolutions deal with such relatively limited matters as the correction of errors in existing law, continuing appropriations, a single appropriation, or the establishment of permanent joint committees. Unlike bills, however, joint resolutions also are used to propose constitutional amendments; these do not require the president's signature and become effective only when ratified by three-fourths of the states. The House designates joint resolutions as H.J. Res., the Senate as S.J. Res. Each house numbers its joint resolutions consecutively in the order of introduction during a two-year Congress.

Journal—The official record of House or Senate actions, including every motion offered, every vote cast, amendments agreed to, quorum calls, and so forth. Unlike the *Congressional Record*, it does not provide reports of speeches, debates, statements, and the like. The Constitution requires each house to maintain a *Journal* and to publish it periodically.

King of the Mountain (or Hill) Rule—(*See Queen of the Hill Rule.*)

Lame Duck—Jargon for a member who has not been reelected, or did not seek reelection, and is serving the balance of his or her term.

Lame Duck Session—A session of a Congress held after the election for the succeeding Congress, so-called after the lame duck members still serving.

Law—An act of Congress that has been signed by the president, passed over the president's veto, or allowed to become law without the president's signature.

Legislative Day—The day that begins when a house meets after an adjournment and ends when it next adjourns. Because the House of Representatives normally adjourns at the end of a daily session, its legislative and calendar days usually coincide. The Senate, however, frequently recesses at the end of a daily session, and its legislative day may extend over several calendar days, weeks, or months. Among other uses, this technicality permits the Senate to save time by circumventing its morning hour, a procedure required at the beginning of every legislative day

Legislative Veto—A procedure, declared unconstitutional in 1983, that allowed Congress or one of its houses to nullify certain actions of the president, executive branch agencies, or independent agencies. Sometimes called congressional vetoes or congressional disapprovals. Following the Supreme Court's 1983 decision, Congress amended several legislative veto statutes to require enactment of joint resolutions, which are subject to presidential veto, for nullifying executive branch actions.

Live Pair—A voluntary and informal agreement between two members on opposite sides of an issue under which the member who is present for a recorded vote withholds or withdraws his or her vote because the other member is absent.

Loan Guarantee—A statutory commitment by the federal government to pay part or all of a loans principal and interest to a lender or the holder of a security in case the borrower defaults.

Lobby—To try to persuade members of Congress to propose, pass, modify, or defeat proposed legislation or to change or repeal existing laws. A lobbyist attempts to promote his or her own preferences or those of a group, organization, or industry. Originally the term referred to persons frequenting the lobbies or corridors of legislative chambers in order to speak to lawmakers. In a general sense, lobbying includes not only direct contact with members but also indirect attempts to influence them, such as writing to them or persuading others to write or visit them, attempting to mold public opinion toward a desired legislative goal by various means, and contributing or arranging for contributions to members election campaigns. The right to lobby stems from the First Amendment to the Constitution, which bans laws that abridge the right of the people to petition the government for a redress of grievances.

Logrolling—Jargon for a legislative tactic or bargaining strategy in which members try to build support for their legislation by promising to support legislation desired by other members or by accepting amendments they hope will induce their colleagues to vote for their bill.

Mace—The symbol of the office of the House sergeant at arms. Under the direction of the Speaker, the sergeant at arms is responsible for preserving order on the House floor by holding up the mace in front of an unruly member, or by carrying the mace up and down the aisles to quell boisterous behavior. When the House is in session, the mace sits on a pedestal at the Speaker's right; when the House is in Committee of the Whole, it is moved to a lower pedestal. The mace is 46 inches high and consists of 13 ebony rods bound in silver and topped by a silver globe with a silver eagle, wings outstretched, perched on it.

Majority Leader—The majority party's chief floor spokesman, elected by that party's caucus—sometimes called floor leader. In the Senate, the majority leader also develops the party's political and procedural strategy, usually in collaboration with other party officials and committee chairmen. He negotiates the Senates agenda and committee ratios with the minority leader and usually calls up measures for floor action. The chamber traditionally concedes to the majority leader the right to determine the days on which it will meet and the hours at which it will convene and adjourn. In the House, the majority leader is the Speaker's deputy and heir apparent. He helps plan the floor agenda and the party's legislative strategy and often speaks for the party leadership in debate.

Majority Whip—In effect, the assistant majority leader, in either the House or Senate. His job is to help marshal majority forces in support of party strategy and legislation.

Manual—The official handbook in each house prescribing in detail its organization, procedures, and operations.

Marking Up a Bill—Going through the contents of a piece of legislation in committee or subcommittee to, for example, consider its provisions in large and small portions, act on amendments to provisions and proposed revisions to the language, and insert new sections and phraseology. If the bill is extensively amended, the committee's version may be introduced as a separate bill, with a new number, before being considered by the full House or Senate. (*See Clean Bill.*)

Method of Equal Proportions—The mathematical formula used since 1950 to determine how the 435 seats in the House of Representatives should be distributed among the 50 states in the apportionment following each decennial census. It minimizes as much as possible the proportional difference between the average district population in any two states. Because the Constitution guarantees each state at least one representative, 50 seats are automatically apportioned. The formula calculates priority numbers for each state, assigns the first of the 385 remaining seats to the state with the highest priority number, the second to the state with the next highest number, and so on until all seats are distributed. (*See Apportionment.*)

Midterm Election—The general election for members of Congress that occurs in November of the second year in a presidential term.

Minority Leader—The minority party's leader and chief floor spokesman, elected by the party caucus; sometimes called minority floor leader. With the assistance of other party officials and the ranking minority members of committees, the minority leader devises the party's political and procedural strategy.

Minority Whip—Performs duties of whip for the minority party. (*See also Majority Whip.*)

Minority Staff—Employees who assist the minority party members of a committee. Most committees hire separate majority and minority party staffs, but they also may hire nonpartisan staff.

Motion—A formal proposal for a procedural action, such as to consider, to amend, to lay on the table, to reconsider, to recess, or to adjourn. It has been estimated that at least 85 motions are possible under various circumstances in the House of Representatives, somewhat fewer in the Senate. Not all motions are created equal; some are privileged or preferential and enjoy priority over others. And some motions are debatable, amendable or divisible, while others are not.

Nomination—A proposed presidential appointment to a federal office submitted to the Senate for confirmation. Approval is by majority vote. The Constitution explicitly requires confirmation for ambassadors, consuls, public Ministers (department heads), and Supreme Court justices. By law, other federal judges, all military promotions of officers, and many high-level civilian officials must be confirmed.

Oath of Office—Upon taking office, members of Congress must swear or affirm that they will "support and defend the Constitution . . . against all enemies, foreign and domestic," that they will "bear true faith and allegiance" to the Constitution, that they take the obligation "freely, without any mental reservation or purpose of evasion," and that they will "well and faithfully discharge the duties" of their office. The oath is required by the Constitution; the wording is prescribed by a statute. All House members must take the oath at the beginning of each new Congress.

Obligations—Orders placed, contracts awarded, services received, and similar transactions during a given period that will require payments during the same or future period. Such amounts include outlays for which obligations had not been previously recorded and reflect adjustments for differences between obligations previously recorded and actual outlays to liquidate those obligations.

Omnibus Bill—A measure that combines the provisions of several disparate subjects into a single and often lengthy bill.

One-Minute Speeches—Addresses by House members at the beginning of a legislative day. The speeches may cover any subject but are limited to one minute's duration.

Order of Business (House)—The sequence of events during the meeting of the House on a new legislative day prescribed by a House rule; also called the general order of business. The sequence consists of (1) the chaplain's prayer; (2) approval of the *Journal*; (3) pledge of allegiance (4) correction of the reference of public bills; (5) disposal of business on the Speaker's table; (6) unfinished business; (7) the morning hour call of committees and consideration of their bills (largely obsolete); (8) motions to go into Committee of the Whole; and (9) orders of the day (also obsolete). In practice, on days specified in the rules, the items of business that follow approval of the *Journal* are supplanted in part by the special order of business (for example, the corrections, discharge, or private calendars or motions to suspend the rules) and on any day by other privileged business (for example, general appropriation bills and special rules)

or measures made in order by special rules. By this combination of an order of business with privileged interruptions, the House gives precedence to certain categories of important legislation, brings to the floor other major legislation from its calendars in any order it chooses, and provides expeditious processing for minor and noncontroversial measures.

Order of Business (Senate)—The sequence of events at the beginning of a new legislative day prescribed by Senate rules. The sequence consists of (1) the chaplain's prayer; (2) *Journal* reading and correction; (3) morning business in the morning hour; (4) call of the calendar during the morning hour; and (5) unfinished business.

Outlays—Amounts of government spending. They consist of payments, usually by check or in cash, to liquidate obligations incurred in prior fiscal years as well as in the current year, including the net lending of funds under budget authority. In federal budget accounting, net outlays are calculated by subtracting the amounts of refunds and various kinds of reimbursements to the government from actual spending.

Override a Veto—Congressional enactment of a measure over the president's veto. A veto override requires a recorded two-thirds vote of those voting in each house, a quorum being present. Because the president must return the vetoed measure to its house of origin, that house votes first, but neither house is required to attempt an override, whether immediately or at all. If an override attempt fails in the house of origin, the veto stands and the measure dies.

Oversight—Congressional review of the way in which federal agencies implement laws to ensure that they are carrying out the intent of Congress and to inquire into the efficiency of the implementation and the effectiveness of the law. The Legislative Reorganization Act of 1946 defined oversight as the function of exercising continuous watchfulness over the execution of the laws by the executive branch.

Pairing—A procedure that permits two or three members to enter into voluntary arrangements that offset their votes so that one or more of the members can be absent without changing the result. The names of paired members and their positions on the vote (except on general pairs) appear in the *Congressional Record*. Members can be paired on one vote or on a series of votes.

Parliamentarian—The official advisor to the presiding officer in each house on questions of procedure. The parliamentarian and his assistants also answer procedural questions from members and congressional staff, refer measures to committees on behalf of the presiding officer, and maintain compilations of the precedents. The House parliamentarian revises the House Manual at the beginning of every Congress and usually reviews special rules before the Rules Committee reports them to the House. Either a parliamentarian or an assistant is always present and near the podium during sessions of each house.

Party Caucus—Generic term for each party's official organization in each house. Only House Democrats officially call their organization a caucus. House and Senate Republicans and Senate Democrats call their organizations conferences. The party caucuses elect their leaders, approve committee assignments

and chairmanships (or ranking minority members, if the party is in the minority), establish party committees and study groups, and discuss party and legislative policies. On rare occasions, they have stripped members of committee seniority or expelled them from the caucus for party disloyalty.

Petition—A request or plea sent to one or both chambers from an organization or private citizens' group asking support of particular legislation or favorable consideration of a matter not yet receiving congressional attention. Petitions are referred to appropriate committees.

Pocket Veto—The indirect veto of a bill as a result of the president withholding approval of it until after Congress has adjourned sine die. A bill the president does not sign, but does not formally veto while Congress is in session, automatically becomes a law 10 days (excluding Sundays) after it is received. But if Congress adjourns its annual session during that 10-day period, the measure dies even if the president does not formally veto it.

Point of Order—A parliamentary term used in committee and on the floor to object to an alleged violation of a rule and to demand that the chair enforce the rule. The point of order immediately halts the proceedings until the chair decides whether the contention is valid.

Pork or Pork Barrel Legislation—Pejorative terms for federal appropriations, bills, or policies that provide funds to benefit a legislator's district or state, with the implication that the legislator presses for enactment of such benefits to ingratiate himself or herself with constituents rather than on the basis of an impartial, objective assessment of need or merit.

The terms are often applied to such benefits as new parks, post offices, dams, canals, bridges, roads, water projects, sewage treatment plants, and public works of any kind, as well as demonstration projects, research grants, and relocation of government facilities. Funds released by the president for various kinds of benefits or government contracts approved by him allegedly for political purposes are also sometimes referred to as pork.

Postcloture Filibuster—A filibuster conducted after the Senate invokes cloture. It employs an array of procedural tactics rather than lengthy speeches to delay final action. The Senate curtailed the postcloture filibusters effectiveness by closing a variety of loopholes in the cloture rule in 1979 and 1986.

President of the Senate—The vice president of the United States in his constitutional role as presiding officer of the Senate. The Constitution permits the vice president to cast a vote in the Senate only to break a tie, but he is not required to do so.

President Pro Tempore—Under the Constitution, an officer elected by the Senate to preside over it during the absence of the vice president of the United States. Often referred to as the "pro tem," he is usually the majority party senator with the longest continuous service in the chamber and also, by virtue of his seniority, a committee chairman. When attending to committee and other duties, the president pro tempore appoints other senators to preside.

Previous Question—A nondebatable motion which, when agreed to by majority vote, usually cuts off further debate, prevents the offering of additional amendments, and brings the pending matter to an immediate vote. It is a major debate-limiting device in the House; it is not permitted in Committee of the Whole or in the Senate.

Printed Amendment—A House rule guarantees five minutes of floor debate in support and five minutes in opposition, and no other debate time, on amendments printed in the Congressional Record at least one day prior to the amendment's consideration in the Committee of the Whole. In the Senate, although amendments may be submitted for printing, they have no parliamentary standing or status. An amendment submitted for printing in the Senate, however, may be called up by any senator.

Private Bill—A bill that applies to one or more specified persons, corporations, institutions, or other entities, usually to grant relief when no other legal remedy is available to them. Many private bills deal with claims against the federal government, immigration and naturalization cases, and land titles.

Private Calendar—Commonly used title for a calendar in the House reserved for private bills and resolutions favorably reported by committees. The private calendar is officially called the Calendar of the Committee of the Whole House.

Privilege—An attribute of a motion, measure, report, question, or proposition that gives it priority status for consideration. Privileged motions and motions to bring up privileged questions are not debatable.

Privileged Questions—The order in which bills, motions, and other legislative measures are considered by Congress is governed by strict priorities. A motion to table, for instance, is more privileged than a motion to recommit. Thus, a motion to recommit can be superseded by a motion to table, and a vote would be forced on the latter motion only. A motion to adjourn, however, takes precedence over a tabling motion and thus is considered of the "highest privilege." (*See also Questions of Privilege.*)

Pro Forma Amendment—In the House, an amendment that ostensibly proposes to change a measure or another amendment by moving "to strike the last word" or "to strike the requisite number of words." A member offers it not to make any actual change in the measure or amendment but only to obtain time for debate.

Proxy Voting—The practice of permitting a member to cast the vote of an absent colleague in addition to his own vote. Proxy voting is prohibited on the floors of the House and Senate, but the Senate permits its committees to authorize proxy voting, and most do. In 1995, House rules were changed to prohibit proxy voting in committee.

Public Law—A public bill or joint resolution enacted into law. It is cited by the letters P.L. followed by a hyphenated number. The digits before the hyphen indicate the number of the Congress in which it was enacted; the digits after the hyphen indicate its position in the numerical sequence of public measures that became law during that Congress. For example, the

Budget Enforcement Act of 1990 became P.L. 101-508 because it was the 508th measure in that sequence for the 101st Congress. (*See also Private Bill.*)

Queen of the Hill Rule—A special rule from the House Rules Committee that permits votes on a series of amendments, especially complete substitutes for a measure, in a specified order, but directs that the amendment receiving the greatest number of votes shall be the winning one. This kind of rule permits the House to vote directly on a variety of alternatives to a measure. In doing so, it sets aside the precedent that once an amendment has been adopted, no further amendments may be offered to the text it has amended. Under an earlier practice, the Rules Committee reported "king of the hill" rules under which there also could be votes on a series of amendments, again in a specified order. If more than one of the amendments was adopted under this kind of rule, it was the last amendment to receive a majority vote that was considered as having been finally adopted, whether or not it had received the greatest number of votes.

Questions of Privilege—These are matters affecting members of Congress individually or collectively. Matters affecting the rights, safety, dignity, and integrity of proceedings of the House or Senate as a whole are questions of privilege in both chambers.

Questions involving individual members are called questions of "personal privilege." A member rising to ask a question of personal privilege is given precedence over almost all other proceedings. An annotation in the House rules points out that the privilege rests primarily on the Constitution, which gives a member a conditional immunity from arrest and an unconditional freedom to speak in the House. (*See also Privileged Questions.*)

Quorum—The minimum number of members required to be present for the transaction of business. Under the Constitution, a quorum in each house is a majority of its members: 218 in the House and 51 in the Senate when there are no vacancies. By House rule, a quorum in Committee of the Whole is 100. In practice, both houses usually assume a quorum is present even if it is not, unless a member makes a point of no quorum in the House or suggests the absence of a quorum in the Senate. Consequently, each house transacts much of its business, and even passes bills, when only a few members are present.

For House and Senate committees, chamber rules allow a minimum quorum of one-third of a committee's members to conduct most types of business.

Ramseyer Rule—A House rule that requires a committee's report on a bill or joint resolution to show the changes the measure, and any committee amendments to it, would make in existing law.

Readings of Bills—Traditional parliamentary procedure required bills to be read three times before they were passed. This custom is of little modern significance. Normally a bill is considered to have its first reading when it is introduced and printed, by title, in the *Congressional Record*. In the House, its second reading comes when floor consideration begins. (This is the most likely point at which there is an actual reading of the bill, if there is any.) The second reading in the Senate is supposed to occur on the legislative day after the measure is introduced, but

before it is referred to committee. The third reading (again, usually by title) takes place when floor action has been completed on amendments.

Reapportionment—(*See Apportionment.*)

Recess—(1) A temporary interruption or suspension of a meeting of a chamber or committee. Unlike an adjournment, a recess does not end a legislative day. Because the Senate often recesses from one calendar day to another, its legislative day may extend over several calendar days, weeks, or even months. (2) A period of adjournment for more than three days to a day certain, especially over a holiday or in August during odd-numbered years.

Recognition—The power of recognition of a member is lodged in the Speaker of the House and the presiding officer of the Senate. The presiding officer names the member who will speak first when two or more members simultaneously request recognition.

Recommit—To send a measure back to the committee that reported it; sometimes called a straight motion to recommit to distinguish it from a motion to recommit with instructions. A successful motion to recommit kills the measure unless it is accompanied by instructions.

Reconciliation—A procedure for changing existing revenue and spending laws to bring total federal revenues and spending within the limits established in a budget resolution. Congress has applied reconciliation chiefly to revenues and mandatory spending programs, especially entitlements. Discretionary spending is controlled through annual appropriation bills.

Reconsider a Vote—A motion to reconsider the vote by which an action was taken has, until it is disposed of, the effect of putting the action in abeyance. In the Senate, the motion can be made only by a member who voted on the prevailing side of the original question or by a member who did not vote at all. In the House, it can be made only by a member on the prevailing side.

A common practice in the Senate after close votes on an issue is a motion to reconsider, followed by a motion to table the motion to reconsider. On this motion to table, senators vote as they voted on the original question, which allows the motion to table to prevail, assuming there are no switches. The matter then is finally closed and further motions to reconsider are not entertained. In the House, as a routine precaution, a motion to reconsider usually is made every time a measure is passed. Such a motion almost always is tabled immediately, thus shutting off the possibility of future reconsideration, except by unanimous consent.

Motions to reconsider must be entered in the Senate within the next two days of actual session after the original vote has been taken. In the House they must be entered either on the same day or on the next succeeding day the House is in session.

Recorded Vote—(1) Generally, any vote in which members are recorded by name for or against a measure; also called a record vote or roll-call vote. The only recorded vote in the Senate is a vote by the yeas and nays and is commonly called a roll-call vote. (2) Technically, a recorded vote is one demanded in the House of Representatives and supported by at least one-fifth of a quorum (44 members) in the House sitting as the House or at least 25 members in Committee of the Whole.

Report—(1) As a verb, a committee is said to report when it submits a measure or other document to its parent chamber. (2) A clerk is said to report when he or she reads a measure's title, text, or the text of an amendment to the body at the direction of the chair. (3) As a noun, a committee document that accompanies a reported measure. It describes the measure, the committee's views on it, its costs, and the changes it proposes to make in existing law; it also includes certain impact statements. (4) A committee document submitted to its parent chamber that describes the results of an investigation or other study or provides information the committee is required to provide by rule or law.

Reprimand—A formal condemnation of a member for misbehavior, considered a milder reproof than censure. The House of Representatives first used it in 1976. The Senate first used it in 1991. (*See also Censure, Code of Official Conduct, Expulsion.*)

Rescission—A provision of law that repeals previously enacted budget authority in whole or in part. Under the Impoundment Control Act of 1974, the president can impound such funds by sending a message to Congress requesting one or more rescissions and the reasons for doing so. If Congress does not pass a rescission bill for the programs requested by the president within 45 days of continuous session after receiving the message, the president must make the funds available for obligation and expenditure. If the president does not, the comptroller general of the United States is authorized to bring suit to compel the release of those funds. A rescission bill may rescind all, part, or none of an amount proposed by the president, and may rescind funds the president has not impounded.

Resolution—(1) A simple resolution; that is, a nonlegislative measure effective only in the house in which it is proposed and not requiring concurrence by the other chamber or approval by the president. Simple resolutions are designated H. Res. in the House and S. Res. in the Senate. Simple resolutions express nonbinding opinions on policies or issues or deal with the internal affairs or prerogatives of a house. (2) Any type of resolution: simple, concurrent, or joint. (*See Concurrent Resolution, Joint Resolution.*)

Revise and Extend One's Remarks—A unanimous consent request to publish in the *Congressional Record* a statement a member did not deliver on the floor, a longer statement than the one made on the floor, or miscellaneous extraneous material.

Rider—Congressional slang for an amendment unrelated or extraneous to the subject matter of the measure to which it is attached. Riders often contain proposals that are less likely to become law on their own merits as separate bills, either because of opposition in the committee of jurisdiction, resistance in the other house, or the probability of a presidential veto. Riders are more common in the Senate.

Rule—(1) A permanent regulation that a house adopts to govern its conduct of business, its procedures, its internal organization, behavior of its members, regulation of its facilities, duties of an officer, or some other subject it chooses to govern in that form. (2) In the House, a privileged simple resolution reported by the Rules Committee that provides methods and conditions for floor consideration of a measure or, rarely, several measures.

Secretary of the Senate—The chief administrative and budgetary officer of the Senate. The secretary manages a wide range of functions that support the operation of the Senate as an organization as well as those functions necessary to its legislative process, including recordkeeping, document management, certifications, housekeeping services, administration of oaths, and lobbyist registrations.

Select or Special Committee—A committee established by a resolution in either house for a special purpose and, usually, for a limited time. Most select and special committees are assigned specific investigations or studies, but are not authorized to report measures to their chambers.

Senate—The house of Congress in which each state is represented by two senators; each senator has one vote. Article V of the Constitution declares that "No State, without its Consent, shall be deprived of its equal Suffrage in the Senate." The Constitution also gives the Senate equal legislative power with the House of Representatives. Although the Senate is prohibited from originating revenue measures, and as a matter of practice it does not originate appropriation measures, it can amend both. Only the Senate can give or withhold consent to treaties and nominations from the president. It also acts as a court to try impeachments by the House and elects the vice president when no candidate receives a majority of the electoral votes. It is often referred to as "the upper body," but not by members of the House.

Senate Manual—The handbook of the Senate's standing rules and orders and the laws and other regulations that apply to the Senate, usually published once each Congress.

Senatorial Courtesy—The Senate's practice of declining to confirm a presidential nominee for an office in the state of a senator of the president's party unless that senator approves.

Sequestration—A procedure for canceling budgetary resources that is, money available for obligation or spending to enforce budget limitations established in law. Sequestered funds are no longer available for obligation or expenditure.

Sine Die—(*See Adjournment Sine Die.*)

Slip Law—The first official publication of a measure that has become law. It is published separately in unbound, single-sheet form or pamphlet form. A slip law usually is available two or three days after the date of the law's enactment.

Speaker—The presiding officer of the House of Representatives and the leader of its majority party. The Speaker is selected by the majority party and formally elected by the House at the beginning of each Congress. Although the Constitution does not require the Speaker to be a member of the House, in fact, all Speakers have been members.

Special Session—A session of Congress convened by the president, under his constitutional authority, after Congress has adjourned sine die at the end of a regular session. (*See Adjournment Sine Die.*)

Spending Authority—The technical term for backdoor spending. The Congressional Budget Act of 1974 defines it as

borrowing authority, contract authority, and entitlement authority for which appropriation acts do not provide budget authority in advance. Under the Budget Act, legislation that provides new spending authority may not be considered unless it provides that the authority shall be effective only to the extent or in such amounts as provided in an appropriation act.

Sponsor—The principal proponent and introducer of a measure or an amendment.

Standing Committee—A permanent committee established by a House or Senate standing rule or standing order. The rule also describes the subject areas on which the committee may report bills and resolutions and conduct oversight. Most introduced measures must be referred to one or more standing committees according to their jurisdictions.

Standing Vote—An alternative and informal term for a division vote, during which members in favor of a proposal and then members opposed stand and are counted by the chair. (*See Division Vote.*)

Star Print—A reprint of a bill, resolution, amendment, or committee report correcting technical or substantive errors in a previous printing; so called because of the small black star that appears on the front page or cover.

Statutes at Large—A chronological arrangement of the laws enacted in each session of Congress. Though indexed, the laws are not arranged by subject matter nor is there an indication of how they affect or change previously enacted laws. The volumes are numbered by Congress, and the laws are cited by their volume and page number. The Gramm-Rudman-Hollings Act, for example, appears as 99 Stat. 1037.

Strike from the *Record*—Expunge objectionable remarks from the *Congressional Record*, after a member's words have been taken down on a point of order.

Strike Out the Last Word—A motion whereby a House member is entitled to speak for five minutes on an amendment then being debated by the chamber. A member gains recognition from the chair by moving to "strike out the last word" of the amendment or section of the bill under consideration. The motion is proforma, requires no vote, and does not change the amendment being debated.

Substitute—A motion, amendment, or entire bill introduced in place of the pending legislative business. Passage of a substitute measure kills the original measure by supplanting it. The substitute also may be amended. (*See also Amendment in the Nature of a Substitute.*)

Sunshine Rules—Rules requiring open committee hearings and business meetings, including markup sessions, in both houses, and also open conference committee meetings. However, all may be closed under certain circumstances and using certain procedures required by the rules.

Super Majority—A term sometimes used for a vote on a matter that requires approval by more than a simple majority of those members present and voting; also referred to as extraordinary majority.

Supplemental Appropriation Bill—A measure providing appropriations for use in the current fiscal year, in addition to those already provided in annual general appropriation bills. Supplemental appropriations are often for unforeseen emergencies.

Suspension of the Rules (House)—An expeditious procedure for passing relatively noncontroversial or emergency measures by a two-thirds vote of those members voting, a quorum being present.

Suspension of the Rules (Senate)—A procedure to set aside one or more of the Senate's rules; it is used infrequently, and then most often to suspend the rule banning legislative amendments to appropriation bills.

Table a Bill—Motions to table, or to "lay on the table," are used to block or kill amendments or other parliamentary questions. When approved, a tabling motion is considered the final disposition of that issue. One of the most widely used parliamentary procedures, the motion to table is not debatable, and adoption requires a simple majority vote.

In the Senate, however, different language sometimes is used. The motion may be worded to let a bill "lie on the table," perhaps for subsequent "picking up." This motion is more flexible, keeping the bill pending for later action, if desired. Tabling motions on amendments are effective debate-ending devices in the Senate.

Teller Vote—A voting procedure, formerly used in the House, in which members cast their votes by passing through the center aisle to be counted, but not recorded by name, by a member from each party appointed by the chair. The House deleted the procedure from its rules in 1993, but during floor discussion of the deletion a leading member stated that a teller vote would still be available in the event of a breakdown of the electronic voting system.

Treaty—A formal document containing an agreement between two or more sovereign nations. The Constitution authorizes the president to make treaties, but he must submit them to the Senate for its approval by a two-thirds vote of the senators present. Under the Senate's rules, that vote actually occurs on a resolution of ratification. Although the Constitution does not give the House a direct role in approving treaties, that body has sometimes insisted that a revenue treaty is an invasion of its prerogatives. In any case, the House may significantly affect the application of a treaty by its equal role in enacting legislation to implement the treaty.

Trust Funds—Special accounts in the Treasury that receive earmarked taxes or other kinds of revenue collections, such as user fees, and from which payments are made for special purposes or to recipients who meet the requirements of the trust funds as established by law. Of the more than 150 federal government trust funds, several finance major entitlement programs, such as Social Security, Medicare, and retired federal employees' pensions. Others fund infrastructure construction and improvements, such as highways and airports.

Unanimous Consent—Without an objection by any member. A unanimous consent request asks permission, explicitly or implicitly, to set aside one or more rules. Both houses and their

committees frequently use such requests to expedite their proceedings.

Unanimous Consent Agreement—A device used in the Senate to expedite legislation. Much of the Senate's legislative business, dealing with both minor and controversial issues, is conducted through unanimous consent or unanimous consent agreements. On major legislation, such agreements usually are printed and transmitted to all senators in advance of floor debate. Once agreed to, they are binding on all members unless the Senate, by unanimous consent, agrees to modify them. An agreement may list the order in which various bills are to be considered, specify the length of time bills and contested amendments are to be debated and when they are to be voted upon, and, frequently, require that all amendments introduced be germane to the bill under consideration. In this regard, unanimous consent agreements are similar to the "rules" issued by the House Rules Committee for bills pending in the House.

Unfunded Mandate—Generally, any provision in federal law or regulation that imposes a duty or obligation on a state or local government or private sector entity without providing the necessary funds to comply. The Unfunded Mandates Reform Act of 1995 amended the Congressional Budget Act of 1974 to provide a mechanism for the control of new unfunded mandates.

Union Calendar—A calendar of the House of Representatives for bills and resolutions favorably reported by committees that raise revenue or directly or indirectly appropriate money or property. In addition to appropriation bills, measures that authorize expenditures are also placed on this calendar. The calendar's full title is the Calendar of the Committee of the Whole House on the State of the Union.

U.S. Code—Popular title for the *United States Code: Containing the General and Permanent Laws of the United States in Force on. . . .* It is a consolidation and partial codification of the general and permanent laws of the United States arranged by subject under 50 titles. The first six titles deal with general or political subjects, the other 44 with subjects ranging from agriculture to war, alphabetically arranged. A supplement is published after each session of Congress, and the entire Code is revised every six years.

Veto—The president's disapproval of a legislative measure passed by Congress. He returns the measure to the house in which it originated without his signature but with a veto message stating his objections to it. When Congress is in session, the president must veto a bill within 10 days, excluding Sundays, after he has received it; otherwise it becomes law without his signature. The 10-day clock begins to run at midnight following his receipt of the bill. (*See also Committee Veto, Item Veto, Override a Veto, Pocket Veto.*)

Voice Vote—A method of voting in which members who favor a question answer aye in chorus, after which those opposed answer no in chorus, and the chair decides which position prevails.

War Powers Resolution of 1973—An act that requires the president "in every possible instance" to consult Congress before he commits U.S. forces to ongoing or imminent hostilities. If he commits them to a combat situation without congressional consultation, he must notify Congress within 48 hours. Unless Congress declares war or otherwise authorizes the operation to continue, the forces must be withdrawn within 60 or 90 days, depending on certain conditions. No president has ever acknowledged the constitutionality of the resolution.

Whip—The majority or minority party member in each house who acts as assistant leader, helps plan and marshal support for party strategies, encourages party discipline, and advises his leader on how his colleagues intend to vote on the floor. In the Senate, the Republican whip's official title is assistant leader.

Without Objection—Used in lieu of a vote on noncontroversial motions, amendments, or bills that may be passed in either the House or Senate if no member voices an objection.

Yeas and Nays—A vote in which members usually respond "aye" or "no" (despite the official title of the vote) on a question when their names are called in alphabetical order. The Constitution requires the yeas and nays when a demand for it is supported by one-fifth of the members present, and it also requires an automatic yea-and-nay vote on overriding a veto. Senate precedents require the support of at least one-fifth of a quorum, a minimum of 11 members with the present membership of 100.

Yielding—When a member has been recognized to speak, no other member may speak unless he or she obtains permission from the member recognized. This permission is called yielding and usually is requested in the form, "Will the gentleman yield to me?" While this activity occasionally is seen in the Senate, the Senate has no rule or practice to parcel out time.

Constitution of the United States

We the People of the United States, in Order to form a more perfect Union, establish Justice, insure domestic Tranquility, provide for the common defence, promote the general Welfare, and secure the Blessings of Liberty to ourselves and our Posterity, do ordain and establish this Constitution for the United States of America.

ARTICLE I

Section 1. All legislative Powers herein granted shall be vested in a Congress of the United States, which shall consist of a Senate and House of Representatives.

Section 2. The House of Representatives shall be composed of Members chosen every second Year by the People of the several States, and the Electors in each State shall have the Qualifications requisite for Electors of the most numerous Branch of the State Legislature.

No Person shall be a Representative who shall not have attained to the age of twenty five Years, and been seven Years a Citizen of the United States, and who shall not, when elected, be an Inhabitant of that State in which he shall be chosen.

[Representatives and direct Taxes shall be apportioned among the several States which may be included within this Union, according to their respective Numbers, which shall be determined by adding to the whole Number of free Persons, including those bound to Service for a Term of Years, and excluding Indians not taxed, three fifths of all other Persons.][1] The actual Enumeration shall be made within three Years after the first Meeting of the Congress of the United States, and within every subsequent Term of ten Years, in such Manner as they shall by Law direct. The Number of Representatives shall not exceed one for every thirty Thousand, but each State shall have at Least one Representative; and until such enumeration shall be made, the State of New Hampshire shall be entitled to chuse three, Massachusetts eight, Rhode-Island and Providence Plantations one, Connecticut five, New-York six, New Jersey four, Pennsylvania eight, Delaware one, Maryland six, Virginia ten, North Carolina five, South Carolina five, and Georgia three.

When vacancies happen in the Representation from any State, the Executive Authority thereof shall issue Writs of Election to fill such Vacancies.

The House of Representatives shall chuse their Speaker and other Officers; and shall have the sole Power of Impeachment.

Section 3. The Senate of the United States shall be composed of two Senators from each State, [chosen by the Legislature thereof,][2] for six Years; and each Senator shall have one Vote.

Immediately after they shall be assembled in Consequence of the first Election, they shall be divided as equally as may be into three Classes. The Seats of the Senators of the first Class shall be vacated at the Expiration of the second Year, of the second Class at the Expiration of the fourth Year, and of the third Class at the Expiration of the sixth Year, so that one third may be chosen every second Year; [and if Vacancies happen by Resignation, or otherwise, during the Recess of the Legislature of any State, the Executive thereof may make temporary Appointments until the next Meeting of the Legislature, which shall then fill such Vacancies.][3]

No Person shall be a Senator who shall not have attained to the Age of thirty Years, and been nine Years a Citizen of the United States, and who shall not, when elected, be an Inhabitant of that State for which he shall be chosen.

The Vice President of the United States shall be President of the Senate, but shall have no Vote, unless they be equally divided.

The Senate shall chuse their other Officers, and also a President pro tempore, in the Absence of the Vice President, or when he shall exercise the Office of President of the United States.

The Senate shall have the sole Power to try all Impeachments. When sitting for that Purpose, they shall be on Oath or Affirmation. When the President of the United States is tried, the Chief Justice shall preside: And no Person shall be convicted without the Concurrence of two thirds of the Members present.

Judgment in Cases of Impeachment shall not extend further than to removal from Office, and disqualification to hold and enjoy any Office of honor, Trust or Profit under the United States: but the Party convicted shall nevertheless be liable and subject to Indictment, Trial, Judgment and Punishment, according to Law.

Section 4. The Times, Places and Manner of holding Elections for Senators and Representatives, shall be prescribed in each State by the Legislature thereof; but the Congress may at any time by Law make or alter such Regulations, except as to the Places of chusing Senators.

The Congress shall assemble at least once in every Year, and such Meeting shall [be on the first Monday in December],[4] unless they shall by Law appoint a different Day.

Section 5. Each House shall be the Judge of the Elections, Returns and Qualifications of its own Members, and a Majority of each shall constitute a Quorum to do Business; but a smaller Number may adjourn from day to day, and may be authorized to compel the Attendance of absent Members, in such Manner, and under such Penalties as each House may provide.

Each House may determine the Rules of its Proceedings, punish its Members for disorderly Behaviour, and, with the Concurrence of two thirds, expel a Member.

Each House shall keep a Journal of its Proceedings, and from time to time publish the same, excepting such Parts as may in their Judgment require Secrecy; and the Yeas and Nays of the Members of either House on any question shall, at the Desire of one fifth of those Present, be entered on the Journal.

Neither House, during the Session of Congress, shall, without the Consent of the other, adjourn for more than three days, nor to any other Place than that in which the two Houses shall be sitting.

Section 6. The Senators and Representatives shall receive a Compensation for their Services, to be ascertained by Law, and paid out of the Treasury of the United States. They shall in all Cases, except Treason, Felony and Breach of the Peace, be privileged from Arrest during their Attendance at the Session of their respective Houses, and in going to and returning from the same; and for any Speech or Debate in either House, they shall not be questioned in any other Place.

No Senator or Representative shall, during the Time for which he was elected, be appointed to any civil Office under the Authority of the United States, which shall have been created, or the Emoluments whereof shall have been encreased during such time; and no Person holding any Office under the United States, shall be a Member of either House during his Continuance in Office.

Section 7. All Bills for raising Revenue shall originate in the House of Representatives; but the Senate may propose or concur with Amendments as on other Bills.

Every Bill which shall have passed the House of Representatives and the Senate, shall, before it become a Law, be presented to the President of the United States; If he approve he shall sign it, but if not he shall return it, with his Objections to that House in which it shall have originated, who shall enter the Objections at large on their Journal, and proceed to reconsider it. If after such Reconsideration two thirds of that House shall agree to pass the Bill, it shall be sent, together with the Objections, to the other House, by which it shall likewise be reconsidered, and if approved by two thirds of that House, it shall become a Law. But in all such Cases the Votes of both Houses shall be determined by yeas and Nays, and the Names of the Persons voting for and against the Bill shall be entered on the Journal of each House respectively. If any Bill shall not be returned by the President within ten Days (Sundays excepted) after it shall have been presented to him, the Same shall be a Law, in like Manner as if he had signed it, unless the Congress by their Adjournment prevent its Return, in which Case it shall not be a Law.

Every Order, Resolution, or Vote to which the Concurrence of the Senate and House of Representatives may be necessary (except on a question of Adjournment) shall be presented to the President of the United States; and before the Same shall take Effect, shall be approved by him, or being disapproved by him, shall be repassed by two thirds of the Senate and House of Representatives, according to the Rules and Limitations prescribed in the Case of a Bill.

Section 8. The Congress shall have Power To lay and collect Taxes, Duties, Imposts and Excises, to pay the Debts and provide for the common Defence and general Welfare of the United States; but all Duties, Imposts and Excises shall be uniform throughout the United States;

To borrow Money on the credit of the United States;

To regulate Commerce with foreign Nations, and among the several States, and with the Indian Tribes;

To establish an uniform Rule of Naturalization, and uniform Laws on the subject of Bankruptcies throughout the United States;

To coin Money, regulate the Value thereof, and of foreign Coin, and fix the Standard of Weights and Measures;

To provide for the Punishment of counterfeiting the Securi-

ties and current Coin of the United States;

To establish Post Offices and post Roads;

To promote the Progress of Science and useful Arts, by securing for limited Times to Authors and Inventors the exclusive Right to their respective Writings and Discoveries;

To constitute Tribunals inferior to the supreme Court;

To define and punish Piracies and Felonies committed on the high Seas, and Offences against the Law of Nations;

To declare War, grant Letters of Marque and Reprisal, and make Rules concerning Captures on Land and Water;

To raise and support Armies, but no Appropriation of Money to that Use shall be for a longer Term than two Years;

To provide and maintain a Navy;

To make Rules for the Government and Regulation of the land and naval Forces;

To provide for calling forth the Militia to execute the Laws of the Union, suppress Insurrections and repel Invasions;

To provide for organizing, arming, and disciplining, the Militia, and for governing such Part of them as may be employed in the Service of the United States, reserving to the States respectively, the Appointment of the Officers, and the Authority of training the Militia according to the discipline prescribed by Congress;

To exercise exclusive Legislation in all Cases whatsoever, over such District (not exceeding ten Miles square) as may, by Cession of particular States, and the Acceptance of Congress, become the Seat of the Government of the United States, and to exercise like Authority over all Places purchased by the Consent of the Legislature of the State in which the Same shall be, for the Erection of Forts, Magazines, Arsenals, dock-Yards, and other needful Buildings; — And

To make all Laws which shall be necessary and proper for carrying into Execution the foregoing Powers, and all other Powers vested by this Constitution in the Government of the United States, or in any Department or Officer thereof.

Section 9. The Migration or Importation of such Persons as any of the States now existing shall think proper to admit, shall not be prohibited by the Congress prior to the Year one thousand eight hundred and eight, but a Tax or duty may be imposed on such Importation, not exceeding ten dollars for each Person.

The Privilege of the Writ of Habeas Corpus shall not be suspended, unless when in Cases of Rebellion or Invasion the public Safety may require it.

No Bill of Attainder or ex post facto Law shall be passed.

No Capitation, or other direct, Tax shall be laid, unless in Proportion to the Census or Enumeration herein before directed to be taken.[5]

No Tax or Duty shall be laid on Articles exported from any State.

No Preference shall be given by any Regulation of Commerce or Revenue to the Ports of one State over those of another; nor shall Vessels bound to, or from, one State, be obliged to enter, clear, or pay Duties in another.

No Money shall be drawn from the Treasury, but in Consequence of Appropriations made by Law; and a regular Statement and Account of the Receipts and Expenditures of all public Money shall be published from time to time.

No Title of Nobility shall be granted by the United States: And no Person holding any Office of Profit or Trust under them, shall, without the Consent of the Congress, accept of any present, Emolument, Office, or Title, of any kind whatever, from any King, Prince, or foreign State.

Section 10. No State shall enter into any Treaty, Alliance, or Confederation; grant Letters of Marque and Reprisal; coin Money; emit Bills of Credit; make any Thing but gold and silver Coin a Tender in Payment of Debts; pass any Bill of Attainder, ex post facto Law, or Law impairing the Obligation of Contracts, or grant any Title of Nobility.

No State shall, without the Consent of the Congress, **lay** any Imposts or Duties on Imports or Exports, except what may be absolutely necessary for executing it's inspection Laws: and the net Produce of all Duties and Imposts, laid by any State on Imports or Exports, shall be for the Use of the Treasury of the United States; and all such Laws shall be subject to the Revision and Controul of the Congress.

No State shall, without the Consent of Congress, lay any Duty of Tonnage, keep Troops, or Ships of War in time of Peace, enter into any Agreement or Compact with another State, or with a foreign Power, or engage in War, unless actually invaded, or in such imminent Danger as will not admit of delay.

ARTICLE II

Section 1. The executive Power shall be vested in a President of the United States of America. He shall hold his Office during the Term of four Years, and, together with the Vice President, chosen for the same Term, be elected, as follows

Each State shall appoint, in such Manner as the Legislature thereof may direct, a Number of Electors, equal to the whole Number of Senators and Representatives to which the State may be entitled in the Congress: but no Senator or Representative, or Person holding an Office of Trust or Profit under the United States, shall be appointed an Elector.

[The Electors shall meet in their respective States, and vote by Ballot for two Persons, of whom one at least shall not be an Inhabitant of the same State with themselves. And they shall make a List of all the Persons voted for, and of the Number of Votes for each; which List they shall sign and certify, and transmit sealed to the Seat of the Government of the United States, directed to the President of the Senate. The President of the Senate shall, in the Presence of the Senate and House of Representatives, open all the Certificates, and the Votes shall then be counted. The Person having the greatest Number of Votes shall be the President, if such Number be a Majority of the whole Number of Electors appointed; and if there be more than one who have such Majority, and have an equal Number of Votes, then the House of Representatives shall immediately chuse by Ballot one of them for President; and if no Person have a Majority, then from the five highest on the list the said House shall in like Manner chuse the President. But in chusing the President, the Votes shall be taken by States, the Representation from each State having one Vote; A quorum for this Purpose shall consist of a Member or Members from two thirds of the States, and a Majority of all the States shall be necessary to a Choice. In every Case, after the Choice of the President, the Person having the greatest Number of Votes of the Electors shall be the Vice President. But if there should remain two or more who have equal Votes, the Senate shall chuse from them by Ballot the Vice President.][6]

The Congress may determine the Time of chusing the Electors, and the Day on which they shall give their Votes; which Day shall be the same throughout the United States.

No Person except a natural born Citizen, or a Citizen of the United States, at the time of the Adoption of this Constitution, shall be eligible to the Office of President; neither shall any Person be eligible to that Office who shall not have attained to the Age of thirty five Years, and been fourteen Years a Resident within the United States.

In Case of the Removal of the President from Office, or of his Death, Resignation, or Inability to discharge the Powers and Duties of the said Office,[7] the Same shall devolve on the Vice President, and the Congress may by Law provide for the Case of Removal, Death, Resignation or Inability, both of the President and Vice President, declaring what Officer shall then act as President, and such Officer shall act accordingly, until the Disability be removed, or a President shall be elected.

The President shall, at stated Times, receive for his Services, a Compensation, which shall neither be encreased nor diminished during the Period for which he shall have been elected, and he shall not receive within that Period any other Emolument from the United States, or any of them.

Before he enter on the Execution of his Office, he shall take the following Oath or Affirmation: — "I do solemnly swear (or affirm) that I will faithfully execute the Office of President of the United States, and will to the best of my Ability, preserve, protect and defend the Constitution of the United States."

Section 2. The President shall be Commander in Chief of the Army and Navy of the United States, and of the Militia of the several States, when called into the actual Service of the United States; he may require the Opinion, in writing, of the principal Officer in each of the executive Departments, upon any Subject relating to the Duties of their respective Offices, and he shall have Power to grant Reprieves and Pardons for Offences against the United States, except in Cases of Impeachment.

He shall have Power, by and with the Advice and Consent of the Senate, to make Treaties, provided two thirds of the Senators present concur; and he shall nominate, and by and with the Advice and Consent of the Senate, shall appoint Ambassadors, other public Ministers and Consuls, Judges of the supreme Court, and all other Officers of the United States, whose Appointments are not herein otherwise provided for, and which shall be established by Law: but the Congress may by Law vest the Appointment of such inferior Officers, as they think proper, in the President alone, in the Courts of Law, or in the Heads of Departments.

The President shall have Power to fill up all Vacancies that may happen during the Recess of the Senate, by granting Commissions which shall expire at the End of their next Session.

Section 3. He shall from time to time give to the Congress Information of the State of the Union, and recommend to their Consideration such Measures as he shall judge necessary and expedient; he may, on extraordinary Occasions, convene both Houses, or either of them, and in Case of Disagreement between them, with Respect to the Time of Adjournment, he may adjourn them to such Time as he shall think proper; he shall receive Ambassadors and other public Ministers; he shall take Care that the Laws be faithfully executed, and shall Commission all the Officers of the United States.

Section 4. The President, Vice President and all civil Officers of the United States, shall be removed from Office on Impeachment for, and Conviction of, Treason, Bribery, or other high Crimes and Misdemeanors.

ARTICLE III

Section 1. The judicial Power of the United States, shall be vested in one supreme Court, and in such inferior Courts as the Congress may from time to time ordain and establish. The Judges, both of the supreme and inferior Courts, shall hold their

Offices during good Behaviour, and shall, at stated Times, receive for their Services, a Compensation, which shall not be diminished during their Continuance in Office.

Section 2. The judicial Power shall extend to all Cases, in Law and Equity, arising under this Constitution, the Laws of the United States, and Treaties made, or which shall be made, under their Authority; — to all Cases affecting Ambassadors, other public Ministers and Consuls; — to all Cases of admiralty and maritime Jurisdiction; — to Controversies to which the United States shall be a Party; — to Controversies between two or more States; — between a State and Citizens of another State;[8] — between Citizens of different States; — between Citizens of the same State claiming Lands under Grants of different States, and between a State, or the Citizens thereof, and foreign States, Citizens or Subjects.

In all Cases affecting Ambassadors, other public Ministers and Consuls, and those in which a State shall be Party, the supreme Court shall have original Jurisdiction. In all the other Cases before mentioned, the supreme Court shall have appellate Jurisdiction, both as to Law and Fact, with such Exceptions, and under such Regulations as the Congress shall make.

The Trial of all Crimes, except in Cases of Impeachment, shall be by Jury; and such Trial shall be held in the State where the said Crimes shall have been committed; but when not committed within any State, the Trial shall be at such Place or Places as the Congress may by Law have directed.

Section 3. Treason against the United States, shall consist only in levying War against them, or in adhering to their Enemies, giving them Aid and Comfort. No Person shall be convicted of Treason unless on the Testimony of two Witnesses to the same overt Act, or on Confession in open Court.

The Congress shall have Power to declare the Punishment of Treason, but no Attainder of Treason shall work Corruption of Blood, or Forfeiture except during the Life of the Person attainted.

ARTICLE IV

Section 1. Full Faith and Credit shall be given in each State to the public Acts, Records, and judicial Proceedings of every other State. And the Congress may by general Laws prescribe the Manner in which such Acts, Records and Proceedings shall be proved, and the Effect thereof.

Section 2. The Citizens of each State shall be entitled to all Privileges and Immunities of Citizens in the several States.

A Person charged in any State with Treason, Felony, or other Crime, who shall flee from Justice, and be found in another State, shall on Demand of the executive Authority of the State from which he fled, be delivered up, to be removed to the State having Jurisdiction of the Crime.

[No Person held to Service or Labour in one State, under the Laws thereof, escaping into another, shall, in Consequence of any Law or Regulation therein, be discharged from such Service or Labour, but shall be delivered up on Claim of the Party to whom such Service or Labour may be due.][9]

Section 3. New States may be admitted by the Congress into this Union; but no new State shall be formed or erected within the Jurisdiction of any other State; nor any State be formed by the Junction of two or more States, or Parts of States, without the Consent of the Legislatures of the States concerned as well as of the Congress.

The Congress shall have Power to dispose of and make all needful Rules and Regulations respecting the Territory or other Property belonging to the United States; and nothing in this Constitution shall be so construed as to Prejudice any Claims of the United States, or of any particular State.

Section 4. The United States shall guarantee to every State in this Union a Republican Form of Government, and shall protect each of them against Invasion; and on Application of the Legislature, or of the Executive (when the Legislature cannot be convened) against domestic Violence.

ARTICLE V

The Congress, whenever two thirds of both Houses shall deem it necessary, shall propose Amendments to this Constitution, or, on the Application of the Legislatures of two thirds of the several States, shall call a Convention for proposing Amendments, which, in either Case, shall be valid to all Intents and Purposes, as Part of this Constitution, when ratified by the Legislatures of three fourths of the several States, or by Conventions in three fourths thereof, as the one or the other Mode of Ratification may be proposed by the Congress; Provided [that no Amendment which may be made prior to the Year One thousand eight hundred and eight shall in any Manner affect the first and fourth Clauses in the Ninth Section of the first Article; and][10] that no State, without its Consent, shall be deprived of its equal Suffrage in the Senate.

ARTICLE VI

All Debts contracted and Engagements entered into, before the Adoption of this Constitution, shall be as valid against the United States under this Constitution, as under the Confederation.

This Constitution, and the Laws of the United States which shall be made in Pursuance thereof; and all Treaties made, or which shall be made, under the Authority of the United States, shall be the supreme Law of the Land; and the Judges in every State shall be bound thereby, any Thing in the Constitution or Laws of any State to the Contrary notwithstanding.

The Senators and Representatives before mentioned, and the Members of the several State Legislatures, and all executive and judicial Officers, both of the United States and of the several States, shall be bound by Oath or Affirmation, to support this Constitution; but no religious Test shall ever be required as a Qualification to any Office or public Trust under the United States.

ARTICLE VII

The Ratification of the Conventions of nine States, shall be sufficient for the Establishment of this Constitution between the States so ratifying the Same.

Done in Convention by the Unanimous Consent of the States present the Seventeenth Day of September in the Year of our Lord one thousand seven hundred and Eighty seven and of the Independence of the United States of America the Twelfth. IN WITNESS whereof We have hereunto subscribed our Names,

George Washington,
President and
deputy from Virginia.

New Hampshire:	John Langdon
	Nicholas Gilman.
Massachusetts:	Nathaniel Gorham,
	Rufus King.
Connecticut:	William Samuel Johnson,
	Roger Sherman.

New York: Alexander Hamilton.
New Jersey: William Livingston,
David Brearley,
William Paterson,
Jonathan Dayton.
Pennsylvania: Benjamin Franklin,
Thomas Mifflin,
Robert Morris,
George Clymer,
Thomas FitzSimons,
Jared Ingersoll,
James Wilson,
Gouverneur Morris.
Delaware: George Read,
Gunning Bedford Jr.,
John Dickinson,
Richard Bassett,
Jacob Broom.
Maryland: James McHenry,
Daniel of St. Thomas Jenifer,
Daniel Carroll.
Virginia: John Blair,
James Madison Jr.
North Carolina: William Blount,
Richard Dobbs Spaight,
Hugh Williamson.
South Carolina: John Rutledge,
Charles Cotesworth Pinckney,
Charles Pinckney,
Pierce Butler.
Georgia: William Few,
Abraham Baldwin.

[The language of the original Constitution, not including the Amendments, was adopted by a convention of the states on September 17, 1787, and was subsequently ratified by the states on the following dates: Delaware, December 7, 1787; Pennsylvania, December 12, 1787; New Jersey, December 18, 1787; Georgia, January 2, 1788; Connecticut, January 9, 1788; Massachusetts, February 6, 1788; Maryland, April 28, 1788; South Carolina, May 23, 1788; New Hampshire, June 21, 1788.

Ratification was completed on June 21, 1788.

The Constitution subsequently was ratified by Virginia, June 25, 1788; New York, July 26, 1788; North Carolina, November 21, 1789; Rhode Island, May 29, 1790; and Vermont, January 10, 1791.]

Amendments

Amendment I

(First ten amendments ratified December 15, 1791.)

Congress shall make no law respecting an establishment of religion, or prohibiting the free exercise thereof; or abridging the freedom of speech, or of the press; or the right of the people peaceably to assemble, and to petition the Government for a redress of grievances.

Amendment II

A well regulated Militia, being necessary to the security of a free State, the right of the people to keep and bear Arms, shall not be infringed.

Amendment III

No Soldier shall, in time of peace be quartered in any house, without the consent of the Owner, nor in time of war, but in a manner to be prescribed by law.

Amendment IV

The right of the people to be secure in their persons, houses, papers, and effects, against unreasonable searches and seizures, shall not be violated, and no Warrants shall issue, but upon probable cause, supported by Oath or affirmation, and particularly describing the place to be searched, and the persons or things to be seized.

Amendment V

No person shall be held to answer for a capital, or otherwise infamous crime, unless on a presentment or indictment of a Grand Jury, except in cases arising in the land or naval forces, or in the Militia, when in actual service in time of War or public danger; nor shall any person be subject for the same offence to be twice put in jeopardy of life or limb; nor shall be compelled in any criminal case to be a witness against himself, nor be deprived of life, liberty, or property, without due process of law; nor shall private property be taken for public use, without just compensation.

Amendment VI

In all criminal prosecutions, the accused shall enjoy the right to a speedy and public trial, by an impartial jury of the State and district wherein the crime shall have been committed, which district shall have been previously ascertained by law, and to be informed of the nature and cause of the accusation; to be confronted with the witnesses against him; to have compulsory process for obtaining witnesses in his favor, and to have the Assistance of Counsel for his defence.

Amendment VII

In Suits at common law, where the value in controversy shall exceed twenty dollars, the right of trial by jury shall be preserved, and no fact tried by a jury, shall be otherwise re-examined in any Court of the United States, than according to the rules of the common law.

Amendment VIII

Excessive bail shall not be required, nor excessive fines imposed, nor cruel and unusual punishments inflicted.

Amendment IX

The enumeration in the Constitution, of certain rights, shall not be construed to deny or disparage others retained by the people.

Amendment X

The powers not delegated to the United States by the Constitution, nor prohibited by it to the States, are reserved to the States respectively, or to the people.

Amendment XI (Ratified February 7, 1795)

The Judicial power of the United States shall not be construed to extend to any suit in law or equity, commenced or prosecuted against one of the United States by Citizens of another State, or by Citizens or Subjects of any Foreign State.

Amendment XII (Ratified June 15, 1804)

The Electors shall meet in their respective states and vote by ballot for President and Vice-President, one of whom, at least, shall not be an inhabitant of the same state with themselves; they shall name in their ballots the person voted for as President, and in distinct ballots the person voted for as Vice-President, and they shall make distinct lists of all persons voted for as President, and of all persons voted for as Vice-President, and of the number of votes for each, which lists they shall sign and certify, and transmit sealed to the seat of the government of the United States, directed to the President of the Senate; — The President of the Senate shall, in the presence of the Senate and House of Representatives, open all the certificates and the votes shall then be counted; — The person having the greatest number of votes for President, shall be the President, if such number be a majority of the whole number of Electors appointed; and if no person have such majority, then from the persons having the highest numbers not exceeding three on the list of those voted for as President, the House of Representatives shall choose immediately, by ballot, the President. But in choosing the President, the votes shall be taken by states, the representation from each state having one vote; a quorum for this purpose shall consist of a member or members from two-thirds of the states, and a majority of all the states shall be necessary to a choice. [And if the House of Representatives shall not choose a President whenever the right of choice shall devolve upon them, before the fourth day of March next following, then the Vice-President shall act as President, as in the case of the death or other constitutional disability of the President. —][11] The person having the greatest number of votes as Vice-President, shall be the Vice-President, if such number be a majority of the whole number of Electors appointed, and if no person have a majority, then from the two highest numbers on the list, the Senate shall choose the Vice-President; a quorum for the purpose shall consist of two-thirds of the whole number of Senators, and a majority of the whole number shall be necessary to a choice. But no person constitutionally ineligible to the office of President shall be eligible to that of Vice-President of the United States.

Amendment XIII (Ratified December 6, 1865)

Section 1. Neither slavery nor involuntary servitude, except as a punishment for crime whereof the party shall have been duly convicted, shall exist within the United States, or any place subject to their jurisdiction.

Section 2. Congress shall have power to enforce this article by appropriate legislation.

Amendment XIV (Ratified July 9, 1868)

Section 1. All persons born or naturalized in the United States, and subject to the jurisdiction thereof, are citizens of the United States and of the State wherein they reside. No State shall make or enforce any law which shall abridge the privileges or immunities of citizens of the United States; nor shall any State deprive any person of life, liberty, or property, without due process of law; nor deny to any person within its jurisdiction the equal protection of the laws.

Section 2. Representatives shall be apportioned among the several States according to their respective numbers, counting the whole number of persons in each State, excluding Indians not taxed. But when the right to vote at any election for the choice of electors for President and Vice President of the United States, Representatives in Congress, the Executive and Judicial officers of a State, or the members of the Legislature thereof, is denied to any of the male inhabitants of such State, being

twenty-one years of age,[12] and citizens of the United States, or in any way abridged, except for participation in rebellion, or other crime, the basis of representation therein shall be reduced in the proportion which the number of such male citizens shall bear to the whole number of male citizens twenty-one years of age in such State.

Section 3. No person shall be a Senator or Representative in Congress, or elector of President and Vice President, or hold any office, civil or military, under the United States, or under any State, who, having previously taken an oath, as a member of Congress, or as an officer of the United States, or as a member of any State legislature, or as an executive or judicial officer of any State, to support the Constitution of the United States, shall have engaged in insurrection or rebellion against the same, or given aid or comfort to the enemies thereof. But Congress may by a vote of two-thirds of each House, remove such disability.

Section 4. The validity of the public debt of the United States, authorized by law, including debts incurred for payment of pensions and bounties for services in suppressing insurrection or rebellion, shall not be questioned. But neither the United States nor any State shall assume or pay any debt or obligation incurred in aid of insurrection or rebellion against the United States, or any claim for the loss or emancipation of any slave; but all such debts, obligations and claims shall be held illegal and void.

Section 5. The Congress shall have power to enforce, by appropriate legislation, the provisions of this article.

Amendment XV (Ratified February 3, 1870)

Section 1. The right of citizens of the United States to vote shall not be denied or abridged by the United States or by any State on account of race, color, or previous condition of servitude.

Section 2. The Congress shall have power to enforce this article by appropriate legislation.

Amendment XVI (Ratified February 3, 1913)

The Congress shall have power to lay and collect taxes on incomes, from whatever source derived, without apportionment among the several States, and without regard to any census or enumeration.

Amendment XVII (Ratified April 8, 1913)

The Senate of the United States shall be composed of two Senators from each State, elected by the people thereof, for six years; and each Senator shall have one vote. The electors in each State shall have the qualifications requisite for electors of the most numerous branch of the State legislatures.

When vacancies happen in the representation of any State in the Senate, the executive authority of such State shall issue writs of election to fill such vacancies: *Provided*, That the legislature of any State may empower the executive thereof to make temporary appointments until the people fill the vacancies by election as the legislature may direct.

This amendment shall not be so construed as to affect the election or term of any Senator chosen before it becomes valid as part of the Constitution.

Amendment XVIII (Ratified January 16, 1919)[13]

Section 1. After one year from the ratification of this article the manufacture, sale, or transportation of intoxicating liquors within, the importation thereof into, or the exportation thereof

from the United States and all territory subject to the jurisdiction thereof for beverage purposes is hereby prohibited.

Section 2. The Congress and the several States shall have concurrent power to enforce this article by appropriate legislation.

Section 3. This article shall be inoperative unless it shall have been ratified as an amendment to the Constitution by the legislatures of the several States, as provided in the Constitution, within seven years from the date of the submission hereof to the States by the Congress.

Amendment XIX (Ratified August 18, 1920)

The right of citizens of the United States to vote shall not be denied or abridged by the United States or by any State on account of sex.

Congress shall have power to enforce this article by appropriate legislation.

Amendment XX (Ratified January 23, 1933)

Section 1. The terms of the President and Vice President shall end at noon on the 20th day of January, and the terms of Senators and Representatives at noon on the 3d day of January, of the years in which such terms would have ended if this article had not been ratified; and the terms of their successors shall then begin.

Section 2. The Congress shall assemble at least once in every year, and such meeting shall begin at noon on the 3d day of January, unless they shall by law appoint a different day.

Section 3.[14] If, at the time fixed for the beginning of the term of the President, the President elect shall have died, the Vice President elect shall become President. If a President shall not have been chosen before the time fixed for the beginning of his term, or if the President elect shall have failed to qualify, then the Vice President elect shall act as President until a President shall have qualified; and the Congress may by law provide for the case wherein neither a President elect nor a Vice President elect shall have qualified, declaring who shall then act as President, or the manner in which one who is to act shall be selected, and such person shall act accordingly until a President or Vice President shall have qualified.

Section 4. The Congress may by law provide for the case of the death of any of the persons from whom the House of Representatives may choose a President whenever the right of choice shall have devolved upon them, and for the case of the death of any of the persons from whom the Senate may choose a Vice President whenever the right of choice shall have devolved upon them.

Section 5. Sections 1 and 2 shall take effect on the 15th day of October following the ratification of this article.

Section 6. This article shall be inoperative unless it shall have been ratified as an amendment to the Constitution by the legislatures of three-fourths of the several States within seven years from the date of its submission.

Amendment XXI (Ratified December 5, 1933)

Section 1. The eighteenth article of amendment to the Constitution of the United States is hereby repealed.

Section 2. The transportation or importation into any State, Territory, or possession of the United States for delivery or use therein of intoxicating liquors, in violation of the laws thereof, is hereby prohibited.

Section 3. This article shall be inoperative unless it shall have been ratified as an amendment to the Constitution by

conventions in the several States, as provided in the Constitution, within seven years from the date of the submission hereof to the States by the Congress.

Amendment XXII (Ratified February 27, 1951)

Section 1. No person shall be elected to the office of the President more than twice, and no person who has held the office of President, or acted as President, for more than two years of a term to which some other person was elected President shall be elected to the office of the President more than once. But this Article shall not apply to any person holding the office of President when this Article was proposed by the Congress, and shall not prevent any person who may be holding the office of President, or acting as President, during the term within which this Article become operative from holding the office of President or acting as President during the remainder of such term.

Section 2. This article shall be inoperative unless it shall have been ratified as an amendment to the Constitution by the legislatures of three-fourths of the several States within seven years from the date of its submission to the States by the Congress.

Amendment XXIII (Ratified March 29, 1961)

Section 1. The District constituting the seat of Government of the United States shall appoint in such manner as the Congress may direct:

A number of electors of President and Vice President equal to the whole number of Senators and Representatives in Congress to which the District would be entitled if it were a State, but in no event more than the least populous State; they shall be in addition to those appointed by the States, but they shall be considered, for the purposes of the election of President and Vice President, to be electors appointed by a State; and they shall meet in the District and perform such duties as provided by the twelfth article of amendment.

Section 2. The Congress shall have power to enforce this article by appropriate legislation.

Amendment XXIV (Ratified January 23, 1964)

Section 1. The right of citizens of the United States to vote in any primary or other election for President or Vice President, for electors for President or Vice President, or for Senator or Representative in Congress, shall not be denied or abridged by the United States or any State by reason of failure to pay any poll tax or other tax.

Section 2. The Congress shall have power to enforce this article by appropriate legislation.

Amendment XXV (Ratified February 10, 1967)

Section 1. In case of the removal of the President from office or of his death or resignation, the Vice President shall become President.

Section 2. Whenever there is a vacancy in the office of the Vice President, the President shall nominate a Vice President who shall take office upon confirmation by a majority vote of both Houses of Congress.

Section 3. Whenever the President transmits to the President pro tempore of the Senate and the Speaker of the House of Representatives his written declaration that he is unable to discharge the powers and duties of his office, and until he transmits to them a written declaration to the contrary, such powers and duties shall be discharged by the Vice President as Acting President.

Section 4. Whenever the Vice President and a majority of either the principal officers of the executive departments or of such other body as Congress may by law provide, transmit to the President pro tempore of the Senate and the Speaker of the House of Representatives their written declaration that the President is unable to discharge the powers and duties of his office, the Vice President shall immediately assume the powers and duties of the office as Acting President.

Thereafter, when the President transmits to the President pro tempore of the Senate and the Speaker of the House of Representatives his written declaration that no inability exists, he shall resume the powers and duties of his office unless the Vice President and a majority of either the principal officers of the executive department or of such other body as Congress may by law provide, transmit within four days to the President pro tempore of the Senate and the Speaker of the House of Representatives their written declaration that the President is unable to discharge the powers and duties of his office. Thereupon Congress shall decide the issue, assembling within forty-eight hours for that purpose if not in session. If the Congress, within twenty-one days after receipt of the latter written declaration, or, if Congress is not in session, within twenty-one days after Congress is required to assemble, determines by two-thirds vote of both Houses that the President is unable to discharge the powers and duties of his office, the Vice President shall continue to discharge the same as Acting President; otherwise, the President shall resume the powers and duties of his office.

Amendment XXVI (Ratified July 1, 1971)

Section 1. The right of citizens of the United States, who are eighteen years of age or older, to vote shall not be denied or abridged by the United States or by any State on account of age.

Section 2. The Congress shall have power to enforce this article by appropriate legislation.

Amendment XXVII (Ratified May 7, 1992)

No law varying the compensation for the services of the Senators and Representatives shall take effect, until an election of Representatives shall have intervened.

Notes

1. The part in brackets was changed by section 2 of the Fourteenth Amendment.
2. The part in brackets was changed by the first paragraph of the Seventeenth Amendment.
3. The part in brackets was changed by the second paragraph of the Seventeenth Amendment.
4. The part in brackets was changed by section 2 of the Twentieth Amendment.
5. The Sixteenth Amendment gave Congress the power to tax incomes.
6. The material in brackets has been superseded by the Twelfth Amendment.
7. This provision has been affected by the Twenty-fifth Amendment.
8. These clauses were affected by the Eleventh Amendment.
9. This paragraph has been superseded by the Thirteenth Amendment.
10. Obsolete.
11. The part in brackets has been superseded by section 3 of the Twentieth Amendment.
12. See the Nineteenth and Twenty-sixth Amendments.
13. This Amendment was repealed by section 1 of the Twenty-first Amendment.
14. See the Twenty-fifth Amendment.

SOURCE: U.S. Congress, House, Committee on the Judiciary, *The Constitution of the United States of America, as Amended,* 100th Cong., 1st sess., 1987, H Doc 100-94.

Congressional Information on the Internet

A huge array of congressional information is available for free at Internet sites operated by the federal government, colleges and universities, and commercial firms. The sites offer the full text of bills introduced in the House and Senate, voting records, campaign finance information, transcripts of selected congressional hearings, investigative reports, and much more.

THOMAS

The most important site for congressional information is THOMAS (*http://thomas.loc.gov*), which is named for Thomas Jefferson and operated by the Library of Congress. THOMAS's highlight is its databases containing the full text of all bills introduced in Congress since 1989, the full text of the *Congressional Record* since 1989, and the status and summary information for all bills introduced since 1973.

THOMAS also offers special links to bills that have received or are expected to receive floor action during the current week and newsworthy bills that are pending or that have recently been approved. Finally, THOMAS has selected committee reports, answers to frequently asked questions about accessing congressional information, publications titled *How Our Laws Are Made* and *Enactment of a Law*, and links to lots of other congressional Web sites.

House of Representatives

The U.S. House of Representatives site (*http://www.house.gov*) offers the schedule of bills, resolutions, and other legislative issues the House will consider in the current week. It also has updates about current proceedings on the House floor and a list of the next day's meeting of House committees. Other highlights include a database that helps users identify their representative, a directory of House members and committees, the House ethics manual, links to Web pages maintained by House members and committees, a calendar of congressional primary dates and candidate-filing deadlines for ballot access, the full text of all amendments to the Constitution that have been ratified and those that have been proposed but not ratified, and lots of information about Washington, D.C., for visitors.

Another key House site is The Office of the Clerk On-line Information Center (*http://clerkweb.house.gov*), which has records of all roll-call votes taken since 1990. The votes are recorded by bill, so it is a lengthy process to compile a particular representative's voting record. The site also has lists of committee assignments, a telephone directory for members and committees, mailing label templates for members and committees, rules of the current Congress, election statistics from 1920 to the present, biographies of Speakers of the House, biographies of women who have served since 1917, and a virtual tour of the House Chamber.

One of the more interesting House sites is operated by the Subcommittee on Rules and Organization of the House

Committee on Rules (*http://www.house.gov/rules/crs_reports. htm*). Its highlight is dozens of Congressional Research Service reports about the legislative process. Some of the available titles include *Legislative Research in Congressional Offices: A Primer, How to Follow Current Federal Legislation and Regulations, Investigative Oversight: An Introduction to the Law, Practice, and Procedure of Congressional Inquiry*, and *Presidential Vetoes 1789–1996: A Summary Overview*.

A final House site is the Internet Law Library (*http://uscode. house.gov*). This site has a searchable version of the U.S. Code, which contains the text of public laws enacted by Congress, and a tutorial for searching the Code. There also is a huge collection of links to other Internet sites that provide state and territorial laws, laws of other nations, and treaties and international laws.

Senate

At least in the Internet world, the Senate is not as active as the House. Its main Web site (*http://www.senate.gov*) has records of all roll-call votes taken since 1989 (arranged by bill), brief descriptions of all bills and joint resolutions introduced in the Senate during the past week, and a calendar of upcoming committee hearings. The site also provides the standing rules of the Senate, a directory of senators and their committee assignments, lists of nominations that the president has submitted to the Senate for approval, links to Web pages operated by senators and committees, and a virtual tour of the Senate.

Information about the membership, jurisdiction, and rules of each congressional committee is available at the U.S. Government Printing Office site (*http://www.access.gpo.gov/congress/index.html*). It also has transcripts of selected congressional hearings, the full text of selected House and Senate reports, and the House and Senate rules manuals.

General Reference

The U.S. General Accounting Office, the investigative arm of Congress, operates a site (*http://www.gao.gov*) that provides the full text of its reports from 1996 to the present. The reports cover a wide range of topics: aviation safety, combating terrorism, counternarcotics efforts in Mexico, defense contracting, electronic warfare, food assistance programs, Gulf War illness, health insurance, illegal aliens, information technology, long-term care, mass transit, Medicare, military readiness, money laundering, national parks, nuclear waste, organ donation, student loan defaults, and the year 2000 computing crisis, among others.

The GAO Daybook is an excellent current awareness tool. This electronic mailing list distributes a daily list of reports and testimony released by the GAO. Subscriptions are available by sending an E-mail message to *majordomo@www.gao.gov*, and in the message area typing "subscribe daybook" (without the quotation marks).

Current budget and economic projections are provided at the Congressional Budget Office Web site *(http://www.cbo.gov)*. The site also has reports about the economic and budget outlook for the next decade, the president's budget proposals, federal civilian employment, Social Security privatization, tax reform, water use conflicts in the West, marriage and the federal income tax, and the role of foreign aid in development, among other topics. Other highlights include monthly budget updates, historical budget data, cost estimates for bills reported by congressional committees, and transcripts of congressional testimony by CBO officials.

Campaign Finance

Several Internet sites provide detailed campaign finance data for congressional elections. The official site is operated by the Federal Election Commission *(http://www.fec.gov)*, which regulates political spending. The site's highlight is its database of campaign reports filed from May 1996 to the present by House and presidential candidates, political action committees, and political party committees. Senate reports are not included because they are filed with the Secretary of the Senate. The reports in the FEC's database are scanned images of paper reports filed with the commission.

The FEC site also has summary financial data for House and Senate candidates in the current election cycle, abstracts of court decisions pertaining to federal election law from 1976 to 1997, a graph showing the number of political action committees in existence each year from 1974 to the present, and a directory of national and state agencies that are responsible for releasing information about campaign financing, candidates on the ballot, election results, lobbying, and other issues. Another useful feature is a collection of brochures about federal election law, public funding of presidential elections, the ban on contributions by foreign nationals, independent expenditures supporting or opposing a candidate for federal office, contribution limits, filing a complaint, researching public records at the FEC, and other topics. Finally, the site provides the FEC's legislative recommendations, its annual report, a report about its first twenty years in existence, the FEC's monthly newsletter, several reports about voter registration, election results for the most recent presidential and congressional elections, and campaign guides for corporations and labor organizations, congressional candidates and committees, political party committees, and nonconnected committees.

The best online source for campaign finance data is FECInfo *(http://www.tray.com/fecinfo)*, which is operated by former Federal Election Commission employee Tony Raymond. FECInfo's searchable databases provide extensive itemized information about receipts and expenditures by federal candidates and political action committees from 1980 to the present. The data, which are obtained from the FEC, are quite detailed. For example, for candidates contributions can be searched by Zip Code. The site also has data on soft money contributions, lists of the top political action committees in various categories, lists of the top contributors from each state, and much more.

Another interesting site is Campaign Finance Data on the Internet *(http://www.soc.american.edu/campfin)*, which is operated by the American University School of Communication. It provides electronic files from the FEC that have been reformatted in .dbf format so they can be used in database programs such as Paradox, Access, and FoxPro. The files contain data on PAC, committee, and individual contributions to individual congressional candidates.

More campaign finance data is available from the Center for Responsive Politics *(http://www.opensecrets.org)*, a public interest organization. The center provides a list of all "soft money" donations to political parties of $100,000 or more in the current election cycle and data about "leadership" political action committees associated with individual politicians. Other databases at the site provide information about travel expenses that House members received from private sources for attending meetings and other events, activities of registered federal lobbyists, and activities of foreign agents who are registered in the United States.

Index

Index

Index